Democracy in Modern Europe

European Conceptual History

Editorial Board:
Michael Freeden, University of Oxford
Diana Mishkova, Centre for Advanced Study Sofia
Javier Fernández-Sebastián, Universidad del País Vasco, Bilbao
Willibald Steinmetz, University of Bielefeld
Henrik Stenius, University of Helsinki

The transformation of social and political concepts is central to understanding the histories of societies. This series focuses on the notable values and terminology that have developed throughout European history, exploring key concepts such as parliamentarianism, democracy, civilization and liberalism to illuminate a vocabulary that has helped to shape the modern world.

Conceptual History in the European Space
Edited by Willibald Steinmetz, Michael Freeden
and Javier Fernández-Sebastián

Parliament and Parliamentarism: A Comparative History of a European Concept
Edited by Pasi Ihalainen, Cornelia Ilie and Kari Palonen

European Regions and Boundaries: A Conceptual History
Edited by Diana Mishkova and Balázs Trencsényi

Basic and Applied Research: The Language of Science Policy in the Twentieth Century
Edited by David Kaldewey and Désirée Schauz

Democracy in Modern Europe: A Conceptual History
Edited by Jussi Kurunmäki, Jeppe Nevers and Henk te Velde

Democracy in Modern Europe

A Conceptual History

Edited by
Jussi Kurunmäki, Jeppe Nevers and Henk te Velde

berghahn
NEW YORK • OXFORD
www.berghahnbooks.com

First published in 2018 by
Berghahn Books
www.berghahnbooks.com

© 2018, 2025 Jussi Kurunmäki, Jeppe Nevers and Henk te Velde
First paperback edition published in 2025

All rights reserved. Except for the quotation of short passages
for the purposes of criticism and review, no part of this book
may be reproduced in any form or by any means, electronic or
mechanical, including photocopying, recording, or any information
storage and retrieval system now known or to be invented,
without written permission of the publisher.

Library of Congress Cataloging-in-Publication Data

A C.I.P. cataloging record is available from the Library of Congress

British Library Cataloguing in Publication Data

A catalogue record for this book is available from the British Library

ISBN 978-1-78533-847-2 hardback
ISBN 978-1-83695-048-6 paperback
ISBN 978-1-83695-166-7 epub
ISBN 978-1-78533-848-9 web pdf

https://doi.org/10.3167/9781785338472

Contents

Introduction 1
Jussi Kurunmäki, Jeppe Nevers and Henk te Velde

CHAPTER 1 'Democracy' from Book to Life: The Emergence of
the Term in Active Political Debate, to 1848 16
Joanna Innes and Mark Philp

CHAPTER 2 Democracy and the Strange Death of Mixed Government
in the Nineteenth Century: Great Britain, France and the Netherlands 42
Henk te Velde

CHAPTER 3 Another 'Sonderweg'? The Historical Semantics
of 'Democracy' in Germany 65
Jörn Leonhard

CHAPTER 4 Birthplaces of Democracy: The Rhetoric of Democratic
Tradition in Switzerland and Sweden 88
Jussi Kurunmäki and Irène Herrmann

CHAPTER 5 Concepts of Democracy from a Russian Perspective:
Debates in the Late Imperial Period (1905–17) 113
Benjamin Beuerle

CHAPTER 6 A Conceptual History of Democracy in Spain
since 1800 135
Javier Fernández-Sebastián and José María Rosales

CHAPTER 7 The First World War, the Russian Revolution and
Varieties of Democracy in Northwest European Debates 160
Pasi Ihalainen

CHAPTER 8 The Edges of Democracy: German, British and
American Debates on the Dictatorial Challenges to Democracy
in the Interwar Years 182
Marcus Llanque

CHAPTER 9 A Nation Allied with History: Czech Ideas of
Democracy, 1890–1948   208
Peter Bugge

CHAPTER 10 Democracy in Western Europe after 1945   231
Martin Conway

CHAPTER 11 Political Participation and Democratization in
the 1960s: The Concept of Participatory Democracy and
its Repercussions   257
Ingrid Gilcher-Holtey

CHAPTER 12 Democracy and European Integration:
A Transnational History of the Danish Debate   281
Jeppe Nevers

Index   300

Introduction

Jussi Kurunmäki, Jeppe Nevers and Henk te Velde

This is a book about the different meanings of 'democracy' in nineteenth- and twentieth-century Europe. It puts these meanings into the context of European history and thereby tracks a range of similarities as well as differences in the development of the language of democracy. It is the claim of this book that knowledge of the languages of democracy and their interconnections is indispensable for understanding the development and complexity of democracy. Concentrating on language also helps us to uncover lost meanings and forgotten stages in that development.

'Democracy' was one of the most prominent battle cries of the twentieth century. Two world wars were partly fought in its name, and at the beginning of the twenty-first century, the Americans still legitimized their attack on Iraq by arguing that they were bringing democracy. In the twentieth century, democracy became the central political value, claimed by everyone everywhere. At the beginning of the century, only a few republics self-identified as democracies; at the end of the century, only a few dictatorships did not. In the interwar years, fascists could still look down on plutocratic and weak democracy, but they could also claim to represent 'true democracy', and after 1945 Western liberals and Eastern communists alike claimed to be 'democrats'. But what could be the meaning of a word that was used by liberal democracies as well as people's democracies? Was it more than an empty shell? In 1940 T.S. Eliot wrote: 'When a term has become so universally sanctified as "democracy" now is, I begin to wonder whether it means anything, in meaning too many things.'[1]

After 1989, there was a brief moment when many people thought that the answer to that question was obvious: people's democracies were a sham, and liberal democracy was the real thing. Francis Fukuyama even argued that its victory over communism almost announced the end of history as we knew it, that is, the end of 'mankind's ideological evolution'.[2] It later turned out that this was just a fleeting, passing moment. One of the things that it showed, though, was the extent to which 'democracy' could now be claimed to be a quality of (liberal, capitalist) government institutions. While elements of this conception can be traced back to liberal theory in the nineteenth century, it rose to complete dominance only in the second half of the twentieth century, especially under Anglo-Saxon influence.[3] This development has also been termed the taming or domestication of democracy and 'making democracy safe for the world'.[4]

The postvictory moment lasted longer after 1945 than after 1989. Until the 1960s, an institutional and constitutionalist conception of democracy dominated, underlining the importance of the rule of law, stability and prosperity. Then it was challenged, particularly in the 1960s, in the name of participation and autonomy. Whereas its adherents framed participatory democracy as 'more' democracy, it was first and foremost a call for another democracy, less institutional and less formal. It was also a return – in a completely different form – to a more social conception of democracy that concentrated on civil society, as Alexis de Tocqueville and his likes had done in the nineteenth century. When these ideas resurfaced in the 1960s in a completely new form, they became dominant and mainstream for the first, albeit a rather short, time. After 1989 and after 9/11 in particular, liberal democracy has been challenged again, not only by Islamist terrorists who did not like democracy, but also in the name of 'the people'. Political movements and parties that were called 'populist' by their liberal opponents often considered themselves the true democrats who would rescue democracy from the hands of the corrupt elite. This rhetoric has also been used in a backlash against liberal democracy as a government philosophy, an attempt to save democratic dreams from democratic governance and as a sign of the distrust of liberal-democratic governments in the sense that they do not do what they pretend to do.[5]

It is debatable whether the populist dreams are a travesty of democracy or still belong to the 'potent form of wishful thinking' that democracy is.[6] However this may be, it is clear that the label 'democracy' has not only become, but still is, very attractive. It has been used almost as easily to legitimate as to challenge virtually any regime. The word has incredible mobilizing power, and 'democracy as a political value' constantly subverts the legitimacy of democracy as 'an already existing form of government'.[7] This is, of course, more than just a matter of words. Obviously, there is much more to the history of democracy than the history of a word. Recently, it has become quite common to argue that it is more important to look for democratic practices than for democracy as a word, if you want to trace the origin and development of democracy.[8] If you stick only to the word, you run the risk of 'recycl[ing] the Eurocentric story' or reproducing definitions by 'white, wealthy, Anglo-American men'.[9] However, it is only by analysing the history of the word and the conceptions that were connected to that word that you can begin to understand the history of democracy as a slogan, as a political ideal and as the apparently almost inevitable legitimating idea of modern society. By tracing the history of the use of the concept 'democracy' and related terms, this book is a contribution to the study of democratic rhetoric as well as democracy in general. When, why and how did people use the word 'democracy', and what did this mean? It is the central claim of this book that answering such questions leads us to a nonlinear image of democracy in modern Europe and to a rich history of ruptures and differences. In order to show this history of ruptures, the authors of this book devote considerable attention to the use of 'democracy' in institutionalized political forums, public debate in printed press, and political theory. This is not because the authors believe that this is the only possible story, but because they think that starting from established politics will give us a point of departure for a history of democracy as a concept, which could subsequently be broadened.

Moments and Ruptures

When tracing the development of democracy, most contemporary authors underline an open end of the 'unfinished journey' of democracy.[10] They often also mention the two sides of democracy, on the one hand, the often tedious and unconvincing reality of the administration of liberal democracies and, on the other, the dreams that mobilize and energize people: two sides that are often at odds with each other.[11] Today, we often use two different words for those two sides: democracy as in liberal democracy, and populism for the less genteel aspects of the rule of the people. However, the work of, for instance, Pierre Rosanvallon suggests that differing interpretations and continuing tensions belong to the essence of democracy because pure rule by the people is an ideal that is impossible to realize. In this sense, the history of democracy is certainly not one of simple, let alone linear, progress. Hardly anybody would nowadays argue that it is, but more often than not, an implicit idea of progress still prevails, if only because almost all those writing about democracy would applaud the final victory of democracy in some sense. The standard story is also about the modern, representative form of democracy that first emerged in the late eighteenth century. This book does not claim that democratic practices started to prevail from that period onwards. What is clear, however, is that the word 'democracy' travelled 'from book to life' during the so-called *Sattelzeit* from the end of the eighteenth century to the middle of the nineteenth century, denoting the alleged transitional period between early modern and modern political concepts.[12] Although it was around 1848 still 'a rarefied word for a popular thing', it was no longer uncommon to have 'democratic' ideals.[13]

Until the end of the eighteenth century, 'democracy' was a theoretical and historical concept without much practical value. Ancient Athens was seen as an example of what went wrong if you had a 'pure democracy' untempered by monarchy and aristocracy: fickle, noisy and excessive mob rule. But this was a phenomenon of ancient times; pure democracy was gone for good. In the classical tradition of political thought, 'democracy' was evaluated positively as a useful element only in a mixed constitution, consisting of monarchical, aristocratic and democratic elements. During the French Revolution, these old semantic structures changed profoundly. Edmund Burke immediately condemned the first French Republic as a completely 'democratic' regime with all the negative qualities that this entailed. A few years later, some revolutionaries, including the radical Robespierre, proudly started to call their regime 'democratic' themselves – in fact, implying some sort of representative democracy. After the Terror, this usage gave the concept a setback and, in the early nineteenth century, it strengthened the old tradition of using 'democracy' and 'democrat' as pejoratives.

However, from the French Revolution onwards, the concept began to change from a theoretical and bookish word into a word with practical meaning in actual politics. It changed into a modern concept that pointed towards the future. Importantly, an increased use of 'democracy' also led to attempts of creating (often national) roots for the modern democracy.[14] In the middle of the nineteenth century, the radical British historian George Grote changed the interpretation of Athens from an outdated example of unruly and despised democracy to the admired cradle of modern democracy. Much more important still was another shining light, distant not in time like Athens, but in space: American democracy. In his book about the American democracy, Alexis de Tocqueville looked at the country as a kind of futurist laboratory of all the elements of democracy that were promoted or feared in Europe in the first half of the nineteenth century. He was concerned about the consequences of 'the Age of the Democratic Revolution',[15] but reconciled himself to the inevitable democratic conditions of modern society and studied the nature of this society. And he was part of a tradition of interpreting democracy as a condition of society rather than a political regime.[16] When Tocqueville travelled across the Atlantic, it was an important part of his linguistic baggage that the fall of the *ancien régime* led to a democratic social state, an état social démocratique.[17] A democratic society was a society without formal estates and without (a strong) aristocracy, but was also a society that did not necessarily have a democratic political system. Tocqueville was convinced by his experience in America that democracy could work in the modern world, a viewpoint that in the decades after the French Revolution and Napoleon, not many people had shared. The perspective shifted from the past to the future and from the ancient to the modern world. America was, like the ancient world, quite easy to connect to European history, but as a distant cousin who had a different tradition. The United States was a country without a tradition of monarchy and aristocracy, and with a different rhythm in its history. The development of democracy in Europe was influenced by the concrete example of American democracy – which was, however, used most of the time to warn about the possible dangers of mass democracy. America was not Europe, and European contemporaries did not regard America as part of their own world. The French and the English did not see people from Eastern Europe as part of their universe either, but there were European-wide monarchical, aristocratic and diplomatic networks, and even if there was a centre–periphery divide, the alternation between the two was gradual, and intellectuals in Russia and elsewhere followed British, French and German cultural and political life closely. So, there certainly were many national differences, but, besides certain commonalities in the Atlantic world, there was also a common European discourse about democracy. To a surprising extent, authors in all parts of Europe used the same language, even if they gave it a different connotation and frequency.

For instance, the French conservative liberal, prime minister, historian and opponent of democracy François Guizot was read everywhere in Europe. Immediately after the Revolution of 1848, which had resulted in his downfall, he wrote that 'democracy' had become the most effective rhetorical concept of his Age. No government could do without it anymore, he said.[18] After a setback in the postrevolutionary years, 'democracy' had become an almost indispensable part of political language in France. The constitution defined the Second Republic of 1848 – which sparked a wave of revolutions and uprisings across Europe – as a republic as well as a democracy. Its most prominent feature was universal male suffrage. This meant political rights for citizens and, as such, it also carried a symbolic load of an 'investiture' or 'crowning' of social inclusion that could tame its participatory implications.[19]

Even if the Revolution of 1848 seemed to spell the victory of 'democracy', and the late 1840s saw a rise of democratic rhetoric and of self-identified 'democrats' in many countries, this was a rather short-lived boom. Even if liberals could think that a constitutional monarchy should contain a 'democratic element' as a part of a mixed constitution, there were still not many supporters of a 'pure democracy'. In most European countries, it was still a radical position to call oneself a 'democrat'. Later in the nineteenth century, it was no longer unusual to invoke the concept of 'democracy' in the political battles that took place in different countries. In Denmark, for instance, the most common use of the concept in the second half of the nineteenth century was as a definite noun, 'the democracy', *Demokratiet*. This term signified the common people and their representatives of the Left (*Venstre*) in the lower chamber of the parliament fighting for political reforms towards the end of the century, most notably for parliamentarism. In 1901, 'the democracy' achieved what it had been fighting for, but this did not mean that Denmark in general was conceived of as a democracy or that the king had lost his role in Danish politics.[20]

The First World War is another example of a breakthrough or a rupture in the history of 'democracy'. The war was not started as a war for democracy, but it certainly ended as a victory for democracy. The idea of a 'Western democracy' emerged.[21] Universal suffrage was introduced in a number of countries. After the war, a range of parliamentary democracies were established from the Baltic Sea to the Balkans. Political and legal theorists built theories of the new political order. Hans Kelsen published the first version of his well-known *Vom Wesen und Wert der Demokratie* (1920) and, in 1921, the British scholar and liberal statesman James Bryce talked about the 'universal acceptance of democracy as the normal and natural form of government' in his classic work on *Modern Democracies*.[22] Democracy was on everybody's lips, but it was certainly not a concept with a fixed meaning and, as we all know, many of the new democracies in the 1920s and the 1930s proved rather fragile. Out of those European countries that gained independence during and after the First World War, only Ireland, Finland and Czechoslovakia did not become autocracies or dictatorships during the interwar years.[23] Criticism was directed in particular at the workings and nature of parliamentary government across the continent. Many books and articles appeared about the 'crisis' of parliamentary politics and the 'crisis' of democracy. In the interwar years, many detested parliamentary politics as a talking-shop, but sometimes at the same time supported 'true democracy', whether that was communist, fascist, authoritarian or monarchical in character.[24] In addition, some parties, factions and intellectuals of different persuasions rejected this ancient (and, according to them, outdated) concept, for a variety of reasons besides the nineteenth-century fear of a tyranny of the majority.

After the Second World War, democracy, in the sense of universal suffrage, majority rule and now also the rule of law and parliamentary politics, had become a generally accepted concept.[25] Even much more than the First World War, the Second World War meant a victory for democracy as a concept and, in the West, for parliamentary or liberal democracy as a practice. This was a disciplined democracy that distrusted mass participation. The omnipresence of the concept in postwar Europe did not mean an 'end of ideology', as it was postulated in a number of accounts, and the concept of democracy was still highly contested. The difficulty of even finding common ground for understanding democracy was illustrated, for example, by the voluminous The United Nations Educational, Scientific and Cultural Organisation (UNESCO) report *Democracy in a World of Tensions*, which demonstrated the ideological divide that marked the Cold War era.[26] Within the field of political philosophy, W.B. Gallie famously used democracy as one of his prime examples of his category of 'essentially contested' concepts.[27] In the late 1960s and in the 1970s, Western liberal democracies were vehemently criticized again, this time in the name of 'more' or 'participatory' democracy.[28] By the end of the twentieth century, the issue of the 'democratic deficit' in the European Union, on the one hand, and the theoretical attempts of furthering global democracy, on the other, called into question the nation state as the sole locus of democracy.[29] In many European countries populist movements have challenged the important role of the rule of law and the protection of minorities in liberal democracy. Instead, they focus on the voice of 'the people' as a guiding principle of majority rule.

Differences and Transfers

A conceptual history not only avoids viewing just one period as 'formative' in the construction of modern democracy; it also shows significant differences and trajectories in different countries and in different spheres of society. Once research gets away from the fixation on a mainly Anglo-Saxon history of democracy and concentrates on the history of the concept in different national contexts instead, it turns out that the history of the concept is much richer than we knew. Instead of being 'a latecomer to the laurels of democracy', it turns out that Spain was one of the first countries to have a lively debate about 'democracy'.[30] The Netherlands, on the other hand, which has often been portrayed as a pioneering country in the world of democracy, is revealed as a latecomer if you look at the daily use of the term. There were isolated texts with the term in the early modern period and a short-lived popularity of related terms around 1800, it is true, but until the very end of the nineteenth century, the word was hardly used in the Dutch Parliament at all.[31] Popular sovereignty was rejected. The Dutch case shows that we should be very careful about equating a strong civil society or even the rule of law with democracy in the sense of the power of the people at large.

The pace at which the concept of 'democracy' gained support in the second half of the nineteenth century also varied from country to country. In France, the Revolution in 1848 strengthened an already existing discourse of democracy, and in the 1870s the Third Republic sealed the victory of 'democracy' as a concept. In Britain the breakthrough period was in the 1880s, and in the Netherlands in around 1900. From then on, the concept was no longer used to scare people, but rather to convince them not only of the claims of the opposition but also of the legitimacy of parliamentary and government politics. Suffrage movements, now also including demands for women's right to vote, were on the political agenda throughout Europe.

Looking at different national traditions also helps us to understand the ambiguous interplay between concepts related to democracy and to 'the people'. Every language had its own expressions referring to the people and its power, from the Russian *narod* to the German *Volk* and *Volksherrschaft*, from the French *souveraineté du peuple* to the Finnish *kansanvalta* or 'the power of the people', including in an ethnic sense, and from the nineteenth-century Spanish expression 'la Democracia es el pueblo' (the democracy is the people) to the modern Danish *folkestyre* with its connotations of participatory democracy. These all had their different connotations and their different rhythms of popularity, and they all demonstrated strategies to give national connotations to democracy or democratic connotations to nationalism. They helped democracy gain legitimacy or fortify democracy when it had become the name of the regime, or they were used by different parties as an additional argument for their specific interpretation of what democracy was. The vernacular expressions also show that democracy did not necessarily belong to the political left; associating it with national traditions made it easier for conservatives to use it as well. These national expressions were used to rhetorically underline the specific national 'roots' of democracy. Paradoxically, some of these national traditions, such as the Swiss one, were also used in a common European discourse about the development and different faces of democracy. Studying these traditions helps us to see that democracy was never necessarily a 'left-wing' force (see, for instance, Switzerland); it could also be part of a conservative movement, aimed at strengthening the bond between the king and the people (as in Sweden).[32]

This book is, of course, not the first to deal with the conceptual history of democracy. The best-known attempts are, however, designed as auxiliaries to other types of history, such as the articles about democracy in the conceptual dictionaries *Geschichtliche Grundbegriffe* and the *Handbuch politisch-sozialer Grundbegriffe in Frankreich*. They also concentrate on the period before the mid nineteenth century, the 'Sattelzeit', as coined by Reinhart Koselleck. There are also other contributions on this period, the most comprehensive being *Re-imagining Democracy in the Age of Revolutions*, edited by Joanna Innes and Mark Philp, which adds a wider range of countries into the picture.[33]

This book draws on these studies, but it shifts the attention to the nineteenth and twentieth centuries, focusing on later moments of change as well as differences and transfers between different countries: what did 'democracy' mean at various points in time and in various places? What were the experiences and expectations that dominated the shifting understandings of the concept? Who were the 'democrats' and what political goals were they fighting for? Who were their opponents and what did they think of democracy? What was the relationship between the rule of law and the concept of democracy in political and legal theory as well as in political discourse? How was 'democracy' defined in terms of geographical identifications – as 'Nordic' or 'Western' democracy'? Various researchers have addressed some of these questions, but there is no major systematic study in English or any other major language covering the entire period, let alone one with a general European and comparative perspective.[34] The institutional-political part of this history of democracy in modern Europe is well known, but there is no conceptual history of democracy in modern Europe from the Age of Revolution to the present. If literature on conceptions of democracy has covered both the nineteenth and twentieth centuries, such as in the important works by Pierre Rosanvallon and John Dunn, it has not concentrated on the variations of the history of the concept in different parts of Europe.[35]

Theorists from Tocqueville and Guizot to Kelsen, Bryce and Carl Schmitt have on many occasions announced the definitive victory of (some sort of) democracy. Every time this announcement has proved to be premature. Political debates over voting rights, the principle and practice of parliamentarism, constitutional design, industrial relations and so forth demonstrated the disputed nature of democracy more than anything else. We examine such debates and show the contested meaning of the concept and its strategic use. In order to do so, we take debates about democracy in national assemblies, in political movements and at particular (revolutionary) moments as our starting points. As continuous serial sources, the many digitized parliamentary proceedings are a particularly useful point of departure. Thus, this is a volume about the semantics and pragmatics of 'democracy' in modern Europe, with special attention being paid to actual political history as well as relevant political and legal theory in a political context. Obviously, it would have been possible to write a book on the same topic using a different range of sources, from religion to fiction, or with a focus on sources discussing economic and industrial relations. We also could have paid more attention to the relationship between democracy and gender. Our ambition has been to include a gender perspective in the volume by discussing in several chapters how 'universal suffrage' developed from an exclusively male content in the mid nineteenth century to a slogan of women's movements in the late nineteenth century, but this is no substitute for a separate or in-depth discussion of the topic. In addition to the gendered aspect of the concept of 'democracy', more focus on the relationship between racial arguments and democracy will be needed in the future. Instead, we have chosen to concentrate on the still rather unknown story of the huge national differences in the use of the concept of 'democracy' in order to make it possible to draw conclusions about European similarities as well as differences.

This book seeks to contribute to a transnational history of 'democracy' and to a history of the transfer of concepts, as well as to a history of the rhetoric of models and 'roots' of democracy. But we cannot ignore the fact that most political debates took place in a national context, and therefore we have chosen to take national debates as our point of departure. Democracy as a regime has until now also been confined to national states; European democracy, for instance, has run into a lot of trouble because it has not conformed to this national pattern. However, we link these national cases to conceptual developments in other countries, which served as models or as export destinations, or that we simply use for comparative reasons. Moreover, the case studies are chosen with care. Until now, most histories of democracy in Europe have, often implicitly, taken countries such as Britain and France as their yardstick. This book pays attention to countries that often disappear in such stories: the Nordic countries, Spain, Russia and the Czech Republic. It contains one contribution devoted to an overview of two centuries of 'democracy' in one particular country, and it immediately turns out that the country chosen, Spain, is much more interesting from the point of view of the history of democracy than many people would expect. It appears that there is no single mainstream development of democracy, but instead an abundance of democratic rhetoric in countries that commonly have not been regarded as 'core countries' of democratization.

By investigating many different countries, we discovered that there was already in the nineteenth century a strikingly common discourse about democracy, but also that there remained salient national peculiarities and surprising differences. Moreover, besides contributions about one or two individual countries, the book also contains a number of more comparative essays to underline commonalities and to highlight more general developments and a number of key moments in the history of the concept. In many of these cases the tensions within the concept of democracy are visible. One of the lessons of the history of the concept is that we should not conclude too quickly that older patterns are superseded, let alone surpassed, by new ones. After 1989, and partly already after 1945, the victory of liberal democracy seemed complete, but it has become clear that this idea was premature. That is the story of democracy: on many occasions, it seemed to be beaten or its victory seemed to be secured for good, but each time new developments showed that its history had not ended. Nor should we assume too easily that a feature of democracy is really new. It may be true that the notion of 'stability' is particularly suited to characterize post-1945 politics and that it had entered the language of politics only in the nineteenth century.[36] However, much that it entailed after 1945 reminds us of the balance that was considered crucial for the mixed constitution of the early nineteenth century. Also, the post-1945 attempt at domesticating democracy by adding judicial review and European institutions to check national democracy, including the preference of the rule of law over democracy, suggests a return to nineteenth-century discussions about the mixed constitution and the separation of powers. Yet, history never repeats itself, and these new discussions were mostly conducted under the aegis of democracy. Democracy had become the supreme value, whereas in the idea of a mixed constitution, it was only one of the elements contributing to a social balance. However, the similarities are striking, and they are an example of what we see if we look at the history of democracy through the lens of concepts and without the assumption of progress. It is a history of rhetoric, a history of practices; it is a history of the neverending search for ways to ensure the rule and participation of the people, a history of democracy and its discontents.

Jussi Kurunmäki is Associate Professor of Political Science, working at the Department of Cultures, University of Helsinki, and at the Institute of Contemporary History, Södertörn University, Stockholm. His authored and coedited books include *Representation, Nation and Time: The Political Rhetoric of the 1866 Parliamentary Reform in Sweden* (2000), *Käsitteet liikkeessä. Suomen poliittisen kulttuurin käsitehistoria* (2003), *Zeit, Geschichte und Politik; Time, History and Politics: Zum achtzigsten Geburtstag von Reinhart Koselleck* (2003) and *Rhetorics of Nordic Democracy* (2010). He is one of the guest editors of a special issue on the political rhetoric of -isms. He is also the chairperson of the network Concepta – Research Seminars in Conceptual History and Political Thought.

Jeppe Nevers is Professor of History at the University of Southern Denmark in Odense. He has written on a variety of topics in modern Danish and European history, including democracy, liberalism and industrial society. His books include *Fra skældsord til slagord: Demokratibegrebet i dansk politisk historie* (2011) and *Det produktive samfund: Seks kapitler af industrialiseringens idéhistorie* (2013). He has also contributed to comparative and collective volumes as well as international journals, and he is a board member of Concepta – Research Seminars in Conceptual History and Political Thought.

Henk te Velde is Professor of History at Leiden University. He has written a number of monographs on the history of political culture in the Netherlands, such as *Stijlen van Leiderschap: Persoon en Politiek van Thorbecke tot Den Uyl* (2010). *Sprekende politiek: Redenaars en hun publiek in de parlementaire gouden* *eeuw* is about nineteenth-century British and French parliamentary rhetoric and culture (2015). He recently coedited *Organizing Democracy: Reflections on the Rise of Political Organizations in the 19th Century* (2017), which has appeared as the first volume in the new book series 'Palgrave Studies in Political History', which he is coediting. He is also one of the editors of the *Journal of Modern European History* and is a founding member of the international Association for Political History.

Notes

1. Thomas S. Eliot, *The Idea of a Christian Society* (New York: Harcourt, Brace and Company, 1940), 11–12.
2. Francis Fukuyama, 'The End of History?', *The National Interest* 16 (1989), 3–18.
3. Paul Nolte, *Was ist Demokratie? Geschichte und Gegenwart* (Munich: Beck, 2012), 447.
4. Charles S. Maier, 'Democracy since the French Revolution', in John Dunn (ed.), *Democracy: The Unfinished Journey* (Oxford: Oxford University Press, 1992), 126; Tom Buchanan and Martin Conway, 'The Politics of Democracy in Twentieth-Century Europe: Introduction', *European History Quarterly* 32 (2002), 7–12; Henk te Velde, 'De domesticatie van democratie in Nederland', *BMGN – Low Countries Historical Review* 127 (2012), 3–27.
5. See e.g. the oeuvre of Pierre Rosanvallon.
6. John Keane, *The Life and Death of Democracy* (London: Pocket Books, 2009), ix.
7. John Dunn, *Setting the People Free* (London: Atlantic Books, 2005), 171.
8. E.g. Keane, *Life and Death of Democracy*.
9. Benjamin Isakhan and Stephen Stockwell (eds), *The Edinburgh Companion to the History of Democracy* (Edinburgh: Edinburgh University Press, 2012), 9–10.
10. Dunn (ed.), *Democracy: The Unfinished Journey*.
11. Margaret Canovan, 'Trust the People!: Populism and the Two Faces of Democracy', *Political Studies* 47(1) (1999), 2–16.
12. Reinhart Koselleck, 'Einleitung', in Otto Brunner, Werner Conze, and Reinhart Koselleck (eds), *Geschichtliche Grundbegriffe. Historisches Lexikon zur politisch-sozialen Sprache in Deutschland,* Band 1 A-D (Stuttgart: Klett-Cotta, 1972), xiii–xxvii.
13. See the chapter by Joanna Innes and Mark Philp in this volume.
14. See the chapter by Jussi Kurunmäki and Irène Herrmann in this volume.
15. Robert Roswell Palmer, *The Age of the Democratic Revolution: A Political History of Europe and America, 1760–1800* (Princeton: Princeton University Press, 1959–64), vols 1–2.
16. Cf. e.g. Aurelian Craiutu, *Liberalism under Siege: The Political Thought of the French Doctrinaires* (Lanham: Lexington Books, 2003); Annelien de Dijn, *French Political Thought from Montesquieu to Tocqueville: Liberty in a Levelled Society?* (Cambridge: Cambridge University Press, 2008).

17. Melvin Richter, 'Tocqueville and Guizot on Democracy: From a Type of Society to a Political Regime', *History of European Ideas* 30 (2004), 61–82.
18. François Guizot, *De la démocratie en France (janvier 1849)* (Paris: Meline, 1849); see also Christian Meier et al., 'Demokratie', in *Geschichtliche Grundbegriffe* (1972), 874.
19. Pierre Rosanvallon, *Le sacre du citoyen: Histoire du suffrage universel en France* (Paris: Éditions Gallimard, 1992).
20. Jeppe Nevers, *Fra skældsord til slagord: Demokratibegrebet i dansk politisk historie* (Odense: University Press of Southern Denmark, 2011).
21. Marcus Llanque, *Demokratisches Denken im Krieg: Die deutsche Debatte im Ersten Weltkrieg* (Berlin: De Gruyter, 2000), 104 ff.
22. James Bryce, *Modern Democracies* (London: Macmillan, 1921), vol. I, 4.
23. Giovanni Capoccia, *Defending Democracy. Reactions to Extremism in Interwar Europe* (Baltimore: Johns Hopkins University Press, 2005), 6–9, 41–46.
24. For arguments in which 'democracy' was used against liberal democracy, see the chapter by Marcus Llanque in this volume; for the defence of parliamentary democracy, see e.g. Jussi Kurunmäki, '"Nordic Democracy" in 1935. On the Finnish and Swedish Rhetoric of Democracy', in Jussi Kurunmäki and Johan Strang, *Rhetorics of Nordic Democracy* (Helsinki: Finnish Literature Society, 2010), 37–82.
25. See Martin Conway's chapter in this book; see also Martin Conway, 'Democracy in Post-War Western Europe: The Triumph of a Political Model', *European History Quarterly* 32 (2000), 59–84.
26. Richard McKeon and Stein Rokkan (eds), *Democracy in a World of Tensions: A Symposium Prepared by UNESCO* (Paris: UNESCO, 1951).
27. Walter Bruce Gallie, 'Essentially Contested Concepts', *Proceedings of the Aristotelian Society* 56 (1956), 167–98.
28. See the chapter by Ingrid Gilcher-Holtey in this volume.
29. See e.g. Barry Holden (ed.), *Global Democracy: Key Debates* (London: Routledge, 2000).
30. Cf. Guy Hermet, 'A Latecomer to the Laurels of Democracy', in Antoine de Baecque (ed.), *A History of Democracy in Europe* (New York: Columbia University Press, 1995), 150–63 with the chapter by Javier Fernández-Sebastián and José María Rosales in this volume.
31. Cf. Keane, *Life and Death of Democracy,* 242, 250, 254–57, 277, 455–56, 467, 475 with te Velde, 'Domesticatie van democratie in Nederland'.
32. See the chapter by Kurunmäki and Herrmann in this volume.
33. Joanna Innes and Mark Philp: *Re-imagining Democracy in the Age of Revolution* (Oxford: Oxford University Press 2013). See also Pasi Ihalainen, *Agents of the People: Democracy and Popular Sovereignty in British and Swedish Parliamentary and Public Debates, 1734–1800* (Leiden: Brill, 2010).
34. E.g. Heiko Bollmeyer, *Der steinige Weg zur Demokratie: Die Weimarer Nationalversammlung zwischen Kaiserreich und Republik* (Frankfurt: Campus Verlag, 2007); Llanque, *Demokratisches Denken im Krieg*; Nevers, *Fra skældsord til slagord*; Matti

Hyvärinen, '"The People's Power" (Democracy) as an Argument in Finnish Party Manifestos', *Finnish Yearbook of Political Thought* 7 (2003), 36–67. Jens A. Christophersen, *The Meaning of 'Democracy' as Used in European Ideologies from the French to the Russian Revolution* (Oslo: Oslo University Press, 1968); Jan-Werner Müller, *Contesting Democracy: Political Ideas in Twentieth-Century Europe* (New Haven: Yale University Press, 2011).

35. Dunn (ed.), *Democracy: The Unfinished Journey*; Dunn, *Setting the People Free*; Pierre Rosanvallon, 'The History of the Word "Democracy" in France', *Journal of Democracy* 6 (1995), 140–54; Rosanvallon, *La démocratie inachevée*.
36. Müller, *Contesting Democracy*, 143–44, 221.

Bibliography

Bollmeyer, H. 2007. *Der steinige Weg zur Demokratie: Die Weimarer Nationalversammlung zwischen Kaiserreich und Republik*. Frankfurt: Campus Verlag.

Bryce, J. 1921. *Modern Democracies*, vol. I. London: Macmillan.

Buchanan, T., and M. Conway. 2002. 'The Politics of Democracy in Twentieth-Century Europe: Introduction', *European History Quarterly* 32, 7–12.

Canovan, M. 1999. 'Trust the People!: Populism and the Two Faces of Democracy', *Political Studies* 47(1), 2–16.

Capoccia, G. 2005. *Defending Democracy. Reactions to Extremism in Interwar Europe*, Baltimore: Johns Hopkins University Press.

Christophersen, J.A. 1968. *The Meaning of 'Democracy' as Used in European Ideologies from the French to the Russian Revolution*. Oslo: Oslo University Press.

Conway, M. 2000. 'Democracy in Post-War Western Europe: The Triumph of a Political Model', *European History Quarterly* 32, 59–84.

Craiutu, A. 2003. *Liberalism under Siege: The Political Thought of the French Doctrinaires*. Lanham: Lexington Books.

de Dijn, A. 2008. *French Political Thought from Montesquieu to Tocqueville: Liberty in a Levelled Society?* Cambridge: Cambridge University Press.

Dunn, J. 2005. *Setting the People Free*. London: Atlantic Books.

Eliot, T.S. 1940. *The Idea of a Christian Society*. New York: Harcourt, Brace and Company.

Fukuyama, F. 1989. 'The End of History?', *The National Interest* 16, 3–18.

Gallie, W.B. 1956. 'Essentially Contested Concepts', *Proceedings of the Aristotelian Society* 56, 167–98.

Guizot, F. 1849. *De la démocratie en France (janvier 1849)*. Paris: Meline.

Hermet, G. 1995. 'A Latecomer to the Laurels of Democracy', in Antoine de Baecque (ed.), *A History of Democracy in Europe*. New York: Columbia University Press, 150–63.

Holden, B. (ed.). 2000. *Global Democracy: Key Debates*. London: Routledge.

Hyvärinen, M. 2003. '"The People's Power" (Democracy) as an Argument in Finnish Party Manifestos', *Finnish Yearbook of Political Thought* 7, 36–67.

Ihalainen, P. 2010. *Agents of the People: Democracy and Popular Sovereignty in British and Swedish Parliamentary and Public Debates, 1734–1800*. Leiden: Brill.
Innes, J., and M. Philp. 2013. *Re-imagining Democracy in the Age of Revolution*. Oxford: Oxford University Press.
Isakhan, B., and S. Stockwell (eds). 2012. *The Edinburgh Companion to the History of Democracy*. Edinburgh: Edinburgh University Press.
Keane, J. 2009. *The Life and Death of Democracy*. London: Pocket Books.
Koselleck, R. 'Einleitung', in O. Brunner, W. Conze and R. Koselleck (eds), *Geschichtliche Grundbegriffe. Historisches Lexikon zur politisch-sozialen Sprache in Deutschland*, Band 1 A-D. Stuttgart: Klett-Cotta, 1972, xiii–xxvii.
Kurunmäki, J., and J. Strang. 2010. *Rhetorics of Nordic Democracy*. Helsinki: Finnish Literature Society.
Llanque, M. 2000. *Demokratisches Denken im Krieg: Die deutsche Debatte im Ersten Weltkrieg*. Berlin: De Gruyter.
Maier, C.S. 1992. 'Democracy since the French Revolution', in J. Dunn (ed.), *Democracy: The Unfinished Journey*. Oxford: Oxford University Press, 125–153.
McKeon, R., and S. Rokkan (eds). 1951. *Democracy in a World of Tensions: A Symposium Prepared by UNESCO*. Paris: UNESCO.
Meier, C. et al. 1972. 'Demokratie', in O. Brunner, W. Conze and R. Koselleck (eds), *Geschichtliche Grundbegriffe. Historisches Lexikon zur politisch-sozialen Sprache in Deutschland*, Band 1 A-D. Stuttgart: Klett-Cotta, 821–99.
Müller, J-W. 2011. *Contesting Democracy: Political Ideas in Twentieth-Century Europe*. New Haven: Yale University Press.
Nevers, J. 2011. *Fra skældsord til slagord: Demokratibegrebet i dansk politisk historie*. Odense: University Press of Southern Denmark.
Nolte, P. 2012. *Was ist Demokratie? Geschichte und Gegenwart*. Munich: Beck.
Palmer, R.R. 1959–64. *The Age of the Democratic Revolution: A Political History of Europe and America, 1760–1800*. Princeton: Princeton University Press.
Richter, M. 2004. 'Tocqueville and Guizot on Democracy: From a Type of Society to a Political Regime', *History of European Ideas* 30, 61–82.
Rosanvallon, P. 1992. *Le sacre du citoyen: Histoire du suffrage universel en France*. Paris: Éditions Gallimard.
Rosanvallon, P. 1995. 'The History of the Word "Democracy" in France', *Journal of Democracy* 6, 140–54.
te Velde, H. 2012. 'De domesticatie van democratie in Nederland', *BMGN – Low Countries Historical Review* 127, 3–27.

Chapter 1

'Democracy' from Book to Life

The Emergence of the Term in Active Political Debate, to 1848

Joanna Innes and Mark Philp

Between the sixteenth and the mid nineteenth centuries, the Greek and subsequently medieval Latin word 'democratia' was naturalized in most European languages; the term came to be employed in domestic political debate and was increasingly avowed as an aspiration. In the revolutionary era of 1848–49 it was widely endorsed. Nevertheless, even then, it probably had little currency outside the circles of political activists. It remained, ironically, a rarefied word for a popular thing.

This chapter traces the word's emergence in European political argument. It draws upon a wealth of single-language studies, welding them into a broad survey. It suggests that there were phases of development in the frequency and character of the word's use, but also that it acquired different resonances in different national and local contexts, as it was adapted to differing institutional settings and deployed in particular debates. It was always open to a variety of appropriations: it could be used to describe, to analyse, to recommend, to disparage or as a badge of identity. However, its basic referents – popular government and equality – were sufficiently stable for diverse uses to be intelligible, shades of meaning being conveyed by context.

Contestation around 'democracy' was episodic. Most scholarly attention has focused on the word's eruption into political debate in the late eighteenth century, but, following this surge in use (if often defamatory use), it lost currency. There were fewer phenomena to which it could be pinned, but also its association with French revolutionary excess made it hard to invoke to positive effect. After 1830, it regained favour; we try both to chart and to explain this shift by identifying the changes in political life that made 'democracy' and cognate words ones that people wanted and felt able to use. This phase climaxed during the mid nineteenth-century European revolutions, when these terms were unprecedentedly widely endorsed. Yet these events brought new complications in their wake, for not only did mid-century revolutions reinforce old doubts about the merits of giving the people a voice in government, but their medium-term outcomes also disappointed many who had once been proud to call themselves democrats. Such people were prompted to reconsider how to give their aspirations form and whether to continue to term them 'democratic'.

'Democracy', in *Ancien Régime* Europe

During the seventeenth and eighteenth centuries, 'democracy' and cognate terms acquired diverse applications and associations in modern European languages, fitting them for a variety of political appropriations.

The ancient-world associations of 'democracy' coloured its early modern use. It was often used historically, to refer to Greek states or indeed to the Roman Republic. Following Aristotle and Polybius, it was also used analytically, to categorize possible forms of political order. Democracy was contrasted with monarchy and aristocracy – though all three elements could be combined in a 'mixed government' or 'mixed constitution'. Democracy was believed to be a rarity in the modern world: even constitutions identified as mixed might (like the Holy Roman Empire) contain only monarchical and aristocratic elements; only a few Swiss cantons were consistently identified as democratic. But it was a standard category of analysis, deployed in both historical and geographical educational texts, and, as such, must have been familiar to many with a more than elementary education. As in the ancient world, these categories were sometimes applied to social groups: just as a nobility could be termed 'the aristocracy', so the common people could be termed 'the democracy'. Ancient ideas about the political culture of democracies also affected usage: democracies were understood to be turbulent, characterized by crowd activity, demagoguery and popular violence, and in their relations with other polities, to be overweening, bellicose and unstable. They were also thought to be prone to degenerate into tyranny – of the majority, of a demagogue or of a strong man who might offer salvation from democracy.[1]

The Greek-derived 'democracy' and the Latin-derived 'republic' – the latter the subject of much early modern theorizing – sometimes converged in use. Montesquieu, writing in the mid eighteenth century, divided contemporary European states into monarchies, headed by single, often but not necessarily hereditary, rulers, and republics, ruled by a corporate group. Republics, he said, could be aristocratic or democratic, depending on how many were admitted to the privileges of rule. He identified virtue as pre-eminently the principle of democratic republics, for without virtue, defined as 'the love of one's country, that is, the love of equality', such republics were bound to fail. Yet virtue, he believed, was in scant supply in the modern world, and democratic republics were essentially vestiges of the past, of little relevance to modern conditions.[2] Attempts to renovate republican forms in Corsica in the 1750s and 1760s and in America in the 1770s and 1780s encouraged some observers to wonder if 'democracy' might yet find new niches for itself in the modern world, though it seemed unlikely that the experience of such marginal places could be generalized.[3] If the essence of a republic was taken to be orientation to the common good, then even 'patriotic monarchies' could qualify as republics – and if they achieved that orientation by overcoming the self-interest of the nobility, then such a monarchy might be considered a species of democracy: so reasoned the Marquis d'Argenson, writing in mid eighteenth-century France, adumbrating a scheme that had more obvious potential.[4] However, these were exceptional formulations. Rousseau said that such a perfect form of government was not fit for men.[5]

Overall, few suggested that democracy, however imagined, had much of a role to play in modern states. In an era of waxing historicism, it indeed became common to characterize it as a primitive form. The influential late seventeenth-century natural law theorist Pufendorf suggested that democracy was the natural form of first governments, established by agreement among previously ungoverned peoples.[6]

During the seventeenth and eighteenth centuries, democracy figured in current debate mainly in mixed-constitutional and republican settings, since it was in those contexts that it had most obvious purchase. Reference was often to elements of the constitution that stood proxy for the people. In England, during the seventeenth-century Civil War, royal apologists argued that monarchy had an essential part to play balancing aristocratic and democratic elements. In the 1730s, opponents of the extremely powerful Prime Minister Robert Walpole argued that the independence of the House of Commons, the democratic part of the constitution, needed enhancement.[7] In the city-republic of Geneva, an early eighteenth-century defender of its relatively oligarchical institutions claimed that they bore comparison with those of 'the most eminent democracies in Europe', notably England; the English example showed (he said) that it was perfectly proper in a democracy for the people's power to be channelled through representatives.[8] In Sweden in the 1760s, such talk about democracy as there was took place mainly in the noble house, nobles being most familiar with this erudite terminology: while most invoked democracy as a bogey, one speaker argued that it might be given workable form in plenary sessions of the Estates.[9]

'Democracy' was also sometimes identified with the people out of doors, challenging the oligarchic character of assemblies or forgetting their place. In mid and late seventeenth-century England, some troublemakers were termed 'democratics'.[10] In the 1750s and again in the 1780s, popular agitations against unpopular religious groups (Jews, Catholics) were described as 'democratic/al' (though it remained more common to attribute democratic leanings to political factions flirting with a wider public).[11] In Sweden in the 1770s, 'democracy' became associated with critical pressure on the estate system from without (in which context, members of the noble estate lost sympathy with the cause).[12] In the 1760s, Genevan (and in the 1780s Dutch) critics of republican oligarchies were termed democrats – though this was more a matter of abusive labelling than self-description: the Genevans called themselves *représentants*, while the Dutch used 'patriots'; the Dutch affirmed the merits of 'representative democracy', but also expressed the hope that their programme would put an end to 'democratic disorders'.[13] In North America, when the founders set about establishing a republic, they represented themselves as establishing *not* democracy, but its modern analogue, representative government. The charge of being 'democrats' was levelled against those who took part in protests out of doors against fiscal and other policies of the new regime.[14]

'Democracy' during the French Revolution and its Aftermath

The French Revolution did more than any other single historical event to raise the profile of democracy and cognate terms in the European and indeed the American lexicon.[15] This was in the first instance chiefly the achievement of its critics, pre-eminently the British politician and writer Edmund Burke, who claimed that what had been instituted, when the National Assembly voted away noble privilege on 4 August 1789, was 'a pure democracy': 'Our present danger from the example of a people, whose character knows no medium, is . . . a danger of being led through an admiration of successful fraud and violence, to an imitation of the excesses of an irrational, unprincipled, proscribing, confiscating, plundering, ferocious, bloody, and tyrannical democracy.'[16] Burke was alarmed more quickly than most, but events in France, culminating in the Terror, realized many observers' worst fears. Both French revolutionaries and their sympathisers elsewhere were attacked as 'democrats', in polemic pitched at a variety of audiences. In England, the term was employed in songs aimed at tavern groups and ordinary villagers, though if it thereby gained any hold in popular consciousness, it does not seem to have stuck.[17]

Insofar as democracy was invoked positively in the early years of the Revolution, it was chiefly in relation to social status: democrats were contrasted to aristocrats. In this context, to be a democrat was to defend equality and to oppose privilege, feudal rights, corporate monopolies and perhaps also the hierarchies of gender, age or race. Satirical engravings produced early on in the French Revolution contrasted simple, plebeian democrats with bejewelled aristocrats.[18] In England, those who came (in private if not in public) to avow a name originally pinned on them by their enemies used it among themselves to signify their hopes for the introduction of more equal manners. In the United States, where the Federal Constitution of 1787 formally barred the establishment of a nobility, opposition to aristocracy could be seen as expressing American values. This helps to explain why, from 1793, American sympathizers with France established societies formally titled 'Democratic' or 'Democratic-Republican', a practice not echoed in Europe. From the federal election of 1800, 'democracy' was more widely endorsed as an American value – with important if mixed consequences for European perceptions when, with the ending of the Napoleonic Wars in 1815, the United States drew more European visitors, curious to discover what democracy might look like in modern dress.[19]

Once France became a republic in 1792, as aristocracy was discredited through its associations with *émigrés* and counter-revolutionaries, and spontaneous popular action won acceptance as – at least sometimes – a legitimate exercise of power, new imaginative space opened for discussion of political options. But even then, though reactionaries depicted France as teeming with 'democratic' phenomena, the term was rarely deployed by revolutionaries. In the National Convention, Robespierre and his followers Billaud-Varennes and St Just were among the few occasionally to use it – perhaps because they knew that they were denigrated as democrats and wanted to appropriate the term for their own purposes. Robespierre, in his speech on public morality on 5 February 1794, indicated that arrangements such as those set out in the 1793 Constitution *could* be termed democratic, but then qualified what he meant: 'Democracy is not a state in which the people, continually meeting, regulate for themselves all public affairs . . . Democracy is a state in which the sovereign people, guided by laws which are of their own making, do for themselves all that they can do well, and by their delegates do all that they cannot do for themselves.' He suggested that instituting democracy was, even so, essentially a project for the future, for as things were, one could only seek 'to lay the foundations of democracy among us and to consolidate it . . . [since first] we must finish the war of liberty against tyranny and safely cross through the storms of the revolution'. Robespierre also positively glossed democracy by (following Montesquieu) associating it with virtue: 'Not only is virtue the soul of democracy, but it can exist only under this government.'[20] Other revolutionary sympathizers who evoked democracy at this time associated it with popular activity supportive of the new regime, dwelling, for example, on the challenge – and the possible innovative solutions to the challenge – of making government accountable, perhaps through popular surveillance of officials.[21]

It is slightly easier to find affirmations of democracy after the fall of Robespierre, the promulgation of the Constitution of 1795/Year III and the re-establishment of a regular system of government, with an executive Directory and bicameral, elected legislature. In France itself, the Directory, keen to emphasize that it was taming but not renouncing the revolutionary impulse, affirmed (against pure democracy) 'representative democracy', though patterns in the use of this phrase need more study.[22] Democracy was invoked differently by some critics of the regime, who identified the governing clique as a new aristocracy, which challenged their own democratic aspirations. These critics included Pierre Antoine Antonelle, who edited a short-lived journal, *Démocrate Constitutionnel*.[23] A more marginal figure, though better remembered subsequently, was the journalist 'Gracchus' Babeuf. During the famine years 1795–96, appalled by popular suffering, Babeuf called for a social revolution; at his trial for conspiracy, he held forth on the true (essentially egalitarian) nature of democracy – carrying that faith to the guillotine. Philippe Buonarroti (a scion of Tuscan nobility), who like many of Babeuf's circle was deported, sought to keep this radical form of democratic commitment alive into the new century. Yet it is striking how much more insistently the term was invoked in Buonarroti's account of Babeuf and his conspiracy, published in 1828, than it was by Babeuf himself in his writings or at his trial. The term was in Babeuf's lexicon, but he did not make it a slogan.[24]

Democracy and its cognates achieved more prominence in the late 1790s in the 'sister republics' of the Netherlands and Italy.[25] Republican political traditions (in the case of Italy, mostly dormant) played a part; emphasizing that new republics were democratic helped to set them apart from their precursors. In the Batavian Republic, broadly Francophile Dutchmen renounced the demagoguery of the Terror, which they said demonstrated what might go wrong if government were not given a proper constitutional base. They aimed to establish a new centralized republic (contrasting with the old federal republic); in its single legislature, all inhabitants would be equally represented via a wide franchise. This position was supported by a newly founded newspaper, *De Democraten*. When the French ambassador intervened to help members of the deadlocked Dutch constituent assembly formulate new institutional arrangements (to France's taste), his version was rejected on the grounds that the Dutch were capable of more democracy than the French. (The Dutch version provided a greater role for direct election, limited the power of the upper house and provided scope for popular initiative to amend the Constitution). Some adherents of the new north Italian republics displayed notable zeal for the work of 'democratization'. This entailed more than just the introduction of republican institutions; it meant promoting democratic manners and elevating the common people so as to fit them for citizenship. However, enthusiasm fell away in the face of counter-revolution in Naples (in which the common people played a prominent and brutal part) and changes in the French governing style associated with the rise of Napoleon Bonaparte.

In Germany, by contrast, though democratic principles were the subject of discussion in enlightened and academic circles, they found little practical application in persistently monarchical political cultures. Christoph Wieland critically examined democracy in his literary periodical *Teutsche Merkur*. Immanuel Kant distinguished between (desirable) underlying republican principles and (impractical) democratic governmental forms – though some of his followers elided republic and democracy, and began to talk about democracy as a desirable underlying principle. This usage spread from the academy to at least the higher levels of the civil service; thus, the Prussian reformer Hardenberg in 1807 stated: 'Democratic principles in a monarchical government: this seems to me to be the appropriate form in the current climate.' The course of Prussian history did not, however, immediately favour a shift towards a more republican version of monarchy.[26]

What emerges is that the French Revolution helped to make democracy a talking point. Initially, 'democratic' features of the Revolution were largely condemned. By the later 1790s, the term was more often given a positive spin, but its applications remained diverse. It was sometimes taken to imply that the people should vigilantly oversee officials. Some equated democracy with the election of officials or of legislatures. Some understood democracy as a principle or spirit – the principle of directing government to the general good; thus understood, democracy was compatible with almost any overarching institution. Those who thought that the mass of working people and the poor had been poorly served by most past governments sometimes interpreted democracy as entailing above all an undertaking to do better by those masses.

The 1800s–1820s: 'Democracy', in Eclipse

In the first few decades of the new century, there was little institutional encouragement in any European context for positive talk about democracy. Under Napoleon, the French regime at home and abroad lost interest in positively promoting 'democracy' (though the notion that the regime channelled and expressed the sovereignty of the people continued to be affirmed: at the lowest levels, officials continued to be elected, candidates for other offices were nominated through complex electoral processes, and some constitutional changes were subject to plebiscites).[27] Those who opposed the Revolution meanwhile argued that it had exposed the horrors of democracy for all to see: one Jesuit prophesied that the word would disappear from dictionaries.[28] Among those who kept faith with some of the initial objectives of the Revolution but were critical of Napoleon, few had time for democracy, believing that it had opened the way to tyranny. Following the fall of Napoleon, the cause of democracy seemed as dead and impossible to revive as the cause of communism would appear after the fall of the Berlin Wall.

This is not to imply that democracy had no advocates. The English 'philosophical radical' Jeremy Bentham began to champion it at this time; it continued to hold critical potential for those who saw contemporary governments as so many partial, self-serving power blocs.[29] Yet its associations were too problematic to commend it as a mobilizing slogan for almost any position; among the less educated, it perhaps entirely lacked resonance.

In France, 'liberal' was the term that left-wing critics of Napoleon had made their own; now they tried to infuse the Restoration regime with a 'liberal' spirit. Some among them argued that, in one important sense, France was now 'democratic', because privilege had not been restored, and in terms of civil rights, all French were equal. Yet they argued that a democratic *society* needed something other than democratic *government*.[30] Democratic government might have suited the needs of the ancient world, but in the modern world, where liberty was universally enjoyed (in the form of security, private property and freedom to pursue personal happiness), this desirable state of things was most likely to be preserved by a system in which ministers were accountable to a legislature elected from the educated and capable by the educated and capable. Some saw a role for a wider 'public opinion' to inform public debate, but the 'Doctrinaire' liberal theorist and politician François Guizot doubted even that, arguing that reason must prevail.

French liberal arguments for a narrow, educated and propertied franchise gradually won wide support in Europe, but not immediately from liberals everywhere. In around 1820, many continued to adhere to visions associated with earlier phases of the Revolution and accordingly favoured a wide (though usually indirect) franchise. That way of giving institutional form to 'national sovereignty' had been written into the Spanish Constitution of 1812 (the constitution under which the Spanish rallied against absorption into the Napoleonic Empire). This constitution was implemented in Spain once more, in defiance of the wishes of the restored monarch, in 1820; it was adopted (pending agreement on a local version) against the background of revolutions in Portugal in the same year, and also in Naples and Piedmont. The Greeks, revolting against Ottoman rule from 1821, wrote popular sovereignty into their early revolutionary constitutions. However, none of these regimes lasted more than a few years; by 1833, even the Greeks had come under the rule of a Bavarian monarch who heeded no constitution.[31]

In any case, 'democracy' was not the watchword of these efforts: constitution, liberty and national sovereignty were preferred slogans. A Portuguese professor explained why constitutional government was superior to democracy: 'Constitutional Government is the best medium between two extremes: Monarchy and Democracy . . . Constitutional Government is necessary to make the two powers act and react equally, so as to conserve an equilibrium.'[32] Balance thus continued to be valued. Even members of republican secret societies, though they sometimes – under Babouvist or other influence – talked about democracy among themselves, did not flourish the term when circumstances allowed them to make their case in public; they judged 'liberty' more likely to rouse the people.[33]

From the Revolutions of 1830 to 1848: The Revival of Talk about 'Democracy'

Breaking out at a point when the forces of reaction had seemed to be gaining the upper hand, the revolutions of 1830–31 marked a striking reversal, suggesting that the party of movement could not easily be contained. Risings in France, Belgium, Poland and in central Italy brought the people, sometimes in the form of armed militias, on to the streets, while reform movements in Britain, Norway, Denmark, some German states and some Swiss cantons mobilized public support, entailing at least threats of mass disturbance. Within a few years, new monarchs in both Spain and Portugal also backed the constitutionalist cause (though they then had to vindicate it in civil wars).[34] Yet, as in the immediately preceding decades, talk of democracy was initially rare. Moreover, though some of those promoting change endorsed radical aims (in France the institution of a republic, in Spain the reinstatement of the broadly based 1812 Constitution), when protestors succeeded in permanently changing the institutional base of rule, its social base changed only modestly. Property or tax qualifications for voting were endorsed everywhere; in Spain they were newly introduced.

Between 1830 and 1848, 'democracy' and cognate terms nonetheless started to figure more widely and more positively than ever before in European political discourse. This development has neither been fully charted nor clearly explained. We attempt now to identify some reasons why the term gained currency. Its applications remained diverse: what 'democrats' stood for varied according to the context. Again, as in the past, the term was probably most often a slogan, a 'fighting word', rather than being asked to do precise analytical work. But positive uses multiplied and, in that context, the term acquired some new associations.

Though 'democracy' retained problematic associations, the spread of constitutional monarchy, associated with representative assemblies and increasingly with liberal values, created a climate that encouraged both supporters and critics of these regimes to debate the concept. Given that conservatives often denigrated such regimes as democratic, liberals had reason to blunt the charge by explaining that the term could be positively construed. In Britain, proponents of the 1831–32 'Reform Bill', which aimed to rationalize and extend the parliamentary franchise, argued back to Tory critics that there was an advantage in strengthening the democratic element within the British constitution, and in any case neither history nor recent British experience suggested that the minor concessions to 'democracy' that they proposed would prove disastrous.[35] In Spain and Portugal, defenders of constitutional monarchy with a representative component acknowledged that this institutional set-up indeed had a democratic aspect, though within a mixed context, which made it positively desirable, since this was a recognized, effective constitutional form; in Portugal it was argued that what was at issue was a good form of democracy 'legal, pacific, progressive, orderly', as opposed to a turbulent 'proletarian democracy'.[36]

The new Liberal regimes also offered their own provocations: they provided a new 'other' for proponents of radical change to define themselves against. These provocations included the deliberate and reasoned exclusion from active citizenship of a significant majority of men who did not meet property and educational criteria, and (especially in Britain and France) the repression of workers' organizations, seen as would-be privileged bodies obstructing the free play of market forces. In Britain it was after the 1832 Reform Act that 'democracy' was widely endorsed as a goal outside Parliament by people who regarded themselves as having been betrayed by liberals who had talked about democracy, but failed to deliver it. One of the first post-Reform proponents of 'democracy', the Irish radical Bronterre O'Brien, published his own translation of Buonarroti's account of Babeuf's Conspiracy of Equals in 1836. Operating in a liberal environment, O'Brien did not see a need to resort to conspiracy, but he was attracted by Babeuf's insistence that democracy should entail social equality.[37] In Portugal, 'setembristas', who emerged following the liberal resolution of the Portuguese civil wars, championed their cause in periodicals including *O Democrata* (1839–40). They called for a return to the more radical constitutional principles of the early 1820s and attention to 'problemas sociais'.[38] Unlike British Chartists, they did not aim to extend the franchise, focusing instead on strengthening the lower house of the legislature.

In France, democrats were to be found especially amongst those who disliked the bourgeois aristocracy that underpinned the July Monarchy; they were often termed 'radicals', though some were republicans wary of avowing that seditious name. Among left critics of the status quo, there was in effect a tussle over strategy at this time. Some looked to political solutions, perhaps in the wake of a new revolution: Auguste Blanqui was an influential voice for insurrection.[39] Others emphasized social ills and favoured peaceful methods. The Fourierist Victor Considérant disapproved of the 'brutal' revolutionary spirit, which had (as he saw it) fuelled risings in Paris and Lyon in 1834, and in Paris in 1839; he favoured *La Démocratie Pacifique* (giving that title to a newspaper that he founded in 1843). He argued that, with the return of social peace: 'Democracy would soon reacquire that large, general and comprehensive significance which it was destined to receive as it came to express the fundamental spirit of the century.'[40]

We have noted German philosophers identifying democracy with the Zeitgeist at the start of the century. In the 1830s and 1840s, the idea that democracy was not primitive but modern seems to have made headway. Perhaps the most influential promoter of this view was Alexis de Tocqueville, who joined the steady trickle of European literary visitors to the United States. Tocqueville's *De la démocratie en Amérique* (the first volume of which appeared in 1835) identified in the modern world a general tendency towards the equalization of social condition. Like other French liberals, he termed this state of affairs 'democracy' – though he also probed American 'democratic' political institutions and practices. He implied that Europe had something to learn from these practices, which had preserved individual liberty under democratic conditions. Tocqueville's was not a directly political intervention. Yet it was broadly liberal in conception and was received as such: more conservative French liberals criticized it, while British conservatives preferred the deceased New Englander Fisher Ames's splenetic diatribe on American political manners, repackaged and published in London in the same year as *The Influences of Democracy on Liberty, Property and the Happiness of Society Considered*. Tocqueville both reflected and helped to shape developing liberal discourses about how to respond to democracy as an ineluctable force in modern times. His book was widely read in the original French, speedily translated into numerous other languages (English, Spanish and German), and excerpted and discussed in newspapers and periodicals.[41]

As democracy came to be located in the future, its past was also refashioned. It came to be credited with Greek origins (as if set in a continuing lineage) and was also equipped with a modern past, peopled by men portrayed as having striven to give the ideal modern form. Demosthenes, Rousseau, Paine and Robespierre helped to stock a pantheon of democratic forebears, even though the last three had habitually presented themselves in other terms.⁴²

Alongside other changes in representations of democracy, there developed in this period an important strain of religiously infused democratic rhetoric. In the course of the first French Revolution and successor revolutions, some priests had grasped the chance to reform the church as well as the state and had held up for imitation the example set by Christ in attending to the needs of the poor. In the context of widespread reaction against the French Revolution and its legacies, the Catholic cause was often identified with counter-revolution, among others by the influential writers Bonald and de Maistre. However, the statist Catholicism of the Restoration era was not to everyone's taste.

Among those who tried to forge links between Catholicism and democracy, there was a spectrum between those chiefly interested in developing populist underpinnings for traditional authority structures by challenging liberals' and radicals' monopoly on the rhetoric, and those whose commitment to new forms of politics was wholehearted. The case of the Irish Catholic lawyer-turned-political-activist Daniel O'Connell – who achieved fame throughout Europe and both Americas – illustrates these complexities. O'Connell extended the originally aristocratic, middle-class and urban base of an existing Irish campaign for enhanced Catholic political rights to a mass rural base, succeeding in wringing concessions from the British government. While campaigning, he built links with British parliamentary reformers. Having entered Parliament in 1830 as Ireland's first Catholic MP, he was both early and unusually forthright in proclaiming himself a 'democrat'. Later he led another (this time unsuccessful) mass campaign for the repeal of the Anglo-Irish parliamentary union, in which he agitated the cause before 'monster meetings', in the Irish countryside. Yet O'Connell accepted restriction of the franchise, excluding the poorest voters as the price for Catholic entry to Parliament; he concentrated control of his movement in his own hands, denying initiative to the rank and file, and his meetings were carefully choreographed so as to emphasize that goals were shared across the social hierarchy. Coming from a country with a tradition of peasant vigilantism, O'Connell had no intention of giving the people their head.⁴³

O'Connell's activities nonetheless inspired others to link Catholic and democratic causes. The most influential clerical exponent of Catholic democracy was the French priest Félicité de Lammenais. Against the background of the French 1830 Revolution, Lammenais edited the periodical *L'Avenir*, which invoked democracy to positive effect and endorsed (along with an enlarged suffrage and rights of local self-government) separation of church and state, along with freedom of conscience, instruction, assembly and the press –

though some of his associates thought he went too far and the Pope ultimately condemned his views. Nonetheless, his influence helped to channel other priests into radical politics: the Jesuit Gioacchino Ventura, for example, began his career as a proponent of the counter-revolutionary ideas of de Maistre, then passed, through admiration for Daniel O'Connell and association with Lammenais to support the Sicilian revolution of 1848 and the Roman Republic.[44]

Catholic democracy was a political chameleon. In Spain and Portugal, Catholic rural populations flocked to absolutist claimants to the throne in a series of civil wars, enabling absolutists and their clerical supporters to assert that their cause was the truly democratic one. Some Spanish and Portuguese liberals in this context gained a new appreciation of the reservations of French liberals and became wary of democracy. Yet overall, the association of democracy with Christianity, sometimes a very loosely conceived Christianity, perhaps an undogmatic 'true Christianity', eased the way for a broader reception of democracy as an ideal in 1848.[45]

One important context in which talk of democracy gained currency between 1830 and 1848 was that of exile politics. The failed revolutions of the early 1820s and of 1830–31 flung exiles far and wide. Some went to other sites of contestation; others clustered in the relatively hospitable Paris and London. Exiles interacted with their exiled compatriots, with audiences in their countries of origin and with exiles from other states (insofar as their language skills allowed); they were in principle well placed to pick up new ideas, forge new syntheses and disseminate them. There were exiles of all political colourings, from absolutists to radical egalitarians. The 1830s saw the emergence of the 'democrat' as one identity that exiles might assume to locate themselves in a fluid and often fractious political landscape.[46] Polish exiles were both early and stalwart promoters of 'democratic' identity. The Polish National Democratic Association diagnosed Polish nobles' failure to bond with the peasantry as a key reason for the failure of their attempt to throw off the Russian yoke through revolution in 1830. They added to the developing European account of 'social problems' an agrarian component especially relevant to still largely rural and legally stratified Central and Eastern Europe.[47]

In London and Paris, the 'democratic' cause provided a pole around which a variegated set of radicals arrayed themselves. French republican, neo-Babouvist and communist exiles in London founded a *Société démocratique française* (French Democratic Society, SDF) there in 1835. Keenly observing the British Chartist movement as it took shape in the late 1830s, they apostrophized the 1839 Chartist Convention with an address to the 'Democrats of Great Britain!', in which they urged international brotherhood. German communists who had supported the failed 1839 uprising in France took refuge in

London and formed links with the SDF, meeting in the same premises and sometimes jointly, for example, to celebrate Bastille Day. In the 1840s, British Chartists of various shades of opinion strove to incorporate these and other exiles into international associations. The moral-force Chartist William Lovett founded the Democratic Friends of All Nations in 1844; it seems to have been in such circles that Mazzini first came to call himself a democrat. A more militant successor, the Fraternal Democrats, was launched by G.J. Harney, who had earlier founded the first eponymous British democratic society (the East London Democratic Association); he had links to Polish as well as French and German democrats. The new grouping – which described itself as not 'a society or party, but merely an assemblage of men belonging to different countries, for the purpose of mutual information' – was formally instituted in 1845 at a meeting called to celebrate the first French Republic: a symbol of enduring hopes, but also of a previous phase of radical internationalism. Late in 1847, Harney corresponded with Marx and Engels, then in Brussels, about setting up an international organization with branches abroad. Together with the French labour advocate Alexandre Ledru-Rollin, they planned an international democratic congress for 1848.[48]

The 1848 Revolutions and 'Democracy'

During the European revolutionary wave that unfolded from 1848, democratic language proliferated. More people espoused causes termed 'democratic' than ever before. The developments just sketched had prepared the way: democracy had gained new legitimacy and new associations over the preceding twenty years. Moreover, these revolutions overwhelmed liberal as well as absolutist regimes; participants needed new political lexicons to delineate new horizons of expectation. The political strategies developed in this period extended power to the people to a striking degree, and a ferment of politicization ensued: the revolutionary epoch was saturated with phenomena of a kind easy to characterize as democratic, further encouraging talk about democracy. In this context, many at least occasionally saw reason to embrace democracy – though the term continued to be available for negative use, and some negative associations were reinforced. Yet to be a 'democrat' was also, and often increasingly as the revolutions unfolded, to assume a partisan identity: to profess a particular stance within the wide-ranging constitutional and policy debates that the revolutions triggered.

Developments in France illustrate this shift from a shared to a more partisan use of the term. When the July Monarchy fell in 1848, the political classes quickly decided that a new constitution was needed and that, inasmuch as power had reverted to the people, the Constituent Assembly should be elected on the basis of manhood suffrage. The Assembly proclaimed France a *république démocratique* (while rejecting one of its members' calls to define what the phrase meant). It proclaimed civil equality and political equality for adult males: 'universal suffrage', a slogan of about fifty years' standing, acquired authoritative endorsement from one of Europe's leading and still culturally most prestigious states. The new French state's self-description did much to make democracy a talking point in subsequent revolutions elsewhere. But if the French political order became democratic, that did not mean that all its leaders now saw themselves as 'democrats'. In the autumn of 1848, the 'Social Democrats' emerged as a distinct political grouping. Ledru Rollin, their leader, had long been associated with the 'democratic' cause, but the party was a new venture, representing a regrouping on the left in the wake of divisions that had emerged against the background of the workers' rising, the 'June Days'. As left parliamentarians who had not supported the uprising as it happened reassessed the cost of letting their ties to the working masses fray, a hyphenated democratic identity, that of the 'social democrat', was developed, with a view to establishing a left bulwark in a political environment that increasingly threatened a return to the status quo.[49]

The revolutions of 1848–49 affected different parts of Europe to different degrees.[50] France apart, they generally had less radical effects in states that already had liberal or constitutional regimes. In some such states, the revolutions encouraged talk about democracy or mobilizations on the part of those who already conceived of themselves as democrats, but these did not significantly destabilize politics. In Spain, a group on the *exaltado* wing of the liberal spectrum reaffirmed its members' identities as democrats;[51] in Britain, the Chartists, the chief 'democratic' critics of liberal government, mobilized and petitioned for reform, but were seen by the government chiefly as a threat to public order. There was by this point a well-established extraparliamentary discourse about the need for more democracy in Britain; the more notable if transient effect of this new French revolution was to encourage 'republican' talk.[52]

In some other states, constitutional and initially nonconstitutional monarchs managed to keep the situation more or less under control, though at the price of sometimes significant concession: notably in Scandinavia, the Netherlands, Prussia and Piedmont. Talk of democracy played a part in political agitation and in processes of reconstituting authority in most of these contexts – though apparently not in the Netherlands (the king's speedy appointment of a leading liberal to head a constitutional commission may have helped to keep the genie in the bottle).[53] In Germany, by contrast, Democratic Societies (*Demokratische Vereine*) appeared early and prospered, especially in south German constitutional states.[54] In Norway, during the Parliament that opened in February 1848, Ingebrigt Sæter, a farmer representative, wrote to his brother: 'I was scared that the representatives should show themselves weak Democrats. I was wrong. Radical ideas seem to be very well represented.'[55]

In the German Confederation and the Habsburg Empire, the constitutionalist dynamic spiralled in more dramatic ways, as the presiding Habsburgs failed to contain their first really serious political-reforming challenge. In the summer of 1848, would-be reformers set about reconstituting authority: elections were held for a pan-German constituent assembly; constituent assemblies were also summoned in the Habsburg Monarchy and then – in defiance of the Viennese provisional government's designs – in its increasingly loosely appended provinces of Hungary and Croatia. Wide franchises operated everywhere (though in Hungary the requirement that voters speak Magyar disenfranchised sizeable ethnic groups). For the first time in German lands, as one observer put it: 'Democracy made the move from books into life.'[56] Those who succeeded in riding this democratic wave (and many landowners found they could ride it more easily than they had feared) had some basis for claiming democratic authority.

Here again, however, the cause of democracy acquired a narrower definition as the constitutional process unfolded, increasingly connoting a position within contentious debates. In Germany's National Assembly in Frankfurt, for example, democrats crystallized into a recognized group; their watchword was 'popular sovereignty'. Democratic clubs shed liberal members and forged their own federal structures, linking deputies to an extraparliamentary base; they organized a national congress and promulgated a programme echoing an influential manifesto from Baden democrats.[57] In Ottoman but semi-independent Wallachia, Wallachian radicals who had studied in France sought to promote a constitution and (as elsewhere in Central and Eastern Europe) to alleviate the hardships of the peasantry. It seems that it was chiefly in exile, as they sought to make common cause with France's newly instituted Social Democrats, that they represented their cause as the cause of democracy.[58]

The first of the 1848 revolutions had broken out in Naples. Italy also staged the revolutionary era's final act: the rise and fall of the Roman Republic. Democratic factions, notably in Tuscany, initially strove to broaden the social base of Italy's several moderate-liberal revolutions, but as plans to convene a pan-Italian constituent assembly got under way, the cause of 'democracy' came to be rhetorically elided with that of 'the people' and 'the nation'. In 1849, as counter-revolutionary forces began to regain control, Rome became a place of refuge for democrats. Departing from the trend merely to sloganize democracy, which had taken hold elsewhere in the peninsula, some of these men set about laying the foundations for a thoroughgoing democratic polity: this revolutionary wave's most radical constitutional experiment. Roman democrats drew on revolutionary French reworkings of ancient models: a provisional triumvirate presided alongside a constitution-making process. Though the draft constitution firmly endorsed representative democracy, it was nonetheless envisaged that citizens would play a part not only in electing representatives but also in approving the laws that they devised.[59]

In 1848–49, democracy was endorsed by people across the European continent as never before, but it remains doubtful whether, even at this juncture, the term was widely understood or employed by ordinary people. By the spring of 1849, there were some 1,400 *Demokratische Vereine* across Germany. But while democratic sentiments apparently penetrated some German calendars – widely circulated publications – explicit references to 'Demokratie' within them seem to have been rare.[60]

Moreover, the episode also reinforced anti-democratic perspectives. Guizot was apoplectic: 'Today's chaos hides behind one word, "democracy." This word is sovereign, universal. All parties seek to appropriate it . . . A fatal idea, which arouses and incessantly foments war in our midst: social war. It is this idea that must be extirpated.' His *De la démocratie en France* went through many French editions and was republished in the same year in at least twenty-one other European and American cities, in seven other languages.[61] French liberals' habitual warnings that democracy would produce demagogic public opinion and warring factions could be held to have been justified by events.

Overall, the revolutions strengthened the belief – whether held hopefully or (as often) fearfully – that the future lay with democracy. Yet the revolutionary experience also bred disillusionment among erstwhile supporters. The difficulties of instituting 'democracy', in practice had been made manifest. The election of Louis Napoleon in France, followed by his dispatch of troops to put down the Roman Democratic Republic, was particularly disillusioning for those who had imagined that manhood suffrage would advance liberty and progress. The following years accordingly saw 'democratic' programmes rethought by some former sympathizers, with new emphasis on the decentralization of power to local contexts, in which something more like direct democracy might be achievable. More emphasis was also placed on the need to elect men who had emerged from the ranks of the people, men who were not just rhetorically but also experientially democrats. The embryonic alliance between socialism and democracy came to look fragile, especially as socialist thinking evolved.[62] Louis Napoleon had triumphed in part because rural voters had objected to a new tax to fund work for the urban unemployed; no political change effected anywhere showed serious promise of generating answers to the problems of the urban and industrial working classes. Though some form of democracy – perhaps a more devolved, deliberative kind – might be thought to have potential to support radical social change, the events of these years suggested that the determined social revolutionary might need to look elsewhere than to the recently assembled corpus of modern 'democratic' thought and practice to find ways of carrying that set of hopes forwards.

Conclusion

Between the seventeenth and eighteenth, and mid nineteenth centuries, democracy acquired new associations. Whereas it had connoted the past, it came to connote the future. It came to be linked with the 'modern' constitutional form, representative government. A repertoire of new or newly refurbished forms of popular political activity developed to which it could relate: organized mass meetings; petitioning campaigns; newspapers and other expressions of 'public opinion'. Both the Christian credentials of democracy and the democratic credentials of Christianity were repeatedly affirmed (though they were not universally accepted). However, 'democracy' also continued to carry negative connotations and it remained unclear whether – within complex and stratified European societies – it could be embodied in any stable institutional frame. Furthermore, the challenge of achieving sufficient social equality to make democracy meaningful became if anything more acute once it had become clear that the abolition of privilege did no more than reframe the question. Conceived as the future to which Europe was tending, 'democracy' set the terms of a problem; it embodied as yet little more than the hope of a solution.

Joanna Innes is Professor of Modern History at the University of Oxford, and fellow and tutor at Somerville College. She is a former editor and continuing member of the editorial board of the journal *Past and Present*. Her authored and coedited books include: with Arthur Burns, *Rethinking the Age of Reform: Britain 1780–1850* (2003), *Inferior Politics: Social Problems and Social Policies in Eighteenth-Century Britain* (2009); and, edited with Mark Philp, *Re-imagining Democracy in the Age of Revolutions: America, France, Britain, Ireland 1750–1850* (2013). A companion volume to the last, with Mark Philp, *Re-imagining Democracy in the Mediterranean, 1780–1860*, is forthcoming in 2018.

Mark Philp is Professor of History and Politics at the University of Warwick, and an Emeritus Fellow of Oriel College, University of Oxford. He has worked extensively in the field of political corruption and realist political theory as well as in the history of political thought, and late eighteenth and early nineteenth-century European history. His recent publications include *Political Conduct* (2007); *Reforming Political Ideas in Britain: Politics and Language in the Shadow of the French Revolution* (2013); and, edited with Joanna Innes, *Re-imagining Democracy in the Age of Revolutions: America, France, Britain, Ireland 1750–1850* (2013).

Notes

The authors would like to acknowledge the contribution made to this chapter by their involvement in a Leverhulme Trust-funded international network, IN-084.

1. John Dunn, *Setting the People Free: The Story of Democracy* (London: Atlantic Books, 2005), 237–70; Christian Meier et al., 'Demokratie', in Otto Brunner, Werner Conze, and Reinhart Koselleck (eds), *Geschichtliche Grundbegriffe. Historisches Lexikon zur politisch-sozialen Sprache in Deutschland*, Band 1 A–D (Stuttgart: Klett-Cotta, 1972), 839–47; Bo Lindberg, *Den antika skevheten: politiska ord och begrepp i det tidig-moderna Sverige* (Stockholm: K. Vitterhets Historie och Antikvitetsakademien, 2006), 195–213; Jennifer Tolbert Roberts, *Athens on Trial: The Antidemocratic Tradition in Western Thought* (Princeton: Princeton University Press, 1994).
2. Montesquieu, *L'Esprit des Lois* orig. 1748, many editions. The passage cited comes from the author's Advertisement, sometimes called Explanatory Notes, added in the 1757 edition.
3. Marco Cini, 'Democracy, Republicanism and Constitution in Corsica', in Mauro Lenci and Carmelo Calabrò (eds), *Democracy and Risorgimento* (Pisa: Edizioni ETS, 2011), 59–66; Johann Christian Schmohl, *Über Nordamerika und Demokratie: Ein Brief aus England* (Copenhagen: W.J. Röhrig Verlag, 1782).
4. Published posthumously as Marquis d'Argenson, *Considérations sur le gouvernement ancien et présent de la France* (Amsterdam: s.n. [in fact Paris], 1784); Jay M. Smith, *Nobility Reimagined: The Patriotic Nation in Eighteenth-Century France* (Ithaca, NY: Cornell University Press, 2005), 61–64.
5. Jean-Jacques Rousseau, *Du contrat social*, many editions (orig. Amsterdam [in fact Paris], 1762), Book 3, ch 4.
6. Samuel von Pufendorf, *De jure naturae et gentium*, many editions (orig. Lund, 1672), Chapter 5, section 4; Lindberg, *Den antika skevheten*, 208–9.
7. *His Majesties Answer to the Nineteen Propositions of both Houses of Parliament* (Cambridge, 1642); *The Craftsman* (London, 1726–33).
8. Richard Whatmore, *Against War and Empire: Geneva, Britain, and France in the Eighteenth Century* (New Haven: Yale University Press, 2012), 34–35.
9. Pasi Ihalainen, *Agents of the People: Democracy and Popular Sovereignty in British and Swedish Parliamentary and Public Debates, 1734–1800* (Leiden: Brill, 2010), 203–39.
10. E.g. Thomas Hobbes, *Behemoth* (London, 1681), five such references.
11. *Gentleman's Magazine* 23 (1953), 477; *Parliamentary Register* (1781), 29.

12. Ihalainen, *Agents of the People*, 220–26.
13. Whatmore, *Against War*, 54–97; Maarten Prak, 'Citizen Radicalism and Democracy in the Dutch Republic: The Patriot Movement of the 1780s'. *Theory and Society* 20(1) (1991), 73–102.
14. Seth Cotlar, 'Languages of Democracy in America from the Revolution to the Election of 1800', in Joanna Innes and Mark Philp (eds), *Re-imagining Democracy in the Age of Revolutions: America, France, Britain, Ireland 1750–1850* (Oxford: Oxford University Press, 2013), 15–21; Terry Bouton, *Taming Democracy: The People, the Founders, and the Troubled Ending of the American Revolution* (New York: Oxford University Press, 2007).
15. R.R. Palmer, 'Notes on the Use of the Word "Democracy" 1789–1799', *Political Science Quarterly* 68(2) (1953), 203–26 remains a useful starting point.
16. Edmund Burke, *Substance of the Speech, on the Army Estimates* (London: J. Debrett, 1790), 12. Richard Bourke, 'Enlightenment, Revolution and Democracy', *Constellations* 15(1) (2008), 10–32.
17. E.g. in 'Church and King' *Antigallican Songster II* (London, 1793) and in *The Pop-Gun Plot Found Out* (London, 1794).
18. Bibliothèque Nationale de la France, Collection Vinck, 4204, retrieved 31 January 2018 from http://catalogue.bnf.fr/ark:/12148/cb40249928p.
19. Cotlar, 'Languages'; Ruth Scurr, 'Varieties of Democracy in the French Revolution' and Mark Philp, 'Talking about Democracy: Britain in the 1790s', in Innes and Philp, *Re-imagining Democracy*.
20. Pierre Rosanvallon, 'The History of the Word "Democracy" in France', *Journal of Democracy* 6(4) (1995), 143–48 and *La démocratie inachevée: histoire de la souveraineté du peuple en France* (Paris: Gallimard, 2000), 47–100; Jens Christophersen, *The Meaning of 'Democracy' as Used in European Ideologies from the French to the Russian Revolution* (Oslo: Universitetsforlaget, 1966), 7–12. The last clause in the first passage cited also echoes Montesquieu, *L'Esprit*, Book 2, Chapter 2, save for the use of 'delegates' rather than 'ministers'
21. Scurr, 'Varieties', 67.
22. Pierre Serna, *Antonelle: aristocrate révolutionnaire, 1747–1817* (Paris: Éditions de Félin, 1997), 252. For Italy, see Luciano Guerci, 'Democrazia rappresentativa: Definizioni e discussion nell'Italia del triennio republicano (1796–99)', in Paolo Alatri (ed.), *L'Europa tra Illuminismo e Restaurazione: Scritti in Onore di Furio Diaz* (Rome: Bulzoni, 1993), 227–77; for Germany, see Christian Meier et al., 'Demokratie', 849. For the intellectual context, see Nadia Urbinati, *Representative Democracy: Principles and Genealogy* (Chicago: University of Chicago Press, 2006).
23. Serna, *Antonelle*, 349.
24. Jean-Marc Schiappa, *Gracchus Babeuf avec les Egaux* (Paris: Ouvrieres, 1991); Philippe Buonarroti, *Conspiration pour l'égalité dite de Babeuf* (Brussels: A la Librairie romantique, 1828).
25. Joris Oddens, Mart Rutjes and Erik Jacobs (eds), *The Political Culture of the Sister Republics* (Amsterdam: Amsterdam University Press, 2013).

26. Reinhart Koselleck, in Christian Meier et al., 'Demokratie', 850–53.
27. Malcolm Crook, *Napoleon Comes to Power: Democracy and Dictatorship in Revolutionary France, 1795–1804* (Cardiff: University of Wales Press, 1998).
28. Javier Fernández-Sebastián, 'Democracia', in Javier Fernández-Sebastián and Juan Francisco Fuentes (eds), *Diccionario político y social del siglo XIX español* (Madrid: Alianza editorial, 2002), 216.
29. Philip Schofield, *Utility and Democracy: The Political Thought of Jeremy Bentham* (Oxford: Oxford University Press, 2006).
30. Annelien de Dijn, *French Political Thought from Montesquieu to Tocqueville: Liberty in a Levelled Society?* (Cambridge: Cambridge University Press, 2008), 68–154; Rosanvallon, 'The History of the Word', 148–51; Rosanvallon, *La démocratie inachevée*, 101–38.
31. Richard Stites, *The Four Horsemen: Riding to Liberty in Post-Napoleonic Europe* (New York: Oxford University Press, 2013).
32. For Spanish wariness of democratic terminology, Gonzalo Capellán and Rocío García Ruiz, 'Una poderosa pequeñez: El concepto Democracia en España 1750–1870', *Alcores: Revista de Historia Contemporánea* 9 (2010), 50–54, though they note increasing use in the 1820s; Rui Ramos, 'Entre revolução política e evolução social: uma história do conceito de democracia (Portugal, século XIX)', *Ariadna histórica. Lenguajes, conceptos, metáforas* 1 (2012), 168.
33. *Costituzione del Popolo Carbonaro della repubblica lucana orientale, Anno I* (1820), republished as an appendix in *La Carboneria Lucana Artefice della prima Costituzione in Italia* (Potenza: Editrice Ermes, 2009).
34. Clive H. Church, *Europe in 1830: Revolution and Political Change* (London: Allen & Unwin, 1983).
35. Joanna Innes, Mark Philp and Robert Saunders, 'Democratic Discourse in the Reform Era: Britain in the 1830s and 40s', in Innes and Philp, *Re-imagining Democracy*, 116–19.
36. For Spain, see Fernández-Sebastián, 'Democracia', 219–20; Capellán and García Ruiz, 'Una poderosa pequeñez', 54–56. For Portugal, see Ramos, 'Entre revolução', 174.
37. Innes, Philp and Saunders, 'Democratic Discourse', 120–21.
38. Ramos, 'Entre revolução', 175.
39. Rosanvallon, *La démocratie inachevée*, 141–67.
40. *La démocratie pacifique* 1(1) (1843).
41. There is a library of works on Tocqueville. He is set in French intellectual context by de Dijn, *French Political Thought*, 129–54.
42. Innes, Philp and Saunders, 'Rise of Democratic Discourse', 123–24, 127; Florencia Peyrou, 'The Role of Spain and the Spanish in the Creation of Europe's Transnational Democratic Political Culture, 1840–70', *Social History* 40(4) (2015), 506–9.
43. Laurent Colantonio, '"Democracy" and the Irish People, 1830–48', in Innes and Philp, *Re-imagining Democracy*, 162–73.

44. Frédéric Lambert and René Rémond. *Théologie de la république: Lamennais, prophète et législateur* (Paris: L'Harmattan, 2001); Eugenio Guccione (ed.), *Gioacchino Ventura e il pensiero politico d'ispirazione cristiana dell'ottocento* (Florence: Casa editrice Leo S. Olschki, 1991).
45. For Quinet and Lamartine on this theme, see Christophersen, *Meaning of 'Democracy'*, 102–7.
46. Peyrou, 'The Role of Spain' provides a good introduction to the larger subject.
47. Kenneth F. Lewalski, 'Fraternal Politics: Polish and European Radicalism during the Great Emigration', in M.B.B. Biskupski and James S. Pula (eds), *Polish Democratic Thought* (New York: East European Monographs, 1990), 93–108. The Manifesto of the Polish Democratic Society, published in Poitiers in 1836 appears in this collection as Document 7, 199–220.
48. Salvo Mastellone, *Mazzini and Marx: Thoughts upon Democracy in Europe* (Westport, CT: Praeger, 2003). This account is also indebted to Fabrice Bensimon's unpublished paper 'French and German Exiles, London Chartists and the Fraternal Democrats (c. 1840–8)'.
49. Maurice Agulhon, *The Republican Experiment, 1848–1852* (Cambridge: Cambridge University Press, 1983).
50. Jonathan Sperber, *The European Revolutions, 1848–1851* (Cambridge: Cambridge University Press, 1994); Dieter Dowe et al. (eds), *Europe in 1848: Revolution and Reform* (New York: Berghahn Books, 2001).
51. Florencia Peyrou, 'La formación del Partido demócrata español: crónica de un conflicto anunciado?' *Historia Contemporánea* 37 (2011), 343–72.
52. Innes, Philp and Saunders, 'Rise of Democratic Discourse', 125
53. Henk te Velde, 'De Domesticatie van Democratie in Nederland. Democratie als Strijdbegrip van de Negentiende Eeuw tot 1945'. *BMGN – Low Countries Historical Review* 127 (2012), 5–11; Horst Lademacher, 'The Netherlands and Belgium: Notes on the Causes of Abstinence from Revolution', in Dowe et al. (eds), *Europe in 1848*, 260–72.
54. Michael Wettengel, 'Party Formation in Germany: Political Associations in the Revolution of 1848', in Dowe et al. (eds), *Europe in 1848*, 530–57.
55. Anne-Lise Seip, 'The Revolution of 1848 on the Norwegian Scene', in Dowe et al. (eds), *Europe in 1848*, 314–15.
56. Christian Meier et al., 'Demokratie', 862.
57. Heinrich Best, 'Structures of Parliamentary Representation in the Revolutions of 1848', in Dowe et al. (eds), *Europe in 1848*, 475–505; and Wettengel, 'Party Formation' in the same volume. For the Baden programme, see: http://www.offenburg.de/html/13_forderungen_des_volkes.html.
58. See Angela Jianu, *A Circle of Friends: Romanian Revolutionaries and Political Exile, 1840–1859* (Leiden: Brill, 2011), p. 161 for their cause as that of 'democratic Europe'.
59. Enrico Francia, *1848: la rivoluzione del Risorgimento* (Bologna: Il Mulino, 2012), 309–22.

60. James M. Brophy, *Popular Culture and the Public Sphere in the Rhineland 1800–50* (Cambridge: Cambridge University Press, 2007), 36–49 cites *Der Wanderer am Rhein* for its democratic line, but in 1848 the word 'Demokratie' appeared only once and 'Demokratisch' not at all. French Montagnards gave it more prominence in their *Almanach démocratique et social*: Michel Cordillot, 'Les fouriéristes et l'émergence de la coalition démoc-soc à l'automne 1848', *Cahiers Charles Fourier* 13 (2003), retrieved 31 January 2018 from http://www.charlesfourier.fr/spip.php?article55.
61. François Guizot, *De la démocratie en France* (Paris: Victor Masson, 1849), 9–11. For surviving copies, see https://www.worldcat.org.
62. For Proudhon's conversion to the rhetoric of 'democracy' only in the course of 1848, and Marx and Engels's ambivalence, see Christophersen, *Meaning of 'Democracy'*, 118–25, 131–49.

Bibliography

1642. *His Majesties Answer to the Nineteen Propositions of both Houses of Parliament.* Cambridge.
1726–33. *The Craftsman.* London.
1820. *Costituzione del Popolo Carbonaro della repubblica lucana orientale, Anno I.*
1990. Manifesto of the Polish Democratic Society (Poitiers, 1836). Reprinted in M.B.B. Biskupski and J.S. Pula (eds), *Polish Democratic Thought.* New York: East European Monographs, 199–220.
2009. *La Carboneria Lucana Artefice della prima Costituzione in Italia.* Potenza: Editrice Ermes.
Agulhon, M. 1983. *The Republican Experiment, 1848–1852.* Cambridge: Cambridge University Press.
Best, H. 'Structures of Parliamentary Representation in the Revolutions of 1848', in Dowe et al., *Europe in 1848*, 475–505.
Bourke, R. 2008. 'Enlightenment, Revolution and Democracy', *Constellations* 15(1), 10–32.
Bouton, T. 2007. *Taming Democracy: The People, the Founders, and the Troubled Ending of the American Revolution.* New York: Oxford University Press.
Brophy, J.M. 2007. *Popular Culture and the Public Sphere in the Rhineland 1800–50.* Cambridge: Cambridge University Press.
Buonarroti, P. 1828. *Conspiration pour l'égalité dite de Babeuf.* Brussels: A la Librairie romantique.
Burke, E. 1790. *Substance of the Speech, on the Army Estimates.* London: J. Debrett.
Capellán, G., and R.García Ruiz. 2010. 'Una poderosa pequeñez: El concepto democraco en Espana 1750–1870', *Alcores: Revista de Historia Contemporánea* 9, 50–54.
Christophersen, J. 1966. *The Meaning of 'Democracy' as Used in European Ideologies from the French to the Russian Revolution.* Oslo: Universitetsforlaget.
Church, C.H. 1983. *Europe in 1830: Revolution and Political Change.* London: Allen & Unwin.

Cini, M. 2011. 'Democracy, Republicanism and Constitution in Corsica', in Mauro Lenci and Carmelo Calabrò (eds), *Democracy and Risorgimento*. Pisa: Edizioni ETS, 59–66.

Colantonio, L. 2013. '"Democracy" and the Irish People, 1830–48', in Innes and Philp, *Re-imagining Democracy*, 162–73.

Cordillot, M. 2003. 'Les fouriéristes et l'émergence de la coalition démoc-soc à l'automne 1848', *Cahiers Charles Fourier* 13. Retrieved 31 January 2018 from http://www.charlesfourier.fr/spip.php?article55.

Cotlar, S. 'Languages of Democracy in America from the Revolution to the Election of 1800', in Innes and Philp, *Re-imagining Democracy*, 13–27.

Crook, M. 1998. *Napoleon Comes to Power: Democracy and Dictatorship in Revolutionary France, 1795–1804*. Cardiff: University of Wales Press.

Dijn, A. de. 2008. *French Political Thought from Montesquieu to Tocqueville: Liberty in a Levelled Society?* Cambridge: Cambridge University Press.

Dowe, D. et al. (eds). 2001. *Europe in 1848: Revolution and Reform*. New York: Berghahn Books.

Dunn, J. 2005. *Setting the People Free: The Story of Democracy*. London: Atlantic Books.

Fernández-Sebastián, J. 2002. 'Democracia', in J. Fernández-Sebastián and J.F. Fuentes (eds), *Diccionario político y social del siglo XIX español*. Madrid: Alianza editorial, 216–28.

Francia, E. 2012. *1848: la rivoluzione del Risorgimento*. Bologna: Il Mulino.

Guccione, E. (ed.). 1991. *Gioacchino Ventura e il pensiero politico d'ispirazione cristiana dell'ottocento*. Florence: Casa editrice Leo S. Olschki.

Guerci, L. 1993. 'Democrazia rappresentativa: Definizioni e discussioni nell'Italia del triennio republicano (1796–99)', in Paolo Alatri (ed.), *L'Europa tra Illuminismo e Restaurazione: Scritti in Onore di Furio Diaz*. Rome: Bulzoni, 227–77.

Guizot, F. 1849. *De la démocratie en France*. Paris: Victor Masson.

Hobbes, T. 1681. *Behemoth*. London.

Ihalainen, P. 2010. *Agents of the People: Democracy and Popular Sovereignty in British and Swedish Parliamentary and Public Debates, 1734–1800*. Leiden: Brill.

Innes, J., and M. Philp (eds). *Re-imagining Democracy in the Age of Revolutions: America, France, Britain, Ireland 1750–1850*. Oxford: Oxford University Press, 2013.

Innes, J., M. Philp and R. Saunders. 2013. 'Democratic Discourse in the Reform Era: Britain in the 1830s and 40s', in Innes and Philp, *Re-imagining Democracy*, 114–28.

Jianu, A. 2011. *A Circle of Friends: Romanian Revolutionaries and Political Exile, 1840–1859*. Leiden: Brill.

Lademacher, H. 2001. 'The Netherlands and Belgium: Notes on the Causes of Abstinence from Revolution', in Dowe et al. (eds), *Europe in 1848*, 260–72.

Lambert, F., and R. Rémond. 2001. *Théologie de la république: Lamennais, prophète et législateur*. Paris: L'Harmattan.

Lewalski, K.F. 1990. 'Fraternal Politics: Polish and European Radicalism during the Great Emigration', in M.B.B. Biskupski and J.S. Pula (eds), *Polish Democratic Thought*. New York: East European Monographs, 93–108.

Lindberg, B. 2006. *Den antika skevheten: politiska ord och begrepp i det tidig-moderna Sverige.* Stockholm: K. Vitterhets Historie och Antikvitetsakademien.
Marquis d'Argenson. 1784. *Considérations sur le gouvernement ancien et présent de la France.* Amsterdam: s.n. [in fact Paris].
Mastellone, S. 2003. *Mazzini and Marx: Thoughts upon Democracy in Europe.* Westport, CT: Praeger.
Meier, C. et al. 1972. 'Demokratie', in O. Brunner, W. Conze and R. Koselleck (eds), *Geschichtliche Grundbegriffe. Historisches Lexikon zur politisch-sozialen Sprache in Deutschland,* Band 1 A-D. Stuttgart: Klett-Cotta, 821–99.
Oddens, J., M. Rutjes and E. Jacobs (eds). 2013. *The Political Culture of the Sister Republics.* Amsterdam: Amsterdam University Press.
Palmer, R.R. 1953. 'Notes on the Use of the Word "Democracy" 1789–1799', *Political Science Quarterly* 68(2), 203–26.
Peyrou, F. 2011. 'La formación del Partido demócrata español: crónica de un conflicto anunciado?', *Historia Contemporánea* 37, 343–72.
———. 2015. 'The Role of Spain and the Spanish in the Creation of Europe's Transnational Democratic Political Culture, 1840–70', *Social History* 40(4), 506–9.
Philp, M. 2013. 'Talking about Democracy: Britain in the 1790s', in Innes and Philp, *Re-imagining Democracy,* 101–113.
Prak, M. 1991. 'Citizen Radicalism and Democracy in the Dutch Republic: The Patriot Movement of the 1780s', *Theory and Society* 20(1), 73–102.
Pufendorf, S. von. 1672. *De jure naturae et gentium,* many editions, orig. Lund.
Ramos, R. 2012. 'Entre revolução política e evolução social: uma história do conceito de democracia (Portugal, século XIX)', *Ariadna histórica. Lenguajes, conceptos, metáforas* 1: 163–193.
Rosanvallon, P. 1995. 'The History of the Word "Democracy" in France', *Journal of Democracy* 6(4), 143–48.
———. 2000. *La démocratie inachevée: histoire de la souveraineté du peuple en France.* Paris: Gallimard.
Rousseau, J-J. 1762. *Du contrat social,* many editions, orig. Amsterdam [in fact Paris].
Schiappa, J-M. 1991. *Gracchus Babeuf avec les Egaux.* Paris: Ouvrieres.
Schmohl, J.C. 1782. *Über Nordamerika und Demokratie: Ein Brief aus England.* Copenhagen: W.J. Röhrig Verlag.
Schofield, P. 2006. *Utility and Democracy: The Political Thought of Jeremy Bentham.* Oxford: Oxford University Press.
Scurr, R. 2013. 'Varieties of Democracy in the French Revolution', in Innes and Philp, *Re-imagining Democracy,* 57–68.
Seip, A-L. 2001. 'The Revolution of 1848 on the Norwegian Scene', in Dowe et al., *Europe in 1848,* 313–324.
Serna, P. 1997. *Antonelle: aristocrate révolutionnaire, 1747–1817.* Paris: Éditions de Félin.
Smith, J.M. 2005. *Nobility Reimagined: The Patriotic Nation in Eighteenth-Century France.* Ithaca, NY: Cornell University Press.

Sperber, J. 1994. *The European Revolutions, 1848–1851*. Cambridge: Cambridge University Press.
Stites, R. 2013. *The Four Horsemen: Riding to Liberty in Post-Napoleonic Europe*. New York: Oxford University Press.
Tolbert Roberts, J. 1994. *Athens on Trial: The Antidemocratic Tradition in Western Thought*. Princeton: Princeton University Press.
Urbinati, N. 2006. *Representative Democracy: Principles and Genealogy*. Chicago: University of Chicago Press.
Velde, H. te. 2012. 'De Domesticatie van Democratie in Nederland. Democratie als Strijdbegrip van de Negentiende Eeuw tot 1945', *BMGN – Low Countries Historical Review* 127, 5–11.
Wettengel, M. 2001. 'Party Formation in Germany: Political Associations in the Revolution of 1848', in Dowe et al., *Europe in 1848*, 530–57.
Whatmore, R. 2012. *Against War and Empire: Geneva, Britain, and France in the Eighteenth Century*. New Haven: Yale University Press.

Chapter 2

Democracy and the Strange Death of Mixed Government in the Nineteenth Century
Great Britain, France and the Netherlands

Henk te Velde

In recent years, interest in the aristocratic dimension of democracy and in mixed government or mixed constitutions has grown. This interest is historical, but it is related to current conceptions of democracy. Philosopher and historian Frank Ankersmit has argued that it would be easier to understand the current problems of 'representative democracy' if we accepted that we live in an 'elective aristocracy'.[1] In his well-known analysis of 'representative government', political philosopher Bernard Manin underlined the aristocratic elements of our current democracy. In the last sentence of his book, he concludes that 'representative government' is 'the mixed constitution of modern times'.[2] Manin traces ideas about representation from antiquity until today, and he refers to the classical theories about mixed government. These form the explicit starting point for Mogens Herman Hansen, a specialist in ancient Greek politics. He suggests that we should return to the ideas of the mixed constitution in order to understand modern democracy.[3] The conclusion of the comprehensive synthesis of the development of the idea of the mixed constitution by Swiss political scientist Alois Riklin is that modern democracy is, in fact, a mixed constitution: 'the mixed constitution is not dead'.[4]

These recent publications suggest that the old mixed constitution has not been irrevocably superseded by democracy. They show an awareness that modern democracy is a rather ambiguous concept. The advent and victory of the concept of 'democracy' in nineteenth-century Britain have recently been described not as a 'conversion', but rather a 'prolonged negotiation between the language of democracy and the established principles of British politics'.[5] 'But why should we have to call it democracy?', John Dunn asks.[6] Yes, why do we not call it mixed government, for instance? This raises the question of what happened with the mixed constitution during the nineteenth century. At the beginning of the twentieth century, hardly anybody was still referring to the concept and, if they did, it was to argue that it had gone forever.[7] However, this did not mean that aristocratic or monarchical elements had disappeared from the constitution or that the country had turned into a 'pure' democracy. How and why did the concept and words of the 'mixed constitution' lose their attraction? Retracing the debate about the mixed constitution or mixed government may help to explain why, on the one hand, the victory of the word 'democracy' was so complete, whereas the current political system could, on the other, still be described as a sort of mixed constitution after all.

This contribution concentrates on a small number of central issues, and it shall argue that a shift in the hierarchy of political values and a concomitant reinterpretation of democracy are neglected clues to understanding the rise of 'democracy' and the demise of the mixed constitution.[8] When the democratic revolution of 1848 had unseated the French monarchy and its Prime Minister François Guizot, Guizot wrote his well-known pamphlet about 'democracy in France'. He famously equated democracy with class war and 'chaos', and he sang the praises of the British mixed system with the three constitutional powers – monarchy, House of Lords and House of Commons – in his eyes the sole guarantee of good and stable government.[9] At least since Edmund Burke, posing an opposition between savage democracy and prudent mixed government had been quite common. In the 1830s it was not uncommon in Britain to denounce 'the mad attempt at substituting a wild democracy for our mixed constitution'.[10] The ultimate triumph of democracy became possible through the discovery that it need *not* be the opposite of stability, balance and freedom, and that it could even serve as a protection against despotism. This triumph was also brought about by a change of political values: once people started to think that government should not be primarily 'stable' and 'balanced', but rather vigorous, mixed government lost its attraction.

The British Mixed Constitution and its Exportation

The classic references of the literature of the mixed constitution are, of course, Aristotle and, in particular, Polybius. Polybius perfected the classic scheme of the mixed constitution, that is, the ideal mix of monarchical, aristocratic and democratic elements, a stable balance that could avoid the degeneration of its separate 'pure' parts into tyranny, oligarchy and ochlocracy or mob rule, respectively. In early modern Europe, his scheme was applied to many countries. The 'aristocratic republics' of Venice and the Dutch Republic, for instance, allegedly had mixed constitutions because they also included a monarchical element, such as the Prince of Orange in the Dutch case.[11] In Scandinavia, mixed government was sometimes understood in terms of dualism, between the monarch and the people. This conception was often anti-aristocratic and idealized the role of the peasants or the common people.

By the eighteenth century, Britain was by far the most famous example.[12] In no other country was the notion of the mixed constitution so pervasive. After the Glorious Revolution of 1688, politicians often argued that the 'constitution of England' with the king, the House of Lords and the House of Commons presented a 'mixture of monarchical, aristocratical, and democratical power, blended together in one system'.[13] It is obvious that this type of political language was not simply descriptive but also performative. The central issue in constitutional debates was the struggle between the king's executive power and the power of Parliament. The language of the mixed constitution could be used to hold executive power in check, avert royal absolutism and assert the power of the House of Commons. In that sense it supported the *change* of the constitution, away from a preponderant monarchy, and moving in the direction of a larger role for the House of Commons. The connection with present-day British politics was so obvious that the classic references were no longer necessary and disappeared from at least the more popular discussions of the mixed constitution. It is questionable whether those who used the concept had read the ancient authors.

When at the end of the eighteenth century power had shifted to the Commons, a parliamentary variety of the theory was developed. The balance politicians talked about was no longer primarily a balance between the independent powers of king, Lords and Commons, but rather a balance within the Commons, where king and Lords had their 'influence', but 'where all the powers of government and legislature ultimately lie'.[14] For some time this was the theory most Whigs adhered to (although around the time of the Reform Bill of 1832, they rejected the idea of 'influence', which was then defended by the Tories).

So the political implications of the mixed constitution and the theory itself were somewhat in flux. However, the terms constitutional theorists used to describe the British constitution remained the same: 'balance', 'equilibrium', 'mutual check' and 'stability'.[15] The ideal constitution was a flexible balance. According to Whig leader Charles James Fox, amongst others, the aristocratic House of Lords maintained 'the balance that equalized and meliorated the powers of the other two branches, and gave stability and firmness to the whole'. As a constitutional historian put it: 'The desideratum of this mechanism was not progress but stability.'[16] This served political purposes, of course, such as curtailing the position of the king and afterwards legitimizing the role of the aristocratic and liberal Whigs in politics. But the interesting thing is that it was always the argument of stability and balance that was used. This balance was equally important for avoiding the two dangers of democracy, on the one hand, and despotism, on the other. The mixed constitution was a safeguard against both.

Stability and balance were also used by eighteenth-century French critics of the mixed constitution. Not all commentators were as enthusiastic about the British constitution as Montesquieu. Some thought that it was a complicated, burdensome system, while others predicted that the different powers would collide and suffer from 'discordes intestines' and 'conflits perpétuels'. Mixed government would therefore result in 'anarchy', 'a thousand times worse than despotism', and in civil war. All wars in British history resulted from this imbalanced system.[17] Also, those who wanted to criticize the British constitution used the argument of stability and balance, but now *against* it. In 1817 French lawyer Jean Chas used these arguments to counter the promotion of mixed government by French liberals. The divided sovereignty of mixed government produced distrust, 'perpetual combat', and even civil war and anarchy. The British mixed government model would inevitably result in 'democratic government' built on 'the debris of the monarchy'.[18] In 1810 Chas had used the same arguments to defend the authoritarian regime of Napoleon and to attack the British constitution. According to him, only monarchy would bring peace and stability. The mixed constitution and the system of maintaining balance between the powers led to confusion, factious politics and clashes. The British system had produced despotism and corruption.[19]

The *Edinburgh Review* was flabbergasted by this defence of Napoleon. A few years earlier, Francis Jeffrey, the Whig editor of the *Review*, had vigorously defended the parliamentary variety of the mixed constitution – the 'influence' of aristocracy and monarchy within the House of Commons maintained the balance of the constitution.[20] He agreed with Chas that unmitigated aristocracy, let alone pure democracy, did not work, but he was ready to fight for 'the fair form of mixed government'.[21] The self-confidence of British politics soared after the fall of Napoleon. It has sometimes been assumed that the mixed constitution was outdated after the French Revolution and was replaced by ideals of liberal parliamentarianism and democracy.[22] The truth is that the British form of mixed government was never as admired as in the years after the fall of Napoleon. King, Lords and Commons formed the prestigious regime of the greatest power. It was the prime example for countries that had to build up a new political system after the revolutionary period.

This new prestige, however, came at a price. The concept of mixed government was narrowed down. In the eighteenth century it was used not only to describe institutional politics as a mix of rule by one, rule by the few and rule by the many, but also as the representation or balance of different societal 'interests'.[23] The balance ensured that the British 'constitutional nobility' did not 'become an aristocracy like that of Holland'; it would be unfair to compare them to 'these little tyrants'.[24] When after the fall of Napoleon the British system of mixed government was exported to the continent, this was, however, as a system of government only. In order to be ready to be implemented, the 'modularity' of mixed government was useful: there was a kind of political package of constitutional monarchy with a two-chamber system that could be used abroad.[25] Continental commentators usually complained that the social conditions of the British system did not apply in their case. In particular, the introduction of a sort of senate or House of Lords was difficult. According to French conservatives, for example, the nobility could no longer fulfil its social role and thus no real aristocracy existed anymore. Liberals did not mind because they were looking for a new type of 'aristocracy'. Both agreed, however, that the social underpinning of the political constitution was important but problematic.[26]

In any case, in practice the British constitution was used as a model only for the state-structure. The Netherlands, for instance, was turned into a constitutional monarchy and at first tried to keep many elements of the older republican constitution, including the single, small and quiet, deliberative chamber. When the Belgians joined the Dutch in the united Kingdom of the Netherlands (1815–30), a bicameral system was introduced. The supporters of this system argued that a senate should be introduced to accommodate the Belgian nobility, but also to get a balanced constitution that would avoid the risks of an over-ambitious single chamber, such as the revolutionary French National Assembly had been, and to allow for sophisticated and moderate deliberation of political issues. Although the system was introduced without thorough theoretical debates, it is clear that the British example of the mixed constitution was in everybody's mind. Because of its mixed constitution, Britain was the cradle, the home, of 'well-ordered liberty'.[27] The introduction of an aristocratic senate – which was called the 'First Chamber' in the Dutch system – without the societal role of the British aristocracy was later considered to be a failure. Yet, the idea of a balance ('evenwigt') was prominent, at least until 1848.[28] In that year direct elections to the lower house, the 'Second Chamber', were introduced. According to conservatives, this would disturb the balance and 'firmness' of the Dutch Constitution. The aristocratic element was in danger, and this could cause problems for the monarchy as well. After the liberal revision of the Constitution of 1848, many conservatives left parliament and, with them, their ideas of balance and stability disappeared. The liberals who had written the new constitution wanted 'representation', not 'democracy', but they hardly referred to the mixed constitution anymore. In the parliament, one of them still said that 'constitutional government' consisted of three elements that could not exist separately: (pure) monarchy, aristocracy and democracy.[29] This was an isolated comment and, significantly, he did not use the term 'mixed constitution', but the liberal expression 'constitutional government' (even though he quoted the famous theorist of the mixed constitution, William Blackstone). Liberals also advocated a balanced constitution and opposed pure democracy, but in their fight against aristocratic conservatives, they did not want to appeal to the mixed constitution. As in other countries, the separation of powers and the rule of law took the place of the balance between social powers as the guarantee of well-ordered and free government. The mixed constitution disappeared from parliamentary and other debates.

A remarkable feature of the debate about the mixed constitution was the lack of references to the Dutch past. The kingdom of the nineteenth century was presented as a 'restoration' because the Orange family returned after Napoleon had left. The main author of the Constitutions of 1814 and 1815, Gijsbert Karel van Hogendorp, was inspired by Montesquieu and theories about the mixed constitution, and tried to argue using historical precedents in support of his arguments, but only very few commentators really used the old ideas about the mixed constitution of the Dutch Republic to legitimate the new king.[30] The mixed constitution was not a reflection of Dutch societal groups, but an imported attempt to devise a new political system with checks and balances.

France

The same was true for Restoration France.[31] In around 1800, Swiss author Jean Simonde de Sismondi belonged to the circle of Madame de Staël and Benjamin Constant. He referred to his native Geneva in defending the mixed constitution as a protection of freedom against the threats of an overpowering popular sovereignty. He was influenced by the comments on the British constitution of his fellow countryman Jean-Louis Delolme, and the British system of representative government was his obvious albeit implicit model.[32]

When after the revolutionary and Napoleonic periods a new political system had to be devised for France, the prestigious British system was the natural point of reference. 'The whole of Europe appears to be inclined to adopt the [British] system of moderate monarchy', conservative leader René de Chateaubriand opined. He tried to argue that the mix of monarchical, aristocratic and democratic elements was an original French system that would save France from democracy and despotism. He was referring to Aristotle and Polybius, but this could not hide the British inspiration, which he tried to ignore because nationalism was more popular than foreign inspiration.[33] France would probably not have introduced the bicameral system with an aristocratic Chambre des Pairs if it had not been for the concrete example on the other side of the Channel.[34] Already at the beginning of the French Revolution, aristocratic liberals had advocated a bicameral system along British lines. Some argued that this was an original French system that had been copied by the British, while others did not hide the fact that they wanted to introduce the British system.[35] Their proposal did not stand a chance because of the outcry against everything that was 'aristocratic' that dominated the Revolution, and that partly explains the emergence and popularity of the new term 'democrat(ic)'.[36] 'Aristocracy' was at the heart of constitutional debates in the first part of the nineteenth century. Was aristocracy synonymous with a selfish oligarchy and was it the greatest obstacle on the way to a modern republic, as many revolutionaries thought? Or was it crucial for a well-ordered society, freedom and a balanced political system?

Before the Revolution, the nobility had routinely assumed that they were the only real safeguard against despotism, on the one hand, and democracy, on the other, and that only they could assure a 'balanced' representation of all 'interests'. But they could argue this only as a force or class in society, which was not yet matched by an institutional political arrangement. On the eve of the Revolution, the nobles spent their energy on the defence of a 'social rather than an institutional equilibrium'.[37] The Revolution demonstrated the importance of proper political institutions. After the experience of the Terror, the debate about the bicameral system acquired a new dimension. A system with just one chamber would easily derail, as the National Convention had demonstrated during the Revolution.[38] A representative system needed checks and balances, and at the beginning of the Restoration, the adoption of a Chambre des Pairs was almost self-evident. According to liberal theorists, this was rather the introduction of a proper 'aristocracy', and the reflection and recognition of social differences, than the restoration of a narrow caste of 'nobility', let alone formal privileges. The Chambre des Pairs was allegedly needed to maintain the balance between the monarchy and the democratic element in the Chambre des Députés. In practice, it was only a formal political institution, regardless of the social position of the nobility.

Even advanced liberals such as Benjamin Constant thought that a hereditary senate should serve as a 'counterweight' to unpredictable 'democratic tendencies'.[39] In particular, doctrinaire or conservative liberals were fond of the hereditary Chambre des Pairs. In what amounted to a defence of mixed government, leading doctrinaire liberal Royer-Collard argued that 'representation' should not be taken too literally as it was just a 'metaphor'. The Chambre des Députés was a constitutional 'power', the 'democratic part of the constitution'. Representation was a mere means to establish this power. France was a 'mixed monarchy', which was 'called' representative government, where several powers cooperated with the royal power.[40] The Chambre des Pairs was an indispensable element of this mixed government.

The July Revolution of 1830 propelled the doctrinaire liberals into the centre of power, but the debate about the hereditary Chambre des Pairs showed that their conception of government encountered considerable opposition. The liberal Charles de Rémusat thought that the Chambre des Pairs was an artificial creation, but that the debate about it was a nice symbolic way to channel revolutionary passions.[41] Indeed, the abolition of hereditary peers did not change much in the short run, but the outcome of the debate was important for the downfall of the theory of mixed government. Doctrinaire liberals realized their defeat; they criticized the 'commonplaces of democracy', the 'democratic clamor' and 'democratic rancour' of their opponents who presented the debate about the peers as the last combat between feudalism and the modern egalitarian spirit.[42]

Shortly after the introduction of the Chambre des Pairs, its liberal advocates had already realized that it was unlikely that the peers would get the social position that their political role in fact presupposed. The abolition of the hereditary peers turned their chamber for all practical purposes into a chamber of reflection as part of a parliamentary system instead of one of three powers in a mixed government. This did not mean that the (doctrinaire) liberals abandoned the idea of a mixed government, in the sense of balanced government. They advocated parliamentary government, not as a means to (directly) represent the 'people' or introduce democracy, but as a guarantee of good government, and this meant first and foremost 'moderate' government.[43]

The doctrinaire liberals were champions of 'representative government', and Guizot was famous for his work on the subject.[44] However, in order to demonstrate that 'representation' did not really mean that the people decided, arguments drawn from the mixed constitution were particularly useful, as Royer-Collard had already made clear. In the 1860s, Guizot's more left-wing pupil Rémusat still tried to use the mixed constitution in order to moderate or mitigate a democratic system. As 'passions' could endanger freedom, political moderation was its best guarantee. Moderation was not a virtue of 'simple' or 'pure' systems such as political democracy, but of mixed systems. Only mixed systems could maintain an equilibrium based on an institutional structure that regulated conflicts. An aristocratic second chamber was the best example. Rémusat realized that the social basis for such a system did not exist, and his argument was not about society, but about the political system. At the end of the nineteenth century, this type of conservative liberalism was swept away by the Third Republic. It seemed to confirm the opinion of critics who argued that mixed governments did not last. The only example of a lasting mixed government was Great Britain. In other cases it was just a transitory phase on the road to the real thing: democracy.[45] Conservative liberals resigned themselves to democracy; their new motto was: 'to constitute democracy, is to moderate it' ('Constituer la démocratie, c'est la modérer').[46]

Rémusat's biographer points out that the mixed constitution was originally part of a cyclic and pessimist political philosophy, such as that advocated by Polybius. Every pure form of government would degenerate into its bad counterpart, and the best that could be achieved was to avoid evil. The most valuable quality of mixed government was its stability. However, stability was rather hard to reconcile with a progressive philosophy of history and with progress as the aim of politics, and this was one of the reasons why the philosophy of mixed government would disappear. Philosopher and liberal MP John Stuart Mill also said that the idea of a mixed constitution of Aristotle, 'a Liberal Conservative' or rather 'a moderate aristocratical politician, at Athens' was 'a philosophic consecration of existing facts', and that he was more interested in 'stability' than in 'improvement'. This was due to the fact that 'none of the ancient politicians or philosophers believed in progress; their highest hopes were limited to guarding society against its natural tendency to degeneration'. It was not Mills' favoured form of politics.[47]

'Progress' also became a strong argument for democracy and against the mixed constitution in popular circles and in newspapers. 'It is a stereotyped argument, in favour of the complicated character of the "British constitution", that the royal and aristocratic ingredients act as a "check" upon the popular, or democratic, element.' You only needed to 'check' something if it was bad or uncouth, but 'the *progress* of the English people is *upwards*, and not *downwards*'. If this were true, the crown and the nobility had checked the upward progress of the people of England. The conclusion could only be that it was time for democracy.[48]

Great Britain

It is not easy to determine when conceptions of mixed government lost their appeal in Britain. It had always been a rather bookish, theoretical term. But in particular from the 1830s to the 1870s in Britain – unlike France or other countries – the ideas about mixed government became part of newspaper debates about the nature of the constitution. It has often been asserted that the Reform Act of 1832 marked the defeat of mixed government and that there was a parallel between developments in France (the end of the hereditary peers in 1831) and Britain, where the Reform Act affected the position of the House of Lords. By passing the Reform Bill, the Whigs 'involuntarily destroyed mixed government' (Weston) and instituted 'parliamentary government'. In the House of Commons in the 1860s, however, Prime Minister Palmerston could still refer as a matter of course to 'a mixed Constitution like ours'. And Weston also writes that Delolme's theory of British mixed government remained popular until it was superseded by Walter Bagehot's popular conceptions – and his *English Constitution* was published only in 1867.[49] It seems safe to conclude that the period from the 1830s to about 1870 was a phase of discussion. This is corroborated by an overview of newspaper hits of 'mixed constitution' and 'mixed government', which reached a peak in exactly this period, when the discussion over mixed constitution and democracy was apparently most heated.[50] Aristocrats defended the mixed constitution, while radicals attacked it (in the name of progress, democracy and popular influence), and for a couple of decades mixed constitution no longer seemed such a bookish expression, but an ordinary part of political debates.

Already by around 1800, radicals had criticized the system. In 1791 Thomas Paine wrote that mixed government was irresponsible and corrupt, but then it was still very hard to 'imagine' the alternative of a practical democratic system.[51] Another critic who has often been mentioned,[52] Jeremy Bentham, published his most interesting comments decades later, with the existing American example in mind: 'there, all is democracy, all is regularity, tranquility, prosperity, security: continual security', no aristocracy or monarchy in sight. It was clearly nonsensical to equate this democracy with anarchy. The American example inspired Bentham to try to check the overbearing aristocratic and monarchical interest in Britain. 'Mixture' was fine as long as it did not hinder the 'efficiency' of the one constitutional element that mattered – the democratic part. Nobody should think that government should be balanced: 'in a machine of any kind, when forces balance each other, the machine is at a stand'. 'Immobility' would be fatal: 'when motion ceases, the body dies'.[53]

A country could not afford to have such an inefficient 'machine for standing still';[54] progress should be made. This criticism was new. Bentham and his adherents wanted a strong government that could efficiently solve the problems of a modern society. Until then, inefficiency had not been a major problem in the theory of mixed government. On the contrary, some of its conservative adherents saw it as an advantage that it provided 'a check to the too great facility and rapidity of legislation': 'Change of law is in itself an evil, and should never be admitted but from unavoidable necessity.'[55] It is true that after 1800 both the doctrinaire liberals in France and the Whigs in Britain no longer advocated a balance between independent elements (a possible interpretation of mixed government) because this threatened to result in paralysis or even a kind of 'civil war' between these elements. Instead, the Whigs a dvocated the close cooperation among or even fusion of monarchy, aristocracy and democracy in the lower house. According to Guizot, the mixed constitution was not a system of mere negative checks and balances; the three powers should work together closely in order to make government function properly.[56] There was no doubt that these admirers of the mixed constitution were enthusiastic supporters of a representative government with a modest role for the king. For them, representative government meant responsible and moderate government. For the legitimacy of a more powerful executive government, they could have appealed to the king, but as liberals they did not want that solution.

The moderate liberals rejected the alternative source of legitimacy, democracy. Their concept of representative government did not imply democratic rule by the representatives of the people. According to traditional political theory, 'democracy' ran the risk of degenerating into either anarchy or despotism. The period of the French Revolution had changed the meaning of the concept, but the revolutionary experience also seemed to confirm these age-old fears. Mark Philp argues that Edmund Burke's *Reflections on the Revolution in France* (1790) gave a wider and more popular currency to the until then rather academic concept of 'democracy'. Burke did this, of course, by contrasting the anarchy and despotism of French revolutionary democracy with the wise, mixed and tempered British constitution in particular, and solidity, stability and balance in general.[57]

Time and again, the fears about democracy seemed to be confirmed by its European practice. In France, the democratic revolution of 1848 ended in the authoritarian regime of Napoleon III. According to *The Times*, Napoleon's destruction of constitutional rights belonged to 'the ordinary results of democratic revolution'.[58] Walter Bagehot saw Napoleon III's regime as democratic despotism and famously called it 'the best finished democracy which the world has ever seen'. Bagehot also referred to Bentham's conception of efficient democratic government by calling Napoleon III a 'Benthamite despot. He is for the "greatest happiness of the greatest number"'.[59] Bagehot was intrigued by the way Napoleon III ruled his country. He did not like either democracy or despotism, but he favoured strong government. This helps to explain why Bagehot symbolically sealed the fate of mixed government.

Bagehot was a journalist, and his work was more convincing than really original or new. His *The English Constitution* starts with an attack on the idea of the 'balanced union of three powers'. Bagehot uses a rhetorical trick because the old Whig Lord Brougham was one of the last people to really defend the classic idea of mixed government with its completely separate powers. He thought that its incomparable 'stability' depended on the principle 'that each of the orders or estates should remain separate from the other'.[60]

To a certain extent, Bagehot summarized current ideas. According to some comments, he was meanwhile looking for a new balance, in the Whig tradition. It is clear that he did not attack mixed government in the name of democracy. He was 'exceedingly afraid of the ignorant multitude' in Britain and thought that democracy had brought the United States 'an almost unmitigated ochlocracy'. He wanted to legitimate responsible and strong executive government. He thought that the recent broadening of the suffrage at least had the advantage that the 'now secure predominance of popular power must greatly mitigate our traditional jealousy of the Executive Government'. He did not like democracy, but democracy could serve to legitimate strong government. British government should follow the modern French and Prussian regimes, both 'new machines, made in civilized times to do their appropriate work'.[61]

The end of mixed government was not the end of the ideal of stable and balanced government. Bagehot loved the idea of an 'equilibrium'[62] in politics, exactly the ideal of mixed government. However, the hierarchy of values had changed. A combination of democracy and executive government became dominant. The answer to the question why mixed government disappeared and democracy won is not that the checks and balances had now gone and the people now ruled. The authors quoted at the start of this chapter explain that what we call 'democracy' today is more akin to mixed government than to 'pure' democracy.

In the first half of the nineteenth century, the form of government in Britain, France and the Netherlands was called representative government, but representation did not mean reproduction of the wishes of the people. In explicit contrast to 'democracy', it implied the independence of representatives, once they were chosen by the select group of voters.[63] The efforts to make representatives more responsive to the electorate and also to enlarge the electorate were increasingly symbolized by the word 'democracy'. When it became common to use the adjective 'democratic' to describe the regime in Britain, France or the Netherlands, this was parliamentary or representative democracy. However, the new popularity of the term – in France after 1848, and again after 1870, in Britain from the second but mostly the third Reform Bill, and in the Netherlands from around 1900 – was the expression of a shift in politics. The old independence of representatives was gone, and now they continuously had to justify their actions to the people and to political parties. Parties now mobilized and organized the people, and their dominance in many countries is a sure sign that the meaning of representation had changed. Conservatives and conservative liberals had used the virtues of 'mixed government' as an argument to prevent the change of representative government. In 1816 a prominent conservative politician said in the French Parliament that representative government meant the cooperation of royal, aristocratic and democratic powers in order to defend the common interest and the balance and security of the state. At the same time, another conservative parliamentarian doubted whether such a representative system existed in France because the balance between the powers was disturbed by the lack of power of the aristocracy.[64] They equated 'representative' with 'mixed' government. When mixed government lost its attraction, 'representative government' was also contaminated, so that now even conservatives had to come to terms with democracy. To a certain extent, the same was true for 'parliamentary government' in Britain, which in the middle of the nineteenth century was also defended as a moderate and balanced government.[65]

On the other hand, 'democracy' increasingly included liberal notions of rule of law and separation of powers, which took over the moderating functions of a balance of powers within the mixed constitution. It is no coincidence that the well-known history of the theory of the separation of powers by Maurice Vile reads as a history of the theory of mixed government until the story reaches the middle of the nineteenth century. In the nineteenth century, the main opponent of 'democracy' was 'aristocracy', and thus democracy almost self-evidently implied an attack on the social foundation and legitimation of mixed government. The struggle against totalitarianism of the 1930s and 1940s would result in the new antinomy of democracy and dictatorship, which definitely made the rule of law the heart of democracy. It brought democracy closer to mixed government again.

A second change was related to the legitimation of government and was popularized by the work of Walter Bagehot. The change from mixed government to democracy did not mean the end of checks and balances, but government could remain legitimate only by calling the new balance 'democracy'. In addition, executive government required a new legitimation too. The idea of balance and equilibrium was completed and sometimes even overruled by the idea that a modern society needed vigorous government. Bagehot's 'description' of the British constitution was an acknowledgement of the importance of executive government. He still thought that a deferential attitude of the population would suffice as popular support for this government. But soon it appeared that this was a miscalculation. It was no coincidence that future liberal leader William Gladstone complained about the 'declining efficiency of parliament' (*Quarterly Review*, September 1856) and was at the same time arguing for a broadening of the suffrage.[66] In the short run, the extension of the suffrage perhaps seemed to hinder executive government, but it appeared that legitimation of power by 'democracy' was very effective. This was particularly the case once it had become clear that democracy did not mean 'ochlocracy' or mob rule, but suffrage for those who were – as Gladstone said in the House of Commons in 1864 – 'morally entitled to come within the pale of the Constitution'. Accepting democracy was a process of, on the one hand, parliamentarization of democracy and, on the other, democratization of parliament. In the meantime (general, male) suffrage became the main element of democracy. In the mixed constitution, suffrage had not been very important, and its prominence in political debates was one of the signs of the end of the mixed constitution, as well as of parliamentary government as an opposite of democracy.

Even more clearly than Gladstone, his radical opponent Joseph Chamberlain combined 'democracy' with strong executive government. It became hard to distinguish the two: for him, 'democratic' meant 'representation of the will of the majority', and this in turn meant that the 'executive' should mirror this majority.[67] This could just as well mean that he used democracy as legitimation for strong executive government. The first criterion for good government was no longer stability, but vigorous execution of the wishes of the majority. This was perhaps a democratic claim, but it certainly was anti-aristocratic, and it could build on older doubts about the efficiency of aristocratic government.[68]

Conclusion

After the fall of Napoleon I, the British version of the mixed constitution was attractive for opinion leaders in many countries. Only in Britain, however, was it part of popular debates and perceived as a 'national' form of government. According to MP and historian Macaulay, the French Chambre des Pairs – an essential element of mixed government – 'was a mere exotic transplant from our island'.[69] However that may be, in countries such as the Netherlands and France, as well as in Britain, defence of the mixed constitution became a strategy to hold democracy at bay; representative government was interpreted as merely virtual or metaphoric representation. For those who wanted to interpret representation in a democratic way, the mixed constitution had become a defence of aristocratic interest. Democracy, moreover, was a battle cry that could mobilize the people; the mixed constitution mainly remained an idea for the connoisseurs. It was used quite a lot in parliament, but, setting aside a short period in Britain, hardly in mass meetings. If politics was for everyone, then it should be democratic; the mixed constitution was something for the social elite and political insiders.

The values of stability and balance that were attached to the mixed constitution were gradually transferred to democracy and also became less prominent. Democracy demanded progressive government that would improve society. The changed interpretation of representation as well as of executive government helps to explain the victory of democracy over mixed government. When during the nineteenth century both the input of popular influence and the output of government action were redefined, and the links between politics and society were strengthened and restructured, democracy replaced the mixed constitution. This did not mean that all aristocratic or mixed elements disappeared from the political system – far from it. Key virtues of the concept in its original shape such as stability, balance and a safeguard against despotism were to a certain extent transferred to democracy. Current debates between liberal democracy and populism sometimes recall the old opposition between the mixed constitution and democracy. Hardly anybody would really like to return to the old system, but if you want to understand modern democracy, you are well advised to review the arguments used for and against the mixed constitution.

Henk te Velde is Professor of History at Leiden University. He has written a number of monographs on the history of political culture in the Netherlands, such as *Stijlen van Leiderschap: Persoon en Politiek van Thorbecke tot Den Uyl* (2010). *Sprekende politiek: Redenaars en hun publiek in de parlementaire gouden eeuw* is about nineteenth-century British and French parliamentary rhetoric and culture (2015). He recently coedited *Organizing Democracy: Reflections on the Rise of Political Organizations in the 19th Century* (2017), which has appeared as the first volume in the new book series 'Palgrave Studies in Political History', which he is coediting. He is also one of the editors of the *Journal of Modern European History* and is a founding member of the international Association for Political History.

Notes

1. Frank Ankersmit, 'What if Our Representative Democracies are Elective Aristocracies?', *Redescriptions: Political Thought, Conceptual History and Feminist Theory* 15 (2011), 21–44. The original Dutch text is Frank Ankersmit, *De representatieve democratie is een electieve aristocratie*, Afscheidscollege, 12 April 2010 (Groningen s.a.).
2. Bernard Manin, *The Principles of Representative Government* (Cambridge: Cambridge University Press, 1997), 238.
3. Mogens Herman Hansen, 'The Mixed Constitution versus the Separation of Powers: Monarchical and Aristocratic Aspects of Modern Democracy', *History of Political Thought* 31 (2010), 509–31. Hansen and Manin refer to each other's work.

4. Alois Riklin, *Machtteilung. Geschichte der Mischverfassung* (Darmstadt: Wissenschaftliche Buchgesellschaft, 2006), 423. Riklin was inspired by a rather isolated essay by the German political scientist Dolf Sternberger (1984).
5. Robert Saunders, 'Democracy', in D. Craig and J. Thompson (eds), *The Languages of Politics in Modern British History* (Basingstoke: Palgrave Macmillan, 2013), 162.
6. John Dunn, *Setting the People Free: The Story of Democracy* (London: Atlantic Books, 2005), 155.
7. E.g. Conservative Lord Hugh Cecil, Hansard's House of Commons, 12 March 1913: 'At present we have no Parliamentary government or representative government, or what our ancestors used to be proud of – the old mixed government in which the Crown and the aristocracy and the democracy took a share. We have none of this now. Instead, we have Cabinet government and Cabinet autocracy.' This is a result of searching historical Hansard for 'mixed constitution' and 'mixed government'.
8. Cf. the first sentence of Aurelian Craiutu, *A Virtue for Courageous Minds: Moderation in French Political Thought, 1748–1830* (Princeton: Princeton University Press, 2012), 1: 'There is no agreement about what is the supreme political virtue.' He argues that 'moderation' is this virtue, which would fit very well into mixed government.
9. François Guizot, *De la démocratie en France (janvier 1849)* (Paris: Masson, 1849).
10. *London Evening Standard*, 12 November 1835.
11. E.g. Vittorio Conti, 'The Mechanisation of Virtue: Republican Rituals in Italian Political Thought in the Sixteenth and Seventeenth Centuries', in Martin van Gelderen and Quentin Skinner (eds), *Republicanism: A Shared European heritage* II (Cambridge: Cambridge University Press, 2002), 74–79; Wyger R.E. Velema, '"That a Republic is Better than a Monarchy": Anti-monarchism in Early Modern Dutch Political Thought', in van Gelderen and Skinner, *Republicanism* I, 9–41 (12); G.O. van de Klashorst, '"Metten schijn van monarchie getempert": De verdediging van het stadhouderschap in de partijliteratuur, 1650–1686', in H.W. Blom and I.W. Wildenberg (eds), *Pieter de la Court in zijn tijd: Aspecten van een veelzijdig publicist (1618–1685)* (Amsterdam/Maarssen: APA/Holland University Press, 1986), 93–136; Jill Stern, *Orangism in the Dutch Republic in Word and Image* (Manchester: Manchester University Press, 2010).
12. E.g. Riklin, *Machtteilung*, 12, 353.
13. Bolingbroke, quoted by David Lieberman, 'The Mixed Constitution and the Common Law', in Mark Goldie and Robert Wokler (eds), *The Cambridge History of Eighteenth-Century Political Thought* (Cambridge: Cambridge University Press, 2006), 319.
14. Thomas Pitt, *A Dialogue on the Actual State of Parliament* (1783), quoted by J.A.W. Gunn, 'Influence, Parties and the Constitution: Changing Attitudes, 1783–1832', *Historical Journal* XVII (1974), 301–28, at 308. In 1785 William Paley formulated a variety of this idea in his comments on the constitution.
15. Lieberman, 'Mixed Constitution', 325, 337 (quotations from William Blackstone, Jean Louis Delolme, etc.).

16. Corinne Comstock Weston, *English Constitutional Theory and the House of Lords 1556–1832* (Abingdon: Routledge, 2010), 129 (referring to Delolme) and 160 (quotation of Fox in the 1790s).
17. A list of critics in Gabriel Bonno, *La constitution britannique devant l'opinion française de Montesquieu à Bonaparte* (New York: Lenox Hill, 1971), 9, 11, 26, 59, 87, 97 and passim.
18. J. Chas, *Des gouvernemens représentatif et mixte* (Paris: Villet, 1817), 18–19, 21, 28, 37; 16 against Guizot.
19. J. Chas, *Sur la souveraineté*, 2nd edn. (Paris: Egron, 1810): this edition contains a critique of British mixed government.
20. Gunn, 'Influence, Parties and the Constitution', 320.
21. *Edinburgh Review* (1811), 409–28 (review of Chas with extensive quotations).
22. Riklin, *Machtteilung*, 425, footnote 1 refers only to developments in the nineteenth century. Like democracy, the concepts of both parliamentarianism and liberalism have their own (complicated) history: see the respective volumes about them in this same Berghahn series.
23. Angus Hawkins, *Victorian Political Culture: 'Habits of Heart and Mind'* (Oxford: Oxford University Press, 2015), 35.
24. Brook Boothby (1792), quoted by Amanda Goodrich, *Debating England's Aristocracy in the 1790s: Pamphlets, Polemics and Political Ideas* (Woodbridge: Boydell, 2005), 94; Amanda Goodrich, 'Understanding a Language of "Aristocracy", 1700–1850', *Historical Journal* 56(2) (2013), 369–98 about the difficult conceptual history of the term.
25. Historical sociologist Tarrow uses 'modularity' in his analysis of the transfer of concrete organizational elements of social movements, also around 1800; see e.g. Sidney Tarrow, *Power in Movement. Social Movements and Contentious Politics* (Cambridge: Cambridge University Press, 2011).
26. E.g. Annelien de Dijn, *French Political Thought from Montesquieu to Tocqueville: Liberty in a Levelled Society?* (Cambridge: Cambridge University Press, 2008); Lucien Jaume, 'Tocqueville face au thème de la "nouvelle aristocratie" : La difficile naissance des partis en France', *Revue française de science politique* 56 (2006), 969–84; Lucien Jaume, *L'individu effacé ou le paradoxe du libéralisme français* (Paris: Fayard, 1997), 143, 165, 288–320; Pierre Rosanvallon, *La démocratie inachevée : Histoire de la souveraineté du peuple en France* (Paris: Gallimard, 2000), 108–16; Pierre Rosanvallon, *Le moment Guizot* (Paris: Gallimard, 1985), 107–20 ('la nouvelle aristocratie'). See e.g. contemporary comments by J. Fiévée, *Histoire de la session de 1815* (Paris: Normant, 1816), 31–51 ('Du Pouvoir aristocratique').
27. Conservative G.W. Vreede, *De regtstreeksche verkiezingen tot de nationale vertegenwoordiging bestreden* (Amsterdam: Schleijer,1848), 27. Cf. for these paragraphs Henk te Velde, 'De domesticatie van democratie in Nederland: Democratie als strijdbegrip van de negentiende eeuw tot 1945', *BMGN – Low Countries Historical Review* 127 (2012), 3–27, esp. 9–10.
28. E.g. Donker Curtius van Tienhoven, *Handelingen Tweede Kamer 1832–1833*, 11 June 1833, 246.

29. A.F. Jongstra, *Handelingen Tweede Kamer 1852–1853*, 23 November 1852, 169.
30. But cf. Olivarius [Floris Adriaan van Hall], *Staatkundige opmerkingen* (Amsterdam: Van Kampen, 1848).
31. For that reason, Pierre Rosanvallon, *La monarchie impossible : Les Chartes de 1814 et 1830* (Paris: Fayard, 1994), 175–77 argues that a mixed constitution was in fact impossible or 'unthinkable' in France.
32. Emmanuelle Paulet-Grandguillot, *Libéralisme et démocratie: De Sismondi à Constant, à partir du Contrat social (1801–1806)* (Geneva: Slatkine, 2010), 266–70 and passim.
33. François-René de Chateaubriand, *Écrits politiques (1814–1816)*, ed. Colin Smethurst (Geneva: Droz, 2002), 165–76; quotation from 200 (cf. footnote 138); François-René de Chateaubriand, 'Polémique', in *Oeuvres politiques (l'édition intégrale)*, e-artnow 2015: e-pub.
34. Benjamin Constant, 'Principes de politique', in Benjamin Constant, *Écrits politiques*, ed. Marcel Gauchet (Paris: Gallimard, 1997), 325: 'Comme il est toujours utile de sortir des abstractions par les faits, nous citerons la constitution anglaise.'
35. Emmanuel de Waresquiel, *Un groupe d'hommes considérables. Les pairs de France et la Chambre des pairs héréditaire de la Restauration 1814–1831* (Paris: Fayard, 2006), 25 ff.
36. Pierre Rosanvallon, 'L'histoire du mot démocratie à l'époque moderne', in *La pensée politique. Situations de la démocratie* (Paris: Gallimard, 1993), 17–18, 23. Cf. Raymonde Monnier, 'Démocratie et Révolution française', *Mots* 59 (1999), 47–68, esp. 50. Joanna Innes and Mark Philp (eds), *Re-imagining Democracy in the Age of Revolutions: America, France, Britain, Ireland 1750–1850* (Oxford: Oxford University Press, 2013), in particular 57, 61, 149–50, 157, 169, 199.
37. Vivian R. Gruder, *The Notables and the Nation: The Political Schooling of the French, 1787–1788* (Cambridge, MA: Harvard University Press, 2007), Chapter 3, in particular 66, 70, 77–80; quotations from 79 and 80.
38. Waresquiel, *Groupe d'hommes*, 59: Benjamin Constant was one of the first to use this argument.
39. Constant, 'Principes de politique', 535.
40. Prosper de Barante, *La vie politique de Royer-Collard : Ses discours et ses écrits*, 2 vols (Paris: Didier, 1863) I, 222, 227–28; II, 223; Darío Roldán, *Charles de Rémusat : Certitudes et impasses du libéralisme doctrinaire* (Paris: L'Harmattan, 1999), 127. Cf. Rosanvallon, *Démocratie inachevée*, 102–4.
41. Waresquiel, *Groupe d'hommes*, 319.
42. Guizot and Broglie, quoted by Waresquiel, *Groupe d'hommes*, 330.
43. De Dijn, *French Political Thought*, 72–73, 133; François Guizot, 'De la démocratie dans les sociétés modernes', *Revue française* (1837), 193–225; Jean-François Jacouty, 'Une aristocratie dans la démocratie? Le débat politique sur la chambre des pairs au début de la Monarchie de Juillet (et ses conditions historiques et théoriques)', *Revue d'histoire du XIXe siècle* 20–21 (2000), 93–116, esp. 115–16 and 95: a memoir Guizot wrote as a civil servant in 1816 about parliamentary government.

44. François Guizot, *Histoire des origines du gouvernement représentatif en Europe*, 2 vols (Paris: Didier, 1851): this was based on lectures from the early 1820s. See for this paragraph Roldán, *Rémusat*, 248–55.
45. Étienne Vacherot, *La démocratie* (Paris: Chamerot, 1860), 15–18, 349–50. Vacherot addresses his criticism to the doctrinaires he had once belonged to himself; at the end of the nineteenth century, he would return to monarchism.
46. Charles de Rémusat, 'De l'esprit de réaction. Royer-Collard et Tocqueville', *Revue des Deux Mondes* 35 (1861), 812; cf. Roldán, *Rémusat*, 251.
47. Roldán, *Rémusat*, 249; John Stuart Mill, 'Grote's Aristotle' (1873), in John Stuart Mill, *The Collected Works* XI (Toronto: Toronto University Press/London: Routledge, 1978), 473–510, retrieved 31 January 2018, http://oll.libertyfund.org/titles/248.
48. Northumbrian, 'Our Mixed Constitution', *Reynold's Newspaper*, 16 January 1859 (letter to the editor of this radical, post-Chartist newspaper).
49. Weston, *English Constitutional Theory*, 242 and passim (quotation from 244; 129 about Delolme); Jacouty, 'Aristocratie', 108–9 and footnote 79; Hawkins, *Victorian Political Culture*; Hansard, House of Commons, 11 April 1864 (Palmerston).
50. Cf. http://www.britishnewspaperarchive.co.uk/search/results?basicsearch=%22mixed%20constitution%22 (April 2016): before and after 1830–70, in the tens each decade, in between in the (many) hundreds. In comparison, a search of the category 'la presse et les revues' of 'gallica' (Bibliothèque Nationale de France) for 'gouvernement mixte' yielded far fewer results and more purely intellectual analysis or ancient history.
51. Cf. Mark Philp, *Reforming Ideas in Britain: Politics and Language in the Shadow of the French Revolution, 1789–1815* (Cambridge: Cambridge University Press, 2014), 122–23.
52. E.g. by Weston, *English Constitutional Theory*; and M.J.C. Vile, *Constitutionalism and the Separation of Powers* (Indianapolis: Liberty Fund, 1998).
53. Jeremy Bentham, *Plan for Parliamentary Reform* (London: Hunter, 1817).
54. Bentham's adherent John Arthur Roebuck, quoted by Weston, *English Constitutional Theory*, 238.
55. John Headlam, *Attachment to the Established Forms of Our Civil and Ecclesiastical Constitution* (York: Blanchard, 1813), 23.
56. In the introduction to the edition of his parliamentary speeches, François Guizot, *Histoire parlementaire de la France : Recueil complet des discours prononcés dans les chambres de 1819 à 1848* I (Paris: Michel Lévy, 1863), 29–32; this is a long quotation from François Guizot, *Du Gouvernement représentatif et de l'état actuel de la France* (Paris: Maradan, 1816), 25–31. Cf. Vile, *Constitutionalism*, 221.
57. Mark Philp, 'Talking about Democracy: Britain in the 1790s', in Innes and Philp, *Re-imagining Democracy*, 104–5; see also 200; Burke, *Reflections*.
58. *The Times*, 8 December 1851, quoted by Saunders, *Democracy*, 139; cf. J.P. Parry, 'The Impact of Napoleon III on British Politics, 1851–1880', *Transactions of the Royal Historical Society* 11 (2001), 147–75.

59. Walter Bagehot, 'Caesarism as it Now Exists' (1865), in Walter Bagehot, *Collected Works* IV, ed. Norman St. John-Stevas (London: The Economist, 1968), 111–12.
60. Henry Brougham, *The British Constitution: Its History, Structure, and Working* (London: Griffin & Bohn, 1861), 26, 104. Brougham was Bagehot's most probable target: Vile, *Constitutionalism*, 237; Miles Taylor in Walter Bagehot, *The English Constitution* (Oxford: Oxford University Press, 2001), xxii; cf. Paul Smith in Walter Bagehot, *The English Constitution* (Cambridge: Cambridge University Press 2001), xiv (see xviii–xxv for 'a new balance').
61. Bagehot, quoted by Vile, *Constitutionalism*, 247 and by Taylor in Bagehot, *Constitution*, xvii; Walter Bagehot, 'What May Be in America' (1861), in Bagehot, *Collected Works* IV, 272–73; letter to R.H. Hutton, 24 June 1867, in Bagehot, *Collected Works* XIII, 617; Bagehot, *Constitution*, 150.
62. Taylor in Bagehot, *Constitution*, xxviii.
63. E.g. the Dutch Liberal leader Thorbecke, c. 1848, in Johan Rudolf Thorbecke, *De briefwisseling*, eds G.J. Hooykaas and F.J.P. Santegoets (The Hague: ING, 1996), vol. V, 532.
64. Étienne-Denis Pasquier, Chambre des Députés, 14 February 1816; Pierre Béraud, *Souvenirs parlementaires* (Moulins: Desrosiers, 1841), 379.
65. E.g. Henry George Grey, *Parliamentary Government Considered with References to a Reform of Parliament* (1858; London: Bentley, 1864).
66. Richard Shannon, *Gladstone*, 2 vols (London: Penguin, 1982–99) underlines executive government. H.C.G. Matthew, *Gladstone*, 2 vols (Oxford: Clarendon, 1986–95); Roy Jenkins, *Gladstone* (London: Macmillan, 1995); and Eugenio Biagini, *Liberty, Retrenchment and Reform: Popular Liberalism in the Age of Gladstone, 1860–1880* (Cambridge: Cambridge University Press, 1992) concentrate on the charismatic leader, orator and popular politician.
67. J. Chamberlain, 'The Caucus', *Fortnightly Review* (1878), 721–41, esp. 724, 731.
68. Cf. David Craig, 'Statesmanship', in Craig and Thompson (eds), *Languages*, 147–48.
69. Macaulay, *Speeches*, quoted by Annelien de Dijn, 'Balancing the Constitution: Bicameralism in Post-Revolutionary France, 1814–31', *European Review of History* 12 (2005), 249–68, esp. 261.

Bibliography

Ankersmit, F. 2011. 'What if Our Representative Democracies are Elective Aristocracies?', *Redescriptions: Political Thought, Conceptual History and Feminist Theory* 15, 21–44.

Bagehot, W. 1968. 'What May Be in America' (1861), in *Collected Works* IV, Norman St. John-Stevas (ed.). London: The Economist, 272–73.

———. 1968. 'Caesarism as it Now Exists' (1865), in *Collected Works* IV, 111–12.

———. 2001. *The English Constitution* (1867). Cambridge: Cambridge University Press.

Barante, P. de. 1863. *La vie politique de Royer-Collard. Ses discours et ses écrits.* Paris: Didier.
Bentham, J. 1817. *Plan for Parliamentary Reform.* London: Hunter.
Béraud, P. 1841. *Souvenirs parlementaires.* Moulins: Desrosiers.
Biagini, E. 1992. *Liberty, Retrenchment and Reform. Popular Liberalism in the Age of Gladstone, 1860–1880.* Cambridge: Cambridge University Press.
Bonno, G. 1971. *La constitution britannique devant l'opinion française de Montesquieu à Bonaparte.* New York: Lenox Hill.
Brougham, H. 1861. *The British Constitution. Its History, Structure, and Working.* London: Griffin & Bohn.
Chamberlain, J. 1878. 'The Caucus', *Fortnightly Review*, 721–41.
Chas, J. 1810. *Sur la souveraineté*, 2nd edn. Paris: Egron.
———. 1817. *Des gouvernemens représentatif et mixte.* Paris: Villet.
Comstock Weston, C. 2010. *English Constitutional Theory and the House of Lords 1556–1832.* Abingdon: Routledge.
Constant, B. 1997. 'Principes de politique', in B. Constant, *Écrits politiques*, M. Gauchet (ed.). Paris: Gallimard, 303–588.
Conti, V. 2002. 'The Mechanisation of Virtue: Republican Rituals in Italian Political Thought in the Sixteenth and Seventeenth Centuries', in M. van Gelderen and Q. Skinner (eds), *Republicanism: A Shared European Heritage.* Cambridge: Cambridge University Press, 73–83.
Craig, D. 2013. 'Statesmanship', in D. Craig and J. Thompson (eds), *The Languages of Politics in Modern British History.* Basingstoke: Palgrave Macmillan, 44–68.
Craiutu, A. 2012. *A Virtue for Courageous Minds: Moderation in French Political Thought, 1748–1830.* Princeton: Princeton University Press.
Dijn, A. de 2005. 'Balancing the Constitution: Bicameralism in Post-Revolutionary France, 1814–31', *European Review of History* 12, 249–68.
———. 2008. *French Political Thought from Montesquieu to Tocqueville: Liberty in a Levelled Society?* Cambridge: Cambridge University Press.
Dunn, J. 2005. *Setting the People Free: The Story of Democracy.* London: Atlantic Books.
Fiévée, J. 1816. *Histoire de la session de 1815.* Paris: Normant.
Goldie, M., and R. Wokler (eds). 2006. *The Cambridge History of Eighteenth-Century Political Thought.* Cambridge: Cambridge University Press.
Goodrich, A. 2005. *Debating England's Aristocracy in the 1790s: Pamphlets, Polemics and Political Ideas.* Woodbridge: Boydell.
———. 2013. 'Understanding a Language of "Aristocracy", 1700–1850', *Historical Journal* 56(2), 369–98.
Grey, H.G. 1864. *Parliamentary Government Considered with References to a Reform of Parliament.* London: Bentley.
Gruder, V.R. 2007. *The Notables and the Nation: The Political Schooling of the French, 1787–1788.* Cambridge, MA: Harvard University Press.
Guizot, F. 1816. *Du Gouvernement représentatif et de l'état actuel de la France.* Paris: Maradan.

———. 1837. 'De la démocratie dans les sociétés modernes', *Revue française*, 193–225.
———. 1849. *De la démocratie en France (janvier 1849)*. Paris: Masson.
———. 1851. *Histoire des origines du gouvernement représentatif en Europe*. Paris: Didier.
———. 1863. *Histoire parlementaire de la France: Recueil complet des discours prononcés dans les chambres de 1819 à 1848* I. Paris: Michel Lévy.
Gunn, J.A.W. 1974. 'Influence, Parties and the Constitution: Changing Attitudes, 1783–1832', *Historical Journal* XVII, 301–28.
Hansen, H. 2010. 'The Mixed Constitution versus the Separation of Powers: Monarchical and Aristocratic Aspects of Modern Democracy', *History of Political Thought* 31, 509–31.
Hawkins, A. 2015. *Victorian Political Culture: 'Habits of Heart and Mind'*. Oxford: Oxford University Press.
Headlam, J. 1813. *Attachment to the Established Forms of Our Civil and Ecclesiastical Constitution*. York: Blanchard.
Innes, J., and M. Philp (eds). 2013. *Re-imagining Democracy in the Age of Revolutions: America, France, Britain, Ireland 1750–1850*. Oxford: Oxford University Press.
Jacouty, J-F. 2000. 'Une aristocratie dans la démocratie? Le débat politique sur la chambre des pairs au début de la Monarchie de Juillet (et ses conditions historiques et théoriques)', *Revue d'histoire du XIXe siècle* 20–21, 93–116.
Jaume, L. 2006. 'Tocqueville face au thème de la "nouvelle aristocratie" : La difficile naissance des partis en France', *Revue française de science politique* 56, 969–84.
Jenkins, R. 1995. *Gladstone*. London: Macmillan.
Klashorst, G.O. van de. 1986. '"Metten schijn van monarchie getempert". De verdediging van het stadhouderschap in de partijliteratuur, 1650–1686', in H.W. Blom and I.W. Wildenberg (eds), *Pieter de la Court in zijn tijd: Aspecten van een veelzijdig publicist (1618–1685)*. Amsterdam/Maarssen: APA/Holland University Press, 93–136.
Laume, L. 1997. *L'individu effacé ou le paradoxe du libéralisme français*. Paris: Fayard.
Manin, B. 1997. *The Principles of Representative Government*. Cambridge: Cambridge University Press.
Matthew, H.C.G. 1988–1995. *Gladstone*. Oxford: Clarendon.
Mill, J.S. 1978. 'Grote's Aristotle' (1873), in J.S. Mill, *The Collected Works* XI. Toronto: Toronto University Press/London: Routledge, 473–510.
Monnier, R. 1999. 'Démocratie et Révolution française', *Mots* 59, 47–68.
Parry, J.P. 2011. 'The Impact of Napoleon III on British Politics, 1851–1880', *Transactions of the Royal Historical Society* 11: 147–75.
Paulet-Grandguillot, E. 2010. *Libéralisme et démocratie: De Sismondi à Constant, à partir du Contrat social (1801–1806)*. Geneva: Slatkine.
Philp, M. 2013. 'Talking about Democracy: Britain in the 1790s', in Innes and Philps, *Re-imagining Democracy*, 101–13.
———. 2014. *Reforming Ideas in Britain: Politics and Language in the Shadow of the French Revolution, 1789–1815*. Cambridge: Cambridge University Press.

Rémusat, C. de. 1861. 'De l'esprit de réaction. Royer-Collard et Tocqueville', *Revue des Deux Mondes* 35, 777–813.
Riklin, A. 2006. *Machtteilung: Geschichte der Mischverfassung.* Darmstadt: Wissenschaftliche Buchgesellschaft.
Roldán, D. 1999. *Charles de Rémusat: Certitudes et impasses du libéralisme doctrinaire.* Paris: L'Harmattan.
Rosanvallon, P. 1985. *Le moment Guizot.* Paris: Gallimard.
———. 1993. 'L'histoire du mot démocratie à l'époque moderne', in *La pensée politique. Situations de la démocratie.* Paris: Gallimard, 11–29.
———. 1994. *La monarchie impossible : Les Chartes de 1814 et 1830.* Paris: Fayard.
———. 2000. *La démocratie inachevée : Histoire de la souveraineté du peuple en France.* Paris: Gallimard.
Saunders, R. 2013. 'Democracy', in Craig and Thompson, *The Languages of Politics*, 142–167.
Shannon, R. 1982–1999. *Gladstone.* London: Penguin.
Stern, J. 2010. *Orangism in the Dutch Republic in Word and Image.* Manchester: Manchester University Press.
Tarrow, S. 2011. *Power in Movement: Social Movements and Contentious Politics.* Cambridge: Cambridge University Press.
Thorbecke, J.R. 1996. In G.J. Hooykaas and F.J.P. Santegoets (eds), *De briefwisseling*, vol. V. The Hague: ING.
Vacherot, É. 1860. *La démocratie.* Paris: Chamerot.
Velde, H. te. 2012. 'De domesticatie van democratie in Nederland. Democratie als strijdbegrip van de negentiende eeuw tot 1945', *BMGN – Low Countries Historical Review* 127, 3–27.
Velema, W.R.E. 2002. '"That a Republic is Better than a Monarchy": Anti-monarchism in Early Modern Dutch Political Thought', in M. van Gelderen and Q. Skinner (eds), *Republicanism: A Shared European Heritage* I. Cambridge: Cambridge University Press, 9–41.
Vile, M.J.C. 1998. *Constitutionalism and the Separation of Powers.* Indianapolis: Liberty Fund.
Vreede, G.W. 1848. *De regtstreeksche verkiezingen tot de nationale vertegenwoordiging bestreden.* Amsterdam: Schleijer.
Waresquiel, E. de. 2006. *Un groupe d'hommes considérables. Les pairs de France et la Chambre des pairs héréditaire de la Restauration 1814–1831.* Paris: Fayard.

Chapter 3

Another 'Sonderweg'?

The Historical Semantics of 'Democracy' in Germany

Jörn Leonhard

At first sight, the historical evolution of the terms 'Demokratie', 'demokratisch' and 'Demokraten' in Germany seems to fit into Reinhard Koselleck's paradigm of the saddle epoch ('Sattelzeit') in the development of basic concepts in political and social language.[1] The semantic field expanded, with the concept's meaning becoming more ideologically polarized and its usage more popular in the period following the French Revolution and during the first decades of the nineteenth century. But this general trend says nothing about the peculiarities of different societies. Was there a 'Sonderweg' in the semantics of 'democracy' in modern German history?

In a *longue durée* perspective, for much of the Middle Ages 'democracy' was not used to describe a particular regime.[2] As in the case of Marsilius of Padua, for many political thinkers, the concept rather referred to a panorama of crisis and decline of order.[3] Democracy formed part of ideal and degenerated types of political rule, as in the works of Engelbert of Admont, who developed Aristotle's three ideal types into four pairs: 'regnum/tyranny', 'aristocracy/oligarchy', 'olicratie/clerotis' and 'democracy/barbarie'.[4] It was characteristic of this early typology of constitutional forms that the 'res publica' was often directly compared with the individual household and the family. The relationship between the father and his wife was seen as aristocratic, that between father and children as monarchical, that between the father and his younger brothers as oligarchic and that between different households as democratic.

Variants of 'Democracy' until 1815: Traditions and Impulses

Until the later eighteenth century, 'democracy' remained a concept within the boundaries of enlightened discourse and the vocabulary of learned political theory.[5] German uses from the sixteenth to eighteenth centuries referred to the rule by the majority of the people and served as a synonym of 'politeia'. In 1755 'Demokratie' was defined as 'regime of the whole people'.[6] This semantic structure was still a major point of reference after the revolution in France had changed Europe's political landscape. Thus, in 1793 August Ludwig von Schlözer offered the following definition: 'Only one has sovereignty, – monarchy. Or a committee, – aristocracy. Or the majority, which is consulted at every act of government specifically, – democracy.'[7] This focus on ideal types and their degenerated forms of government stood in contrast to discourses on 'democracy' in Britain and North America. Here the concept was interpreted as one element of a mixed constitution, which John Adams had in mind in 1775: 'Is not the democracy as essential to the English Constitution as the monarchy or aristocracy?'[8] This idea of 'democracy' as part of a balance of constitutional elements would become more relevant after 1815 in continental European societies and would replace older references in the Aristotelian tradition, while pointing to cyclical changes in constitutional forms.

A closer view reveals that already in the context of the late eighteenth century and the French Revolution, new connotations had developed: on the one hand, 'democracy' was regarded as an impossible form of government, highlighting the difference between political theory and practice. Writing under the impression of Jacobin Terror in France, Immanuel Kant in 1795 identified pure democracy with 'despotism, because it institutes an executive power in which all decide over – and if need be against – one (who therefore does not take part in the decision), and consequently all and yet not all; which is a contradiction of the common will with itself and with freedom'.[9] Kant referred to the problem of the majority's tyranny against the individual among the minority whose liberty was questioned by the majority. In contrast to this polemical interpretation of direct democracy, Kant favoured what he called 'Republikanism', in which he found a safeguard for every individual's free will. It was based on the rule of law, a system of constitutional checks and balances as well as on elements of political representation. Any form of government that included these elements could be qualified as a republic. Hence, even a monarchy could be republican. The contrast between ideal types of government as normative constitutional models and the practice of political rule, i.e. between 'forma imperii' and 'forma regiminis', was vital and became a leitmotif in later refutations of 'democracy' in Germany.[10]

Even before the outbreak of the French Revolution, European contemporaries distinguished between apparently legitimate and degenerated forms of 'democracy', a semantic operation that made it possible to interpret historical change, ideological polarization and political instrumentalization of vocabularies without dropping the concept altogether. This process accompanied the semantic pluralization and segmentation of 'democracy' as it would characterize the history of other political key concepts such as 'liberal'.[11] It was no accident that these tendencies first became visible in pre-revolutionary France. Thus, René Louis d'Argenson in 1764 distinguished between 'fausse et légitime démocratie' in France.[12] And even before 1789, there were also tendencies of semantic expansion and the development of a new semantic field. 'Democracy' was no longer applied only to forms of government and categories of political order, but was also used to denote a structural change in society: the 'progrès de la démocratie' corresponded to new social aspirations of the Third Estate and the bourgeoisie's demand to be treated equally in French politics.[13] However, before 1789, the French monarchy was not excluded from this interpretation; instead, it could still be regarded as a legitimate institution to contain or even put an end to noble privileges that had lost their function in society. The semantic application of 'democracy' was still relatively open as long as it denoted a restoration of a just order and not a social revolution with a radically different vision of a political and social regime.

The concept's use during the French Revolution clearly changed, and it marked a watershed not only for French political and social vocabularies, but also for other European cases. Different functions of the concept became obvious: first, and against the background of the transformation from monarchical constitutionalism to social republicanism, 'démocratie' and 'république' became synonyms, as Maximilien Robespierre observed in February 1794. For him, the 'démocratie' included direct forms and elements of political representation, but more important was the particular virtue of each individual associated with 'démocratie', which Robespierre found in the 'amour d'égalité' as a 'vertu publique'.[14] Second, 'democracy' was no longer primarily applied to constitutional categories and a typology of political regimes, but to a particular social composition and collective dispositions associated with social groups. In that way the positive connotation of 'démocratie' in the works of Mignet, Lamartine and Michelet developed into one of the Revolution's hallmarks and had lasting impact on nineteenth-century historiography: 'la démocratie personnelle' became a synonym for the lower classes and their role in politics.[15] Third, the use of the concept allowed a particular temporalization in history, a historical self-positioning vis-à-vis past and future. In that way contemporaries quoted 1793 as the 'second year of democracy'.[16]

The transnational dynamics of these semantic impulses became visible in the course of the 1790s, for instance in Italy, but also in the German states, provoking critique and refutations. A good example is the negative connotation derived from interpretations by Edmund Burke and Friedrich Gentz as Burke's German translator. Here 'democracy' was identified as a political rule in which the people as its own sovereign would accept any violation of power. According to Burke and Gentz, the results were inevitably uncontrollable masses, anarchy and chaos, as demonstrated by France in the 1790s.[17] In Britain and the United States, positive references could be found in the speeches and publications of Fox and Paine, but in most British references the concept was associated with revolutionary developments on the European continent challenging political stability and social order. Yet these negative meanings catalysed the ideological self-positioning of those who identified positively with 'democracy' – a mechanism of critique and counter-critique similar to the semantics of 'liberal' and 'liberalism', and indicating the dynamic expansion of a spectrum of competing ideological movements.[18]

The French Revolution created a common point of reference for contemporary attempts to define the concept's meaning. The competing definitions contributed to 'democracy's' popularization and politicization in European societies.[19] 'Democracy' was no longer confined to learned discourses and enlightened vocabularies, but became a concept in concrete political and social actions, in political pamphlets and parliamentary debates, as well as in the political discourse of the middle classes, as represented in dictionaries and encyclopaedias. An ideological differentiation took place, in which the choice of vocabulary was used to structure the complexity of political movements, factions and parties. In German-speaking territories, the antagonism between 'Demokrat' and 'Aristokrat' served as an ideological marker, obviously modelled after the French 'démocrat' and 'aristocrat'.[20] Friedrich Gentz in 1794 distinguished between a 'demokratische und antidemokratische Partei', and in 1809 Freiherr von Aretin spoke of 'Ultra-Demokraten und Ultra-Aristokraten'.[21]

As in the case of other concepts, the historical events in France provoked a critical view of the concept in Germany – an example of entangled semantics made possible by networks of correspondents and translations. 'Universal-Demokratie' as observed in revolutionary France could be repudiated as barbarous, and 'Demokratisierung' became identified with a major challenge to peace and political stability.[22] Indirectly, this critique underlined the very expansion of 'democracy' from a rather marginalized concept into an essential one, denoting an ever-growing set of political anticipations and social projections. 'Demokratie' in German political language became a concept of expectations, no longer based primarily on perceptions of past cycles of constitutional change and references to ancient Greece or Rome. In other words, the temporal structure of the meaning changed from past past to a past future, an imagined and anticipated future by which the present status in history could be defined. By associating utopian qualities with 'Demokratie', a surplus of expectations developed, which allowed past contemporaries to identify and explain the deficiencies of their own political and social situation.

As mentioned above, Immanuel Kant had distinguished between constitutional types and practices of governing, advocating a republic based on a representative system. Applying evolutionary reforms would qualify a monarchy as republican. Whereas Kant had insisted on the difference between 'Demokratie' as 'forma imperii' and 'Republikanism' as 'forma regiminis', other authors in around 1800 reflected upon the political and social changes in France. They concluded that 'Republikanismus' and 'Demokratismus' had interrelated meanings. In the words of Friedrich Schlegel in 1796: 'Therefore republicanism is necessarily democratic, and the unproven paradox that democratism/democracy is necessarily despotic cannot be correct.'[23]

German meanings of 'Demokratie' around 1800 showed different trends: the traditional Kantian antagonism between republicanism and 'Demokratismus' was overcome. At the same time, many authors remained sceptical towards pure democracy. Searching for alternatives, they were particularly interested in differentiations between 'democracy' and 'democratic principles'. Given the challenge of Napoleonic France and the Revolution's progressive legacy for German territorial states, a new connotation developed: progressive Prussian reformers favoured a mixture of democratic and monarchical elements under the auspices of evolutionary reforms initiated by the state as a response to Prussia's catastrophic defeat by Napoleon in 1806. In his Riga Memorandum of 1807, a key document of the Prussian reform era, the Prussian State Minister Karl-August von Hardenberg spoke of 'democratic principles of a monarchical government: to me this seems to be the form suitable to the current spirit of the age'.[24] In contrast to the political polarization around the holistic meaning of 'democracy', the use of 'democratic principles' was attractive to politicians seeking to demonstrate their intention to reform while opposing Napoleonic France.

Another consequence of the French Revolution was the development of party names. 'Democrat' became more widespread, but negative connotations dominated in Germany as well as in other contexts. In Britain and the United States, the use of the party name 'democrat' was first seen as a denunciation if not stigmatization of political factions as Jacobin and anarchic. Only in the late 1820s would this constellation begin to change, and a positive meaning was fuelled by 'Jacksonian Democracy' and the official party name 'democrat'. As in the case of other party names (notably 'liberals'), the origin of 'democrat' had been an invention by its ideological opponents.[25]

The Post–1815 Complexities of 'Democracy'

In post–1815 France, the inflation of political party names reflected different layers of polarization. In this context a contemporary political observer distinguished between two extremes: those 'known under the name of ultra-royalist' and those under the name of 'libéraux'. But since this denomination seemed more 'of an accolade than a qualification . . . because there can nonetheless be liberality in the doctrines', the author referred to the concept 'démocratique' to highlight the ideological antagonism between what he regarded as the two main political parties of France: 'I would prefer to call democratic the party whose views are opposed to those of the first; because from liberalism – as it is understood – to democracy there is a gentle slope and a quite slippery track.'[26]

This semantic connection between 'liberal' and 'democratic' was a consequence of polarizing revolutionary legacies, which continued to influence French political culture well after 1815. Identifying with or distancing from the restored monarchy served as a dividing line and allowed the political camps to be structured in a bipolar way:

> Here we have the two parties that exist and will exist in France like in England: the royalist party, which supports the monarchical ideas and the aristocratic ideas which are inseparable from them; the liberal party, that supports the democratic ideas . . . We counted four parties in France, or rather in parliament; the two liberal varieties composed of the more or less pronounced partisans of the democratic ideas, and which are designated under the name of the left and the center-left; the two royalist varieties, composed of the more or less pronounced partisans of the monarchical and aristocratic ideas, that is to say the right and the center-right.[27]

After the July Revolution of 1830, many pamphlets and articles referred to the continued fragmentation of party names in France, each corresponding to new layers of polarizations that every revolution added:

> Since July 29th, we have seen how constitutional opinions have been modified and formed several varieties which, in time, have become more and more pronounced. This natural effect of the clash of parties always takes place after a victory. Without looking for examples beyond our own political disputes, we may recollect that in the first revolution the democrats divided into Girondins, Montagnards and Jacobins; under the restoration, the royalists became Ultra-Montanes, Monarchists or Oligarchs.[28]

However, in the course of the 1840s, 'démocratie' acquired a more prominent character in French political discourse. On the one hand, the concept was clearly identified with the United States – an effect of the perception of Alexis de Tocqueville's work.[29] On the other hand, the concept's relevance seemed to highlight the importance of social questions and social movements outside parliament and beyond elections, which were based on an ever more reduced franchise. For François Guizot, a leading political figure of the monarchy who was trying to explain the regime's eroding legitimacy in the late 1840s, 'démocratie' had become 'le mot souverain, universel',[30] accepted by all political parties in France as the key to understand the major political and social transformations in France. Written in 1848, this statement reflected the broad anti-monarchical consensus after the two experiments with constitutional regimes that had failed in July 1830 and in February 1848, but also the cult around equality and universal suffrage that characterized the French Second Republic. The concept's universalization in French usage was obvious from the many possible semantic combinations, thereby fusing historical experiences of 1789 and those of 1848. The 'empire of the word democracy' that Guizot referred to camouflaged a still relative fluidity of meaning. 'Démocratie' could be connected with liberty, equality, nation, Christianity or even a reformulation of the Bonapartist Empire by Louis Napoleon after the coup d'état in 1851.

Towards the end of Napoleon III's Second Empire, the opposition against the authoritarian version of Bonapartism assembled around the concept again. Émile Ollivier, the key figure in the transformation from the 'empire autoritaire' into the 'empire libéral', used 'democratie et liberté' as a programmatic motto to describe the change in the regime's political course during the 1860s.[31] A few months before the empire's collapse, he advocated the strength of a government based on the will of the people as proven in plebiscites: 'Who would rise against such a democratic, liberal, progressive government?'[32] On the other hand, being a truly democratic voter could still mean opposing the focus on the social question, which many identified with a democratic party: 'The liberal party confines itself a little too much to the study of pure politics, while the democratic party confines itself to the study of a false social economics.'[33]

The semantic development in Germany was quite different. Despite the French stimuli and the possible amalgamations between reformist approaches and 'democratic principles' in German states, discourses on 'Demokratie' in the first decades of the nineteenth century still contained traditional semantic markers. As the developments in France seemed to demonstrate in the eyes of contemporary observers, pure democracy would sooner or later decline into chaos and anarchy. But a closer look reveals important new trends that came to fruition before 1848/49. First, the meaning of 'demokratisch' and 'Demokratie' was no longer applied to traditional categories and typologies of constitutional change, but made it possible to distinguish between 'pure' and 'moderate' forms of democracy,[34] as visible in the practice of direct and representative democracy, which appeared in encyclopaedias as 'aristocratically tempered, i.e. refined democracy'.[35]

Second, the semantics of 'Demokratie' departed from the traditional view that democracy was possible only in small, homogeneous states, notably in city states like the ancient polis or Rousseau's ideal of Geneva. Now the example of the American Republic became important because it demonstrated a new relationship between democracy and republican nation-state building. In that way, the *Brockhaus Encyclopaedia* of 1838 pointed to the interrelation between the American model of 'democracy' and developments in European societies:

> Democracy as a genuine rule of the people has its place in America; it will surely continue to hold its ground there for a long time and not only develop into the various forms that it is capable of, but also have retroactive effects on old Europe in important ways, and more so to the extent that the European languages gain ground and take root there.[36]

Third, and in contrast to the French uses of 'democracy' during the Revolution, German contemporaries highlighted a semantic balance between monarchy, aristocracy and democracy, and avoided a simple antagonism between these. Hence, Hardenberg's idea of 'democratic principles' as part of a constitutional, enlightened and reform-oriented monarchy, in contrast to Hegel's opposition to any mixing of monarchy and democratic elements,[37] cast a long shadow in Germany prior to the March Revolution of 1848. It reflected the desire to maintain a peaceful coexistence of political interests instead of a revolutionary polarization of antagonistic fractions. In 1857 and after the revolutionary experiences of 1848/49, Bluntschli and Brater in their influential *Staatswörterbuch* advocated an interconnection between monarchy and democracy in order to contain the extremes of both: 'While monarchy quietly acknowledges the natural justification of the democratic element, it finds in it the most secure support while at the same time having the power to ward off the hypertension and excess of this element by means of organic arrangements.'[38]

Fourth, similar to what happened in France but characteristically later, the social connotation of 'democracy' became important in German contexts in the course of the 1840s. Pointing to the needs of the lower classes reflected the social transformations and the crisis of pauperism, caused by demographic dynamics and mass poverty in a society still dominated by traditional economic structures. In 1840 the *Brockhaus Encyclopaedia* defined 'Demokratie' as:

> the rule of the material interests and needs of the masses of the people or the greater part of it, which makes its claims anywhere, under any constitution, because the people demand sustenance and fair and full wages everywhere, which is related to freedom of trade, the possibility of acquisition and legal security, which itself cannot not be conceived of at all without legal equality.

The concept became coupled with a vision of moral cultivation and solidarity between peoples, which was defined as a new function of the state, as a 'rule of the higher spiritual or moral interests, which consist in the ethical elevation of peoples, in justice, truth and the disinterested activity for the good of the whole, and let them be considered the supreme tasks of the life of the state'.[39]

Fifth, the concept served as a means of temporalization, thereby replacing cyclical models of history and historical explanation by categories of a linear *longue durée* and a possible final point in the future. Imagining a future 'Demokratie' thus helped to define the state of politics and society in the present, but it also made it possible to draw lines of historical continuity. The concept's temporalizing function included both possible references in history – no longer the ancient polis as an ideal city state, but rather the ancient German idea of freedom or seventeenth-century Protestantism, both important references for German nation-building after 1815 – and an anticipated future. The traditional idea of learning from historical cycles ('historia magistra vitae') declined – as did the model of ancient republicanism as a reference for defining 'Demokratie' in nineteenth-century Germany.

1848/49 and after: Reformulations and Reconfigurations of 'Democracy'

Compared to France, German discourses around 'Demokratie' in 1848/49 showed a much more antagonistic structure of meanings that continued well after 1848. For a long time, 'Demokratie' did not become as universally accepted as in France, either in 1848/49 or after 1871. It was no 'sovereign, universal word' in Germany, but rather provoked resistance and widespread criticism. In order to understand this difference, it is essential to look into semantic discussions prior to 1848. After 1815, one could observe an expansion of the concept's semantics and possible usages, reflecting the development of constitutional monarchies in several states of the German Confederation based on enlarged, yet still narrowly defined, political participation and at the same time strongly opposed by conservatives. For Hegel, 'Demokratie' represented the result of an artificial revolution resulting in an atomized political and social order, as the radical revolution in France had proved. He also questioned the concept's supposed progressive character and insisted on what he regarded as the really progressive force in history: the reform-oriented Prussian state as the incarnation of an organic concept of state.[40] Hegel's premise would cast a long shadow over the German semantics of 'Demokratie' – not in the sense of a conventional history of elitist ideas, but as a major point of reference that allowed German definitions of 'Demokratie' by highlighting the contrast with West European and transatlantic developments. Without repeating the narrative of the German 'Sonderweg', the semantics of 'democracy' in Germany reflected a particularity, in that 'Demokratie' lacked the integration into an universalistic ideological language, as was the case in France with regard to the French Revolution and its legacy, or Britain with the suggestive Whig interpretation of history and the Glorious Revolution, or the United States' historiography of exceptionalism with its focus on republicanism and revolutionary emancipation identified with 1776.[41] These interpretations made it possible to integrate 'democracy' into a specific ideological universalism, transcending national boundaries and promising a model for other societies.

Despite its territorial fragmentation, the 1830s and 1840s witnessed the evolution of distinct party names in German political discourse, reflecting a broadening spectrum of ideological camps and competing visions of political and social order. Karl Rosenkranz in 1843 pointed to the fact that these new names no longer marked personal or corporatist positions, but programmes that allowed mobilization and identification in a changing society. 'Demokraten' were now a part of the spectrum:

> It is only with such an awareness that the dependence of the individual on the nepotism of the party of family, on the egoism of the guild, the corporation or the estate disappears. The designations of the parties themselves are generalized. Instead of the accidental names of their founders, designations expressing a concept emerge. One speaks of democrats and oligarchs, of republicans and royalists, of liberals and serviles, of radicals and conservatives.[42]

It was against this background of ideological polarization and political pluralization during the 1840s that a positive understanding of 'Demokratismus' could be positioned against liberalism as the dominant political trend of these years. Arnold Ruge developed the most outspoken critique in 1843.[43] For him, the people's fight against Napoleonic occupation and military repression before 1815 was the real birthplace of a democratic party in Germany, the predecessor of the radicals' in Ruge's own days: 'In the Wars of Liberation a nucleus of the new Germany was present: the radical democrats, whose great effectiveness is evident in the regeneration of Prussia and the popular uprising against Napoleon.'[44] Following the course of polemic against constitutional liberals around 1830, especially on the occasion of the Hambach Festival in May 1832, Ruge defined liberalism as a bourgeois movement. It seemed overly oriented towards constitutions and compromises, still hoping for a reform-oriented state to prevent a social revolution, a repetition of violent events as in France, but too narrow to understand the dynamics of the growing proletariat and to respond adequately to the challenges of pauperism as the social question of the day. According to Ruge, liberalism had no future if it was not prepared to accept the new ideal of free man and free people.[45] If liberals of the 1840s still insisted on an integrative understanding of liberalism, a movement and political habitus that would embrace all reasonable political trends, thus avoiding extremes and a revolutionary conflict with existing governments, Ruge demanded liberalism's transformation into 'Demokratismus', 'in one word the dissolution of liberalism into democratism [Demokratismus]'.[46]

The Revolution of 1848/49 in Germany intensified this semantic antagonism between liberalism and 'Demokratismus', between liberal variations of constitutional monarchy and connotations of social democracy.[47] The dividing line between liberals and democratic radicals was a leitmotif inside and outside parliaments. Liberalism was defined as the only movement capable of finding the middle ground between the extremes of absolutism and democratic self-government.[48] In Heinrich Laube's description of the German National Assembly of 1848, the antagonism between liberals and democratic radicals was the most profound aspect: 'For at least a year the liberals of Germany, the liberals of education and patriotism, were not only internally, but also externally separated from the radicals, to whom an abstract concept called democracy, republic or whatever else had priority.'[49] 'Radikale' became associated with democratic ideals such as popular sovereignty, solidarity between European peoples, national unity, universal suffrage and social rights. However, these important differences should not be overestimated: as the work on the German Constitution of 1849 proved, compromises between liberals and democrats were still possible.

Despite the enormous stimulus for politicization and ideological mobilization in parliaments and on the streets, which had a profound impact on vocabularies and the semantics of key concepts, the consequences of the revolutionary experience of 1848/49 can be described as a dual defeat – a failure to achieve a German nation state and a constitutional framework for a German monarchy. This defeat contributed to ever more antagonized definitions of the concept. In that context, 'Demokratie' was written out of discourses on a future German constitution after 1850. Against this background, one can discern two main processes in the semantics of 'democracy' in Germany that had started before 1848, but became ever more obvious in the decades afterwards.

Following from the critique of liberalism as a bourgeois ideology during the 1840s as represented by Arnold Ruge, 'Demokraten' became a positive self-description, identified with connotations of universal suffrage, social rights, social equality and the growing workers' movement as leading principles after 1848/49. In that way, Lorenz von Stein referred to social equality symbolized by universal suffrage as the most relevant trend in politics and society – a process most advanced in France. For Stein, 'soziale Demokratie' was a fact transcending the difference between constitution and administration as he saw it in the French Second Republic.[50] At the same time, he concluded that 'soziale Demokratie' included two alternative options, consisting of social revolution as exemplified by France or social reform and the evolutionary development of a welfare state as a possible means to prevent radical social revolutions.[51]

The more radical view on democracy was offered by Marx and Engels. For them, real democracy could be found only in communism. For them, the Revolution of 1848/49 signified an only temporary alliance between workers and petty bourgeois democrats, as demonstrated in France. In their eyes, the concept of 'democracy' also allowed self-positioning in the historical process; hence, 'pure Demokratie' would be transformed into 'soziale Demokratie' and later into the dictatorship of the proletariat, which would then embody democracy in a communist society.[52] This interpretation proved to be influential among left-wing activists and coloured the concept's perception among the workers' movement. In 1863 Ferdinand Lassalle wrote about the separation between democracy and liberalism: 'Democracy was the unifying bond between the bourgeoisie and the working class. By shaking off and renouncing this name, this unifying bond was cut from this side, and the banner was no longer planted in a democratic, but in a liberal bourgeois movement.'[53] After this separation from liberalism, the working class could be the only basis of democracy.

In contrast to this understanding of 'Demokratie' on the political left, national liberals and progressive liberals maintained a negative connotation of 'Demokratie' after 1848/49. The concept became increasingly identified with Socialists and Social Democrats after the foundation of Second German Empire in 1871. The supposed internationalist orientation of Social Democrats and Roman Catholics seemed to challenge the new nation state's existence. For liberals who regarded themselves as the natural political force behind the emergence of the German nation state of 1871, the *Kulturkampf* as well as the anti-socialist stereotype influenced their understanding of the concept. A strong indication for this negative perception was the fact that neither

'Demokratie' nor 'demokratisch' was used for an official party name of liberal parties or a key aspect in liberals' party programmes before 1918 – with the single exception of a democratic connotation in the South German 'Deutsche Volkspartei', later the 'Fortschrittliche Volkspartei', which was presented as a fusion between liberals and democrats.[54]

Further on the right, polemical critiques of the concept flourished after 1871. Heinrich von Treitschke repudiated the supposedly progressive character of democracy, which he associated with a primitive period in history before the emergence of a monarchical nation state, exemplified by the German Empire of 1871.[55] Connotations of mass culture and universal suffrage could even lead to an understanding of 'Demokratie' as a precondition for cultural decline. Thus, Treitschke contrasted the achievements of what he regarded as grand nation states like Wilhelmine Germany with the 'mediocrity' of small states.[56]

'Democracy' before and after the First World War: New Experiences, New Expectations

However, towards the end of the nineteenth century, important new impulses developed. They were the result of a self-critique by many German liberals, who looked for a reformulation of the liberal paradigm vis-à-vis the growth of Social Democracy in Germany. These attempts, mirrored by the development of New Liberalism in Britain, were greatly stimulated by Friedrich Naumann. He argued that liberalism and socialism were inextricably related to each other by the relevance of democracy in modern industrial societies. The conclusion he drew from this process in late nineteenth-century Germany was to strongly advocate a fusion between social liberalism and democracy. What he called in 1901 the 'innovation of liberalism' had to be founded on universal suffrage ('auf der Grundlage des allgemeinen Wahlrechts') as a bridge between liberals and Social Democrats. Naumann demanded a social opening of liberalism that should go hand in hand with Social Democracy becoming a national and integrative party in the German Empire's political system.[57]

Naumann defined democracy as the natural result of dynamic industrialization and mass politics: 'Democracy is the political expression of the efforts of the new German industrial masses. With the growth of this mass democracy rises.' And he connected the rise of the industrial model and industrialization to the progress of democratic thinking. His key concept was 'democratic industrial policy', denoting higher productivity and workers' social participation, and directed against the self-isolation of both bourgeois democracy and proletarian democracy. The 'Industrievolk' for Naumann would represent progressive 'Demokratismus als Prinzip'.[58]

These attempts to overcome the semantic antagonism between liberalism and democracy marked an important ideological discourse before the First World War, but they did not change the nature of German politics as represented by political parties in the Reichstag.[59] It took many more years and the experience of the war before this trend was taken up again. When war broke out in the summer of 1914, the cultural war between European intellectuals also concentrated on different understandings of political key concepts such as 'democracy'. Numerous university professors, artists and journalists engaged in this debate and defended the German 'ideas of 1914' in contrast to West European and transatlantic understandings of democracy. The German 'ideas of 1914' were associated with a particular understanding of culture and were positioned against the French 'ideas of 1789', associated with mass politics, a fragile republican democracy and a decadent civilization, or against Britain's materialism and cultural decline. During the war, new concepts such as 'Volksgemeinschaft' emerged in Germany that made it possible to integrate connotations of social participation, organic community and war experiences of collective victimhood. But these concepts derived their suggestive power from the ideological antagonism between a German national community and democracy marked by competing interests and social atomization.[60]

When in 1917 the American President Woodrow Wilson presented his vision of a peace without annexations and reparations and in the name of democracy, the German writer Thomas Mann expressed his scepticism, underlining the interrelationship between the new universalism of democracy and the collective experience of excessive numbers of war victims.[61] For him, the triple advent of peace, democracy and a new morality in politics was but a consequence of exhausted war societies – from that perspective, he found it difficult to understand the enthusiasm that greeted Wilson's promises: Philipp Scheidemann, one of the Social Democratic Party's leaders, had remarked to Mann that 'democracy would make stark progress due to the general exhaustion. That is not very honorable for democracy – nor for humanity. For the morality of exhaustion is no very edifying morality'.[62]

This negative meaning and the impression of being forced to accept democracy as something un-German, as a mere precondition for a Wilsonian peace, became major points of reference in German political discourses. Many critical observers would refer to these connotations in critical moments, during the revolution in November 1918 and in the early years of the Weimar Republic, as well as after 1928. The semantic coupling between the stab-in-the-back myth and the new democratic republic, emerging from 9 November 1918, and in the eyes of many Germans responsible for the catastrophic armistice of 11 November 1918 and the traumatic Treaty of Versailles signed in June 1919, prolonged a negative understanding of 'democracy' in Germany.

But as in the history of the concept in the nineteenth century, a sort of dialectical response followed, and new impulses became more influential in practical politics from 1917/18, when members of the Weimar Coalition formed by Social Democrats, Left Liberals and members of the Catholic Center Party tried to embrace a positive connotation of democracy in Germany. The economist Walther Rathenau and the theologian Ernst Troeltsch promoted a 'Demokratischer Volksbund', the 'Deutsche Demokratische Partei' as left liberalism's political organization explicitly used the adjective for its new party name, as did the 'Demokratische Republik Österreich' after the Habsburg monarchy's dissolution in 1918.[63] Troeltsch's actions offer a particularly interesting example of the attempts to reformulate a German understanding of 'democracy' in a radically different political and social context after the war.[64] A staunch supporter of the German 'ideas of 1914' at the beginning of the war when he was still a professor of theology in Heidelberg, he became much more sceptical during the war. In 1919 and during the debates on drafting a new republican constitution, he compared the situation of postwar Germany with that of 1648. Deeply divided over the legacy of a traumatizing war, the country needed to be reintegrated by looking towards the democratic ideals of 1848.[65] For Troeltsch, the end of the war and the revolution had brought about a radical new situation. In a speech given to the Demokratischer Studentenbund in mid December 1918, he stated that overnight Germany had become the most radical of all of Europe's democracies ('zur radikalsten Demokratie Europas geworden').

But Troeltsch insisted that this transformation was more than just a consequence of defeat and revolution in Germany. Instead, it reflected structural processes that had been catalysed by the events in late 1918: if one takes a closer look, it did not happen quite so suddenly. Democracy is the natural consequence of modern population density combined with the popular education, industrialization, mobilization, military reinvigoration and politicization necessary for its sustenance.[66] Strongly opposed to the prospect of an October Revolution in Germany, a radical social revolution following the Bolshevik model, Troeltsch took up earlier approaches to reformulate liberalism before 1914 and demanded the acceptance of social democracy as a historical fact – this relates his understanding of the concept to Arnold Ruge's definition in Germany before the Revolution of 1848 and Friedrich Naumann's position in around 1900. For Troeltsch, 'democracy' seemed to be 'the only means to lead the reverse class rule, the rule of the proletariat, into the course of a healthy and just state formation and to save the healthy nucleus of a state-preserving socialism'. Democracy, according to him, was not the result of a mere political doctrine, but the consequence of a social process, which had been revealed by war and defeat.

Comparing the democracy of his own days in 1919 to the concept's meaning in 1848/49, Troeltsch concluded that in contrast to the mid nineteenth century, it was no longer possible to demand political reforms and new constitutional frameworks as had been the bourgeois democrats' goal in the mid-nineteenth century. Instead, Germans had to focus on the transformation of social order ('It cannot be merely a legally and ethically conceived 'formal democracy''').[67] Troeltsch referred to the United States as a successful synthesis of democratic and conservative elements: 'Thus, a radical democracy is united here with the full freedom of extremely conservative manners and a spiritual life springing from its own sources', made possible by religious pluralism and Puritanism in particular.

Despite Germany's difficult situation after the war, Troeltsch's example underlines that there was no linear semantic 'Sonderweg' of a negative connotation of democracy from the failed revolution in 1848 to the foundation of an authoritarian empire in 1871 to the unwanted republic in 1918 to January 1933 and Hitler's rise to power. Instead, his example highlights a complex, often dialectical process of distancing from, approaching and integrating 'Demokratie' into Germany's ideological vocabulary. In 1919 Troeltsch hoped for a similar synthesis of democratic and conservative elements in Germany as he identified them in the United States and Britain: 'Thus it can and must also become with us. Our classical mental world offers plenty of connections to a spiritual-ethical view of democracy as well.'[68] As historians we should not easily reduce this past future of 1918/19 with its own horizon of expectations in the light of retrospective logic, arguing only from the consequences in 1933 and 1945. The historical semantics of 'democracy'' in Germany seems a good example to demonstrate the advantages of carefully reconstructing the past future instead of accepting the suggestive narrative of a simplistic 'Sonderweg'.[69]

Jörn Leonhard is Professor of Modern European History at the University of Freiburg. His main publications include *Liberalismus: Zur historischen Semantik eines europäischen Deutungsmusters* (2001); coedited with Ulrike von Hirschhausen, *Nationalismen in Europa: West- und Osteuropa im Vergleich* (2001); *Bellizismus und Nation: Kriegsdeutung und Nationalbestimmung in Europa und den Vereinigten Staaten 1750–1914* (2008); *Empires und Nationalstaaten im 19. Jahrhundert* (with Ulrike von Hirschhausen), (2010); coedited with Ulrike von Hirschhausen, *Comparing Empires: Encounters and Transfers in the Long Nineteenth Century* (2012); coedited with Christian Wieland, *What Makes the Nobility Noble? Comparative Perspectives from the Sixteenth to the Twentieth Century* (2011); *Die Büchse der Pandora: Geschichte des Ersten Welt-*

kriegs (2014), English translation: *Pandora's Box: A History of the First World War* (2018). His current project is a monograph on *Overburdened Peace: A Global History 1918–1923*.

Notes

1. See Reinhart Koselleck, 'Einleitung', in Otto Brunner, Werner Conze and Reinhart Koselleck (eds), *Geschichtliche Grundbegriffe: Historisches Lexikon zur politisch-sozialen Sprache in Deutschland,* 7 vols (Stuttgart: Klett-Cotta, 1972–97), vol. 1, xiii–xxvii; see Jörn Leonhard, '"Grundbegriffe" und "Sattelzeiten" – "Languages" and "Discourses": Europäische und anglo-amerikanische Deutungen des Verhältnisses von Sprache und Geschichte', in Rebekka Habermas and Rebekka von Mallinckrodt (eds), *Interkultureller Transfer und nationaler Eigensinn: Europäische und angloamerikanische Positionen der Kulturwissenschaft* (Göttingen: Wallstein, 2004), 71–86.
2. See Christian Meier et al., 'Demokratie', in Brunner et al. (eds), *Geschichtliche Grundbegriffe*, Band 1 A-D, 821–99, at 835.
3. Richard Scholz, 'Marsilius von Padua und die Idee der Demokratie', *Zeitschrift für Politik* 1 (1908), 61 and passim.
4. Engelbert von Admont, 'De regimine principum', quoted in Andreas Posch, *Die staats- und kirchenpolitische Stellung Engelberts von Admont* (Paderborn: F. Schöningh, 1920), 65; see Meier et al., 'Demokratie', 837.
5. See the chapter in this volume by Innes and Philp. See also R.R. Palmer, 'Notes on the Use of the Word "Democracy" 1789–1799', *Political Science Quarterly* 68 (1953), 203–26, at 204; Gustav H. Blanke, 'Der amerikanische Demokratiebegriff in wortgeschichtlicher Bedeutung' *Jahrbuch für Amerikastudien* 1 (1956), 41–52, at 41; see also Meier et al., 'Demokratie', 839.
6. *Wohlmeinender Unterricht für alle diejenigen, welche Zeitungen lesen, worinnen so wohl von dem nützlichen Gebrauche der gelehrten und politischen Zeitungen, als auch von ihrem Vorzuge, den einige vor anderen haben, bescheidentlich gehandelt wird, nebst einem Anhange einiger fremden Wörter, die in den Zeitungen häufig vorkommen* (Leipzig: Chr. Fr. Geßner, 1755), Annex, 19.
7. August Ludwig von Schlözer, *Stats-Gelartheit* (Göttingen: Vandenhoeck & Ruprecht, 1793), vol. 1, 112; see Meier et al., 'Demokratie', 841.
8. Quoted in Samuel E. Morison (ed.), *Sources and Documents Illustrating the American Revolution 1764–1788,* 2nd ed (Oxford: Oxford University Press, 1953), 127.
9. Immanuel Kant, 'Zum ewigen Frieden' (1795), *Erster Definitivartikel, Akademieausgabe* 8 (Berlin/Leipzig: De Gruyter, 1923), 352–53.
10. See Meier et al., 'Demokratie', 842–43.
11. See Jörn Leonhard, *Liberalismus: Zur historischen Semantik eines europäischen Deutungsmusters* (Munich: Oldenbourg, 2001), Chapters III.2 and IV.2; Jörn Leonhard, 'From European Liberalism to the Languages of Liberalisms: The Semantics of Liberalism in European Comparison', *Redescriptions: Yearbook of Political Thought and Conceptional History* 8 (2004), 17–51.

12. René Louis d'Argenson, *Considérations sur le gouvernement ancien et présent de la France* (Yverdon, 1764), 6–7.
13. Ibid., 110–11.
14. Maximilien Robespierre, *Discours et rapports de Robespierre*, ed. C. Vellay (Paris: Charpentier et Fasquelle, 1908), 324–26.
15. See Meier et al., 'Demokratie', 858.
16. Quoted in Palmer, 'Notes', 213; see Meier et al., 'Demokratie', 859.
17. Edmund Burke, *Betrachtungen über die französische [sic!] Revolution, dt. von Friedrich Gentz*, ed. Dieter Henrich (Frankfurt am Main: Suhrkamp, 1967), 156. For the key role of Burke, see also the chapter by Innes and Philp in this volume.
18. See Palmer, 'Notes', 208 and 223–26; Leonhard, *Liberalismus*, Chapter V.2.
19. Joanna Innes and Mark Philp (eds), *Re-imagining Democracy in the Age of Revolutions: America, France, Britain, Ireland 1750–1850* (Oxford: Oxford University Press, 2013).
20. See Meier et al., 'Demokratie', 854.
21. Friedrich von Gentz, *Übersetzung von Jacques Mallet du Pan: Über die Französische Revolution und die Ursachen ihrer Dauer* (Berlin: Vieweg, 1794), xx–xxi; Christoph Freiherr von Aretin, *Die Pläne Napoleons und seiner Gegner* (Munich, 1809), 3; see also Meier et al., 'Demokratie', 856–57.
22. See Meier et al., 'Demokratie', 854–61.
23. Friedrich Schlegel, 'Versuch über den Begriff des Republikanismus' (1796), in *Kritische Friedrich-Schlegel-Ausgabe. Erste Abteilung: Kritische Neuausgabe* (Munich/Paderborn: F. Schöning, 1966), vol. 7, 11–25, at 12–16.
24. Karl August Fürst von Hardenberg, 'Rigaer Denkschrift' (1807), in Georg Winter (ed.), *Die Reorganisation des preußischen Staates unter Stein und Hardenberg* (Leipzig: Hirzel, 1931), vol. 1/1, 306.
25. See Meier et al., 'Demokratie', 854–55; Palmer, 'Notes', 225; Murray S. Stedman Jr., '"Democracy" in American Communal and Socialist Literature', *Journal of the History of Ideas* 12 (1951), 147–54, at 151.
26. *De l'état des partis et des affaires, à l'ouverture de la session de 1819* (Paris: Delaunay, 1819), 2–3.
27. Ibid., 27 and 173.
28. *De l'influence des partis sur les affaires publiques, depuis la révolution de juillet: Par un ami de la liberté* (Paris: Corréard jeune, 1831), 10–11.
29. See Charles Farcy, *Études politiques: De l'aristocratie anglaise, de la démocratie américaine et de la libéralité des institutions françaises* (Paris, 1842).
30. François Guizot, *De la démocratie en France* (Paris, 1849), 9–10.
31. Émile Ollivier, *Démocratie et liberté (1861–1867)* (Paris, 1867).
32. Émile Ollivier, 'Speech Given on 4th April 1870', in *Annales parlementaires: Annales du Corps législatif* (Paris: Administration du Moniteur universel), vol. 3, 309.
33. *Mon Programme: Par un électeur nantais démocrate, anticommuniste, antisocialiste, antiautoritaire* (Nantes, 1869), in *Der Liberalismus und die Arbeiter: Seinen Arbeitskollegen gewidmet von einem Arbeiter* (Berlin, 1906), 20.

34. Karl Heinrich Ludwig Pölitz, *Die Staatswissenschaft im Lichte unserer Zeit* (Leipzig: Hinrichsche, 1823), vol. 1, 441–43.
35. Johann Caspar Bluntschli and Carl Brater (eds), *Deutsches Staatswörterbuch* (Stuttgart and Leipzig: Expedition des Staats-Wörterbuchs, 1857), vol. 2, 699, 704.
36. Brockhaus, *Conversations-Lexicon* (Leipzig: F.A. Brockhaus, 1838), vol. 1, 914.
37. Georg Wilhelm Friedrich Hegel, 'Grundlinien der Philosophie des Rechts' (1821) in Johannes Hoffmeister (ed.), *Hauptwerke in sechs Bänden* (Hamburg: Felix Meiner, 1999), vol. 5, § 273.
38. Bluntschli and Brater, *Staatswörterbuch*, vol. 2, 1857, 712; see Meier et al., 'Demokratie', 866.
39. Brockhaus, *Allgemeine deutsche Real-Encyclopädie für die gebildeten Stände. Conversations-Lexicon*, 8th edn. (Leipzig: F.A. Brockhaus, 1840), vol. 3, 372; see Meier et al., 'Demokratie', 868.
40. G.W.F. Hegel, 'Rechtsphilosophie', §§ 273 and 279 and 'Über die englische Reformbill' (1831), in H. Glockner (ed.), *Sämtliche Werke*, 20 vols (Stuttgart: F. Frommann, 1927–30), here vol. 20 (Stuttgart, 1930), 503.
41. See Meier et al., 'Demokratie', 880.
42. Karl Rosenkranz, *Über den Begriff der politischen Partei: Rede zum 18. Januar 1843, dem Krönungsfeste Preußens. Gehalten in der Königl. Deutschen Gesellschaft* (Königsberg: Theile, 1843), 18.
43. See Leonhard, *Liberalismus*, 442–57.
44. Arnold Ruge, 'Selbstkritik des Liberalismus' (1843) in *Sämtliche Werke*, vol. 4, 2nd edn. (Mannheim: J.P. Grohe, 1847), 76–116, at 81.
45. Ibid., 116.
46. Ibid.
47. See Leonhard, *Liberalismus*, Chapter VI.2 and especially 463–67.
48. See W. Pretzsch, 'Liberalismus', in Robert Blum (ed.), *Volksthümliches Handbuch der Staatswissenschaften und Politik: Ein Staatslexicon für das Volk* (Leipzig: Heinrich Matthes, 1851), vol. 2, 37.
49. Heinrich Laube, *Das erste deutsche Parlament* (Leipzig: Weidmann, 1849), vol. 1, 118.
50. Lorenz von Stein, *Geschichte der sozialen Bewegung in Frankreich von 1789 bis auf unsere Tage* (1850), new edn., ed. Gottfried Salomon (Munich: Drei Masken, 1921), vol. 3, 406; see also Meier et al., 'Demokratie', 869.
51. Stein, *Geschichte*, vol. 1, 122–23; Ernst-Wolfgang Böckenförde, 'Lorenz von Stein als Theoretiker der Bewegung von Staat und Gesellschaft zum Sozialstaat' in *Alteuropa und die moderne Gesellschaft: Festschrift für Otto Brunner* (Göttingen: Vandenhoeck & Ruprecht, 1963), 248–77.
52. Karl Marx, 'Der achtzehnte Brumaire des Louis Bonaparte' (1852), in Karl Marx and Friedrich Engels, *Werke* (Berlin [Ost]: Dietz, 1960), vol. 8, 141; see Meier et al., 'Demokratie', 891.
53. Ferdinand Lassalle, 'Speech of 19th May 1863', in *Gesammelte Reden und Schriften*, vol. 3 (Berlin: P. Cassirer, 1919), 273; see Meier et al., 'Demokratie', 891.

54. Friedrich Naumann, 'Fortschrittliche Volkspartei!' (1910), in Theodor Schieder (ed.), *Politische Schriften*, vol. 5, *Schriften zur Tagespolitik* (Cologne: Westdeutscher Verlag, 1964), vol. 5, 448.
55. Heinrich von Treitschke, *Politik* (Leipzig: Hirzel, 1898), vol. 2, 257.
56. Walter Bussmann, *Treitschke* (Göttingen: Muster-Schmidt, 1952), 231–32; see Meier et al., 'Demokratie', 893.
57. Friedrich Naumann, 'Der Niedergang des Liberalismus: Vortrag auf der 6. Vertretertagung des Nationalsozialen Vereins zu Frankfurt am Main 1901', in Theodor Schieder (ed.), *Politische Schriften*, vol. 4, *Schriften zum Parteiwesen und zum Mitteleuropaproblem* (Cologne: Westdeutscher Verlag, 1964), 215–36 (extracts), quoted in Lothar Gall and Rainer Koch (eds), *Der europäische Liberalismus im 19. Jahrhundert: Texte zu seiner Entwicklung*, 4 vols (Frankfurt am Main: Ullstein, 1981), vol. 4, 254–76, at 258–60 and 262.
58. Friedrich Naumann, 'Demokratie und Kaisertum' (1900), in Theodor Schieder (ed.) *Politische Schriften*, vol. 2, *Schriften zur Verfassungspolitik* (Cologne: Westdeutscher Verlag, 1964), 39, 55–57, 78; see also Meier et al., 'Demokratie', 896; Friedrich Naumann, *Gegenwart und Zukunft des Liberalismus* (Munich: Buchh. Nationalverein, 1911).
59. See for instance Ludwig Haas, *Die Einigung des Liberalismus und der Demokratie* (Frankfurt am Main, 1905); *Der Liberalismus und die Arbeiter: Seinen Arbeitskollegen gewidmet von einem Arbeiter* (Berlin, 1906); Theodor Curti, *Die Reaktion und der Liberalismus: Rede, gehalten in der polizeilich aufgelösten Sitzung des Frankfurter Demokratischen Vereins vom 1. Juli 1878* (Munich, 1912).
60. See Jörn Leonhard, *Die Büchse der Pandora: Geschichte des Ersten Weltkriegs*, 5th edition (Munich: C.H. Beck, 2014), 236–50.
61. See ibid., 803–4.
62. Thomas Mann, 'Weltfrieden?' (27 December 1917), in Hermann Kurzke (ed.) *Große kommentierte Frankfurter Ausgabe*, vol. 15/1, *Essays II 1914–1926* (Frankfurt am Main: S. Fischer, 2002), 212–15, 212; see Marcus Llanque, *Demokratisches Denken im Krieg: Die deutsche Debatte im Ersten Weltkrieg* (Berlin: Akademie, 2000), 103–35.
63. See Meier et al., 'Demokratie', 896.
64. See Jörn Leonhard, '"Über Nacht sind wir zur radikalsten Demokratie Europas geworden" – Ernst Troeltsch und die geschichtspolitische Überwindung der Ideen von 1914', in Friedrich Wilhelm Graf (ed.), *'Geschichte durch Geschichte überwinden': Ernst Troeltsch in Berlin* (Gütersloh: De Gruyter, 2006), 205–30.
65. Ernst Troeltsch, 'Nationalgefühl' (February 1919), in Gangolf Hübinger (ed.) in cooperation with Johannes Mikuleit, *Kritische Gesamtausgabe*, vol. 15, *Schriften zur Politik und Kulturphilosophie (1918–1923)* (Berlin: De Gruyter, 2002), 56 and 59.
66. Ernst Troeltsch, 'Demokratie' (August 1919) in Gangolf Hübinger (ed.) in cooperation with Johannes Mikuleit, *Kritische Gesamtausgabe*, vol. 15, 207–24, at 211.
67. Ibid., 215 and 219.

68. Ibid., 222.
69. See Reinhart Koselleck, *Vergangene Zukunft: Zur Semantik geschichtlicher Zeiten*, 2nd edn. (Frankfurt am Main: Suhrkamp, 1992).

Bibliography

1755. *Wohlmeinender Unterricht für alle diejenigen, welche Zeitungen lesen, worinnen so wohl von dem nützlichen Gebrauche der gelehrten und politischen Zeitungen, als auch von ihrem Vorzuge, den einige vor anderen haben, bescheidentlich gehandelt wird, nebst einem Anhange einiger fremden Wörter, die in den Zeitungen häufig vorkommen.* Leipzig: Chr. Fr. Geßner.

1819. *De l'état des partis et des affaires, à l'ouverture de la session de 1819.* Paris: Delaunay.

1831. *De l'influence des partis sur les affaires publiques, depuis la révolution de juillet. Par un ami de la liberté.* Paris: Corréard jeune.

1906. *Mon Programme: Par un électeur nantais démocrate, anticommuniste, antisocialiste, antiautoritaire* (Nantes, 1869), in *Der Liberalismus und die Arbeiter: Seinen Arbeitskollegen gewidmet von einem Arbeiter.* Berlin.

Aretin, C.F. von. 1809. *Die Pläne Napoleons und seiner Gegner.* Munich.

Blanke, G.H. 1956. 'Der amerikanische Demokratiebegriff in wortgeschichtlicher Bedeutung' *Jahrbuch für Amerikastudien* 1, 41–52.

Bluntschli, J.C., and C. Brater (eds). 1857–1870. *Deutsches Staatswörterbuch*, 11 vols. Stuttgart/Leipzig: Expedition des Staats-Wörterbuchs.

Böckenförde, E-W. 1963. 'Lorenz von Stein als Theoretiker der Bewegung von Staat und Gesellschaft zum Sozialstaat', in *Alteuropa und die moderne Gesellschaft: Festschrift für Otto Brunner.* Göttingen: Vandenhoeck & Ruprecht, 248–77.

Brockhaus. 1840. *Allgemeine deutsche Real-Encyclopädie für die gebildeten Stände: Conversations-Lexicon*, 8th ed., vol. 3. Leipzig: F.A. Brockhaus.

Burke, E. 1967. *Betrachtungen über die französische [sic!] Revolution, dt. von Friedrich Gentz*, Dieter Henrich (ed.), Frankfurt am Main: Suhrkamp, 156.

Bussmann, W. 1952. *Treitschke.* Göttingen: Muster-Schmidt.

Curti, T. 1912. *Die Reaktion und der Liberalismus: Rede, gehalten in der polizeilich aufgelösten Sitzung des Frankfurter Demokratischen Vereins vom 1. Juli 1878.* Munich.

D'Argenson, R.L. 1764. *Considérations sur le gouvernement ancien et présent de la France.* Yverdon.

Farcy, C. 1842. *Études politiques: De l'aristocratie anglaise, de la démocratie américaine et de la libéralité des institutions françaises.* Paris: Chaumerot.

Gall, L., and R. Koch (eds). 1981. *Der europäische Liberalismus im 19. Jahrhundert: Texte zu seiner Entwicklung*, vol. 4. Frankfurt am Main: Ullstein, 254–76.

Gentz, F. von. 1794. *Übersetzung von Jacques Mallet du Pan: Über die Französische Revolution und die Ursachen ihrer Dauer.* Berlin: Vieweg.

Guizot, F. 1849. *De la démocratie en France.* Paris: Victor Masson.

Haas, L. 1905. *Die Einigung des Liberalismus und der Demokratie.* Frankfurt am Main.

Hegel, G.W.F. 1927–30. 'Über die englische Reformbill' (1831), in *Sämtliche Werke*, H. Glockner (ed.), 20 vols. Stuttgart: F. Frommann.

———. 1999. 'Grundlinien der Philosophie des Rechts' (1821), in Johannes Hoffmeister (ed.), *Hauptwerke in sechs Bänden*, vol. 5. Hamburg: Felix Meiner.

Innes, J., and M. Philp (eds). 2013. *Re-imagining Democracy in the Age of Revolutions: America, France, Britain, Ireland 1750–1850*. Oxford: Oxford University Press.

Kant, I. 1923. 'Zum ewigen Frieden' (1795), in *Erster Definitivartikel, Akademieausgabe*. Berlin and Leipzig: De Gruyter, 349–53.

Koselleck, R. 1972. 'Einleitung', O. Brunner, W. Conze and R. Koselleck (eds), *Geschichtliche Grundbegriffe: Historisches Lexikon zur politisch-sozialen Sprache in Deutschland*, 7 vols, vol. 1. Stuttgart: Klett-Cotta, xiii–xxvii.

———. 1992. *Vergangene Zukunft: Zur Semantik geschichtlicher Zeiten*, 2nd edn. Frankfurt am Main: Suhrkamp.

Lassalle, F. 1919. 'Speech of 19th May 1863', in *Gesammelte Reden und Schriften*, vol. 3. Berlin: P. Cassirer.

Laube, H. 1849. *Das erste deutsche Parlament*, vol. 1. Leipzig: Weidmann.

Leonhard, J. 2001. *Liberalismus: Zur historischen Semantik eines europäischen Deutungsmusters*. Munich: Oldenbourg.

———. 2004. 'From European Liberalism to the Languages of Liberalisms: The Semantics of *Liberalism* in European Comparison', *Redescriptions: Yearbook of Political Thought and Conceptional History* 8, 17–51.

———. 2004. '"Grundbegriffe" und "Sattelzeiten" – "Languages" and "Discourses": Europäische und anglo-amerikanische Deutungen des Verhältnisses von Sprache und Geschichte', in R. Habermas and R. von Mallinckrodt (eds), *Interkultureller Transfer und nationaler Eigensinn: Europäische und angloamerikanische Positionen der Kulturwissenschaft*. Göttingen: Wallstein, 71–86.

———. 2006. '"Über Nacht sind wir zur radikalsten Demokratie Europas geworden" – Ernst Troeltsch und die geschichtspolitische Überwindung der Ideen von 1914', in F.W. Graf (ed.), *'Geschichte durch Geschichte überwinden': Ernst Troeltsch in Berlin*. Gütersloh: De Gruyter, 205–30.

———. 2014. *Die Büchse der Pandora: Geschichte des Ersten Weltkriegs*, 5th edn. Munich: C.H. Beck.

Llanque, M. 2000. *Demokratisches Denken im Krieg: Die deutsche Debatte im Ersten Weltkrieg*. Berlin: Akademie.

Mann, T. 2002. 'Weltfrieden?' in *Große kommentierte Frankfurter Ausgabe*, vol. 15/1, *Essays II 1914–1926*, H. Kurzke (ed.). Frankfurt am Main: S. Fischer, 212–15.

Marx, K. 1960. 'Der achtzehnte Brumaire des Louis Bonaparte' (1852) in K. Marx and F. Engels, *Werke*, vol. 8. Berlin: Dietz, 111–207.

Meier, C. et al. 1972. 'Demokratie', in O. Brunner, W. Conze and R. Koselleck (eds), *Geschichtliche Grundbegriffe: Historisches Lexikon zur politisch-sozialen Sprache in Deutschland*, Band 1 A–D. Stuttgart: Klett-Cotta, 821–99.

Morison, S.E. (ed.). 1953. *Sources and Documents Illustrating the American Revolution 1764–1788*, 2nd edn. Oxford: Oxford University Press.

Naumann, F. 1911. *Gegenwart und Zukunft des Liberalismus*. Munich: Buchh. Nationalverein.

———. 1964a. 'Demokratie und Kaisertum' (1900), in *Politische Schriften*, vol. 2, *Schriften zur Verfassungspolitik*, T. Schieder (ed.). Cologne: Westdeutscher Verlag, 39, 55–57, 78.

———. 1964b. 'Der Niedergang des Liberalismus: Vortrag auf der 6. Vertretertagung des Nationalsozialen Vereins zu Frankfurt am Main 1901', in *Politische Schriften*, vol. 4, *Schriften zum Parteiwesen und zum Mitteleuropaproblem*, T. Schieder (ed.). Cologne: Westdeutscher Verlag, 215–36.

———. 1964c. 'Fortschrittliche Volkspartei!' (1910), in *Politische Schriften*, vol. 5, *Schriften zur Tagespolitik*, T. Schieder (ed.). Cologne: Westdeutscher Verlag.

Ollivier, É. 1867. *Démocratie et liberté (1861–1867)*. Paris: A. Lacroix.

———. 'Speech Given on 4th April 1870', in *Annales parlementaires: Annales du Corps législatif*. vol. 3. Paris: Administration du Moniteur universel, 309.

Palmer, R.R. 1953. 'Notes on the Use of the Word "Democracy" 1789–1799', *Political Science Quarterly* 68, 203–26.

Pölitz, K.H.L. 1823. *Die Staatswissenschaft im Lichte unserer Zeit*, vol. 1. Leipzig: Hinrichsche.

Posch, A. 1920. *Die staats- und kirchenpolitische Stellung Engelberts von Admont*. Paderborn: F. Schöningh.

Pretzsch, W. 1851. 'Liberalismus', in R. Blum (ed.), *Volksthümliches Handbuch der Staatswissenschaften und Politik: Ein Staatslexicon für das Volk*, vol. 2. Leipzig: Heinrich Matthes, 37–38.

Robespierre, M. 1908. *Discours et rapports de Robespierre*, C. Vellay (ed.). Paris: Charpentier et Fasquelle.

Rosenkranz, K. 1843. *Über den Begriff der politischen Partei: Rede zum 18. Januar 1843, dem Krönungsfeste Preußens. Gehalten in der Königl. Deutschen Gesellschaft*. Königsberg: Theile.

Ruge, A. 1847. 'Selbstkritik des Liberalismus' (1843), in *Sämtliche Werke*, vol. 4, 2nd edn. Mannheim: J.P. Grohe, 76–116.

Schlegel, F. 1966. 'Versuch über den Begriff des Republikanismus' (1796), in *Kritische Friedrich-Schlegel-Ausgabe. Erste Abteilung: Kritische Neuausgabe*, vol. 7. Munich/Paderborn: F. Schöning, 11–25.

Schlözer, A.L. von. 1793. *Stats-Gelartheit*. Göttingen: Vandenhoeck & Ruprecht.

Scholz, R. 1908. 'Marsilius von Padua und die Idee der Demokratie', *Zeitschrift für Politik* 1, 61–94.

Stedman, Jr., M.S. 1951. '"Democracy" in American Communal and Socialist Literature', *Journal of the History of Ideas* 12, 147–54.

Stein, L. von. 1921. *Geschichte der sozialen Bewegung in Frankreich von 1789 bis auf unsere Tage*, vol. 3. (1850). New edn., ed. Gottfried Salomon. Munich: Drei Masken.

Treitschke, H. von. 1898. *Politik*, vol. 2. Leipzig: Hirzel.

Troeltsch, E. 2002. 'Nationalgefühl' (1919), in *Kritische Gesamtausgabe*, vol. 15, *Schriften zur Politik und Kulturphilosophie (1918–1923)*, G. Hübinger (ed.) in cooperation with J. Mikuleit. Berlin: De Gruyter, 55–59.

Winter, G. (ed.). 1931. *Die Reorganisation des preußischen Staates unter Stein und Hardenberg*, vol. 1/1. Leipzig: Hirzel.

Chapter 4

Birthplaces of Democracy

The Rhetoric of Democratic Tradition in Switzerland and Sweden

Jussi Kurunmäki and Irène Herrmann

Introduction

Attending the Potsdam Conference in 1945, Harry S. Truman noted in his diary that it 'seems that Sweden, Norway, Denmark and perhaps Switzerland have the only real people's governments on the Continent of Europe'.[1] While the war experience certainly was behind this observation, the U.S. President was also able to draw on some seminal accounts of the history of modern democracy in which the homegrown origins of democracy in these countries were pointed out. The notion of a medieval peasant freedom and egalitarian political participation had made both the Swiss cantons and the Scandinavian popular assemblies exemplary cases of the rural origins of democracy. The Swiss cantons had sometimes been described as democratic as early as the sixteenth century,[2] whereas the idea of ancient Nordic constitutional freedom was established around the mid eighteenth century[3] and was developed, in the Swedish case,[4] into an idea of ancient democracy in the early nineteenth century.

However, the very articulation of a medieval or an ancient peasant freedom and popular assemblies in terms of democracy needs to be seen as a part of the formation of modern discourses of democracy rather than as a process that had evolved over centuries. Once more and more states were understood as democracies, there also emerged an increasingly felt need for democratic ancestry.

As several chapters in this volume show, the idea of an age-old democratic past cannot be associated merely with Switzerland and the Scandinavian countries.⁵ Rather, we want to present a mode of rhetoric that has been to varying degrees and in different fashions common to national narratives of democracy. That said, it is also the case that the Swiss cantons and the local ting-assemblies in the Scandinavian countries have gained recognition in some seminal accounts of the history of democracy.

Thomas Erskine May held in his *Democracy in Europe: A History Volume I* (1877), the first major account of the history of democracy in Europe,⁶ that 'Denmark, Norway, and Sweden, whose populations are German and Scandinavian, have been renowned for their free, and even democratic, institutions'.⁷ Yet it was especially the Swiss democracy that was granted a prominent place in the volume, as it was discussed alongside the democracies of ancient Greece and Rome, as well as those of the Italian republics. According to May, the rural cantons in Switzerland had remained examples of a pure democracy. These cantons had 'the simplest form of democracy recorded in the history of the world'.⁸ The particularity of Swiss democracy was further enhanced by James Bryce, who in his influential *Modern Democracies* (1921) maintained that 'among the modern democracies which are true democracies, Switzerland has the highest claim to be studied' because 'it contains communities in which popular government dates farther back than it does anywhere else in the world'.⁹ He noted that Swiss democratic self-government was exceptional as it had developed as early as the fourteenth century. For him, the government of the people by the people was established in Switzerland 'before England's example became known in Continental Europe' and without any knowledge of 'theories of equality and liberty'.¹⁰

In recent times, Robert A. Dahl has emphasized the egalitarian character of the Scandinavian Viking age as one of the sources of democracy. He has pointed out the Icelandic popular assembly, the Althing, as the forerunner of modern democracy, 'foreshadowing the later appearance of national parliaments elsewhere, in 930 C.E'.¹¹ Although he noted that 'we must resist the temptation to exaggerate' and that beneath the freemen, there were slaves,¹² he nevertheless endorsed the Vikings' democratic practice as something that was their own, independent of Athens and Rome: 'The Vikings knew little or nothing, and would have cared less, about the democratic and republican political practices a thousand years earlier in Greece and Rome. Operating from the logic of equality that they applied to free men, they seem to have created assemblies of their own.'¹³

When it is maintained that there is neither a theoretical nor a terminological connection between the classic Greek democracy or modern democracy and these two examples of rural democracy, we may have to pay attention to the criteria that are applied in evaluating what counts as ancient democracy. For Dahl, the decisive criterion for identifying 'democratic tendencies' in the past has been to find places where one can find 'a push toward democratic participation' that has developed out of 'the logic of equality'.[14] Consequently, democracy is not only disentangled from any explicit conceptualizations of the historical actors themselves, but also from canonical contexts of Western civilization and the scholarly language referring to ancient Greek democracy. According to Dahl, 'it would be a mistake to assume that democracy was just invented once and for all, as, for example, the steam engine was invented'. For him, any diffusion from its original inventors to the other groups cannot explain the spreading of democracy, but instead 'democracy can be independently invented and reinvented whenever the appropriate conditions exist'.[15]

This kind of 'anthropological' view of democracy presents certain difficulties, when writing conceptual history of democracy. There may be, as it has been held, 'millions of agricultural communities' that have 'employed some democratic techniques of government'.[16] Instead of trying to judge whether there have been values or practices that can be regarded as democratic by some standards, we present in this chapter a rhetorical perspective on the topic. We examine the emergence and spreading of the very notions of the birthplace of democracy, ancient democracy and democratic tradition in Switzerland and Sweden. Focusing on historical actors' own conceptualizations, we study the ways in which the idea of the ancient roots of democracy has been used in political argumentation for divergent political purposes.

As we will show, the figure of ancient democracy has often been used as an argument against reform-minded opinions. Consequently, this chapter sheds light on the formation and the contested character of the modern concept of democracy. This particular brand of rhetoric has been a part of the politics of democracy, in which present motives and projections towards the future have been merged with recurring redescriptions of the past.[17] As the rhetoric of an ancient democratic past has most often been viewed as separate from the democracy of ancient Athens and even from the Aristotelian notion of democracy as one element of a mixed constitution, this chapter also deals with the making of national traditions of democracy.

The Swiss Democracy

In his *History of the Swiss*, published in 1803, Paul-Henri Mallet explained that, according to some scholars, the Swiss came from Sweden or Denmark. Around 800 AD, they had supposedly settled in the Alps, where they had maintained a specific lifestyle. They notably had continued to gather in assemblies, in which they freely took the necessary decisions on an equalitarian basis. According to Mallet, they enjoyed a commendable democratic system.[18]

Mallet's account was not novel, but in many ways typical of Swiss literary production on Swiss political systems. First, it was inspired by previous Swiss works that, at least since the sixteenth century,[19] had tried to explain the functioning of the cantons in the areas of Alpine Switzerland that were called democratic because they were ruled by *Landsgemeinde*, i.e. regular popular assemblies in which citizens voted on issues of common concern and elected their authorities by showing hands.[20] Second, these accounts were based on a specific conception of history that presented the development of the Swiss Confederation as the place for a genuine aspiration for freedom.[21] Third, they have since then blended the notions of (good) democracy, liberty and their exceptionality, so that it has been very difficult for the Swiss to perceive the fundamental difference between the medieval, organic and historically based conception of democracy and its modern, more individual-based and universally meant counterpart.[22] Finally, most of these laudatory works obviously responded to the contempt such a political system had fostered in the various neighbouring monarchies, whose scholars and leaders considered the Swiss as mere disobedient peasants. Therefore, the cantons attributed to themselves an inverted identity as a political and moral role model for the decadent (Habsburg) aristocracy and, later on, for the whole of humankind.[23] This messianic idea has remained[24] and is closely linked to the idea of Switzerland being the birthplace of good, exemplary and nonchaotic democracy.

The Swiss scholars only erratically interacted with their European counterparts, who, in turn, adopted differentiated views on Swiss democracy. Thus, between 1848 and the beginning of the interwar period – that is, between the transformation of the Confederation of Switzerland's diversely democratic cantons into a federal state based on a representative system and the period during which democracy was repeatedly challenged – hundreds of texts have been written on this topic in the francophone world.[25] This literature provides a good case study for examining the rhetoric of ancient Swiss democracy as a part of the formation of modern democracy. The foreign discourse on Swiss democracy is not only abundant; it is also highly diversified. The assessment of its value ranges from the very negative to the highly positive, and sometimes both extremes coexisted. However, three periods of roughly twenty-five years each may be distinguished: those prior to 1870, after 1870, and the period from 1895 until the 1920s.

Before the Franco-German war of 1870–71, most comments on Swiss democracy underlined its failures and inadequacy compared to the ideals of modern democracy. These texts were obviously influenced by Tocqueville. In *De la démocratie en Amérique* (1835) he did not mention the Swiss cantons, let alone Swiss democracy.[26] Eight years later, the Swiss political scientist Antoine-Elisée Cherbuliez published *De la démocratie en Suisse*. The book was an answer to Tocqueville as well as an analysis of the Swiss political situation, in which he exposed the dangers that democracy posed to his homeland. He challenged both Tocqueville's conception of modern democracy and his conception of America as the best example of democracy.[27] Tocqueville did not notice Cherbuliez's work until January 1848 and eventually replied just nine months before a new constitution, which fulfilled many contemporary criteria of a modern democracy, was introduced in Switzerland, as most male Swiss citizens were granted the right to elect their cantonal and national representatives.

Tocqueville's analysis was critical and clever. He held that most authors confused the republican system of the cantons with true democratic origins and features. According to him, Switzerland was not the cradle of democracy, as there was no country less democratic than the Swiss Confederation. According to him, democracy was not only unable to thrive on Swiss soil because of its lack of genuine roots, but the false belief in the existence of such roots had also prevented thinkers from introducing modern elements of democracy in Switzerland.[28] Tocqueville's statement may be considered an insightful analysis of the Swiss realities prior to the 1848 Constitution. Moreover, his work was soon reissued and became very successful, perhaps explaining why his negative opinion resurfaced almost every time the Swiss system was evoked and why it prevailed at least until 1870. The system was commonly disparaged, albeit in a sometimes contradictory way, depending on the author's ideology. Whereas the right-wing newspaper *Le Figaro* mocked the Swiss civil servants who were supposed to wear clogs,[29] the left-wing *Rappel* ironically reported that there was no true difference between Swiss democracy and British aristocracy.[30]

Most pre-1848 cantonal governments acknowledged that the *Landsgemeinde* was a mere archaism favouring privileges and lineages, admittedly in a nonmonarchical way.[31] So, in this sense, Tocqueville's account was accurate. However, the historical accuracy was not the main reason for a negative view of the Swiss experiences' contribution to democracy. It seems that the evaluation of Swiss democratic roots, at least in the francophone literature, mirrors French fears or hopes. The Bonapartists both despised and dreaded Swiss democracy, whereas the republicans noted its failures and regarded it as not fitting their revolutionary ideals. As long as people thought that 'democracy' had not been achieved in France, it was easier to refer to a largely imaginary and embellished version of the French past or to a complacent theory than to follow the example of one's insignificant neighbour.

After 1870, the overall negative appraisal from outside gave way to mixed evaluations that sometimes praised and sometimes blamed Swiss democracy. This change occurred as Swiss male citizens were given their first direct-democratic right on a national basis: the referendum.[32] Most texts that discussed democracy during this period stressed some failures of the Swiss political system and/or society. However, they also mentioned their good sides, regardless of whether they were considered mere attempts to correct these flaws or qualities per se. Some scholars followed in the footsteps of Tocqueville and lamented the lack of independence of the judiciary,[33] while others stressed the Swiss overdeveloped self-esteem[34] and actual intellectual mediocrity.[35] Most of the time, however, their 'national mores' were supposed to counterbalance the country's political defects.[36] Because of their average poverty, the citizens were seen as simple and deeply concerned about the common good.[37] This argument reappeared precisely at a time when Switzerland was unprecedentedly becoming a rich country. This crucial turning point in Swiss history triggered a well-known mechanism that incites witnesses of changes to stress artificial continuities. Swiss and foreign scholars re-established a progressive democratic linearity that had been denied by Tocqueville several decades before. They considered modern democracy as the progressive and natural outcome of the ancient one, interpreted in terms of evolution rather than opposition.

Presenting Swiss democracy in this way corresponded to the recent development of Swiss historiography. Since the last quarter of the nineteenth century, scholars attempted to show that, at least since the Middle Ages, the cantons had not only been characterized by a genuine appeal for freedom, but that this sense of liberty had also generated a constantly evolving but nonetheless true democracy, the achievement of which was purportedly reached in 1848.[38] Thus, democracy was depicted as starting from an immemorial core that had continuously been extending and improving. This image echoed the representation of the historical formation of Switzerland, which supposedly originated from the centre of the Alps, where pure people lived in a pure landscape, before peacefully reaching its modern territorial limits.[39] In other words, ideology, theories about the cultural effects of their pure air, and geopolitics were tightly intertwined. Although this combination was not especially novel, it was this time allegedly scientifically 'proved' by making references to sources. Yet again, this does not fully explain why this more positive interpretation was increasingly praised outside Switzerland, not only by Anglophone scholars, such as May, but also and above all in once so contemptuous France.

Although the French writers' more positive judgement came along with this recent Swiss historiographical trend, it was hardly known in France. Even the few Swiss historical accounts, which acknowledged the role played by the French Revolution in the moulding of the country's democratic institutions,[40] were barely taken into account. They did not trigger a radical turn in the

French assessment of the historicity of Swiss democracy, but a reinforcement of the previous line of thought. Obviously, in the new French Third Republic, there were many who wanted to grant Switzerland a long and continuous democratic history – regardless of the Swiss historiography and their taking pride in the purported universality of the French Revolution.[41]

In the early 1870s, France and Switzerland were the only republics in Europe. Whereas the Swiss regime was accepted as a harmless eccentricity, this was not the case for its French counterpart. Everybody still had the Revolution of 1789 in mind. Moreover, the Commune in 1871 reawakened the spectre of civil war. In this context, 'inventing' a true and coherent past for Swiss democracy was doubly useful. First, it was a way of legitimizing democracy without stressing its possibly violent outcomes, as they had appeared at the end of the eighteenth century. By underlining the venerable antiquity of Swiss democracy and thus turning the country into the cradle of democracy, the French scholars found a beginning that was not Athenian. The reference to Greece had been abundantly used by the revolutionaries, so that any evocation of it was since then an evocation of them. From this point of view, Swiss democracy was much safer. Second, and more importantly, this mystification reinforced both states. The invention of a common starting point presupposed a consciousness of the existence of a common identity.[42] In this case, the transformation of Switzerland into the birthplace of modern democracy shows that the French writers were willing to symbolically strengthen the links their invention created.

This positive interpretation of Swiss democracy prevailed. Just before and after the First World War, it even dominated the francophone debate on democracy. Unlike what had happened before, most of the few critical accounts during this period stemmed from Swiss authors, particularly in the mid 1890s, when an openly anti-Semitic law had raised fears of democratic demagogy.[43] However, these concerns were rather few and momentary. Quite soon, the discourse on Swiss democracy resumed its course and was developed on two topics. First, the continuity between medieval and modern democracies was not only accentuated but also prolonged. In many respects, Swiss democracy was directly linked with Athenian democracy, so that it was not only the cradle of modern democracy, but was even linked with Europe's most famous political ancestry. This appreciable longevity had several noticeable consequences. It presumably proved the ability of the Swiss to somehow evolve with history. As the monthly magazine *Revue des Deux Mondes* put it in 1895: 'Swiss democracy is a history on the move.'[44] In this context, history was considered not only as past deeds but also as future events.

This also explains why scholars elaborated on a second point: they increasingly depicted Swiss democracy as a true role model. Although this argument was rather old, drawing on the global mission the Swiss had assigned themselves, it was now advocated even by foreign scholars, who considered Switzerland a democratic role model.[45] After the First World War, the discourse, which linked the Swiss democracy's presumed antiquity with its exemplarity, was clearly fixed[46] and even more so during the interwar period in contrast to the Nazi, fascist or communist regimes.[47] However, Swiss democracy was praised despite the fact that Switzerland still denied women the right to vote and was becoming intolerant and xenophobic, and although it was no longer a political exception in Europe. As a matter of fact, this development went along with more detailed accounts of the country's specificities. Not only did writers continue to mention the 'compulsory topoi' on Swiss democracy, evoking its exceptional longevity[48] or the alpine environment in which it was supposedly born; they also stressed the smallness of the country[49] or its plurilingualism. In other words, before the First World War, and even more so after it, the references to Swiss democracy reached a fundamental contradiction.

On the one hand, it was considered a model, and, in many ways, it was used to describe 'realities' the writer wished to address. By underlining the country's natural and historical specificities, most scholars made clear that Switzerland was inimitable. So, on the other hand, this made the reference to Switzerland a void expression that anybody could fill with his or her own wishes and realities. Moreover, the Swiss themselves did nothing to change this and to gain some influence in the world. One of the main features of their national identity was the wish – indeed, sometimes even the bald claim – to be admirable and hence exemplary. However, in order to preserve their self-attributed superiority, they must remain inimitable. Thus, since the scholars' and the Swiss citizens' contradiction regarding their democracy's exemplarity converged, it is little wonder that Switzerland had no international influence and no intention of changing. Notably, the Swiss refused to give women the right to vote until 1971[50] because they considered that they had no lessons to learn from anyone as true representatives of the cradle of modern democracy. While women had been given this right in other countries, Swiss observers had claimed that their country should not follow this example since Switzerland, not the rest of the world, was the ultimate model for democracy![51] However, this label had fooled only the Swiss. The more democratic voting rights were adopted elsewhere, the more stubbornly the Swiss stuck to their role and nurtured their identity as a worldwide democratic role model.

The Swedish Democracy

The rhetoric of an ancient Swedish (and Nordic) democracy was established later than the idea of an ancient Swiss democracy, but when it was taking root in Sweden in the early nineteenth century, it was presented as also the source of Swiss democracy. The Swedish historian Erik Gustav Geijer, the most important promoter of the idea of an ancient Swedish democracy, held that the Swiss people were 'the Swedes of the Alps'.[52] In *Feudalism and Republicanism* (1818-19), he maintained that both of these traditions originated from the social organization of the ancient German tribes, but only two peoples in Europe had managed to avoid feudalism: the Scandinavians and the Swiss. In Scandinavia, this was due to an ancient political system that was built on egalitarian and elected assemblies of free peasants and an elected king, who had to confirm the laws of the community.[53] Importantly, this political relationship between the king and free men not only had a republican character, but also a democratic one. According to him, 'the Nordic constitution' was still in the eleventh century 'purely democratic', except in times of war.[54] Geijer held that traces of the ancient 'national assembly' had survived, even if dimly, until the present day.[55] The main principle of 'the constitution of the free warriors and landowning peasants' was that 'all power and all rights emanated from below, through an assignment from the people'. It was a society based on a contract between equals,[56] and it was thanks to this political arrangement that the Swiss and the Swedish peoples had been able to avoid the yoke of feudal and aristocratic rule.[57]

In fact, the Swedish colony in the Alps had been discussed by one of Geijer's mentors in 1796[58] and by Mallet, who had also been an important disseminator of the idea of ancient freedom in Scandinavia.[59] The notion of ancient democracy was not completely new either when Geijer presented it. Sweden had sometimes been discussed in terms of a mixed monarchy tempered with a democratic element in scholarly works since the seventeenth century, but these treatises did not elaborate any particularly Swedish or Nordic democratic past. However, 'democracy' was increasingly used in debates over the privileges of the nobility towards the end of the 1760s,[60] and it was in this context that one of the radical writers, Johan Hartman Eberhardt, in 1769 attacked the noble privileges by maintaining that a traditionally free people had ended up being treated almost as slaves by a privileged aristocracy. For him, the ancient liberty, which had been based on the free peasants' participation in legislative assemblies as equal members, was characterized by a 'democratic spirit'.[61] This spirit had been destroyed by tenth-century Papism and the subsequent aristocratic usurpation, undermining 'democracy in this realm'.[62]

In the late 1790s, the former secretary of the Patriotic Society, Adolf Modeer, wrote about 'the fortunate times of Sweden' during the Viking rule of the Lodbrok family between the ninth and eleventh centuries, and maintained that the peasants had participated in the rule of the country, which was characteristically 'democratic-monarchical'.[63] According to him, this pagan rule did not recognize any Estates, but all men as free and equal.[64] The idealization of the Viking-age system served a critical opinion after the French Revolution. A revolutionary association was made more explicit in 1809 in the debate over a new constitution, when the radical publicist C.A. Grevensmöhlen defended the extremes of the French Revolution and other 'people's revolutions' as expressions of democracy, which he then linked with 'the most honorable era of Sweden', which was 'the democratic age of the rule of Lodbrok family'. According to him, it was in this period of the rule of Vikings that the superiority of the free people over other peoples had been established in the North.[65]

What these early and rare examples of the rhetoric of ancient democracy had in common is their anti-aristocratic message of political controversy. However, 'ancient democracy' came to be increasingly used as a conservative rhetorical figure during the nineteenth century, not least because of the harmonious and equal relationship between the monarch and the common people it seemed to imply. Geijer's account in 1818–19 influenced both radical and conservative interpretations of the ancient past. In the 1810s, he was one of the leading intellectuals of the national romantic wave that gathered momentum in Sweden after the eastern part of the kingdom, Finland, was ceded to Russia in 1809. He was not arguing in favour of democratic reforms, but was moving in a conservative direction that was characterized by an organic view of the state with a strong emphasis on royalism. He had earlier advocated political ideals that have been described as republican civic virtues,[66] and it is possible that he adopted the language of ancient democracy due to the association he made with Swiss popular freedom, which was, as we have seen, also discussed in terms of ancient democracy. Most likely, nevertheless, he thought within the framework of the Aristotelian constitutional categories, in which democracy was the popular element of a mixed constitution. As a historian, he argued against aristocratic tendencies in Swedish history, and the concept of aristocracy, so to speak, seems to have invited democracy as its counter-concept.

Swedish newspapers bear witness to the fact that the political situation in other countries was sometimes discussed in terms of democracy from the 1830s onwards. News items on the democratic aspects of the British parliamentary politics,[67] as well as Norwegian,[68] Swiss[69] and American democracy,[70] and Tocqueville's account of it,[71] and Guizot's view of democracy[72] were all part of that discursive change. Although this does not explain Geijer's use of 'ancient democracy' as early as 1818, it helps in understanding the popularity of the figure in the following decades.

In 1840, then as a 'liberal', Geijer argued against estate-based representation and held that 'in Sweden the monarchy had been viewed as containing more of the *democratic* element than in most other countries', but he also pointed out that 'conservative advocates of the old institutions' tended to appeal to this fact and use it as their main argument when they claimed that these institutions should remain intact.[73] One of these conservative advocates was another celebrated national romantic, Professor and Bishop Esaias Tegnér. In 1835, he had provoked a debate when he first held that the Swedish 'ancient constitution' had evolved in a special way because its roots were 'democratic in the most beautiful meaning of the word',[74] but then added that the people cannot govern and that 'the Swedish common people' would do best when they 'feared God and honored the King'.[75] The liberal newspaper *Aftonbladet* thought this statement was outrageous and claimed that praising the peasants was, in fact, a camouflage designed to keep 'the educated masses' out of representation.[76] Although the biggest newspaper in the country sometimes regarded the whole figure of ancient democracy as a decoy,[77] the idea of an ancient Swedish democracy seems to have been appealing, as it was held in another article that 'the Swedish people owns . . . in its oldest memories and traditions a heritage of popular sovereignty, which manifested itself in the freedom of odal peasants and in the democratic constitution'. The statement was followed by a description of the decline of the ancient freedom, caused by the noblemen and the priests.[78]

When the reform bill that would abolish the estate-representation was debated in the 1860s, its opponents referred to the domestic origins of the estates, but it was difficult for them to draw on the image of a pre-estate-division age of democracy in this situation. The advocates of the reform of the Diet, in turn, referred to 'the ancient Nordic constitution' in order to expose the decline of the popular freedom of the Swedish people.[79] The figure of ancient Swedish democracy served as a background to the argument that the king should support parliamentary reform, the point being that the people and the monarch had formed a coalition and that this coalition should now be enforced through reform.[80] Their idea was that ancient democracy spoke for modern reforms, but they hardly argued in favour of democracy. While they tried to find a balance between the image of the past and their practical objectives in the present, the conservatives were more resolute in claiming that the ancient past lent the present system its legitimacy.

As the language of democracy became more common towards the end of the nineteenth century, its references became more contemporary. It was even held that one was living in 'the age of democracy'.[81] And when political controversies were conducted in the name of democracy, it became more difficult for those who were against democracy to convincingly refer to 'ancient democracy', whereas a 'democratic' position could be rhetorically backed with it by claiming that 'the Swedish democrats did not want to upset the existing order, only the existing disorder'.[82] In other words, while both the national romantic liberals and the national romantic conservatives had been able to refer to ancient democracy in a monarchist spirit either for reforms or for the status quo, the actuality of the issue of parliamentarism from the late nineteenth century onwards made the conservative rhetoric of ancient democracy somewhat obsolete and misplaced. In the early twentieth century, conservative opponents of parliamentary government referred to the 1809 Constitution and its principle of 'dualism' between the monarch and the Riksdag rather than to an ancient democratic past.[83] The fact that conservatives were uncomfortable with 'democracy' can be seen in the language that was used in the 1914 'Peasant March' and the famous 'Castle Yard Speech' of King Gustav V in connection to that mass demonstration, which was arranged to support military investments and against the policy of the liberal government. The rhetoric of the ancient coalition between the king and the people, as well as the ancient peasant freedom was prominent in the speeches during the conservative demonstration, but not a word was said about ancient democracy;[84] instead, it was held that the peasants had always been a conserving factor in Swedish society.[85]

Now, it would be possible to think that the rhetoric of ancient democracy was too archaic for liberals and socialists, as they, albeit in different ways, drew on the idea of progress. However, the age of mass democratization was also the age of nationalism. When democratization was the most topical issue, the roots of democracy were also invoked. Despite their critique of the bourgeois nature of the established narrative of the Swedish history, the Social Democrats drew on existing historical symbols, although giving them their own reading.[86] As Pasi Ihalainen has shown, the left-wing MPs, in particular, referred to an ancient democratic tradition in the parliamentary debates over parliamentary government and universal suffrage between 1917 and 1919. For instance, Hjalmar Branting, the leader of the Social Democrats, made a link between the medieval German assemblies and his present-day democratic aspirations.[87]

The Swedish Liberals and Social Democrats gained support from a recent study of eighteenth-century constitutional thought by the political scientist Fredrik Lagerroth, who held that the oldest known organization of Swedish society was 'decisively democratic'.[88] According to him, Swedish political life had grown from 'the democratic root' that emanated from 'the soul of the people' and 'all political power was undividedly in the hands of the people'.[89] His main argument was that 'the modern parliamentary government'[90] and 'popular rule'[91] in the eighteenth century had been based on the tradition of ancient democracy.[92] In the opinion of the Liberals and the Social Democrats, the message of the book was that the current situation called for the restoration of the democratic legacy in the form of parliamentarism.

It is noteworthy that, while the figure of ancient democracy had emphasized the harmonious coalition of the monarch and the people in most previous accounts, Lagerroth played down the role of the monarch and emphasized popular rule. The struggle over parliamentarism can be seen as a turning point, in which 'ancient democracy' was no longer associated with the coalition between the monarch and the people in nonconservative rhetoric. It also seems that conservative arguments were presented without references made to 'ancient democracy', but, instead, to 'ancient liberty'.

After the breakthrough of parliamentarism in 1917 and universal suffrage in 1918, the rhetoric of many conservatives featured the expressions 'self-government' or 'popular rule' rather than 'democracy'. Sometimes even 'a strong man' was called for instead of the existing parliamentary democracy.[93] Also, many socialists viewed parliamentary democracy as a bourgeois system and thus as inherently wrong, although it was most often taken as an important phase in a progression towards socialism.[94] By the 1930s, even many sympathetic observers admitted that democracy was in crisis.[95] Although Sweden did not experience right-wing or left-wing extremism to any considerable degree, it is possible to hold that a general acceptance of parliamentary democracy took place only in the mid 1930s, when both the right-wing party and the noncommunist far-left defined dictatorial ideologies as foreign doctrines and the existing democratic institutions as national ones.[96] The idea of ancient Swedish (and Nordic) democracy played a crucial part in this ideological transformation. It was a rhetorical way of defending democracy in times of crisis. When the Social Democrats managed in 1933 to forge a political compromise with the Agrarian Party, which gave the Social Democratic government solid parliamentary support, it was also described as a means of defending 'the ancient democracy and liberty of the nation'.[97]

The celebration of the half-millennial history of the Swedish Parliament and its alleged founder, the fifteenth-century peasant leader Engelbrekt Engelbrektsson, in 1935 illustrates the ways in which an image of a democratic tradition and national independence were linked together. Engelbrekt had in 1434–36 led peasant revolts against King Erik of Pomerania, the king of the Scandinavian Union of Kalmar. In the 1930s, he was widely regarded as a national hero and the man who had united the nation and gathered the Estates together in 1435. Despite some academic critique of the elevation of Engelberkt – it was maintained that he was a fictional figure[98] – he was presented as the symbol of the democratic tradition of the country when the Parliament was celebrated. The first volume of the history of the Swedish Parliament, published in 1931, described him as the leader of 'democratic movement', the one who in the spirit of 'primitive nationalism' demanded a return to an old political order.[99] It is noteworthy that this old political order, which included provincial ting-assemblies, was discussed in a critical historiographical manner without any references to 'ancient democracy' or 'ancient liberty'.[100] The focus seems to have shifted from the Viking-age ancient democracy to a democratic tradition that was closely linked with the emergence of a country-wide institution of political representation in the fifteenth century.

However, when speaking at the celebration of the Riksdag in 1935, the Social Democratic Prime Minister Per Albin Hansson held that 'the Swedish people had been able to maintain their ancient self-government', which also led him to argue that it made it possible to 'further develop our democratic order'.[101] The word 'order' here is telling. In the mid 1930s, any defence of parliamentary democracy was linked to the question of order because parliamentary democracy was everywhere criticized for its alleged weakness and inability to guarantee a firm government. The narrative of a democratic tradition that was based on an ancient democracy supported the existing democratic system by underlining its solid base in the time of Nazi, fascist and Bolshevist totalitarianism. When asked how the Scandinavian countries had managed to maintain their democratic governments, Hansson explained that the 'democratic system had not been seriously threatened in countries that had a democratic tradition'.[102] This idea was also behind the launching of 'Nordic democracy' by the Nordic Social Democratic parties in the mid 1930s.[103]

The interchangeability of 'ancient liberty' and 'ancient democracy' explains much of the success of the latter. For example, the liberal journalist Birger Beckman held in his 1937 volume on the history of popular freedom in Sweden that it was a great strength of Swedish democracy that it had in many ways been synonymous with Swedish popular freedom.[104] Beckman's account is in many ways illustrative of the ambition, and difficulty, of keeping a critical historiographical view of the ancient past and the national tradition. On the one hand, he held that it was easy to find historical evidence that 'our ancient freedom' and 'our ancient democracy' were inadequate expressions; on the other hand, he argued that there were also facts that would speak for the contrary. He held that the Viking Age did not have any notion of democratic popular freedom and that women's free position should be taken with great reservation, that individual freedom had little room in the ancient peasant society, that the ancient ting-democracy was a modern construction and that the sources from the early Middle Ages did not contain any democratic language.[105] But he nevertheless pointed out the popular character of the pre-medieval ting-assemblies because, according to him, all free men were able to participate in them.[106] Despite his reserved attitude towards the ancient democracy, he was nevertheless seeking 'democratic principles' that had manifested themselves since that time in Swedish history.[107]

This kind of endorsement combined with critical reservations also characterized many attempts to promote the image of the particularly democratic tradition of the Nordic countries during the Cold War. For example, a Swedish historian warned in the 1950s against an anachronistic view of ancient Scandinavian democracy and maintained that his purpose was to 'offset recent and often highly idealized versions of the ancient political liberties in Scandinavia'. However, he also stated that there was an unbroken and direct line of 'pre-democratic' tradition in Sweden.[108] A couple of decades later, a specialist on Icelandic sagas concluded, despite his critical account of yeoman freedom, that 'there are distinct threads in modern Nordic democracy which extend all the way back to the Viking Age, and which tie the history of Nordic democracy together' and then added: 'This is perhaps why democracy has found such firm footing in the Nordic nations of today, and has shown such consistent development there since early in the nineteenth century.'[109] The figure of 'ancient democracy', which had served the purpose of defending existing democratic institutions in the 1930s, was in the Cold War era turned into an ingredient of a Nordic national identity and moral superiority.

Concluding Remarks

The rhetoric of the ancient origins of democracy is a crucial aspect of the formation of modern democracy rather than a mere historiographical phenomenon – even if historians have been key actors in producing the arguments. There has been a general search for national roots of democracy during the processes that we normally understand as democratization and the formation of nation states. This phenomenon is not limited to the Swiss and Scandinavian cases only, but has taken place in varied forms everywhere. Nevertheless, we think that the idea of an ancient democratic past has helped a more general proliferation of the language of democracy where this phenomenon has begun particularly early. The Swiss case stands out in this respect, but we may also note that early-nineteenth-century Swedish and Spanish languages of democratic tradition bear similarities and may explain the relative prominence of 'democracy' in these countries.[110] Also, the notion of domestic democratic tradition has had an important impact on the prevalence of the concept of democracy in Czech and Russian early twentieth-century political debates.[111]

The cases analysed in this chapter, as well as the chapters on the Spanish, Russian and Czech democracies in this volume, suggest that the non-Athenian origins of an ancient democratic tradition in Europe are likely to be associated with peasant cultures rather than with urban contexts that are known as places of republican civic liberty. One explanation for this is that the idea of an ancient democratic tradition has been fuelled by the contrast that has been made to feudalism. Moreover, unlike the idea of a mixed constitution, the image of an ancient peasant democracy has characteristically been an anti-aristocratic one, regardless of whether it has been described as having been based on a coalition between the people and the monarch, as in the Nordic case, or whether it has been republican in the sense of being anti-monarchical though pro-Emperor, as in the Swiss cantons. What it has in common with the classic model, though, is that the rhetoric of ancient democracy has been presented as having been based on local popular assemblies in which the participation in decision-making is direct. As the Swedish case shows, the idealized picture was translated into an argument that criticized the estates-based representation for its lack of direct popular anchorage, on the one hand, and into claims that pointed out the existing peasant estate as the guarantee of that anchorage, on the other. A more or less shared view of the past was used in order to demand both reforms of political representation and in favour of the status quo.

Although the rhetoric analysed in this chapter was in many cases put forward to serve reformist and even radical purposes, it had a conservative side as well. In the Swiss case, the figure was used, for example, in order to defend the traditional societal order of the cantons and oppose the supporters of representative democracy; in the Swedish case, for a long time it had a royalist tone. As we have shown, many of the arguments that were made with the help of 'ancient democracy' in the nineteenth century did not originate from the few contemporary 'democrats'. The emphasis was on the orderly common people, who were not inclined to protest or revolt.

Despite the fact that the idea of ancient democracy was at odds with modern parliamentary democracy, it was elevated rather than downplayed after the introduction of democratic reforms in the twentieth century. During the interwar crisis of democracy, its conservative character was used as an argument in defence of the existing institutions of parliamentary democracy. It was held that democracy survived in Switzerland as well as in Sweden (and the Nordic countries) thanks to its ages-old rootedness in the political culture. From this defensive argument, there was only a short (if any) leap to the view that these traditional democracies served as models for other countries. For sure, the Swiss exemplarity had been recognized at home as well as abroad since the eighteenth century, but it was made a major virtue during the European crisis of democracy. As we have argued, this image was self-sufficient to the degree that it was presented as so exceptional that it was virtually impossible to be imitated. At the same time, this collective self-image was less concerned with the democratic credentials of a system that left half of the adult citizens without democratic voting rights. In Sweden and other Nordic countries, in turn, a more self-confident promotion of Nordic traditional democracy gained ascendancy during the Cold War. However, it was the Nordic welfare state rather than democracy that was thought imitable, as the alleged unique roots of democracy were not something that could be exported.

Jussi Kurunmäki is Associate Professor of Political Science, working at the Department of Cultures, University of Helsinki, and at the Institute of Contemporary History, Södertörn University, Stockholm. His authored and coedited books include *Representation, Nation and Time: The Political Rhetoric of the 1866 Parliamentary Reform in Sweden* (2000), *Käsitteet liikkeessä. Suomen poliittisen kulttuurin käsitehistoria* (2003), *Zeit, Geschichte und Politik; Time, History and Politics: Zum achtzigsten Geburtstag von Reinhart Koselleck* (2003) and *Rhetorics of Nordic Democracy* (2010). He is one of the guest editors of a special issue on the political rhetoric of -isms. He is also the chairperson of the network Concepta – Research Seminars in Conceptual History and Political Thought.

Irène Herrmann is Professor of Transnational Swiss History at the University of Geneva. She has coauthored or edited works on humanitarianism, conceptual history, conflict management and the political uses of the past in Switzerland and in post-Soviet Russia, including *L'humanitaire en questions* (2018), *12 septembre 1814: La Restauration* (2016), *Quand le monde a changé* (2016), *Die Fabrikation staatsbürgerlichen Verhaltens* (2011), *Problem Schweizergeschichte?* (2009), *Die Revanche der Opfer?* (2007), *Les cicatrices du passé* (2006), *Историческое знание в современной России* [*Historical Knowledge in Contemporary Russia*] (2005), *Vermittlung von Geschichte* (2004) and *Genève entre république et canton* (2003).

Notes

1. Harry S. Truman, *Off the Record: The Private Papers of Harry S. Truman* (Columbia: University of Missouri Press, 1980), 57.
2. For example, Switzerland was mentioned as a democracy in Luther's *Tischreden* in 1539. See Christian Meier et al., 'Demokratie', in Otto Brunner, Werner Conze, and Reinhart Koselleck (eds), *Geschichtliche Grundbegriffe. Historisches Lexikon zur politisch-sozialen Sprache in Deutschland,* Band 1 A-D (Stuttgart: Klett-Cotta, 1972), 821–99, at 845.
3. The idea of a northern egalitarian peasant freedom and popular assemblies was also noted, beyond Nordic historians, by Montesquieu, and was further elaborated and actively disseminated by the Genevan historian Paul-Henri Mallet, who also wrote several books on Swiss history. See Håkon Evju, *Ancient Consti-*

tutions and Modern Monarchy: Historical Writing and Enlightened Reform in Denmark-Norway, c. 1730–1814 (Oslo: University of Oslo, 2013), 80–100.
4. The selection of the Swedish case is based on the limitations of space and our competence, not on any alleged priority of the Swedish narratives of democracy in comparison to the Norwegian, Danish, Finnish or Icelandic narratives.
5. See, in particular, the chapters on the Spanish, Russian and Czech democracies in this volume.
6. Joanna Innes and Mark Philp, 'Introduction', in Joanna Innes and Mark Philp (eds), *Re-imagining Democracy in the Age of Revolutions: America, France, Britain, Ireland 1750–1850* (Oxford: Oxford University Press, 2013), 4.
7. Thomas Erskine May, *Democracy in Europe: A History Volume I* (New York: W. J. Widdleton, 1878), xlvii.
8. May, *Democracy in Europe*, 355.
9. James Bryce, *Modern Democracies Vol. I* (1921; repr. London: Macmillan & Co., 1929), 367.
10. Ibid., 38, 40.
11. Robert A. Dahl, *On Democracy* (New Haven: Yale University Press, 2000), 20.
12. Ibid., 19.
13. Ibid., 18–19.
14. Ibid., 10.
15. Ibid., 9.
16. Quoted in Steven Muhlberger and Phil Paine, 'Democracy's Place in World History', *Journal of World History* 4(1) (1993), 23–45, at 32.
17. For rhetorical re-descriptions, see Quentin Skinner, *Visions of Politics, Volume 1: Regarding Method* (Cambridge: Cambridge University Press, 2002), 153.
18. Paul-Henri Mallet considered in his *Histoire des Suisses ou Helvétiens: depuis les tems les plus reculés, jusques à nos jours*, vol. 1 (Geneva: Manget, 1803) the three first cantons (Uri, Schwyz and Underwald) as the 'cradle of freedom' (p. 161). According to him, they proved that democracy associated with 'pure morality' is the best of governments, whereas a democratic system associated with corrupt morality is the worst (at 480–81).
19. See, for instance, Josias Simmler, *La république des Suisses*, (Geneva [Lausanne]: Antoine Chuppin & François Le Preux, 1577), 50, 157 and passim.
20. Eike Hinz, *Landsgemeinde und Bundesbriefe: kognitive und politische Anthropologie der Innerschweiz des 13. und 14. Jahrhunderts: 'Gründungszeit von und mit Eidgenossen': Variationen zu Sabloniers Thema 'Gründungszeit ohne Eidgenossen'* (Hamburg: s.n., 2016).
21. Guy P. Marchal, *Schweizer Gebrauchsgeschichte: Geschichtsbilder, Mythenbildung und nationale Identität* (Basel: Schwabe, 2006).
22. Andreas Sutter, 'Direkte Demokratie – historische Reflexionen zur aktuellen Debatte', in B. Adler, *Die Entstehung der direkten Demokratie: Das Beispiel der Landsgemeinde Schwyz 1789–1866* (Zurich: NZZ Verlag, 2006), 219–78; Irène Herrmann, 'Zwischen Angst und Hoffnung. Eine Nation entsteht (1798–1848)', in Georg Kreis (ed.), *Geschichte der Schweiz* (Basel: Schwabe, 2014), 370–421.

23. See e.g. Johan Jakob Scheuchzer, *Beschreibung der Natur-Geschichten des Schweizerlandes*, 3 Theile (Zurich: Schaufelberger/Hradmeyer, 1706–8); Abraham Ruchat, *Les délices de la Suisse* (Leiden: Pierre Van der Aa, 1714); Albrecht von Haller, *Versuch von schweizerischen Gedichten* (Bern: Niclaus Emanuel Haller, 1732).
24. Irène Herrmann, 'Histoire politique', in Peter Knoepfel et al. (eds), *Handbuch der Schweizer Politik / Manuel de la politique suisse* (Zurich: Verlag Neue Zürcher Zeitung, 2014), 95–117.
25. The database at http://www.gallica.fr shows about 300 results with some repetitions. Although it does not indicate all texts on this topic, these results can be considered representative of the existing literature.
26. In the first volume, he mentioned that there was no such thing as Swiss federalism and in the second volume (published in 1840) he merely evoked the reputation of Swiss medieval soldiers.
27. Marc Vuilleumier, 'La Suisse de 1848: l'analyse de Tocqueville', *Revue suisse d'Histoire* 55(2) (2005), 149–74.
28. *La Presse*, 25 January 1848
29. *Le Figaro*, 9 September 1868.
30. *Le Rappel*, 12 September 1869.
31. Irène Herrmann, *Genève entre république et canton* (Geneva: Passé présent/ Quebec City: Presses de l'Université Laval, 2003), 263–64.
32. In 1848, the Swiss citizens were given the right to revise their national Constitution, in 1874 the right of referendum to oppose federal laws and in 1891 the right of initiative to propose changes to the Swiss Constitution. Most of the time, these rights already existed at a cantonal level before being introduced at the national level.
33. G. du Petit-Thouars, *Démocratie, liberté. Réflexions d'un électeur* (Paris: J. Mersch, 1881), 65.
34. Otto von Bismarck, *Correspondance diplomatique* (Paris: E. Plon, 1883), vol. 2, 238.
35. Petit-Thouars, *Démocratie*, 65.
36. *Compte-rendu analytique des séances de la Société d'économie politique* (1887), 381.
37. *La science sociale suivant la méthode de F. Le Play* VIII (1889), 113–19.
38. Marchal, *Gebrauchsgeschichte*, 114.
39. Herrmann, *Genève*, 402–3.
40. Jean Signorel, *Etude de législation comparée sur le 'référendum' législatif et les autres forces de participation directe* (Paris: Rousseau, 1896), 252.
41. Valentine Zuber, *Le culte des droits de l'homme* (Paris: Gallimard, 2014).
42. Guy P. Marchal, 'Nouvelles approches des mythes fondateurs suisses: l'imaginaire historique des Confédérés à la fin du XVe siècle', in Marc Comina (ed.), *Histoire et belles histoires de la Suisse Guillaume Tell, Nicolas de Flüe et les autres, des chroniques au cinéma* (Basel: Schwabe, 1989), 23.
43. *La réforme sociale*, January–June 1895, 111.
44. *Revue des Deux Mondes*, February 1895, 291.

45. See e.g. *Revue socialiste* (1898), 78; *l'Aurore*, 16 September 1901.
46. See e.g. *La Revue bleue*, 1927, 144
47. See e.g. *Le Matin*, 14 February 1939
48. *Revue du monde catholique*, 1903, 319.
49. Jules-Louis Breton, *Les maladies professionnelles* (Paris: Alcan, 1911), 9.
50. Nadine Boucherin, *Les stratégies argumentatives dans les débats parlementaires suisses sur le suffrage féminin (1945–1971)* (s.n., 2012), retrieved 31 January 2018 from http://ethesis.unifr.ch/theses/BoucherinN.pdf.
51. Sarah Kasme, '"Justifier l'injustifiable" ou l'obtention du suffrage féminin à l'étranger vu par les médias suisses-romands (1918–1971)' (BA thesis, University of Geneva, 2012).
52. Erik Gustaf Geijer, 'Feodalism och republikanism', in *Samlade skrifter II* (Stockholm: P.A. Nordstedt & Söner, 1874), 270–379, at 282. Geijer published in 1828 a separate treatise on a Scandinavian colony in Switzerland. See Anton Blanck, *Geijers götiska diktning* (Stockholm: Albert Bonniers Förlag, 1918), 45, 236.
53. Geijer, 'Feodalism och republikanism', 282, 293–94.
54. Ibid., 388.
55. Ibid., 294.
56. Ibid., 295.
57. Ibid., 314–15.
58. See Bengt Henningsson, *Geijer som historiker* (Uppsala: University of Uppsala, 1961), 249.
59. See Evju, *Ancient Constitutions and Modern Monarchy*, 55, 88–101.
60. Bo Lindberg, *Den antika skevheten: Politiska ord och begrepp i det tidig-moderna Sverige* (Stockholm: Kungl. Vitterhets Historie och Antikvitets Akademien, 2006), 205–6, 212–13; Pasi Ihalainen, *Agents of the People: Democracy and Popular Sovereignty in British and Swedish Parliamentary and Public Debates, 1734–1800* (Leiden: Brill, 2010), 157, 166, 195. The period between 1719 and 1772 is commonly known as the 'Age of Liberty' in Sweden. It was characterized by the rule of the four-estate Diet over the weak monarchs. It ended with a coup mounted by King Gustaf III.
61. Quoted in Peter Hallberg, 'The Language of Democracy in Eighteenth-Century Reformist Thought', in Jussi Kurunmäki and Johan Strang (eds), *Rhetorics of Nordic Democracy* (Helsinki: Finnish Literature Society, 2010), 219–22, at 222.
62. Quoted in Peter Hallberg, *Ages of Liberty: Social Upheaval, History Writing and the New Public Sphere in Sweden, 1740–1792* (Stockholm: Stockholm University), 188.
63. Quoted in Anton Blanck, *Den nordiska renässansen i sjuttonhundratalets litteratur: En undersökning av den 'götiska' poesiens allmänna och inhemska förutsättningar* (Stockholm: Albert Bonniers Förlag, 1911), 424.
64. Ibid., 424–25.
65. C. A. Grevensmöhlen, *Påminnelser och Tilläggningar vid några nyligen utkomma politiska skrifter* (Stockholm: Johan Peter Lindh, 1809), 14–15.
66. Blanck, *Geijers götiska diktning*, 50 and passim.

67. *Aftonbladet*, 29 March 1831.
68. *Aftonbladet*, 19 March 1832; 17 April 1829; 1 November 1845; *Post- och Inrikes Tidningar*, 17 October 1845.
69. *Aftonbladet*, 26 October 1836.
70. *Aftonbladet*, 13 August 1836.
71. *Aftonbladet*, 31 December 1836; *Sveriges Stats-Tidning*, 30 January 1840.
72. *Aftonbladet*, 11 November 1831.
73. Erik Gustaf Geijer, 'Representationsfrågan', in *Samlade skrifter III* (Stockholm: P.A. Nordstedt & Söner, 1874), 274.
74. Esaias Tegnér, *Samlade skrifter: Tredje bandet* (Stockholm: Norstedt & Söder, 1860), 328. See also Göte Jansson, *Tegnér och politiken 1815–1840* (Uppsala: Almqvist & Wiksell, 1948), 372.
75. Tegnér, *Samlade skrifter*, 330.
76. *Aftonbladet*, 30 November 1835.
77. *Aftonbladet*, 3 December 1835; see also *Aftonbladet*, 5 January 1836.
78. *Aftonbladet*, 7 December 1843; see also *Aftonbladet*, 15 May 1835.
79. E.g. *Politisk Tidskrift för Sveriges Allmoge*, 5, 1862, 298.
80. *Politisk Tidskrift för Sveriges Allmoge*, 1, 1860, 10–32.
81. *Aftonbladet*, 16 September 1891.
82. *Dagens Nyheter*, 9 July 1883.
83. See, however, Pontus Falhbeck, *Sveriges författning och den moderna parlamentarismen* (Lund: Gleerups, 1904), who referred to the ancient democracy as a background of the 'dualism' between the monarch and the Riksdag.
84. *Fram, Fram, Bondemän! Minnes- och maningsord till Bondetågets ledamöter* (Stockholm, 1914).
85. Ibid., 24–25.
86. Åsa Linderborg, *Socialdemokraterna skriver historia: Historieskrivning som ideologisk maktresurs* (Stockholm: Atlas, 2001), 273, 298–304; Pasi Ihalainen, 'The 18th-Century Traditions of Representation in a New Age of Revolution', *Scandinavian Journal of History* 40(1) (2015), 70–96, at 73.
87. Ihalainen, 'The 18th-Century Traditions', 73.
88. Fredrik Lagerroth, *Frihetstidens författning: En studie i den svenska konstitutionalismens historia* (Stockholm: Albert Bonniers, 1915), 5.
89. Ibid., 6.
90. Ibid., 322.
91. Ibid., 385.
92. Ibid., 280–81.
93. See Rolf Torstendahl, *Mellan nykonservatism och liberalism: Idébrytningar inom högern och bondepartierna 1918–1934* (Stockholm: Svenska bokförlaget, 1969), 103; Jussi Kurunmäki, '"Nordic Democracy" in 1935: On the Finnish and Swedish Rhetoric of Democracy', in Jussi Kurunmäki and Johan Strang (eds), *Rhetorics of Nordic Democracy* (Helsinki: Finnish Literature Society, 2010), 37–82, at 45–48, 76–77.
94. See Kurunmäki, '"Nordic Democracy" in 1935', 49–51, 76–77.

95. See e.g. Herbert Tingsten, *Demokratiens seger och kris: Vår egen tids historia 1880–1930* (Stockholm: Albert Bonniers Förlag, 1933), 17–18.
96. Kurunmäki, '"Nordic Democracy" in 1935', 77.
97. Quoted in *Aftonbladet*, 23 June 1933.
98. Erik Lönnroth, 'Engelbrekt', *Scandia* 7(1) (1934), 1–13, at 13.
99. Sven Tunberg, 'Riksdagens uppkomst och utveckling intill medeltidens slut', *Sveriges Riksdag: Förra avdelningen, Band I* (Stockholm, 1931), 48, 54.
100. Ibid., 7–46.
101. *Riksdagens minnesfest 1935* (Stockholm, 1936), 68.
102. Quoted in *Dagens Nyheter*, 2 January 1935.
103. Kurunmäki, '"Nordic Democracy" in 1935', 74–77.
104. Birger Beckman, *Svensk folkfrihet genom tiderna* (Stockholm: Tidens förlag, 1937), 11.
105. Ibid., 21–24.
106. Ibid., 30–31.
107. Ibid., 79, 99, 120.
108. Ivar Andersson, 'Early Democratic Traditions in Scandinavia', in J.A. Lauwerys (ed.), *Scandinavian Democracy: Development of Democratic Thought & Institutions in Denmark, Norway and Sweden* (Copenhagen: Danish Institute, Norwegian Office of Cultural Relations, Swedish Institute, American-Scandinavian Foundation, 1958), 69–93, at 72 and 93.
109. Sigurđur Líndal, 'Early Democratic Traditions in the Nordic Countries', in Erik Allardt et al. (eds), *Nordic Democracy: Ideas, Issues, and Institutions in Politics, Economy, Education, Social and Cultural Affairs of Denmark, Finland, Iceland, Norway, and Sweden* (Copenhagen: Det Danske Selskab, 1981), 15–41, at 40–41.
110. For the Spanish use of democracy, see the chapter by Javier Fernández-Sebastián and José María Rosales in this volume.
111. For the Czech and the Russian democracies, see the chapters by Peter Bugge and Benjamin Beuerle, respectively.

Bibliography

1887. *Compte-rendu analytique des séances de la Société d'économie politique.*
1889. *La science sociale suivant la méthode de F. Le Play*, vol. VIII.
1914. *Fram, Fram, Bondemän! Minnes- och maningsord till Bondetågets ledamöter.* Stockholm.
Andersson, I. 1958. 'Early Democratic Traditions in Scandinavia', in J.A. Lauwerys (ed.), *Scandinavian Democracy: Development of Democratic Thought & Institutions in Denmark, Norway and Sweden.* Copenhagen: Danish Institute, Norwegian Office of Cultural Relations, Swedish Institute, American-Scandinavian Foundation, 69–93.
Beckman, B. 1937. *Svensk folkfrihet genom tiderna.* Stockholm: Tidens förlag.
Bismarck, O. von. 1883. *Correspondance diplomatique*, vol. 2. Paris: E. Plon.

Blanck, A. 1911. *Den nordiska renässansen i sjuttonhundratalets litteratur: En undersökning av den 'götiska' poesiens allmänna och inhemska förutsättningar.* Stockholm: Albert Bonniers Förlag.

———. 1918. *Geijers götiska diktning.* Stockholm: Albert Bonniers Förlag.

Boucherin, N. 2012. *Les stratégies argumentatives dans les débats parlementaires suisses sur le suffrage féminin (1945–1971).* s.n. Retrieved 31 January 2018 from http://ethesis.unifr.ch/theses/BoucherinN.pdf.

Breton, J-L. 1911. *Les maladies professionnelles.* Paris: Alcan.

Bryce, M. 1929. *Modern Democracies Vol. I* (1921). London: Macmillan & Co.

Dahl, R.A. 2000. *On Democracy.* New Haven: Yale University Press.

Evju, H. 2013. *Ancient Constitutions and Modern Monarchy: Historical Writing and Enlightened Reform in Denmark-Norway, c. 1730–1814.* Oslo: University of Oslo.

Falhbeck, P. 1904. *Sveriges författning och den moderna parlamentarismen.* Lund: Gleerups.

Geijer, E.G. 1874a. 'Feodalism och republikanism' in *Samlade skrifter II.* Stockholm: P.A. Nordstedt & Söner, 270–379.

———. 1874b. 'Representationsfrågan', in *Samlade skrifter III.* Stockholm: P.A. Nordstedt & Söner, 259–314.

Grevensmöhlen, C.A. 1809. *Påminnelser och Tilläggningar vid några nyligen utkomma politiska skrifter.* Stockholm: Johan Peter Lindh.

Hallberg, P. 2003. *Ages of Liberty: Social Upheaval, History Writing and the New Public Sphere in Sweden, 1740–1792.* Stockholm: Stockholm University.

———. 2010. 'The Language of Democracy in Eighteenth-Century Reformist Thought', in J. Kurunmäki and J. Strang (eds), *Rhetorics of Nordic Democracy.* Helsinki: Finnish Literature Society, 219–22.

Haller, A. von. 1732. *Versuch von schweizerischen Gedichten.* Bern: Niclaus Emanuel Haller.

Henningsson, B. 1961. *Geijer som historiker.* Uppsala: University of Uppsala.

Herrmann, I. 2003. *Genève entre république et canton.* Geneva: Passé présent/Quebec City: Presses de l'Université Laval.

———. 2014. 'Histoire politique', in P. Knoepfel et al. (eds), *Handbuch der Schweizer Politik/ Manuel de la politique Suisse.* Zurich: Verlag Neue Zürcher Zeitung, 95–117.

———. 2014. 'Zwischen Angst und Hoffnung: Eine Nation entsteht (1798–1848)', in G. Kreis (ed.), *Geschichte der Schweiz.* Basel: Schwabe, 370–421.

Hinz, E. 2016. *Landsgemeinde und Bundesbriefe: kognitive und politische Anthropologie der Innerschweiz des 13. und 14. Jahrhunderts: 'Gründungszeit von und mit Eidgenossen': Variationen zu Sabloniers Thema 'Gründungszeit ohne Eidgenossen'.* Hamburg: s.n.

Ihalainen, P. 2010. *Agents of the People: Democracy and Popular Sovereignty in British and Swedish Parliamentary and Public Debates, 1734–1800.* Leiden: Brill.

———. 2015. 'The 18th-Century Traditions of Representation in a New Age of Revolution', *Scandinavian Journal of History* 40(1), 70–96.

Innes, J., and M. Philp. 2013. 'Introduction', in J. Innes and M. Philp (eds), *Reimagining Democracy in the Age of Revolutions: America, France, Britain, Ireland 1750–1850*. Oxford: Oxford University Press, 1–10.
Jansson, G. 1948. *Tegnér och politiken 1815–1840*. Uppsala: Almqvist & Wiksell.
Kasme, S. 2012. '"Justifier l'injustifiable" ou l'obtention du suffrage féminin à l'étranger vu par les médias suisses-romands (1918–1971)'. BA thesis, University of Geneva.
Kurunmäki, J. 2010. '"Nordic Democracy" in 1935: On the Finnish and Swedish Rhetoric of Democracy', in J. Kurunmäki and J. Strang (eds), *Rhetorics of Nordic Democracy*, Helsinki: Finnish Literature Society, 37–82.
Lagerroth, F. 1915. *Frihetstidens författning: En studie i den svenska konstitutionalismens historia*. Stockholm: Albert Bonniers.
Líndal, S. 1981. 'Early Democratic Traditions in the Nordic Countries', in E. Allardt et al. (eds), *Nordic Democracy: Ideas, Issues, and Institutions in Politics, Economy, Education, Social and Cultural Affairs of Denmark, Finland, Iceland, Norway, and Sweden*. Copenhagen: Det Danske Selskab, 15–41.
Lindberg, B. 2006. *Den antika skevheten: Politiska ord och begrepp i det tidig-moderna Sverige*. Stockholm: Kungl. Vitterhets Historie och Antikvitets Akademien.
Linderborg, Å. 2001. *Socialdemokraterna skriver historia: Historieskrivning som ideologisk maktresurs*. Stockholm: Atlas.
Lönnroth, E. 1934. 'Engelbrekt', *Scandia* 7(1), 1–13.
Mallet, P-H. 1803. *Histoire des Suisses ou Helvétiens: depuis les tems les plus reculés, jusques à nos jours*, vol. 1. Geneva: Manget.
Marchal, G.P. 1989. 'Nouvelles approches des mythes fondateurs suisses: l'imaginaire historique des Confédérés à la fin du XVe siècle', in M. Comina (ed.), *Histoire et belles histoires de la Suisse Guillaume Tell, Nicolas de Flüe et les autres, des chroniques au cinema*. Basel: Schwabe, 1–23.
———. 2006. *Schweizer Gebrauchsgeschichte: Geschichtsbilder, Mythenbildung und nationale Identität*. Basel: Schwabe.
May, T.E. 1878. *Democracy in Europe: A History Volume I* (1877). York: W. J. Widdleton.
Meier, C. et al. 1972. 'Demokratie', in O. Brunner, W. Conze and R. Koselleck (eds), *Geschichtliche Grundbegriffe. Historisches Lexikon zur politisch-sozialen Sprache in Deutschland*, Band 1 A–D. Stuttgart: Klett-Cotta, 821–99.
Muhlberger, S., and P. Paine. 1993. 'Democracy's Place in World History', *Journal of World History* 4(1), 23–45.
Petit-Thouars, G. du. 1881. *Démocratie, liberté. Réflexions d'un électeur*. Paris: J. Mersch.
Ruchat, A. 1714. *Les délices de la Suisse*. Leiden: Pierre Van der Aa.
Scheuchzer, J.J. 1706–8. *Beschreibung der Natur-Geschichten des Schweizerlandes*, 3 parts. Zurich: Schaufelberger/Hradmeyer.
Signorel, J. 1896. *Etude de législation comparée sur le 'référendum' législatif et les autres forces de participation directe*. Paris: Rousseau.
Simmler, J. 1577. *La république des Suisses*. Geneva [Lausanne]: Antoine Chuppin & François Le Preux.

Skinner, Q. 2002. *Visions of Politics, Volume 1: Regarding Method.* Cambridge: Cambridge University Press.

Sutter, A. 2006. 'Direkte Demokratie – historische Reflexionen zur aktuellen Debatte', in B. Adler, *Die Entstehung der direkten Demokratie: Das Beispiel der Landsgemeinde Schwyz 1789–1866.* Zurich: NZZ Verlag, 219–78.

Tegnér, E. 1860. *Samlade skrifter: Tredje bandet.* Stockholm: Norstedt & Söder.

Tingsten, H. 1933. *Demokratiens seger och kris: Vår egen tids historia 1880–1930.* Stockholm: Albert Bonniers Förlag.

Torstendahl, R. 1969. *Mellan nykonservatism och liberalism: Idébrytningar inom högern och bondepartierna 1918–1934.* Stockholm: Svenska bokförlaget.

Truman, H.S. 1980. *Off the Record: The Private Papers of Harry S. Truman.* Columbia: University of Missouri Press.

Tunberg, S. 1931. 'Riksdagens uppkomst och utveckling intill medeltidens slut', in *Sveriges Riksdag: Förra avdelningen, Band I.* Stockholm: Victor Pettersons Bokindustriaktiebolag.

Vuilleumier, M. 2005. 'La Suisse de 1848: l'analyse de Tocqueville', *Revue suisse d'Histoire* 55(2), 149–74.

Zuber, V. 2014. *Le culte des droits de l'homme.* Paris: Gallimard.

Chapter 5

Concepts of Democracy from a Russian Perspective

Debates in the Late Imperial Period (1905–17)

Benjamin Beuerle

Introduction

Until the beginning of the twentieth century, debates on democracy in Russia were largely confined either to academia or to illegal underground circles. This situation changed considerably with the onset of the Revolution of 1905, which was accompanied by a partial breakdown of censorship, at least in the metropolises of the empire.[1] It was now possible to discuss democracy in public, and quite a large number of politicians and writers made use of this possibility, particularly during the revolutionary years 1905, 1906 and 1917, when the future path of the Russian state was unclear to most and thus was up for discussion. Statements on democracy and its different aspects were relatively frequent during this period. In most cases, these statements in some way referred to Western states or theories.

This chapter endeavours to capture the meanings of the concept of 'democracy' in the political language of this crucial period in Russian history. The chapter draws mainly on Russian pamphlets and publications of this time, political speeches and Russian encyclopaedias.

Most of the elements linked to 'democracy' in the political language of the time did not represent Russian uniqueness, but could be found in Western European states concurrently and earlier. In this sense, the chapter illuminates the adaption, use and importance of Western concepts of democracy in a non-Western environment with (for most of the period) a strong, albeit constitutional, monarchy. At the same time, it describes the development of the concept within a changing political context and the concept's meaning within a multinational empire. It also traces the significance of a certain sociopolitical definition of the 'people' (*narod*) and of 'democracy' itself, both as the 'working masses' and the parties defending their interests, and the political consequences of these concepts in 1917.

Preconditions: Concepts of Democracy before 1905

During the nineteenth century, the use of 'democracy' as a concept in Russia was mostly confined to academic and underground circles. Beginning in the second half of that century, the concept of 'democracy' played an important role in the writings of a number of (liberal) Russian jurists. Most of them – like, most prominently, Boris Chicherin – endorsed a concept that placed an accent on freedom, liberty, parliamentarianism, constitutionalism and the separation of powers. The British form of government was their preferred model. Russian liberal jurists saw a historical universal (although nonlinear) trend towards democracy. Around the beginning of the twentieth century, the concepts of liberal Russian jurists evolved towards postulating the necessity of societal solidarity assured by the state (as a precondition for a stable democracy) in the form of some kind of social welfare.[2]

In doing so, they came close to a similar (positive) concept of democracy held by a majority of social democrats of different currents, a conception that the latter saw as clear progress over the situation in the Russian autocracy and suitable at least for the first (long) stage after an expected 'bourgeois' revolution. Lenin and his followers were the exception in this sense.[3]

When Russian conservatives wrote about democracy before the turn of the twentieth century, they did so in a negative way, designating it as a degenerate, Western form of state whose main elements were the existence of different parties and of a parliament. However, in the first years of the twentieth century, Russian conservatives started to make more nuanced and cautious statements on democracy.[4] After the Revolution of 1905, most of them refrained from elaborating explicitly on this concept at all.

The Discourse on Democracy in Russia between 1905 and 1914/16

Who Spoke about Democracy?
The concepts of 'democracy' and 'democratic' in Russia between 1905 and 1914 were mostly used by those who were in favour of some form of democracy: left-liberals and socialists. At least three of the parties represented in the new Russian Parliament, the State Duma, from 1906 carried 'democratic'

in their name: the Social Democratic Party (i.e. the Mensheviks and Bolsheviks), the (left-liberal) Constitutional Democratic Party and the (centrist-liberal) Party of Democratic Reforms. It is hardly surprising that members of these parties and sympathetic intellectuals referred to 'democracy' and that they did so in a positive way, albeit with different meanings. Most articulate were members and sympathizers of the Constitutional Democratic Party, who were called 'Kadets': This left-liberal party not only emerged from the first two national elections, in the spring of 1906 and early in 1907, as the strongest faction in the Duma, but it also counted among its ranks an impressive number of highly capable and well-known lawyers and writers.[5]

Now, the interesting question is, of course, why most conservatives and rightists were, at least publicly, keeping a rather low profile concerning 'democracy' and were considerably less outspoken in this respect than before the Revolution of 1905. Why did democrats dominate the debate on 'democracy' in Russia between 1905 and 1917?

A first explanation can be found in the fact that, especially during the revolutionary years of 1905, 1906 and 1917, proponents of 'democracy' to a large extent dominated Russian public debate in general. The bulk of the Russian *Intelligentsia* – whose members were the most articulate of the Russian public – opposed the Tsarist regime, even if they were not openly pro-democratic. Moreover, the first national elections in 1906 ended with a landslide victory for democratic forces. Thus, hardly any rightists and very few conservatives were represented in the First Duma. The democrats were even more dominant after the February Revolution of 1917, when the whole political spectrum shifted considerably to the left.[6]

However, this at least partial dominance of public debates by democratic forces is not enough to explain why rightists and conservatives usually did not attack positive conceptions of 'democracy'. After all, the political right was by no means inarticulate and had the support of both the Tsarist court and at least parts of the government. Moreover, conservatives and rightists were in the majority in the State Duma from its third elections (late in 1907) until at least the outbreak of the First World War. Thus, they had every possibility to make themselves heard and read.[7] But the rightists' restraint concerning 'democracy' might be explained by the importance of the concept of the 'people' in the tsarist and rightist ideologies of this time. Although rightists wanted a strong and politically decisive monarchy that would, from a constitutional point of view, be responsible to no one, there nevertheless existed at least a certain ambiguity regarding the place of the people in this political conception. According to the tsarist ideology of the time, there existed a spiritual bond between the Tsar and the people. Nicholas II thought and asserted that the people supported him. Although there were certainly theoretical differences, this conception was not so far from the idea that the Tsar had a popular mandate to rule.[8]

In this respect, it is important to highlight the meaning of the word *narod*, the Russian word for 'people'. While the word can mean all the constituents of a certain state, it was at the time more often used in opposition to *obshchestvo* (educated society). In this sense, the Russian *narod* was constituted exclusively by workers and, in particular, peasants – that is, the bulk of the Russian population at that time.[9] It was with *this* people that Nicholas II was supposed to have had a spiritual bond. It should be noted that by far the largest and most important extreme rightist association during these years called itself the 'Union of the Russian People' (*Soiuz Russkago Naroda*).[10] To be sure, rightists and conservatives still attacked the concept of 'parliamentarianism' – a concept that could be dismissed as being obviously 'Western' and not fit for the Russian context.[11] But arguably because of the positive connotation of the 'people' and its ambiguous position in the political conceptions of rightists and conservatives, they largely refrained from dealing with the concept of 'democracy' instead of criticizing it in a direct way. Even Lev Tikhomirov, a staunch defender of Tsarist autocracy who in the 1890s had published several articles condemning the European trend towards democracy, admitted in 1908 at least the possibility that democratic government might bring positive results.[12]

There were exceptions, such as the well-known historian Vladimir Ger'e, one of the leading figures and intellectuals of the rightist-liberal (or conservative) 'Union of October 17'.[13] In several articles and pamphlets in 1905 and 1906, which were primarily directed against the Constitutional Democrats, he criticized 'democracy' and 'democratic parties' in a way that reflected anti-democratic statements in France and the United States in the late eighteenth century. He equated 'democracy' with the future State Duma. In his view, it was dangerous to give 'democracy' (in this sense) too much power and to leave it unchecked because he thought it to be impulsive, prone to instability and potentially imprudent. Therefore, he called not only for a strong monarchy but also for a strong upper house with the ability to counterbalance the potentially damaging influence of 'democracy'. It was one of the few cases in this period where 'democracy' was used in a 'classical' or Aristotelian way, indicating here a legislature within a mixed constitution that needs to be restrained by the other parts in order to do no harm to the state.[14]

Problems related to democracy were discussed in a number of other publications. For example, the political activists and writers Vodovozov (in 1905) and Ostrogorskii (in 1913) pointed to the critical necessity and task in democracies of somehow protecting the minority from abuses by the majority.[15] Nevertheless, the authors of these and similar statements made it clear that they were for democracy and that the problems they hinted at, if appropriately confronted, could be resolved.

In general, there was widespread belief in the modern and progressive nature of democracy. Lev Shalland, a Russian professor of constitutional law with a doctoral degree from Heidelberg University, confidently stated in 1905 that the 'modern' (or 'contemporary') state was based on 'democratic foundations'. Another author emphasized towards the end of the same year that a historical period was beginning in which it was no longer possible to govern against the will of the people. Vladimir Gessen, one of the leading Kadets, wrote in 1906 that it was by then universally recognized that the state should serve the good of the people and that power should therefore be held by the people themselves. Like Shalland – but more articulately – he stated that one could observe in general a continual historical development towards democracy. He concluded (again) that the 'modern' state was democratic.[16]

To sum up, in Russia between 1905 and 1917, the concepts 'democracy' and 'democratic' were used mainly by democrats. The positive meaning of these concepts – as an ideal, something that Russia should strive for – was thus rarely (explicitly) contested. That said, we can turn to the question that suggests itself at this point in the analysis: what did 'democracy' mean for those Russians who used this concept in public between 1905 and 1917?

One Word, Two Meanings
First, a word on some 'descriptive' definitions and explanations of the concept: two huge Russian encyclopaedias were published during these years, and coincidentally the volume containing the article on 'democracy' appeared in both of them in 1913. Both were written by prominent (left-)liberal authors (Vodovozov and Dzhivelegov), and both defined 'democracy' in an institutional *and* sociopolitical way. It was, first, a form of state in which 'power belongs to the people or in which the interests of [a majority of] the people rank first'. Its antonym in this sense, Dzhivelegov stated, was 'aristocracy', in which the interests of only a minority of the population were upheld. Second, 'democracy' denominated 'the popular masses [constituting the people's majority] themselves' and, according to Dzhivelegov, also 'the groups which tend to it [the people's majority] according to their ideology'.[17] Whereas the latter (sociopolitical) usage of the term was at earlier periods well known in various parts of Western Europe as well, after the turn of the twentieth century, it appears to have been considerably less common there than in Russia.[18]

The largest part of both articles was, however, devoted to an elaboration of the institutional meaning of the word and to the historical development of 'democracy' in this sense. This institutional concept was very common in the political languages in Western European states. Both articles referred to Western historical developments since the Middle Ages and to various Western thinkers and writers, including most prominently Jean-Jacques Rousseau.[19] Notwithstanding a number of differences between the articles, both saw a continuous trend of democratization, especially since the eighteenth century, and both saw as the main element of this trend the successive elimination of legal inequalities between different groups and sectors of the population. Thus, *equality* was then seen as the most important and defining element of modern democracy – in contrast to liberal understandings in nineteenth-century Russia, which ranked liberty first. In addition, it was equality that at the end of both articles linked the first and second definitions of democracy: according to Dzhivelegov, since 1793 the 'popular masses' had replaced the bourgeoisie as the driving force behind democratization. Vodovozov explained that in more recent times, this force had been expanding the 'battle' for democratization from the legal to the socioeconomic sphere and that democracy itself designated 'not any longer the third estate, but the proletariat'.[20]

However, the question of equality constituted not only a link between the two definitions and concepts of democracy, but also an at least potential tension, which was not limited to a sort of affirmative action: if 'democracy' meant the 'working masses', that could lead in extremis to the conclusion that anyone not belonging to these masses should be excluded from 'democracy' in a politico-juridical sense. For the time being, only Lenin and his followers drew this conclusion. Before 1917, they were not able to influence the debate on democracy in a substantial way, not least because Lenin eventually preferred the term 'dictatorship of the proletariat'. It was not quite clear if he held a positive concept of democracy at all.[21] Nevertheless, the sociopolitical definition of 'democracy' itself had deeper roots in Russia and could draw on the abovementioned common understanding of the 'people' (the *narod*) as the 'toiling masses'.

Russia as a 'Peasant Democracy'

In the eyes of many who discussed democracy in Russia between 1905 and 1917, the concept not only implied equality and rule 'by the people', but also rule 'for the people'. Here the 'people' mostly had the connotation of the *narod* in opposition to *obshchestvo*, i.e. it meant peasants and workers. Not surprisingly, Social Democrats in particular argued that any 'democratic' state should primarily defend the interests of the employees (against those of the employers). We can observe this kind of argumentation, for example, in the statements made in the Third Duma by the deputies Predkal'n (a Bolshevik) and Kuznetsov (a Menshevik). However, a number of Kadets held similar ideas. Prince Drutskoi-Liubetskii, one of the delegates at the third Constitutional Democratic Party conference, in the spring of 1906, asked for the expropriation of all large estates. In his opinion, this corresponded to 'democratic principles', because these estates had been real 'centres for the exploitation of peasants'. Here, the 'demos' in 'democratic' was clearly confined to the working masses. Similarly, in 1911, the Duma deputy Stepanov requested on behalf of the Kadet faction that in the projected self-governed health insurance, which was to be jointly financed by employers and employees, only employees should hold voting rights, according to what he called a 'democratic principle'.[22] In these statements the concepts of democracy and rule for the working people ('socio-economic progress') appear closely linked.

Interestingly enough, when it came to naming the most suitable democratic model state for Russia, quite a few Russian democrats had Norway in mind. Many Kadets held this to be the 'most democratic' state in Europe. This was due not only to its political system but also to the fact that, as opposed to France, England and the United States, Norway was said to be a real 'peasants' kingdom'. The Kadet Kotliarevskii explained in the First Duma that there were two types of democracy: one based mostly on city-dwellers and another based on peasants in the form of small landowners. In the latter case – for which Norway was the brightest example – peasants were the main pillars and defenders of democracy. For Kotliarevskii, Russia – whose population consisted mostly of peasants – could develop only into the second type of democracy. It therefore needed a strong, landowning peasantry.[23] Here again, the concept of the 'demos' was very much that of the *narod*.

It should be noted that comparable ideas had been in use elsewhere. Peter Bugge shows that prominent Czech democrats at this time held an analogous (positive) concept of the common people (the *lid*), and something similar could initially be said about the Polish *lud* for Polish democrats. However, whereas for Polish National Democrats, the *lud* later took on the negative meaning of the 'mob' that threatened the national agenda and unity, and thus had to be disciplined, Russian democrats of various shades kept a positive notion of the people in the form of the *narod* in the period from 1905 to 1917.[24]

Whereas this understanding laid strong roots for the sociopolitical definition of 'democracy', the debates on the institutional meaning of this term clearly prevailed prior to 1917.

The Institutional Meaning of Democracy

In their speeches and writings, liberal and most socialist politicians and publicists confirmed the primordial importance of equality in the process of democratization. Thus, the Socialist Revolutionary deputy Tigranian told the Second Duma in 1907 that there should be no privileged classes in democratic states. Fëdor Kokoshkin, another leading Kadet, attributed a Russian particularity to this striving when he explained in a speech before the First State

Duma in the spring of 1906 that in Russia, a specific sentiment for 'democratic equality' had for a long time been rooted in the society and among the masses – whereas Russian legislation was in 'outrageous contradiction' with this sentiment as it was marked by the principle of inequality to a degree unseen in the 'civilized world'.[25]

But what did 'equality' imply? One of the most important criteria for democratic states that everyone in the Russian debates of this time could agree upon was universal manhood suffrage. Practically all those who spoke or wrote about this subject in Russia between 1905 and 1914 agreed that in order for a state to be democratic, suffrage needed to be 'four-tailed': universal (i.e. for all male adults), equal, direct and secret. To name but a few examples, Vodovozov stated in the spring of 1905 that 'four-tailed' suffrage was a necessary condition for any expression of the real will of the people. Shalland agreed and held that there was a historical trend in all countries towards this kind of suffrage. Petr Struve, another well-known Kadet, held the same opinion and argued that any restriction whatsoever on this kind of suffrage was to be repudiated.[26]

Some went further. I. Osipov in 1905 and N. Kabanov in 1906 stated that in order for suffrage to really correspond to democratic standards, all electoral districts should be equal in size (one of the reasons why Osipov thought the German electoral system to be quite flawed). Another criterion mentioned by Osipov and Kabanov and supported in April 1906 by an article in the Kadet organ *Rech'* was that deputies should receive remuneration, as otherwise the right to stand for election would in practice be restricted to the propertied.[27] And there were, of course, those – like Osipov and also a number of Kadets and more radical political activists – who held that universal suffrage was complete only if women were given the right to vote. After all, there was the example of Finland, which – within the realm of the Tsarist Empire and in general – was in the vanguard in this respect. Hardly any democrat explicitly spoke against women's suffrage in principle. However, this criterion was omitted in a number of statements and publications on suffrage and democracy. Before 1917, quite a few Russian liberals at least thought it to be premature to discuss this point in public.[28] In contrast, hardly anyone disputed the necessity of universal, equal, direct and secret manhood suffrage in any democratic state.

The importance of equal and universal suffrage presupposed a decisive parliament. In October 1905, at the height of the revolutionary uproar, the Tsar issued a manifesto in which he promised the introduction of an elected parliament, without whose consent no law should come into effect. Only a couple of months later, shortly before the first national elections, the public was informed that there would be another legislative chamber. The State Council was to receive the same legislative rights as the Duma, and half of its members were to be appointed (and replaced at any given moment) by the Tsar. Many Russian democrats saw this institutional arrangement as a violation of the Tsar's October Manifesto. Thus, a large majority of the First Duma demanded the abolition of the State Council or at least its replacement by a democratically elected upper house.[29]

Two elaborate articles by the prominent Kadet lawyer Vladimir Gessen, appearing in the spring of 1906 in the journals *Rech'* and *Pravo*, can be viewed against this background. Gessen claimed that, notwithstanding assertions to the contrary or the theory of Montesquieu, any bicameral system was in reality incompatible with the 'modern democratic form of state'. The upper chamber was generally intended as a counterweight to 'modern democratic' tendencies, and it had in practice most often 'a decisive and sharply expressed aristocratic or class character' and served as an obstacle to democratic reforms. According to Gessen, the bicameral system was thus undemocratic and should be dismissed (unless its decisions could be overruled by the people's assembly, as in Norway, or it represented the regional entities in a federal state, as in the United States). Gessen was confident that the 'inexorable process of democratization' would sooner or later lead to the implementation of the unicameral system in Europe and beyond.[30]

Gessen was by no means the only one to hold this position in Russia at the time.[31] There was, however, some debate on this position among democrats. The Kadets could not agree to insert the demand for a unicameral system into their party platform. Some of them held that a bicameral system was at least in principle not contradictory to a constitutional democratic form of government, if both chambers were elected on the basis of universal suffrage.[32] However, it seems clear that at least in 1906, democrats who wanted a bicameral system were very much on the defensive.

To be sure, such debates on the kind of suffrage and the nature of parliament to be adopted for a truly democratic state were not unique to Russia and mirrored, albeit with variations (like the strong advocacy for unicameralism), similar debates in (other) European countries both beforehand and thereafter.[33] In contrast, somewhat more peculiar was the nexus between 'democracy' and the 'nationalities question' as discussed in the Russian context.

The Nationalities Question: Democracy in a Multinational Empire
In a multinational empire like the Russian one, the question of democracy was closely linked with the question of nationalities. It is truly remarkable that, in the Russian case, pro-democratic representatives of the hegemonic nationality within a multinational empire were all but unanimous in their opinion that the introduction of democracy presupposed the abolition of legal discriminations on a national basis. The only sort of exception concerned Russian

as a common state language, which many Russian democrats thought to be a necessary prerequisite for a viable federal state.[34]

Thus, the Kadet Shershenevich argued on behalf of his party in 1906 that, in a democratic state, equal rights should also be granted to members of different nationalities. He concluded that school education should be offered in the corresponding national language (instead of in Russian as a matter of course).[35] Shershenevich's statements were only part of a wider discourse according to which, in a democratic state, it should be up to the *local* population (of various nationalities) to deal with their own matters. The Kadet deputy and Polish professor of law Petrazhitskii made a statement to that effect in the First Duma in 1906. In a similar vein, a number of leftist Duma deputies stated in 1907 that any democracy depended on the closeness of the institutions to the population and thus needed small administrative entities for decision-making, as the local population should be able to decide for themselves about their issues.[36]

A text published in 1906 by Vladimir Gessen made the link between the question of democracy and the 'nationalities question' within the empire especially plain: efforts for national self-determination and for democracy were 'like two branches of one tree of freedom', the text explained. If the two came into conflict with each other, it could crush the whole tree, which was why absolutism would make use of national chauvinism for a *divide and conquer* policy. National autonomy, especially in cultural and religious matters, and equal rights for each nationality were thus preconditions for a real democratization of the state. A common language for the state's institutions might be necessary, the author further stated, but in regional and local institutions, it was, on the contrary, necessary to accept the use of the corresponding national languages. These institutions would otherwise be de facto inaccessible to the local population, who would not be able to understand their proceedings, thus hindering the people's effective self-determination.[37] From this perspective, real cultural autonomy for the different nationalities within the empire was a *sine qua non* for its real democratization.

Whereas the aforementioned text emphasized normative and practical reasons for the link between national and democratic demands, this link took on a descriptive and empirical nature in Vodovozov's article on the 'nationalities question', which appeared in 1916 in a well-known encyclopaedia. According to Vodovozov, 'democracy' (defined here implicitly as the 'popular masses') was generally at the forefront of the nationalist movement, as the masses suffered most as a result of the enslaved condition of the corresponding 'nation'. Thus, national movements most often had a democratic character and national demands were combined with democratic ones, e.g. for widespread suffrage. Vodovozov remarked, however, that there was a certain tension in this empirical relationship, since in nearly every national movement 'democratic ambitions' for equal rights for the given dominant nationality were combined with ambitions for dominance over other nationalities.[38] Ironically, in 1905 Vodozov himself had stated some reservations about the principle of legal equality between the different nationalities of the empire (which he generally defended and that was endorsed by most Russian democrats). He held the view that it was impossible to give voting rights to some nomadic tribes and peoples in the Russian Empire, who were in his words mostly illiterate, dispersed across vast territories and alien to Russian culture. In justification he pointed to the United States, which denied voting rights to native peoples who still lived nomadic lifestyles.[39]

Ultimately, the question of how to define the 'rule of the people' within a multinational empire posed a lasting challenge for Russian democrats. It would be discussed even more ardently in 1917, when both 'democracy' and the 'nationalities question' became more concrete and acute in Russia than ever before.

Concepts of Democracy in 1917

In 1917, the word 'democracy' – in an institutional sense – was increasingly used not to designate an ideal to be aspired to, but rather as a denomination for the new Russian state that had come into being with the February Revolution and that quite a few Russians now saw at the forefront of the worldwide movement of democratization.[40] As 'democracy' was thus to become a very concrete form of government to be dealt with in practice on a daily basis, its definition and necessary components became all the more disputed. This can be exemplified by some statements on the interrelated questions of a national educational policy and of national and regional self-determination.

The vital importance of schooling for the survival of the new Russian 'democracy' was a topical issue in 1917. In some ways, an author in the liberal journal *Vestnik Evropy* (*Messenger of Europe*) had delivered the theoretical underpinning for this reasoning in a 1911 article on the 'Young French Democracy', in which he argued that unlike other forms of government, the democratic state could by no means be founded on police power; on the contrary, it depended on the support of its citizens. Hence, the author stated, a democratic state needed democratic schools for the whole population, democratic curricula and democratic-minded teachers.[41]

Accordingly, in 1917, different publications and government commissions time and again reiterated that the new Russian democracy needed a new democratic school system and therefore far-reaching reforms in the educational sector. The report of a government commission established for this purpose claimed that the democratic state had to ensure the education of all the people. It had to overcome the 'darkness' in which the people had lived for centuries, as otherwise all the accomplishments of democracy would be incomplete. Those who discussed reforms to this sector in 1917 agreed that an adequate school system for the democratic state would have to make education accessible to all and should be organized by democratically elected institutions of self-government. However, there was no consensus among democrats regarding the extent to which the democratic principle was applicable or what it meant in practice in the educational sector: Should the people themselves have the right to decide whether to send their children to school? And should different nationalities be free to choose their own language of education? While there were more voices who answered the first question in the negative and the second in the positive, these questions remained disputed up to the Bolshevik coup in October 1917.[42]

The tension inherent in the concept of the 'rule of the people' became very concrete in a debate within the 'State Committee on People's Education', which discussed educational reforms in the summer of 1917. At some point during the discussion, one member of the Committee (V. Nadezhdin) stated that, in a democratic state, the population should decide for itself about its priorities. He argued that compulsory education should therefore not be introduced in Russia. Two other members of the committee, G. Titov and A. Namitokov, profoundly disagreed. They pointed to England as a democratic model state, where in some areas of state concern like education and military service, there were exceptions to the 'democratic' principle of self-determination (which neither Titov nor Namitokov challenged as such). And they stressed that this was certainly necessary, for, they argued, if you were completely consistent with this principle, it would lead to letting children decide whether they wanted to go to school or not.[43] In other words, some limits to the democratic principle of self-determination had to be set, as otherwise no democracy would be viable. The writer A. Iashchenko went further when he declared in 1917 that 'democracy' was the 'kingdom of the will of the people', which in his view naturally meant the rule of the majority. According to him, this implied that everyone had to submit to majoritarian rule. This concerned compulsory schooling and the learning of a common state language (Russian) by all.[44]

While the question of the necessity of a common state language for all public institutions remained disputed, in 1917 (even more than after 1905) hardly anyone contested that each nationality in the empire should otherwise have equal rights. Thus, Kechek'ian wrote in 1917 that 'democracy' was not able to make all national differences disappear, but it could put an end to national antagonisms. The 'nationalities question' could be solved only in 'the spirit of freedom and fraternity'. Therefore, each nationality should be given autonomy and the right to use its own language.[45] S. Avaliani stated in 1917 that in a 'democracy', no nationality should have more rights than others. He promoted complete autonomy for every nationality within the empire.[46] In a similar vein, S. Semkovskii held that a true democratization of the state could lead to a closer link between the nationalities of the empire, whereas the Provisional Government's reluctance to proclaim widespread autonomy for each nationality within the empire before the Constitutional Assembly met was promoting nationalism and endangering the 'revolutionary democracy' and the Russian state as a whole.[47] They, like other Russian democrats, were convinced that unless all nationalities were given the same rights, Russian 'democracy' (and therefore the multinational Russian state itself) would collapse.

It is, however, important to note that several historians dealing with the subject recognize for the year 1917 a predominance of the sociopolitical ('social') concept of 'democracy'. Whereas Kolonitskii and Figes see a continuous trend in that direction, Zhdanova asserts that this concept was accepted by socialists and liberals alike in the spring of 1917. This, Zhdanova argues, changed throughout the summer and autumn, when Liberals, Mensheviks and a number of Socialist Revolutionaries focused their hopes on the constitutional assembly – which was too late to influence the political mood and outcome of the autumn of 1917. In any case, at least during a number of months in 1917, this notion of democracy – whose antonym was not any authoritarian form of government, but the 'bourgeoisie' – found wide acceptance in Russia, at a time when the general mood was overwhelmingly 'democratic'. This very much helped the Bolsheviks at a decisive moment, rendering plausible their slogan 'all power to the Soviets'.[48]

We should note once more the closeness of the sociopolitical concept of 'democracy' to the meaning of the *narod* as the toiling masses. In this sense, the 'social meaning' of democracy had deep roots in a Russian political and societal discourse, which long pre-dated the revolutionary year of 1917. Within the increasingly polarized environment of the new Russian 'democracy', the possible discriminating political implications of this concept became acute. The Bolsheviks were inspired in the first place by Marx, but their success presupposed an environment where their ideas were compatible with certain currents and traditions of thought, and therefore seemed reasonable and understandable to many. In a context where even the liberal Constitutional Democrats were ready to accept that the term 'people' (*narod*) was to be equated with peasants and workers only (thereby largely excluding themselves from it), Lenin's slogans of 'dictatorship of the proletariat' (as equivalent to socialist democracy) and 'all power to the Soviets' (as democratic bodies both constituted and elected by workers and peasants) acquired some plausibility.

Conclusion

When Russian liberals, socialists and conservatives started to discuss democracy in the nineteenth century, they borrowed the concept largely from Western (liberal) thinkers and Western practices. Around the turn of the twentieth century, the Russian 'new liberals', in contrast to the first generation of Russian liberals, stressed the importance of 'social justice' ensured by the state, and by doing so came close to a concept of a democratic state that was also acceptable to a majority of Social Democrats. This was not the case for Lenin and his followers, but for the time being they were just one, rather small, faction within the socialist camp. However, the most important phase for pluralistic debate on democracy in Russia only began in 1905.

The Revolution of 1905 promoted debates on democracy in two respects: with the virtual breakdown of censorship in the metropolises, these debates were now possible in public without restraint and, for the first time in history, the transformation of Russia into a democratic state appeared, to many, to be a real possibility. The resulting debates on the nature and definition of democracy and on the elements that were to be regarded as essential for a democratic state were largely dominated by Russian democrats. These debates were, like most political debates in Russia at the time, informed by Western European reference models.[49] It is thus hardly surprising that the institutional topics they discussed mostly sounded familiar from debates among democrats in Western European states, although the Russian liberal democrats went well beyond most Western European *practices* of their time in their demands for a strong unicameral parliament to be elected on the basis of universal suffrage. In contrast, the importance of the nationalities question in Russia and, even more so, the sociopolitical notion of the *narod* and of 'democracy' itself led to more specifically Russian traits in the debate on democracy. Not only Social Democrats, but also Kadets and other left-liberals postulated that a democratic government would have to primarily (if not exclusively) serve the *narod* and that democracy in Russia would have to be based on peasants and/or workers.

In the special context after the February Revolution of 1917, the broad acceptance of this definition of the 'people' and of the opposition between 'democracy' and the 'bourgeoisie' strengthened the credibility and status of the Soviets within the new dual power structure (consisting basically of the Petrograd Soviet and the Provisional Government) and thus lent some plausibility to the Bolsheviks' slogan 'all power to the Soviets'. In this sense, the Bolsheviks' upswing during 1917 had part of its roots in a concept of the 'people' that was accepted by liberal, conservative and socialist parties alike. Nonetheless, what the Bolsheviks established in Russia after their October coup had very little in common with concepts of 'democracy' as discussed and endorsed by Russian proponents of democracy – both liberals and a majority of socialists – between 1905 and 1917.

Benjamin Beuerle is a Research Fellow at the German Historical Institute Moscow. He has published articles on reform debates and politics in late imperial Russia, and is the author of *Russlands Westen: Westorientierung und Reformgesetzgebung im ausgehenden Zarenreich, 1905–1917* (2016). He is currently working on contemporary Russian environmental history and policy.

Notes

1. M. von Hagen, 'Freedom of the Press after 1861', in M. von Hagen (ed.), *Die russische Freiheit: Wege in ein paradoxes Thema* (Stuttgart: Steiner, 2002), 104–10.
2. T.E. Griaznova, *Idea demokratii v Rossiiskoi liberal'noi pravovoi mysli vtoroi poloviny XIX – pervoi poloviny XX veka*. Summary of dissertation [Avtoreferat dissertatsii na soiskanie uchenoi stepeni doktora iuridicheskikh nauk] (Nizhnii Novgorod [Nizhegor. akad. MVD Rossii], 2010), 18–24; N.V. Deeva, *Evoliutsiia kontseptsii demokratii v Rossiiskoi politicheskoi mysli kontsa XIX – pervoi chetverti XX veka (liberal'noe, konserativnoe i sotsial-demokraticheskoe napravleniia)*. Summary of dissertation [Avtoreferat dissertatsii na soiskanie uchenoi stepeni kandidata politicheskikh nauk] (Moscow [MPGU], 2006), 9–10, 13.
3. See below under the heading 'One Word, Two Meanings'.
4. Deeva, *Evoliutsiia*, 13–17.
5. For short articles on the history of the three mentioned parties, see I. Rozental', 'Rossiiskaia Sotsial-Demokraticheskaia Rabochaia Partiia (RSDRP)', in V. Shelokhaev (ed.), *Politicheskie partii Rossii. Konets XIX – pervaia tret' XX veka* (Moscow: ROSSPEN, 1996), 516–19; N. Kanishcheva, 'Konstitutsionno-Demokraticheskaia Partiia', in Shelokhaev, *Politicheskie partii*, 267–73; N. Khailova, 'Partiia Demokraticheskikh Reform', in Shelokhaev, *Politicheskie partii*, 418–19.
6. See R. Pipes, *Die russische Revolution*, vol. 1, *Der Zerfall des Zarenreiches* (Berlin: Rowohlt, 1992), 109–10, 246–70; A. Ascher, *The Revolution of 1905: Authority Restored* (Stanford: Stanford University Press, 1992), 50–53; R.A. Wade, *The Russian Revolution, 1917* (Cambridge: Cambridge University Press, 2000), 53–86.
7. Pipes, *Revolution*, 319–21; V. Demin, 'Chetvertaia Gosudarstvennaia Duma', in V. Shelokhaev (ed.), *Gosudarstvennaia Duma Rossiiskoi Imperii 1906–1917. Entsiklopediia* (Moscow: ROSSPEN, 2008), 676–79; D. Rawson, *Russian Rightists and the Revolution of 1905* (Cambridge: Cambridge University Press, 1995), 142–51.
8. R. Wortman, *Scenarios of Power. From Alexander II to the Abdication of Nicholas II* (Princeton: Princeton University Press, 2000), 13–14, 365–66, 390, 396–97,

490; F. Wcislo, *Reforming Rural Russia: State, Local Society, and National Politics, 1855–1914* (Princeton: Princeton University Press, 1990), 142–46; cf. Deeva, *Evoliutsiia*, 15.
9. See e.g. 'Narod', in *Bol'shaia entsiklopediia. Slovar' obshchedostupnykh svedenii* ..., vol. 13, *Melaneziitsy – Nerchinskii zavod* (St Petersburg: 'Prosveshchenie', 1903), 661.
10. A. Verner, *The Crisis of Russian Autocracy: Nicholas II and the 1905 Revolution* (Princeton: Princeton University Press, 1990), 89–91; Rawson, *Russian Rightists*, 56–72.
11. See e.g. V.N. L'vov, *Programmnyia rechi i stat'i v Samarskom Otdele Soiuza 17 Oktiabria* (Moscow: t-va skoropech. A.A. Levenson, 1907), 20, 25; cf. E. Birth, *Die Oktobristen (1905–1913). Zielvorstellungen und Struktur* (Stuttgart: Klett, 1974), 148. For a clear repudiation of any 'Western' (and especially the English) form of government, see 'Razboiniki na zakonom osnovanii', *Za Caria i Rodinu. Organ Soiuza Russkago Naroda. Odessa*, N° 50, 5 April 1907.
12. L. Tikhomirov, *Demokratiia liberal'naia i sotsial'naia* (Moscow: Univ. tipogr., 1896); see GARF (= State Archive of the Russian Federation, Moscow) F. 102, dp-4, 1908g., op. 117, d. 251, ll. 107ob, 170.
13. On Ger'e, see D. Pavlov, 'Vladimir Ivanovich Ger'e', in Shelokhaev, *Politicheskie partii*, 151–52; on his party, see D. Pavlov, 'The Union of October 17', in A. Geifman (ed.), *Russia under the Last Tsar: Opposition and Subversion 1894–1917* (Oxford: Blackwell, 1999), 179–98.
14. V.I. Ger'e, *Chego zhe khochet Konstitutsionno-Demokraticheskaia Partija? Ot Soiuza 17 Oktiabria* (Moscow: t-vo 'Pechatnia S.P. Iakovleva', 1906), 6–7; V.I. Ger'e, *O konstitutsii i parlamentarizm v Rossii* (Moscow: Tipogr. 'Russkogo golosa', 1906), 15–17, 31. Cf. Birth, *Oktobristen*, 104. On the Aristotelian concept of democracy and the 'mixed constitution', see the chapter by Henk te Velde in the present volume.
15. V. Vodovozov, *Proportsional'nye vybory ili Predstavitel'stvo Men'shinstva* (St Petersburg: A.K. Veierman, 1905), 10; M. Ostrogorskii, 'Konstitutsionnaia evoliutsiia Anglii (v techenie posledniago poluveka). IV.: Apoteoz monarkhii i torzhestvo demokratii', *Vestnik Evropy* 48(11) (1913), 169–70; *Napadki na Partiiu Narodnoi Svobody i vozrazheniia na nikh*. Pod redaktsiei A.A. Kizevettera (Moscow: Tipogr. G. Lessnera i D. Sobko, 1906), 10.
16. L.V. Shalland, 'Voprosy izbiratel'nago prava', *Pravo (ezhenedel'naia iuridicheskaia gazeta)* (1905), 3139; A.S. Belevskii, *Zemel'nyi vopros i natsionalizatsiia zemli* (Moscow: izd. E.V. Kozhevnikova i E.A. Kolomiitseva, 1906), 9; V. Gessen, 'O dvupalatnoi sisteme', *Pravo* (1906), 1730, 2524–25. On Shalland, see 'Lev Adamirovich Shalland', in *Entsiklopedicheskii slovar'. Dopolnitelnyi tom IIa: Prussiia – Foma. Rossiia* (St Petersburg: Brokgauz-Efron, 1907), 877; on Gessen, see I. Narskii, 'Vladimir Matveevich Gessen', in Shelokhaev, *Politicheskie partii*, 152.
17. V. V., 'Demokratiia', in *Novyi entsiklopedicheskii slovar'*, vol. 15, *Grivna – Desmurgiia* (St Petersburg: Brokgauz-Efron, 1913), 849–51; A. Dzhivelegov, 'Demokratiia', in *Entsiklopedicheskii slovar' t-va 'Br. A. i I. Granat i Ko'*. 7th

completely revised edition, vol. 18, *Darvin–Dorokhov* (Moscow: A. i I. Granat, 1913), 208–15.
18. Cf. O. Figes and B. Kolonitskii, *Interpreting the Russian Revolution: The Language and Symbols of 1917* (New Haven: Yale University Press, 1999), 122. Notably, the sociopolitical concept of democracy appeared neither in the *Encyclopaedia Britannica* of 1910 nor in German encyclopaedias of this time: *The Encyclopaedia Britannica*, 11th ed., vol. 8, *Demijohn to Edward* (Cambridge: Cambridge University Press, 1910), 1–2; *Brockhaus' Conversations-Lexikon*, 13. vollst. überarb. Aufl., Bd. 5: *Deidesheim–Elektra* (Leipzig: Brockhaus, 1883), 41–43; *Meyers Konversations-Lexikon. Ein Nachschlagewerk des allgemeinen Wissens.* Fünfte, gänzlich neubearb. Aufl. Bd. 4: *Chemillé bis Dingelstedt* (Leipzig: Bibliograph. Inst., 1897), 725–26.
19. Ibid.; V. V., 'Demokratiia'; Dzhivelegov, 'Demokratiia'.
20. Ibid.
21. Deeva, *Evoliutsiia*, 9–10, 16–17; V. I. Lenin, *O sovetskoi sotsialisticheskoi demokratii*, 2nd revised edn. (Moscow: Izd-vo Politicheskoi Literatury, 1967), 16–17; cf. D. Priestland, 'Soviet Democracy, 1917–1991', *European History Quarterly* 32(1) (2002), 114–16; R. Miliband, 'Dictatorship of the Proletariat', in T. Bottomore (ed.), *A Dictionary of Marxist Thought*, 2nd edn. (Oxford: Blackwell, 1991), 151–52.
22. Gosudarstvennaia Duma, Convocation III, Session 4, *Stenograficheskie otchety*, vol. 3 (St Petersburg: Gosud. Tipogr., 1911), 2593–94, 2706–09; Gosudarstvennaia Duma, Convocation III, Session 5, *Stenograficheskie Otchety*, vol. 1 (St Petersburg: Gosud. Tipogr., 1911), 1391–93, 1399; *Protokoly III Obshcheimperskago Delegatskago S"ezda Partii Narodnoi Svobody (Konstitutsionno-Demokraticheskoi)* (St Petersburg: Sekretariat TsK Partii Narodnoi Svobody, 1906), 118.
23. Kizevetter (ed.), *Napadki na Partiiu*, 9; Gosudarstvennaia Duma, Convocation I, *Stenograficheskie otchety* (St Petersburg: Gosud. Tipogr., 1906), 722–25; see also Kokoshkin's speech at the Constitutional Democrats' Second Party Convention, in V.V. Shelokhaev et al. (eds), *S"ezdy i konferentsii konstitutsionno-demokraticheskoi partii 1905–1920 gg.*, vol. 1: *1905–1907 gg.* (Moscow: ROSSPEN, 1997), 154.
24. See Peter Bugge's chapter in this volume; for the Polish case, see B.A. Porter, 'Democracy and Discipline in Late Nineteenth-Century Poland', *Journal of Modern History* 71(2) (1999), 346–93.
25. Gosudarstvennaia Duma, Convocation I, *Stenograficheskie otchety*, 1006–7; Gosudarstvennaia Duma, Convocation II, *Stenograficheskie otchety*, vol. 1 (St Petersburg: Gosud. Tipogr., 1907), 167. On Kokoshkin and Tigranian, see N. Kanishcheva, 'Fedor Fedorovich Kokoshkin', in Shelokhaev, *Politicheskie partii*, 257–58; L.G. Protasov, 'Sirakan Faddeevich Tigranian', in Shelokhaev, *Gosudarstvennaia Duma*, 610.
26. Vodovozov, *Proportsional'nye vybory*, 1–7; Shalland, 'Voprosy'; P. S., 'O vseobshchem izbiratel'nom prave v russkikh usloviiakh', *Pravo* (1905), 2028–29. On Struve, see N. Kazakova et al., 'Petr Berngardovich Struve', in Shelokhaev, *Politicheskie partii*, 596–97.

27. I. Osipov, 'Izbiratel'noe pravo v Germanskoi Imperii i v otdel'nykh eia gosudarstvakh', *Vestnik Evropy* 40(6) (1905), 572–75; N.A. Kabanov, *Gosudarstvennoe ustroistvo v Zapadno-evropeiskikh Stranakh* (Rostov-na-Donu: 'Donskaia Rech', 1906), 22, 25; N. B., 'Voznagrazhdenie chlenov Gosudarstvennoi Dumy', *Rech'*, 27 March 1906, 4.
28. Osipov, 'Izbiratel'noe pravo', 569; Vserossiiskii Soiuz uchitelei i deiatelei po narodnomu obrazovaniiu (ed.), *Protokoly III-go delegatskago s"ezda vserossiiskago soiuza ..., 7–10 iiunia 1906 g.* ([n.p.], 1906), 99–100. Cf. on this subject A. Ascher, *The Revolution of 1905: Russia in Dissaray* (Stanford: Stanford University Press, 1988), 193–94, 236; B. Pietrow-Ennker, *Rußlands 'neue Menschen'. Die Entwicklung der Frauenbewegung von den Anfängen bis zur Oktoberrevolution* (Frankfurt am Main: Campus, 1999), 332–51; R. Stites, *The Women's Liberation Movement in Russia. Feminism, Nihilism, and Bolshevism, 1860–1930*, 2nd ed. (Princeton: Princeton University Press, 1991), 198–222.
29. See Ascher, *Revolution* (1988), 226–30; A. Korros, *A Reluctant Parliament: Stolypin, Nationalism, and the Politics of the Russian Imperial State Council, 1906–1911* (Lanham, MD: Rowman & Littlefield, 2002), 13–36; Ascher, *Revolution* (1992), 58–60, 94–95.
30. Vladimir Gessen, 'Russkaia Konstitutsiia. II. Gosudarstvennyi Sovet', *Rech'*, 27 February 1906, 1; Gessen, 'O dvupalatnoi sisteme'.
31. See e.g. Kabanov, *Gosudarstvennoe ustroistvo*, 16–18.
32. Kizevetter (ed.), *Napadki na Partiiu*, 12–20.
33. For analogous (although not identical) discussions on suffrage and (to a lesser extent) on the legislature in other European contexts, see e.g. the chapters by Innes and Philp, te Velde, Bugge, Fernández-Sebastián and Rosales, and Ihalainen in this volume. For its part, the subject of multinationality within one country or empire also plays a role in the chapter by Peter Bugge, dealing with the Habsburg and (then) Czechoslovak case.
34. The differences compared to the Czech case as described by Bugge in this volume are obvious.
35. G.F. Shershenevich, *Programma Partii Narodnoi Svobody (Konstitutsionno-Demokraticheskoi)*, 2nd ed. (Moscow: Nar. pravo, 1906), 20–21.
36. Gosudarstvennaia Duma I, *Stenograficheskie otchety*, 458; the leftist deputies' declaration is printed in V.I. Charnoluskii (ed.), *K shkol'noi reforme* (Moscow: T-vo I. D. Sytina, 1908), 15–17. On Petrazhitskii, see Shelokhaev, *Gosudarstvennaia Duma*, 455.
37. *Avtonomiia, federatsiia i natstional'nyi vopros*, pod redaktsiei Vl. M. Gessena (St Petersburg: 'Obshchestvennaia pol'za', 1906), 2–9.
38. V. Vodovozov, 'Natsional'nyi vopros', in *Novyi entsiklopedicheskii slovar'*, vol. 28: *Narushevich–N'iuton* (Petrograd: Brokgauz-Efron, 1916), 108–12.
39. V. Vodovozov, 'Vseobshchee izbiratel'noe pravo i primenenie ego k Rossii', *Pravo* (1905), 2440.
40. For examples for the use of the word 'democracy' as a synonym for the Russian state after February 1917, see e.g. I.G. Kordo, *Reforma narodnago obrazovaniia v*

svobodnoi Rossii. Doklad ... (Moscow: 'Rus. t-va izd. Dela', 1917), 4; GARF, F. 1803, op. 1, d. 12, l. 297; on the 'Messianism' of Russian democrats after February 1917, cf. B.I. Kolonitskii, '"Democracy" in the Political Consciousness of the February Revolution', *Slavic Review* 57(1) (1998), 97–99.
41. V.O. Belorussov, 'Molodaia Frantsuzskaia Demokratiia. Pis'mo iz Parizha', *Vestnik Evropy* 46(4) (1911), 290–91, 300–1.
42. RGIA (= Russian State Historical Archive, St. Petersburg) F. 733, op. 184, d. 280, l. 21ob; Kordo, *Reforma*, 4–5; RGIA, F. 733, op. 184, d. 281, l. 7; see also GARF, F. 1803, op. 1, d. 12, ll. 9–10.
43. GARF, F. 1803, op. 1, d. 12, ll. 303ob–4.
44. A. Iashchenko, *Kakiia natsional'nyia trebovaniia spravedlivy?* (Petrograd: kruzhok 'Druz'ia svobody', 1917), 14.
45. S.T. Kechek'ian, *Natsional'nyi vopros na zapade i v Rossii* (Moscow: D. Ia. Makovskii, 1917), 8–10.
46. S. Avaliani, *Natsional'nyi vopros v Rossii i ego reshenie v programmakh politicheskikh partii* (Petrograd: 'Blago', 1917), 9.
47. S. Semkovskii, *Natsional'nyi vopros v Rossii* (Petrograd: 'Kniga', [1917]), 7–9, 14, 21–22.
48. I.A. Zhdanova, *Sotsial'no-politicheskie predstavleniia o demokratii v Rossiiskoi periodicheskoj pechati marta – oktjabrja 1917 g.* Summary of dissertation [Avtoreferat dissertatsii na soiskanie uchenoi stepeni kandidata istoricheskikh nauk] (Moscow [RGGU], 2003), 14–15, 18–20; Kolonitskii, '"Democracy"', 96–97, 100–3; Figes and Kolonitskii, *Interpreting the Russian Revolution*, 122–26.
49. Cf. B. Beuerle, *Russlands Westen. Westorientierung und Reformgesetzgebung im ausgehenden Zarenreich, 1905–1917* (Wiesbaden: Harrassowitz, 2016).

Bibliography

1903. 'Narod', in *Bol'shaia Entsiklopediia. Slovar' Obshchedostupnykh Svedenii ...*, vol. 13, *Melaniziitskii – Nerchinskij zavod*. St Petersburg: 'Prosveshchenie', 661.
1907. 'Lev Adamirovich Shalland', in *Entsiklopedicheskii slovar'. Dopolnitelnyi tom IIa: Prussiia – Foma. Rossiia*. St Petersburg: Brokgauz-Efron, 877.
Ascher, A. 1988. *The Revolution of 1905: Russia in Dissaray*. Stanford: Stanford University Press.
———. *The Revolution of 1905: Authority Restored*. Stanford: Stanford University Press.
Avaliani, S. 1917. *Natsional'nyi Vopros v Rossii i Ego Reshenie v Programmakh Politicheskikh Partii*. Petrograd: 'Blago'.
Beuerle, B. 2016. *Russlands Westen: Westorientierung und Reformgesetzgebung im ausgehenden Zarenreich, 1905–1917*. Wiesbaden: Harrassowitz.
Belevskii, A.S. 1906. *Zemel'nyi Vopros i Natsionalizatsiia Zemli*. Moscow: izd. E.V. Kozhevnikova i E.A. Kolomiitseva.
Belorussov, V.O. 1911. 'Molodaia Frantsuzskaia Demokratiia. Pis'mo iz Parizha', *Vestnik Evropy* 46(4), 285–301.

Birth, E. 1974. *Die Oktobristen (1905–1913). Zielvorstellungen und Struktur.* Stuttgart: Klett.
Charnoluskii, V.I. (ed.). 1908. *K shkol'noi Reforme.* Moscow: T-vo I. D. Sytina.
Deeva, N.V. 2006. *Evoliutsiia Kontseptsii Demokratii v Rossiiskoi Politicheskoi Mysli Kontsa XIX – Pervoi Chetverti XX Veka (Liberal'noe Konserativnoe i Sotsialdemokraticheskoe Napravleniia).* Summary of dissertation [Avtoreferat dissertatsii na soiskanie uchenoi stepeni kandidata politicheskikh nauk], Moscow: MPGU.
Demin, V. 2008. 'Chetvertaia Gosudarstvennaia Duma', in V. Shelokhaev (ed.), *Gosudarstvennaia Duma Rossiiskoi Imperii 1906–1917. Entsiklopediia.* Moscow: ROSSPEN, 676–82.
Dzhivelegov, A. 2013. 'Demokratiia', in *Entsiklopedicheskii slovar' t-va 'Br. A. i I. Granat i Ko'.* 7th, completely revised edn., vol. 18: *Darvin–Dorokhov.* Moscow: A. i I. Granat, 208–15.
Figes, O., and B. Kolonitskii. 1999. *Interpreting the Russian Revolution: The Language and Symbols of 1917.* New Haven: Yale University Press.
Ger'e, V.I. 1906a. *Chego zhe Khochet Konstitutsionno-Demokraticheskaia Partiia? Ot Soiuza 17 Oktiabria.* Moscow: t-vo 'Pechatnia S. P. Iakovleva'.
———. 1906b. *O Konstitutsii i Parlamentarizm v Rossii.* Moscow: Tipogr. 'Russkogo golosa'.
Gessen, V. 1906a. 'O dvupalatnoi sisteme', *Pravo*, 1726–38.
———. 1906b. 'Russkaia Konstitutsiia. II. Gosudarstvennyi Sovet', *Rech'*.
Gessen, V.M. (ed.). 1906. *Avtonomiia, Federatsiia i Natstional'nyi Vopros.* St Petersburg: 'Obshchestvennaia pol'za'.
Gosudarstvennaia Duma [State Duma]. 1906. Convocation I. *Stenograficheskie otchety.* St Petersburg: Gosud. Tipogr.
———. 1907. Convocation II. *Stenograficheskie otchety*, vol. 1. St Petersburg: Gosud. Tipogr.
———. 1911a. Convocation III, Session 4. *Stenograficheskie otchety*, vol. 3. St Petersburg: Gosud. Tipogr.
———. 1911b. Convocation III, Session 5. *Stenograficheskie Otchety*, vol. 1. St Petersburg: Gosud. Tipogr.
Griaznova, T.E. 2010. *Idea demokratii v Rossiiskoi Liberal'noi Pravovoi Mysli Vtoroi Poloviny XIX – Pervoi Poloviny XX Veka.* Summary of dissertation [Avtoreferat dissertatsii na soiskanie uchenoi stepeni doktora iuridicheskikh nauk], Nizhnii Novgorod: Nizhegor. akad. MVD Rossii.
Hagen, M. von. 2002. 'Freedom of the Press after 1861', in M. von Hagen (ed.), *Die russische Freiheit. Wege in ein Paradoxes Thema.* Stuttgart: Steiner, 98–113.
Iashchenko, A. 1917. *Kakiia Natsional'nyia Trebovaniia Spravedlivy?* Petrograd: kruzhok 'Druz'ia svobody'.
Kabanov, N.A. 1906. *Gosudarstvennoe Ustroistvo v Zapadno-evropeiskikh Stranakh.* Rostov-na-Donu: 'Donskaia Rech'.
Kanishcheva, N. 1996a. 'Fedor Fedorovich Kokoshkin', in V. Shelokhaev (ed.), *Politicheskie Partii Rossii. Konets XIX – Pervaia Tret' XX veka.* Moscow: ROSSPEN, 257–58.

———. 1996b. 'Konstitutsionno-Demokraticheskaia Partiia', in Shelokhaev, *Politicheskie partii*, 267–73.
Kazakova, N. et al. 1996. 'Petr Berngardovich Struve', in Shelokhaev, *Politicheskie partii*, 596–97.
Kechek'ian, S.T. 1917. *Natsional'nyi Vopros na Zapade i v Rossii*. Moscow: D. Ia. Makovskii.
Khailova, N. 1996. 'Partiia Demokraticheskikh Reform', in Shelokhaev, *Politicheskie partii*, 418–19.
Kizevetter, A.A. (ed.). 1906. *Napadki na Partiiu Narodnoi Svobody i Vozrazheniia na Nikh*. Moscow: Tipogr. G. Lessnera i D. Sobko.
Kolonitskii, B.I. 1998. '"Democracy" in the Political Consciousness of the February Revolution', *Slavic Review* 57(1), 95–106.
Konstitutsionno-Demokraticheskaia Partiia. 1906. *Protokoly III Obshcheimperskago Delegatskago S"ezda Partii Narodnoi Svobody (Konstitutsionno-Demokraticheskoi)*. St Petersburg: Sekretariat TsK Partii Narodnoi Svobody.
Kordo, Ia.G. 1917. *Reforma Narodnago Obrazovaniia v Svobodnoi Rossii. Doklad ...* Moscow: 'Rus. t-va izd. Dela'.
Korros, A. 2002. *A Reluctant Parliament: Stolypin, Nationalism, and the Politics of the Russian Imperial State Council, 1906–1911*. Lanham, MD: Rowman & Littlefield.
Lenin, V.I. 1967. *O Sovetskoi Sotsialisticheskoi Demokratii*, 2nd revised edn. Moscow: Izd-vo Politicheskoi Literatury.
L'vov, V.N. 1907. *Programmnyia Rechi i Stat'i v Samarskom Otdele Soiuza 17 Oktiabria*. Moscow: t-va skoropech. A.A. Levenson.
Miliband, R. 1991. 'Dictatorship of the Proletariat', in T. Bottomore (ed.), *A Dictionary of Marxist Thought*, 2nd ed. Oxford: Blackwell, 151–52.
N. B. 1906. 'Voznagrazhdenie chlenov Gosudarstvennoi Dumy'. *Rech'*, 27 March 1906, 4.
Narskii, I. 1996. 'Vladimir Matveevich Gessen', in Shelokhaev, *Politicheskie partii*, 152.
Osipov, I. 1905. 'Izbiratel'noe pravo v Germanskoi Imperii i v otdel'nykh eia gosudarstvakh', *Vestnik Evropy* 40(6), 567–89.
Ostrogorskii, M. 1913. 'Konstitutsionnaia evoliutsiia Anglii (v techenie posledniago poluveka). IV.: Apoteoz monarkhii i torzhestvo demokratii', *Vestnik Evropy* 48(11), 153–70.
Pavlov, D. 1996. 'Vladimir Ivanovich Ger'e', in Shelokhaev, *Politicheskie partii*, 151–52.
———. 1999. 'The Union of October 17', in A. Geifman (ed.), *Russia under the Last Tsar: Opposition and Subversion 1894–1917*, Oxford: Blackwell, 1999, 179–98.
Pietrow-Ennker, B. 1999. *Rußlands 'neue Menschen': Die Entwicklung der Frauenbewegung von den Anfängen bis zur Oktoberrevolution*. Frankfurt am Main: Campus.
Pipes, R. 1992. *Die russische Revolution*, vol. 1, *Der Zerfall des Zarenreiches*. Berlin: Rowohlt.
Priestland, D. 2002. 'Soviet Democracy, 1917–1991', *European History Quarterly* 32(1), 114–16.

Protasov, L.G. 1996. 'Sirakan Faddeevich Tigranian', in Shelokhaev, *Gosudarstvennaia Duma*, 610.
Rawson, D. 1995. *Russian Rightists and the Revolution of 1905*. Cambridge: Cambridge University Press.
Rozental', I. 1996. 'Rossiiskaia Sotsial-Demokraticheskaia Rabochaia Partiia (RSDRP)', in Shelokhaev, *Politicheskie partii*, 516–19.
Semkovskii, S. 1917. *Natsional'nyi vopros v Rossii*. Petrograd: 'Kniga'.
Shalland, L.V. 1905. 'Voprosy izbiratel'nago prava', *Pravo (ezhenedel'naia iuridicheskaia gazeta)*, 1460–68, 1551–59, 1651–58, 2302–12, 3007–17, 3135–42.
Shelokhaev, V. (ed.). 1996. *Politicheskie partii Rossii. Konets XIX – pervaia tret' XX veka*. Moscow: ROSSPEN.
———. 2008. *Gosudarstvennaia Duma Rossiiskoi Imperii 1906–1917. Entsiklopediia*. Moscow: ROSSPEN.
Shelokhaev, V.V. et al. (eds). 1997. *S"ezdy i Konferentsii Konstitutsionno-demokraticheskoi Partii 1905–1920 gg.*, vol. 1, *1905–1907 gg*. Moscow: ROSSPEN.
Shershenevich, G.F. 1906. *Programma Partii Narodnoi Svobody (Konstitutsionno-Demokraticheskoi)*. 2nd edn., Moscow: 'Nar. pravo'.
Stites, R. 1991. *The Women's Liberation Movement in Russia: Feminism, Nihilism, and Bolshevism, 1860–1930*, 2nd ed. Princeton: Princeton University Press.
Struve, P. 1905. 'O Vseobshchem Izbiratel'nom Prave v Russkikh Usloviiakh', *Pravo*, 2028–34.
Tikhomirov, L. 1896. *Demokratiia Liberal'naia i Sotsial'naia*. Moscow: Univ. tipogr.
Verner, A. 1990. *The Crisis of Russian Autocracy: Nicholas II and the 1905 Revolution*. Princeton: Princeton University Press.
Vodovozov, V. 1905. *Proportsional'nye Vybory ili Predstavitel'stvo Men'shinstvo*. St Petersburg: A.K. Veierman.
———. 1905b. 'Vseobshchee Izbiratel'noe Pravo i Primenenie Ego k Rossii', *Pravo*, 2432–45, 2570–78, 2782–90.
———. 1913. 'Demokratiia', in *Novyi entsiklopedicheskii slovar'*, vol. 15, *Grivna – Desmurgiia*. St Petersburg: Brokgauz-Efro, 849–51.
———. 1916. 'Natsional'nyi vopros', in *Novyi entsiklopedicheskii slovar'*, vol. 28, *Narushevich–N'iuton*. Petrograd: Brokgauz-Efron, 108–12.
Vserossiiskii Soiuz uchitelei i deiatelei po narodnomu obrazovaniiu (ed). 1906. *Protokoly III-go delegatskago s"ezda vserossiiskago soiuza …, 7–10 iiunia 1906 g*. [n.p.].
Wade, R.A. 2000. *The Russian Revolution, 1917*. Cambridge: Cambridge University Press.
Wcislo, F. 1990. *Reforming Rural Russia: State Local Society and National Politics 1855–1914*. Princeton: Princeton University Press.
Wortman, R. 2000. *Scenarios of Power: From Alexander II to the Abdication of Nicholas II*. Princeton: Princeton University Press.
Zhdanova, I.A. 2003. *Sotsial'no-politicheskie Predstavleniia o Demokratii v Rossiiskoi Periodicheskoi Pechati Marta – Oktjabria 1917 g*. Summary of dissertation [Avtoreferat dissertatsii na soiskanie uchenoi stepeni kandidata istoricheskikh nauk], Moscow [RGGU].

Chapter 6

A Conceptual History of Democracy in Spain since 1800

Javier Fernández-Sebastián and José María Rosales

This chapter presents a conceptual history of 'democracy' in Spain from the nineteenth century to the early 1980s, the time marking the end of the transition to a democratic regime begun in 1976. It surveys the semantic changes the concept of democracy underwent from its original, pejorative meaning in the first decades of the nineteenth century, denoting a political ideal opposing liberalism, to its recast sense identifying with a political party and then a programme of government since the 1850s. Its later history unearths a stunning semantic broadening – the adjective 'democratic' expanding to qualify a distinct type of society, party and regime. And so, in spite of the institutional gains achieved through the mid 1870s, the idea of democracy fell into disrepute. A new regime adopted a liberal constitution in 1876, which lasted for almost fifty years.

After decades of scant use, the concept slowly gained scholarly and public prominence at the turn of the twentieth century and by the 1930s designated a fully fledged political ideology, shared by parties from left and right. Over the next four decades, it became rudely distorted to make it describe the Franco dictatorship as an 'organic democracy', argued as an alternative model to the parliamentary democracies of the time. In the path towards regime change, since the second half of the 1970s, 'democracy' denoted a liberal, parliamentary political system.

From then on, democracy not only signified a political regime, but above all the pluralist political culture inspiring it – the vocabulary of civic rights and freedoms informing the new language of politics. Because of its rhetorical capacity, the concept was used as an argumentative means to critically assess the governments of the day, but it was also questioned as an evaluative resource itself. Its semantic contestability became especially apparent during the following decades in the opposition raised between the ideas, or models, of representative and participatory democracy. Such tension was reflected in the language of democracy, gradually wielded as a militant token of a new political culture.

The Democratic Beginning

Many nineteenth-century historians and politicians agreed that 1808 marked the beginning of modern democracy in Spain. In the spring of that year, while the monarchic state was collapsing and the elites were preparing to collaborate with the usurper, Joseph I Bonaparte, the people, bereft of leaders, rose up *en masse* against the Napoleonic occupation and created from the bottom up emergency institutions in order to coordinate the resistance. Newly appointed councils made way for a 'democratic' *Cortes* (parliament representing the people). Once the *Cortes* was summoned in Cadiz, in September 1810, the parliamentary debates brought to light diverse manners of understanding the word democracy. Whilst for the royalists, democracy at that juncture simply meant 'Cortes sin estamentos' (unicameral parliament, without estates), at one point the discussion revolved around whether monarchy and democracy might be reconciled or whether they remained as incompatible as 'fire and water,' as the cleric Inguanzo claimed.[1] Arguably, the Cadiz charter was understood – first by its enemies and later by almost everybody – as a democratic constitution.

Describing the 1812 Constitution as 'democratic' would become a habit in Spain and abroad, particularly after the Liberal Triennium of 1820–23. Indeed, during the 1820s and 1830s, support for, or rejection of, this constitutional text was sufficient to distinguish between left- and right-wing European liberals. Thus, for a German observer, the 1812 Constitution was regarded as either a threat, if they were a conservative liberal, or a worthy combination of monarchy and democracy, allowing the latter a greater weight, if they belonged to the minority of liberal democrats.[2] Meanwhile, the leaders of the emancipation of Spanish America spoke little of democracy. More frequent in their speeches were invocations to 'representative popular government' or even to the old ideal of 'tempered monarchy' or mixed constitution, a model that had been strongly recommended by several second-scholastic theologians and jurists since the sixteenth century and that persisted for several decades in the newly independent countries.

In the meantime, the idea of representative democracy, which initially sounded like an oxymoron, gradually spread through the Iberian world. After 1810, a number of political catechisms, circulating in places as far apart as Spain and Chile, already admitted that in democratic government, sovereignty could reside in the representatives of the people and not necessarily in the people itself.[3] From 1820 onwards, however, several liberal publicists underlined the advantages of representative government and compared it with the turbulence of pure democracy, arguing that in the former, 'the exercise of sovereignty resides not in the nation, but in the persons to whom the nation has been delegated'.[4]

In the European context, the Spanish case was surprisingly precocious in the use of democratic discourse. It is not easy to explain the underlying reasons for the relatively early upsurge in the use of language of this type, but it is possible to point out some peninsular traditions that may have fertilized the flowering of this language. The medieval roots of social egalitarianism, including the old institution of the *concejo abierto* (open council) from the times of the Reconquest, revived in 1808, and interclass relations, which were seemingly plainer and freer than in other countries, are not the only factors to be borne in mind. Although there were also widespread anti-aristocratic attitudes in early modern Spain, from the Catholic Monarchs to the Elightenment kings of the eighteenth century, there is no mistaking the alliance between the crown and some popular sectors, including the lowest ranks of the nobility, against the grandees. But what strikes us as the most decisive and singularly Spanish factor in the first half of the nineteenth century is the stunning emergence of the people as a political actor in the crisis of the Monarchy in 1808. The abdications of Bayonne, forced by Napoleon, which transferred the Spanish crown from the Bourbons to his brother Joseph, were totally rejected by the Spanish population. The vast majority continued to regard the 'captive king' Ferdinand VII as their legitimate monarch, branding Joseph Bonaparte a usurper. In the absence of the political head of the kingdom (*vacatio regis*) and given the unwillingness of the Frenchified elites to fulfil their role as leaders of the patriotic movement, it was people at large who took the initiative. Their sudden emergence on the political scene was described by various observers as a genuine 'apotheosis of democracy', a kind of de facto 'plebeian democracy'.[5]

The fact that the *juntas* (councils) assumed control in practice was supported by some legal traditions deeply rooted in the culture, including scholastic theories of *consensus populi* and of the reversion of sovereignty, which theoretically permitted the people to take action in such circumstances. Consequently, as Donoso Cortés noted, if the 1812 Constitution was understood as democratic, it was largely due to the unusual leading role of the people in the uprising against the Napoleonic army, followed by the ruthless war that served to erode social differences.[6] Unlike other continental countries in Napoleon's grip, Spain never submitted to the French invaders. Later on, the prominent role of the guerrillas and the poorer classes during the war was inevitably translated into a mythification of the people that probably rendered the concept of democracy more acceptable than in other places.

In this respect, the considerable impact of the *Nuevo vocabulario filosófico-democrático* in the Hispanic world is quite revealing. Written in Italy during the Jacobin triennium (1796–99) by the Jesuit Thjulen, it reached a wide readership in the Spanish-speaking world because the word 'democracy' and its derivatives had attained certain positive connotations that they lacked in other countries. For this reason, the counter-revolutionary groups were particularly zealous in their condemnation of a language that they regarded as especially dangerous.[7]

When the Tocquevillian sense of democracy spread from the 1830s onwards, understood as the trend in modern societies towards equal conditions, there was a clear re-emergence of the old idea that Spanish society had been fundamentally democratic since time immemorial. In both political literature and works of fiction, the members of the incipient democratic party would argue time and time again that, on account of both its customs and its idiosyncrasies, 'the Spanish people is one of the most democratic peoples in Europe', in contrast to a small elite perceived as oligarchic and foreign-centred.[8]

Democracy or Liberalism (1833–49)

After the death of Ferdinand VII in 1833, the term 'democracy' was employed again in political debates and newspapers. Transcending both learned circles and revolutionary milieux, it would soon become a protean, polysemic and controversial word, used even by centrist political sectors. Following the French *doctrinaires*, their Spanish counterparts understood democracy as an essential feature of modern societies, characterized by a moderate egalitarianism that would gradually bridge the gap separating the middle classes from the aristocracy.

Most social and political actors used the word 'democracy'. An analysis of the parliamentary minutes from the period 1834–45 reveals that, depending on the circumstances and the rhetorical tactics employed, a speaker might use the term in different ways and with divergent meanings. For example, the liberal-conservative MP Alcalá Galiano repeatedly condemned democracy, understood as mob rule. Both in his *Lectures on Public Law* and in his parliamentary speeches, he established a contrast between 'true liberalism', typical of the educated middle classes, and the 'brutal democracy', which resulted from the power of the crowds. He also advocated a transformation of the old Spanish democratic monarchy into a 'mesocratic' monarchy. But on other occasions he praised 'democracy', equating it with representative government of the middle classes.[9] Another MP, Armendáriz, claimed that in fact 'the most liberal government is absolute democracy'.[10]

Writers and politicians claimed that Spanish society was fundamentally egalitarian and that it had been so since time immemorial. This idea was confirmed by several foreign observers. For example, Georges Villiers, the British Ambassador to Spain during the first Carlist War, wrote in a letter to his brother Edward in 1835 that the Spanish nation, unsuited to a liberal regime, was, however, the freest nation in Europe. Villiers insisted upon the profoundly democratic nature of the Spaniards: there were no barriers between classes, and every position and honour was open to one and all.[11] Much of the literature on this subject explores the country's past in search of clues for this 'anomaly'. Spain has been a basically democratic society since the Middle Ages, we read in these sources, because as a result of the lengthy struggles against the Muslims on the peninsula, there was no real feudalism. It was a considerably weakened aristocracy that emerged from that experience, and local government had been open since ancient times to very broad popular participation.

While the discussion on democracy took place in the political sphere in the first two constitutional periods (1812–14 and 1820–23), many of the debates on democracy moved towards a 'sociological' terrain in the 1830s. In the first three decades of the nineteenth century, the dividing lines in this semantic field were mainly monarchy versus democracy, or democracy versus representation, whereas the strongest tension lay between democracy and aristocracy in the 1830s and 1840s. In a context of discussion that was increasingly international, with references to France and England, debates in the *Cortes* and the press over the extension of suffrage frequently adopted the language of class conflict.

Another inexhaustible source of egalitarian arguments was religion. Both moderate and progressive authors repeatedly noted that, before being incorporated into the vocabulary of politics, concepts such as equality, liberty and fraternity were originally 'gospel maxims'.[12] And many underscored that the clergy was 'largely recruited from among the lower classes of the population', and therefore the Catholic Church – an institution open to talent and merit – had acted for centuries as an instrument of social democratization.[13]

In the 1840s, both conservative and progressivist liberals acknowledged that the 'great ideas of equality, fraternity and common law are gaining ground everywhere, [and] aristocratic institutions are disappearing from the face of the earth'.[14] It was therefore necessary, they argued, to incorporate 'the democratic principle' into institutions. After all, as they held, the Spanish monarchy had throughout the ages been the most democratic in the world.¹⁵ Such statements, frequent in political debates as well as in literature and historiography, were based not only on the conviction that the kings of Spain had historically protected the weak and disadvantaged from the rich and powerful, but above all on the supposed 'democratic' idiosyncrasy of the Spaniards and their simple and egalitarian customs compared with the rigidity and social classism of other European peoples.¹⁶

In 1843, a manifesto entitled 'The Democratic Party to Voters', whose authors introduced themselves as 'passionate defenders of freedom' and of the 'principle of popular sovereignty declared by the nation in September 1810', called upon its supporters to vote.¹⁷ These self-proclaimed 'democrats' employed a new language, different from that of the 'old parties'. Acknowledging that their ideas were not yet very popular, they stressed the need to better guarantee the 'rights of the people'. Given that, paradoxically, most of the population did not subscribe to the principle of popular sovereignty, they sought to persuade people with reason, ruling out any recourse to violence and insurrection.¹⁸ Even though this attempt to establish an electoral 'democratic party' was not successful, it inspired the drafting of the 1849 democratic programme.

Democracy as Political Party and Government Programme (1849–56)

The events of early 1848 in France quickly affected Spain. For the more progressive groups, a horizon of hope arose, encouraging the dissemination of democratic ideas under the impetus of what was happening in Europe. For the traditionalists, declared enemies of such ideas, the events of 1848 confirmed that all liberalisms, from the conservative to the progressivist, eventually led to democracy. In this regard, Guizot's *De la démocratie en France* (1849) contributed to the sensation that democracy had become a threat on an international scale. It had an enormous impact in Spain. In the same year two Spanish translations appeared, in Mexico City and in Madrid, the latter being 'refuted by a Spanish democrat'.¹⁹ Furthermore, its ideas circulated rapidly in journals and newspapers.²⁰ Although the essay rendered the word 'democracy' synonymous with chaos and desolation, it acknowledged that the progress of democracy was irresistible and its empire as 'a sovereign, universal word' was such that 'no party dares to, nor believes it can live without inscribing it on its banner'.²¹ Over the coming years, a democratic party would be created, which meant the rise of a new political actor and a new political language.

The 'ardent democrats' of the journal *El Pueblo* claimed that 'the old progressive party, just like the absolutist and moderate parties, has neither life nor future in our nation'.²² Its propaganda was mainly directed at the youth. Revealingly, some two thousand young craftsmen, writers and factory workers from Madrid signed up in support of the new programme. An associative network woven during previous years across the provinces would be a vehicle of political propaganda and recruitment. This inclusive, popular and egalitarian character already formed part of the concept at an international level, as was reflected in an enlarged translation of Louis-Antoine Pagnerre's 1842 *Dictionnaire politique* by a group of Spanish democrats. It was like a manifesto of the young French republicans assuming the socioeconomic doctrine of the socialist school.²³

The programme of the first democratic party in Spain contained objectives that relied on the radical affirmation of individual rights and freedoms. For republican politician Sixto Cámara, the time had come for left-wing liberals to hand over the baton to the democrats:

> It is necessary [for the liberal party] to assume a new name, in keeping with the progress of time . . . That name is democracy. The liberal idea, which yesterday was called progress [i.e. progressive party], developed over time, is today called democracy.²⁴

Due to the historico-political moment, and due to the connotations born of the recent past of the very concept of democracy, the political programme was deliberately presented in anti-revolutionary terms. For similar reasons, the Spanish democrats assumed both the legitimacy of the hereditary throne of Queen Isabella II and the adoption of Catholicism as the state religion. This posed questions for some of the thorniest when it came to interpreting the meaning of democracy in Spain. One should not forget the effective propaganda deployed after the French Revolution to identify democracy with anti-monarchism (as if it were equivalent to republic) and with anti-Catholicism.

There was a tendency to avoid the clear rejection of the idea of democracy as expressed by the representatives of the Catholic Church, emphasizing Christianity and the figure of Jesus as the embodiment of equality and human fraternity. As these debates reached the *Cortes* in 1854, when the liberal revolution of 1854 had taken young democrats to Parliament, Nicolás Salmerón, one of the would-be presidents of the First Republic and leading advocate of religious freedom, claimed: 'Democracy, gentlemen, and let this be well understood, lays its head on the Gospel'²⁵ – a harmony of the democratic ideal with Christianity that seemed indispensable in a country where, in the opinion of MP Moreno Nieto, 'democracy will not triumph whilst it retains that mantle of atheism it still wears'.²⁶

The initial success of the democratic party was confirmed by its capacity to forge a political identity out of a broad internal range of sensibilities. The new political identity would be displayed in Parliament, the organ that, along with the press, pamphlets and associations, acted as a mouthpiece for the party's ideas. Between 1851 and 1854, more MPs, disappointed as they were with the progressive party, would describe themselves as democrats.

Polemics against Democracy and between Democrats (1856–68)

A series of progressive governments enjoyed extraordinary momentum in 1854–56. Even if they failed to replace the 1845 Constitution, a new party was founded, the Liberal Union, an intermediate option between conservatives and progressives. In the end, the moderate party returned to office, which meant its gradual rightward shift, because of the protection of Queen Isabella II and the electoral retreat of progressives and democrats. These in turn resorted to violent methods, such as military uprising or revolution, in an attempt to overthrow the government. Such political radicalization would unite all the parties, finally culminating in 1868 in a revolution against the reigning Bourbon dynasty.

As a consequence, democracy was identified with violence – a criticism soon responded to by a leading democratic publicist, Nemesio Fernández Cuesta. His pamphlet *Vindication of Spanish Democracy* claimed that 'Democracy is the people' (such usage of the word was indeed common at that time), adding: 'The blood of democracy flows strong through the veins of Spain.'[27] Since the Reconquest (*Reconquista*), the claim proceeded, its customs and instincts have been democratic and what is radically new is a party that embodies those principles. Further to this claim of historical continuity, he also argued for the continuity of the ideas of freedom and progress.

Progressives and democrats differed in relation to the dogma of national sovereignty. That fundamental progressive banner was for the republican politician Emilio Castelar subordinate to the idea of rights. Rights, accordingly, were regarded as prior and superior to any will, be it individual or collective (general, national) – a reason why in Spanish democratic theory, rights were not only absolute, but also unlegislatable. Yet, the real debate had to do with their different ways of understanding democracy, for instance, from individualist or socialist perspectives. In 1860 a group of young people inspired by Krausist philosophy – from the mid nineteenth century onwards a number of leading Spanish scholars had embraced the doctrine of the German philosopher K.C.F. Krause[28] – flew the flag of democracy in the pages of *La Razón*. Castelar participated in this dispute by publishing a series of articles entitled 'Democracy and Socialism' that evidenced the doctrinal distance separating the different socialist groups from the Krausists. He redefined democracy in liberal terms, excluding from its field the 'democratic-socialist' sectors of the two leaders and ideologists Fernando Garrido and Francisco Pi y Margall.

To avoid an internal fracture, a joint manifesto was published by thirty leading democrats who regarded as democratic 'all those who, whatever their opinions in philosophy, in economic and social questions, profess in politics the principle of human personality or of individual, absolute, unlegislatable freedoms and of universal suffrage', the latter referring to adult male suffrage.[29] Yet, the polemic as regards socialism would be revived shortly afterwards and would eventually divide the Spanish democrats into different factions. In a text published in 1861 – the same year that in eastern Andalusia thousands of revolutionaries rose up to the cry of '¡Viva la Democracia!'[30] – the crucial question was asked: anarchists, socialists and communists, are they democrats?

All these internal disputes indicate that there was a need to establish the party's official line. In a manifesto released in 1865, the Central Committee of the Democratic Party justified its initiative in order to avoid misinterpretations and 'declare its proposals to instil in the nation the confidence that it is not only a party of teaching and propaganda, but also a party of government'.[31] Without renouncing the essential programmatic points formulated in 1849, the manifesto synthesized the entire content of democracy into two key concepts that identified it, namely, freedom and equality.

Achieving Democracy: The Glorious Revolution and the 1869 Constitution

In 1865, the progressive politician and journalist Carlos Rubio vouched for strengthening the strategic bond between his own party and that of the democrats, arguing that 'today democracy is the theory of the progressive party; the progressive party is the practice of democracy'.[32] He later encouraged the publication of a new 'Manifesto of Democracy', the outcome of an alliance between progressive liberals and unionists against the conservative regime and the monarchy of Isabella II. Signed by the cream of the democratic movement, it highlighted two central principles of Spanish democracy: the sovereignty of the nation and 'universal [male] suffrage'. Acknowledging a certain diversity of opinions with regard to these principles, there existed neither 'hesitation, doubt, nor fragmentation/split in Democracy'.

By the end of the reign of Isabella II, disputes declined to give way to a rapprochement of former political rivals under the banner of democracy, leading to the so-called Glorious Revolution of 1868. Quarrels resumed again when some of the expectations of the democratic revolutionaries were frustrated by legislative and government action that, in fact, was largely inspired by the old progressive party. One of the bones of contention referred to natural and unlegislatable rights, namely, those prior to any political constitution. They would form the foundations of the new Constitution of 1869, which was regarded by many as democratic since it acknowledged civil and political rights, including religious freedom and universal male suffrage. In the context of the Europe at that time, it can be described as an early establishment of a democratic regime. Certainly no other European nation (including France, Italy, Denmark, Belgium, the Netherlands and the United Kingdom), with Switzerland as the only exception, had at that time so broad an electorate.[33] It is also significant that, whereas in most European languages the peak in the use of the term 'democracy' is reached around 1848–50, in Spanish there is a notable increase of 'democracy' after 1868, with the word hitting its highest peak in 1873.[34]

The tensions between the principles of freedom and democracy, whose merger had been the aspiration of Spanish democrats, were thus relieved. In 1869, a debate arose over another of the historical tensions of the concept, namely, the relationship between monarchy and democracy. The terms of the debate had been formulated since the beginning of the revolution, as illustrated by an article published on 22 October 1868 in the Barcelona-based *La Crónica de Cataluña* entitled 'Is Monarchy Impossible with Democracy? Does Republic Imply Democracy?' The answer sought to relativize the forms of government, which rendered to democracy its original meaning of popular government.

The debate was rekindled in the Constituent *Cortes* during the moments prior to a vote on the future form of government. Also, the pamphlet *Monarchy and Democracy as Connecting Link and the Only Form of Government that Should Be Accepted by Spaniards* by 'a Spanish woman who loved her country', Antonia Cussac y García, was published in 1869.[35] In the end, the democratic monarchy would hold sway, quelling the republican aspirations within Spanish democracy. A final thread of meanings of the concept that became prominent in the debates was the one related to equality – an equality that was not only political but also understood, above all, in a social sense.

The failure of the successive democratic experiences undertaken from 1868 to 1874, first under the form of a constitutional monarchy and then under an ephemeral and turbulent republic, led to the restoration of the monarchy. The new constitutional arrangement, mainly designed by the conservative Antonio Cánovas with the collaboration of liberal P. Mateo Sagasta, gave way to a long period of oligarchic liberalism, which was exceptionally stable compared to the preceding decades. During the last quarter of the nineteenth century, a relative eclipse of 'democracy' is found – a term that, along with those of 'republic' and 'federalism', had lost prestige after the failed expectations of the revolutionary *sexennium*. Only some extraparliamentary left-wing minority parties still embraced democracy as an ideal. Yet, some academic voices, such as that of Professor Moreno Nieto,[36] were raised to claim the fusion of liberalism and democracy. Furthermore, in the last decade of the century, after the electoral law of June 1890 reinstating universal male suffrage, a timid retrieval of political debates on democracy took place.

Democracy and Reformism

Spain's defeat in 1898 by the United States and the subsequent loss of Cuba, Puerto Rico and the Philippines sharply uncovered the real political might of a diminished empire that had definitely fallen apart. The 'disaster' became the leitmotif of a group of intellectuals, the 'generation of '98', who from divergent views thematized the crisis politically. Authors such as Pío Baroja and Azorín mistrusted democracy, arguing that it meant hardly more than a game of votes and had no hope of reversing the tide of political events. The scholar and politician Joaquín Costa offered instead a 'regenerationist' criticism of what he called a Spain of 'oligarchy and patronage', in reference to the oligarchic structure of both economic and political power entrenched throughout the country, badly aided by a deficient administration.[37]

'To Europeanize Spain', Costa's claim in his 1900 essay 'Reconstitution and Europeanization of Spain', was formulated as a programme for a new political party,[38] but the fact that it relied on the charismatic leadership of Costa himself turned out to be a handicap. Some years later, intellectuals of a younger generation resumed that quest. In the views of the generation of 1914, democracy came to epitomize reformist politics. The writer and republican politician Manuel Azaña and the philosopher and liberal intellectual José Ortega y Gasset exemplified that reaction.

'The Spanish Problem' was the title of a lecture Manuel Azaña delivered at a socialist association. There he argued that the response to the Spanish misalignment with European history should entail, among other conditions, the remoralization of politics. And, specifically, it should demand the overhauling of the political system:

> Have we said democracy? Indeed. Don't be tempted by the ridiculous apprehension of fearing it. Let's restore it or, better, let's establish it pulling out from its essential forms all excrescences that disfigure it. Don't hate politics and don't move aside from politics, because without it we shall not be saved.[39]

In his public lecture 'Old and New Politics', Ortega presented the basic ideas of the Spanish League for Political Education, a group of visionaries instilling a kind of political pedagogy that paved the way for the emergence of liberal reformism. Distancing himself from Costa, he argued that under the circumstances of political uncertainty affecting the world:

> it is the generic, eternal ideals of democracy the only thing that remains immutable and irreplaceable; everything else, every means to achieve and putting those democratic ideals into practice at every moment, is transitory.[40]

Yet, for all its public influence, the political impact of the generation of 1914 was initially short-lived. It was limited to the regenerationist question and the need to catch up with the pace of European politics after the isolationist consequences of the country's neutrality in the First World War. Only in the 1930s was its civic impulse resumed, as the group of intellectuals turned into professional politicians defending a liberal and democratic political programme.

Reform vs. Revolution: Arguing the Language of Democracy

During the Restoration's last decade in the 1920s, Spain evinced the exhaustion of a regime identified with the monarchy and mired in institutional stalemate. Ironically, its promise of reform was accomplished in part by a dictatorship imposed in 1923 by General Miguel Primo de Rivera's coup d'état. The new regime softened authoritarian rule with a blend of paternalist social entitlements that secured social peace for some time, until the failure of its economic policies was forcefully contested by workers and until the country approached the brink of chaos at the height of the global financial crisis.

The loss of the support of the military led to Primo de Rivera's resignation in January 1930, which was followed by a new attempt at coalition government by Liberals and Conservatives. Municipal elections were held in 1931, aimed at a gradual reinstatement of the Restoration status quo. However, the strong electoral showing by republican parties, even if an absolute majority was not obtained, led the government to the striking move of yielding power to a provisional government that two days later proclaimed the Republic and called general elections. Before the elections, the provisional government outlined a plan to draft a new constitution, which would be eventually approved by the Constituent *Cortes* in December 1931.

Spain was refounded constitutionally as a 'democratic Republic of workers of every class', but this left-wing imprint, even if all-embracing in principle and aimed primarily at empowering the working class ('in a democracy of the twentieth century, work and citizenship are synonymous terms', argued MP Fernando Valera),[41] never dispelled the doubts of sectarianism. The clearest proof thereof came with the political measures undertaken by the six centre-left governments in office from 1931 to 1933 to reform land property rights, public education (revising in depth the monopoly of the Catholic Church), the military organization and the territorial structure of the state. This pressing legislative pace put a strain on the procedures of the parliamentary regime, and its visionary style provoked an ideological polarization around the democratic character of the Republic – probably its clearest institutional evidence was that Parliament was unicameral for democratic reasons, as argued in the debate on the senate at the October 1931 sessions.

Parliamentary activity was hectic even in moments of political instability. In that sense, it resembled the intricate workings of other parliamentary democracies of the 1930s at the height of anti-parliamentary times, from Italy to France and Germany, from Austria to Belgium, Finland and the Netherlands.[42] It was in the *Cortes* where the most evocative moments in defence of the democratic identity of the Republic took place and where debates forged the new language of democracy.[43] As the priest and Republican MP Ramón Molina eloquently expressed it: 'Democracy, gentlemen, is one of the most sonorous words of the modern vocabulary, of the least understood, of the worst interpreted and, for that reason, one of the most difficult to apply.'[44]

In the early sessions of the Constituent *Cortes*, Republican MP Eduardo Barriobero presented the role of democratic representatives: 'our democracy must treat everyone with fairness, our role being that of mediators and pacifiers'.[45] Representatives became pacifiers in a battle they themselves had helped provoke around the firmness of the constitutional regime. The claim by Socialist Fernando de los Ríos, 'in an autocracy disobedience is a duty; in a democracy, obedience is a necessity',[46] reflected a growing loss of trust in the rule of law. A Law for the Defence of the Republic was passed in October 1931, which was followed by a Law of Public Order in July 1932, further restricting public liberties to degrees approaching states of emergency.

Only by strengthening the state could democracy thrive. 'Democracy is not the people, it is the state of the people and not the people without the state ... democracy is the organized people', the Liberal José Ortega y Gasset argued.[47] The independent MP Jerónimo García Gallego would add that 'more than the state of the people, to me democracy is the people set up as a state'.[48] The Republican Radical Socialist Fernando Valera further claimed: 'We want the state to be strong, because in democracies the state is the embodiment of the people, it is the people itself.'[49]

Acknowledging women's suffrage turned out to be a defining test for the democratic credentials of Socialists and Republicans. The debate was held in October 1931, led by Victoria Kent, then of the Radical Socialist Republican Party, and Clara Campoamor of the republican Radical Party. Whereas Kent advised granting it once women had improved their education, maintaining that 'it is necessary that those who feel the republican fervour, the democratic and liberal republican fervour, stand up to say: it is necessary to postpone women's suffrage',[50] Campoamor advocated universal suffrage, arguing that denying women's political rights was an unlawful act, supported by force and 'not because you [men] have a natural right to marginalize women'.[51] The latter option was finally enshrined in Article 36 of the Constitution.

Throughout the Republic's existence, from 1931 to 1939, representatives in the *Cortes* were still identified according to the old cleavage separating monarchic from republican parties. Such antagonism, inaccurate as it was when monarchic was presented as anti-democratic, had a powerful rhetorical effect on political debates. At times left-wing politicians characterized their monarchic rivals as critics of the Republic, and monarchic politicians had to demonstrate their allegiance to the 'republican democracy'. The antagonism had a far-reaching effect beyond the rhetoric of political naming, as over time it undermined the chances of reaching agreements across the board.

Out of an ebullient atmosphere, the Republic created newborn democrats from all ideological positions. However, the endorsements of democracy were argued in the name of competing views of the Republic as a political regime. Interestingly, monarchic liberals and conservatives stayed loyal to the Republic even when adhering to the old idea of a constitutional monarchy. Moderate liberals, conservatives and socialists identified 'republican democracy' with a parliamentary regime. Left-wing republicans, socialists and communists spoke of 'proletarian democracy' as opposed to 'bourgeois democracy'. Some of the socialists saw the Republic as the chance to achieve a fully egalitarian regime, namely, a 'classless democracy'. Further, unlike the communists, part of the socialists reinterpreted the constitutional blueprint for a 'parliamentary democracy' in terms of a 'revolutionary democracy'.[52]

A major reason for this puzzling situation lies in constitutional politics, since the process of regime change towards a republic was conceptualized ambivalently by declaring the Republic's working-class identity, while at the same time professing an all-inclusive spirit. The course of events, with the rise of government instability, further explains one of its unintended consequences, as the political meaning of the Republic became subject to an entrenched semantic dispute that soon led to the clash of two antagonistic perspectives: revolutionary democracy versus parliamentary democracy. Before long, their rivalry reflected irresolvable claims about governing the Republic, and so every new government's policies were seen by opposition parties as partisan and excluding interpretations of the Constitution.

Political instability and social unrest grew with the passage of time. Efforts were made to preserve unity around the constitutional order. A republican journal highlighted how political pluralism 'suits the Republic, and is required by democracy'.⁵³ In practice, adversarial politics was soon taken to extremes. The wanting performance and parliamentary isolation of successive centre-right governments since 1933 led to anticipated elections in February 1936. The 'Popular Front' coalition of left-wing parties would win. The liberal *El Sol* criticized their electoral campaign: 'their mission is not to strengthen the republican institutions, but to destroy them should they hinder the triumph of integral Marxism'.⁵⁴

Shortly before the Civil War broke out on 18 July 1936, in the wake of General Franco's uprising, democrats from across Parliament forged an alliance in response to mounting violence. Moderate conservatives and liberals underscored the crucial condition of political pluralism and political toleration, which parliamentary democracy made possible. All this was about to be lost as recent disputes had cornered pragmatic moderates. Liberal Manuel Giménez Fernández argued that:

> the presence here of anyone called fascist is, indeed, an acknowledgement of the democratic legality, and the highest success democracy can achieve is that its own enemies acknowledge the existence of a legality and of a popular will, and thus come here to defend their views – which is something much more difficult, Messrs. Representatives, than gaining prestige in front of the ignorant masses of anti-parties . . . Parties, ideas, democracy, the Republic, none has anything to fear from its enemies.⁵⁵

It was an alliance only ephemerally shared in by left-wing parties, which underwent an agonizing fragmentation along revolutionary lines.

Rhetoric of Democracy in a Non-democracy

A number of reasons both domestic and international can be cited to explain the defeat of the Republic: from the poor coordination and solidarity among democratic parties to the radicalization of the republican and socialist leaderships, and the isolation of moderate democrats, to the calculated 'impartiality' of European diplomacy and the rebels' support from fascist regimes. The dictatorship imposed in 1939 rested on the ruins of a devastated country. Its ideological fracture was still further deepened through propaganda depicting the regime as the only feasible escape from war.

Institution-building of the 'new order' was orchestrated to reproduce the features of a fascist regime. A law 'creating the Spanish *Cortes*'⁵⁶ aspired to 'resume glorious Spanish traditions' by adopting the representative institutions of corporatism, which stood as a salient mark of the state's patronage network. Out of a single-party ('Movimiento Nacional') regime, the new non-pluralist Parliament made room for a limited experience of political deliberation, even though the law-making process apparently followed the deliberative conventions of modern parliaments. The law erased most footprints of civic terminology and appealed to the 'Spanish people' in bluntly excluding terms, as the liberals and the left-wingers, to single out the most conspicuous cases, were deemed anti-patriots.

The regime was unmistakably anti-democratic, but the official rhetoric was gradually softened. The dictator himself, General Franco, embodied its changing uses. In his speeches to the *Cortes* from 1943 to 1967, he employed the term *democracia* twenty-four times with varying meanings all through nine legislative periods.[57] If in the second legislature (1946–49) it was to distance the regime from exemplars of 'formalist democracy', which he defined as 'inorganic', in the fifth legislature (1955–58), it was to champion the regime's 'organic democracy', and in the seventh legislature to boost the illusion of governing a comparable political system. In 1946, he held: 'Regarding the allegation of antidemocrats . . . [i]t is paradoxical that the title of democratic is refused to a nation that lives . . . under the principles of Catholic faith . . . that has its representative *Cortes* . . . that has established direct referendum.'[58] The idea of 'inorganic' referred to the loss of the imperative mandate in the principle of representation, whereas the alternative, an 'organic vote', was presented as the true democratic bond between represented and representatives.[59] In spite of the claim that the legislative process was deliberative in the 'organic *Cortes*', nothing was said of the incompatibility between imperative mandate and political deliberation. The Francoist *Cortes* preserved that distinctive feature of medieval parliaments where representation was understood mostly in legal and not in political terms, namely in a contractual sense precluding deliberation.

Almost ten years later, Franco would argue that democracy 'should be active', further upholding the idea that 'proclaiming its principles or the formulation of a system is not enough; it is necessary that through dialogue on different issues, the opinion of the different sectors [of society] can be expressed'.[60] In a pseudo-democracy, words did not mean what they apparently meant, but slowly since the mid 1960s they recovered some of their previous meanings as the regime began to display signs of the 'limited pluralism'[61] characteristic of authoritarian regimes in their twilight.

Retrieving the Civic Language of Democracy

After Franco's death in November 1975, a number of internal factors accelerated the political changes taking place, beginning with a spectacular rise of social claims for democracy, the splitting of the National Movement's political factions along reformist lines and a final, unanticipated negotiation of regime change.⁶² In line with moderate reformists, most notably Torcuato Fernández-Miranda, King Juan Carlos appointed the insider Adolfo Suárez as Prime Minister, charging him with revising the existing blueprint for a 'limited democracy', which had been years in the making.

Regime change proceeded through trial and error, testing the reformist capacity of a blueprint that had to be continuously re-adjusted to political circumstances, which were not always propitious. Conventional narratives of Spain's transition to democracy usually dismiss the enduring weight of political uncertainty,⁶³ since the serious risk of regression lasted until the 1980s and beyond, proving democracy's 'uncertain institutionalization'.⁶⁴

A first set of changes following the introduction of a new legality was aimed at overhauling political institutions. It began with reparliamentarizing politics and ran parallel to repoliticizing professional politicians, mostly trained in a dictatorship, and the citizenry in general. Civic changes would engage different generations, with their dissimilar historical views and political expectations, in a process of joint accommodation of conflictual political views and practices for the upcoming decades.

What kind of democracy came about? Judging by the new language of politics, it was a democracy drawn on a constitutional agreement wider and steadier than that of 1931, arising from a different appreciation of both political dissent and constitutional loyalty or patriotism. Unlike in 1931, the 1978 Constitution relied on the joint support of centre-left and centre-right parties.

It was a paradox that adversarial politics stemmed from a culture of pacts engaging all parties, but the paradox becomes intelligible in light of the contrast with adversarial politics in the Second Republic. By then, debating was mistrusted by political parties insofar as it could lead to compromising their principled stances. Adversarial politics taken to extremes, as was also the case in the final phase of Weimar's parliamentary politics,⁶⁵ provoked the paralysis of the political process and alienated Parliament from society.

The political vocabulary re-entered everyday language, opening up a process of democratization of political concepts.⁶⁶ Along with concepts denoting political freedoms, technical terms such as 'agenda', 'session', 'procedure', 'deliberation', 'debate', 'interpellation', 'motion', 'committee', 'plenary' and 'vote' began to regain their full sense.⁶⁷ The relearning of parliamentary politics denoted the vocabulary of the new language of democracy. But it gained a distinctive qualification from the political process under way by representing the path from dictatorship to democracy as a multiform civic achievement. Syntagmas such as *lucha democrática* (democratic fight), *ruptura democrática* (democratic rupture), *alternativa democrática* (democratic alternative), *reforma democrática* (democratic reform) and *orden democrático* (democratic order)[68] captured its successive moments, which were always perceived as contingent moves. The language of democratic change became the 'cultural idiom', as Pérez-Díaz argued, which made visible 'the integrative role of politics'.[69]

For the first time in years, engaging in politics from adversarial positions was no longer the divisive experience it had been for the previous decades. Politics soon became regarded as the debating activity of the citizenry. Time was needed to establish a new political culture where the constitutional regime relied on and fostered political pluralism, and at the same time appreciated the value of adversarial politics. For some years, remnants of the dictatorship pervaded salient sectors of society, from the political class to the military. The defining test for democracy came with the coup d'état of 23 February 1981, when Parliament was stormed. The reaction by Prime Minister Suárez and King Juan Carlos neutralising the military plot cut short the coup. Their reactions produced a general awareness of democracy being safe.

That same night, when the radio stations broadcast and denounced the coup, the early edition of the centre-left newspaper *El País* bore the front-page headline: 'Coup d'État: The Country [and the newspaper][70] Stands by the Constitution', whereas the centre-right *Diario 16* headed its edition: 'In Defence of the Constitution'. Others followed suit. A huge popular endorsement of democracy spread, producing the effect of a bold legitimation of the regime. However, it marked the end of the politics of constitutional consensus and the beginning of a new path to consolidate it as a working parliamentary democracy. The ensuing language of democracy soon became vibrantly dissensual.

Concluding Remarks

By exploring the term's uses in political debates, this chapter has presented a conceptual history of democracy in Spain over the past two centuries. To broaden the analysis, it has included arguments of democracy's opponents, be they liberals *tout court*, who thought the ideal of democracy irreconcilable with modern times (a view widely shared by moderate Liberals and Conservatives from the 1810s, as well as by Liberal and Conservative politicians during the whole Restoration period from 1876 to 1923), or open anti-democrats (from early nineteenth-century absolutists to Carlists from the 1830s onwards). In the twentieth century, the range of critics grew to take in anarchists and revolutionary Socialists during the Second Republic from 1931 to 1939, fascists and traditionalists supporting the dictatorship of 1939–75, and extremists from the left and the right since the mid 1970s.

Democracy's conceptual history provides a research perspective on its ideological and practical ties with other political concepts. Since the association of 'democratic' and 'liberal' in the 1810s, its changing political uses later arise as 'egalitarian' and 'democratic' in the 1860s and 1870s, 'revolutionary' and 'democratic', 'socialist' and 'democratic' or 'republican' and 'democratic' in the 1930s. By the second half of the 1970s, after almost four decades of repression altering the meanings of the entire political vocabulary in order to present the dictatorship as an idiosyncratic 'democracy', the language of democracy regained its semantic liveliness with the emergence of a pluralist political culture. Since 1977, the concept has identified the constitutional values of pluralism and equality. Some decades afterwards, democracy in Spain would attest to the arrival of alternative political actors out of movement politics, again evoking the condition of an inexhaustible semantic reservoir.

Javier Fernández-Sebastián is Professor of History of Political Thought at the University of the Basque Country in Bilbao. He has published extensively on modern intellectual and conceptual history, in particular on Spain and the Iberian world. Among his recent books are the multivolume *Diccionario político y social del mundo iberoamericano: Conceptos políticos fundamentales* (2009–14), as well as *Conceptual History in the European Space* (2017), co-edited with Willibald Steinmetz and Michael Freeden.

José María Rosales is Professor of Moral and Political Philosophy at the University of Málaga. He has coedited, *Beyond Nationalism? Sovereignty and Citizenship* (2001) with F.R. Dallmayr, *The Ashgate Research Companion to the Politics of Democratization in Europe: Concepts and Histories* (2008) with K. Palonen and T. Pulkkinen, and *Parliamentarism and Democratic Theory: Historical and Contemporary Perspectives* (2015) with K. Palonen. A board member of Concepta, he is the chair of the COST Action 16211 *Reappraising Intellectual Debates on Civic Rights and Democracy in Europe* (RECAST).

Notes

Javier Fernández-Sebastián acknowledges the support of both the project *Temporal and Spatial Dimensions of the Political-Juridical Languages in Euro-American Modernity. An Interdisciplinary Approach* (HAR2017-84032-P, Ministry of Science and Innovation, Government of Spain plus ERDF, EU) and the research group IT615-13. José María Rosales acknowledges the support of the project *Civic Constellation II: Debating Democracy and Rights* (FFI2014-52703-P).

1. *Diario de Sesiones de las Cortes Generales y Extraordinarias* (*Proceedings of General and Extraordinary Parliament* (1810–12), hereinafter *DSCGE*), 12 and 13 September 1811, 1822 and 1834; 1 January 1812, 2517.
2. H. Dippel, 'La significación de la Constitución española de 1812 para los nacientes liberalismo y constitucionalismo alemanes', in J.M. Iñurritegui and J.M. Portillo (eds), *Constitución en España: orígenes y destinos* (Madrid: Centro de Estudios Políticos y Constitucionales, 1998), 287–307.
3. A. de Moya Luzuriaga, *Catecismo de Doctrina Civil* (Cádiz, 1810), in *Catecismos políticos españoles: arreglados a las constituciones del siglo XIX* (Madrid: Comunidad de Madrid, 1989), 57; on Chile, see J. Amor de la Patria, *Catecismo político cristiano* [c. 1810], cited in A. San Francisco, 'Chile', in *Democracia*, G. Caetano (ed.) in J. Fernández-Sebastián (dir.), *Diccionario político y social del mundo iberoamericano. Conceptos políticos fundamentales, 1770–1870* (Madrid: Centro de Estudios Políticos y Constitucionales, 2014), 102–3.
4. *El Censor*, 7 October 1820, 269 and 273. Unless otherwise stated, newspapers cited were published in Madrid.
5. M. Agustín Príncipe, *Tirios y troyanos* (Madrid: Mora y Soler, 1845), 83; A. Alcalá Galiano, *Recuerdos de un anciano* (Madrid: Hernando, 1878), 46.
6. J. Donoso Cortés, *Obras Completas*, Carlos Valverde (ed.) (Madrid: Biblioteca de Autores Cristianos, 1970), vol. I, 247–51.
7. J. Fernández-Sebastián, 'Guerra de palabras. Lengua y política en la Revolución de España', in P. Rújula and J. Canal (eds), *Guerra de ideas. Política y cultura en la España de la Guerra de la Independencia* (Madrid: Marcial Pons, 2012), 251–53.
8. E. Castelar, 'Breve historia de la democracia española', in *Almanaque de 'La Democracia' para 1866* (Madrid: Imprenta Universal, 1866), 45–56; X. Andreu Miralles, 'El pueblo y sus opresores: populismo y nacionalismo en la cultura política del radicalismo democrático, 1844–1848', *Historia y política* 25 (2011), 65–91.
9. *Diario de Sesiones de las Cortes* (Parliamentary Proceedings (1820 to the present), hereinafter *DSC*), 19 January 1836, 491–92; 2 June 1840, 2157; 18 November 1844, 508.
10. *DSC*, 9 April 1837, 2607.
11. See M. Rodríguez Alonso, 'La correspondencia privada de Jorge Villiers referente a España (1833–1839)', *Revista de historia contemporánea* 4 (1985), 57–9.
12. G. Barnosell, 'God and Freedom: Radical Liberalism, Republicanism, and Religion in Spain, 1808–1847', *International Review of Social History* 57 (2011), 37–59.
13. G. G. 1841, vol. II: 83; MP Egaña, *DSC*, 11 January 1845, 1181; see F. Garrido, *Propaganda democrática. Instrucción política del pueblo. Derrota de los viejos partidos políticos. Deberes y porvenir de la democracia española* (Madrid: Librerías de Cuesta, Baylli-Baillierey y Durán, 1849), 16.
14. 'Report of the Commission on Constitutional Reform', *DSC*, Appendix to No. 23, 5 November 1844, 288.
15. MP Donoso Cortés, *DSC*, 16 November 1844, 500–3; see also MP Alcalá Galiano, *DSC*, 18 November 1844, 508, as well as his *Lecciones de Derecho Político*

(1843–44), Ángel Garrorena Morales (ed.) (Madrid: Centro de Estudios Constitucionales, 1984), 103.
16. E. de Ochoa, *París, Londres y Madrid* (Paris: Baudry, 1861), 574ff; M. Menéndez Pelayo, *Historia de los heterodoxos españoles* (1880–82) (Madrid: Biblioteca de Autores Cristianos, 1956), vol. VII; P. Cirujano Martín et al., *Historiografía y nacionalismo español (1834–1868)* (Madrid: CSIC, 1985), 187.
17. *Guindilla*, 24 January 1843.
18. *Eco del Comercio*, 27 January 1843; *El Espectador*, 28 January 1843.
19. F. Guizot, *De la democracia en Francia. Obra traducida y refutada por un escritor liberal* (Madrid: Imprenta de los Señores Andrés y Díaz, 1849).
20. *El Español*, 19 January 1849; *El Heraldo*, 20 January 1849.
21. Guizot, *De la democracia en Francia*, 3.
22. *El Pueblo*, 17 December 1849.
23. L. Frobert, 'Republicanism and Political Economy in Pagnerre's *Dictionnaire politique* (1842)', *History of European Ideas* 37 (2011), 357–64.
24. *La Soberanía Nacional*, 25 November 1855.
25. *DSC*, 26 December 1854, 227.
26. *DSC*, 28 February 1855, 2487.
27. N. Fernández Cuesta, *Vindicación de la democracia española* (Madrid: Imprenta de Manuel Morales y Rodríguez, 1858), 34.
28. J. López-Morillas, *The Krausist Movement and Ideological Change in Spain, 1854–1874* (Cambridge: Cambridge University Press, 1981).
29. G. Rodríguez, 'La democracia y el socialismo', *La Razón* I (1860), 39.
30. G. Thomson, *The Birth of Modern Politics in Spain: Democracy, Association and Revolution, 1854–75* (Basingstoke: Palgrave Macmillan, 2009), 178–79.
31. 'Manifiesto del Comité Central del Partido Democrático', in Miguel Artola, *Partidos y programas políticos: 1808–1936* (Madrid: Aguilar, 1974), vol. II, 74–78.
32. C. Rubio, *Progresistas y demócratas. Cómo y por qué se han unido. ¿Pueden constituir una comunión en el futuro?* (Madrid: Imprenta de La Iberia, 1865), 22.
33. M. Santirso, *España en la Europa liberal (1830–1870)* (Barcelona: Ariel, 2012), 140–48.
34. See Ngram Viewer, 13 July 2016, retrieved 31 January 2018 from https://books.google.com/ngrams/graph?content=democracia&year_start=1800&year_end=1900&corpus=10&smoothing=3&share=&direct_url=t1%3B%2Cdemocracia%3B%2Cc0.
35. A. Cussac y García, *La Monarquía y la Democracia como lazo de unión y única forma de gobierno que deben aceptar los Españoles* (Madrid: Segundo Martínez, 1869).
36. J. Moreno Nieto, *Discursos académicos* (Madrid: Ateneo Científico, Literario y Artístico de Madrid, 1882), 79–80.
37. J. Costa, *Oligarquía y caciquismo como la forma actual de gobierno en España: urgencia y modo de cambiarla* (1901) (Zaragoza: Guara, 1982), vol. I, 131–253.
38. J. Costa, *Reconstitución y europeización de España* (1900), in S. Martín-Retortillo (ed.), *Reconstitución y europeización de España y otros escritos* (Madrid: Instituto de Estudios de Administración Local, 1981).

39. M. Azaña, 'El problema español' (1911), in S. Juliá (ed.), *Obras Completas*, vol. I, 1897–1920 (Madrid: Centro de Estudios Políticos y Constitucionales–Taurus, 2008), 161.
40. J. Ortega y Gasset, 'Vieja y nueva política' (1914), in *Obras Completas*, vol. I, 1902–15 (Madrid: Taurus–Fundación José Ortega y Gasset, 2004), 728.
41. *Diario de Sesiones de las Cortes Constityentes de la República Española* (Parliamentary Proceedings of the Constituent *Cortes* (1931), hereinafter *DSCCRE*), 15 September 1931, 928.
42. J.J. Linz and A. Stepan (eds), *The Breakdown of Democratic Regimes: Europe* (Baltimore: Johns Hopkins University Press, 1978); M. Mazower, *Dark Continent: Europe's Twentieth Century* (London: Allen Lane, 1998), 1–38.
43. J.M. Rosales, 'Parliamentarism in Spanish Politics in the Nineteenth and Twentieth Centuries: From Constitutional Liberalism to Democratic Parliamentarism', in P. Ihalainen, C. Ilie and K. Palonen (eds), *Parliaments and Parliamentarism* (New York: Berghahn Books, 2016), 277–91.
44. *DSCCRE*, 29 September 1931, 1291.
45. *DSCCRE*, 28 July 1931, 186.
46. *DSCCRE*, 3 September 1931, 749.
47. *DSCCRE*, 4 September 1931, 777.
48. *DSCCRE*, 11 September 1931, 873.
49. *DSCCRE*, 15 September 1931, 926.
50. *DSCCRE*, 1 October 1931, 1351–52.
51. *DSCCRE*, 1 October 1931, 1354.
52. See usage examples in J.F. García Santos, *Léxico y política de la Segunda República* (Salamanca: Universidad de Salamanca, 1980), 307–13.
53. *La Libertad*, 1 January 1935, 1.
54. *El Sol*, 29 January 1936, 1.
55. *DSC*, 2 June 1936, 1044.
56. *Boletín Oficial del Estado* (Spain's Official Bulletin), No. 200, 19 July 1942, 5301–3.
57. A. Cillán Apalategui, *El léxico político de Franco en las Cortes españolas* (Zaragoza: Imp. Tipo-Línea, 1970), 155.
58. Franco's speech of 14 May 1946, cited in Cillán Apalategui, *El léxico político de Franco en las Cortes españolas*, 69.
59. Speech of 16 May 1955, 70.
60. Speech of 8 July 1964, 72.
61. J.J. Linz, *Totalitarian and Authoritarian Regimes* (Boulder: Lynne Rienner, 2000), 3–4, 159–65.
62. See e.g. J.M. Maravall and J. Santamaría, 'Political Change in Spain and the Prospects for Democracy', in G. O'Donnell, P.C. Schmitter and L. Whitehead (eds), *Transitions from Authoritarian Rule: Southern Europe* (Baltimore: Johns Hopkins University Press, 1986), 80–4.
63. See e.g. O.G. Encarnación, *Spanish Politics: Democracy after Dictatorship* (Cambridge: Polity, 2008), 31–49; S. Juliá, *Transición: historia de una política española (1937-2017)*. Madrid: Galaxia Gutenberg, 2017.

64. V.M. Pérez-Díaz, *The Return of Civil Society: The Emergence of Democratic Spain* (Cambridge, MA: Harvard University Press, 1993), 40–9.
65. See e.g. T. Mergel, *Parlamentarische Kultur in der Weimarer Republik*, 3rd edn. (Düsseldorf: Droste, 2012), 399–410.
66. J. Fernández-Sebastián, 'Democracia', in J. Fernández-Sebastián and J.F. Fuentes (eds), *Diccionario político y social del siglo XX español* (Madrid: Alianza, 2008), 345–61.
67. J. de Santiago Guervós, *El léxico político de la transición española* (Salamanca: Universidad de Salamanca, 1992), 152–55.
68. De Santiago Guervós, *El léxico político de la transición española*, 147–49.
69. Pérez-Díaz, *The Return of Civil Society*, 39.
70. *País* means country in Spanish.

Bibliography

Agustín Príncipe, M. 1845. *Tirios y troyanos*. Madrid: Mora y Soler.
Alcalá Galiano, A. 1878. *Recuerdos de un anciano*. Madrid: Hernando.
———. 1984. *Lecciones de Derecho Político* (1843–44), Ángel Garrorena Morales (ed.). Madrid: Centro de Estudios Constitucionales.
Andreu Miralles, X. 2011. 'El pueblo y sus opresores: populismo y nacionalismo en la cultura política del radicalismo democrático, 1844–1848', *Historia y política* 25, 65–91.
Azaña, M. 2008. 'El problema español' (1911), in S. Juliá (ed.), *Obras Completas*, vol. I, 1897–1920. Madrid: Centro de Estudios Políticos y Constitucionales–Taurus, 149–64.
Barnosell, G. 2011. 'God and Freedom: Radical Liberalism, Republicanism, and Religion in Spain, 1808–1847', *International Review of Social History* 57, 37–59.
Castelar, E. 1866. 'Breve historia de la democracia española', in *Almanaque de 'La Democracia' para 1866*. Madrid: Imprenta Universal, 45–56.
Cillán Apalategui, A. 1970. *El léxico político de Franco en las Cortes españolas*. Zaragoza: Imp. Tipo-Línea.
Cirujano Martín, P. et al. 1985. *Historiografía y nacionalismo español (1834–1868)*. Madrid: CSIC.
Costa, J. 1981. *Reconstitución y europeización de España* (1900), in S. Martín-Retortillo (ed.), *Reconstitución y europeización de España y otros escritos*. Madrid: Instituto de Estudios de Administración Local.
———. 1982. *Oligarquía y caciquismo como la forma actual de gobierno en España: urgencia y modo de cambiarla* (1901). Zaragoza: Guara.
Cussac y García, A. 1869. *La Monarquía y la Democracia como lazo de unión y única forma de gobierno que deben aceptar los Españoles*. Madrid: Segundo Martínez.
Dippel, H. 1998. 'La significación de la Constitución española de 1812 para los nacientes liberalismo y constitucionalismo alemanes', in J.M. Iñurritegui and J.M. Portillo (eds), *Constitución en España: orígenes y destinos*. Madrid: Centro de Estudios Políticos y Constitucionales, 287–307.

Donoso Cortés, J. 1970. *Obras Completas,* Carlos Valverde (ed.). Madrid: Biblioteca de Autores Cristianos, 2 vols.
Encarnación, O.G. 2008. *Spanish Politics: Democracy after Dictatorship.* Cambridge: Polity.
Fernández Cuesta, N. 1858. *Vindicación de la democracia española.* Madrid: Imprenta de Manuel Morales y Rodríguez.
Fernández-Sebastián, J. 2008. 'Democracia', in J. Fernández-Sebastián and J.F. Fuentes (eds), *Diccionario político y social del siglo XX español.* Madrid: Alianza, 345–61.
———. 2012. 'Guerra de palabras. Lengua y política en la Revolución de España', in P. Rújula and J. Canal (eds), *Guerra de ideas: Política y cultura en la España de la Guerra de la Independencia.* Madrid: Marcial Pons, 237–80.
Frobert, L. 2011. 'Republicanism and Political Economy in Pagnerre's *Dictionnaire politique* (1842)', *History of European Ideas* 37, 357–64.
G. G. 1841. 'De la democracia en España', *Revisita de Madrid, 1841,* vol. II, 81–93.
García Santos, J.F. 1980. *Léxico y política de la Segunda República.* Salamanca: Universidad de Salamanca.
Garrido, F. 1849. *Propaganda democrática. Instrucción política del pueblo. Derrota de los viejos partidos políticos. Deberes y porvenir de la democracia española.* Madrid: Librerías de Cuesta, Baylli-Baillierey y Durán.
Guizot, F. 1849. *De la democracia en Francia: Obra traducida y refutada por un escritor liberal.* Madrid: Imprenta de los Señores Andrés y Díaz.
Juliá, S. 2017. *Transición: historia de una política española (1937–2017).* Madrid: Galaxia Gutenberg.
Linz, J.J. 2000. *Totalitarian and Authoritarian Regimes.* Boulder: Lynne Rienner.
Linz, J.J., and A. Stepan (eds). 1978. *The Breakdown of Democratic Regimes: Europe.* Baltimore: Johns Hopkins University Press.
López-Morillas, J. 1981. *The Krausist Movement and Ideological Change in Spain, 1854–1874.* Cambridge: Cambridge University Press.
'Manifiesto del Comité Central del Partido Democrático', in M. Artola, *Partidos y programas políticos: 1808–1936.* Madrid: Aguilar, 1974, vol. II, 74–78.
Maravall, J.M. and J. Santamaría. 1986. 'Political Change in Spain and the Prospects for Democracy', in G. O'Donnell, P.C. Schmitter and L. Whitehead (eds), *Transitions from Authoritarian Rule: Southern Europe,* Baltimore: Johns Hopkins University Press, 71–108.
Mazower, M. 1998. *Dark Continent: Europe's Twentieth Century.* London: Allen Lane.
Menéndez Pelayo, M. 1956. *Historia de los heterodoxos españoles* (1880–82). Madrid: Biblioteca de Autores Cristianos.
Mergel, T. 2012. *Parlamentarische Kultur in der Weimarer Republik,* 3rd edn. Düsseldorf: Droste.
Moreno Nieto, J. 1882. *Discursos académicos.* Madrid: Ateneo Científico, Literario y Artístico de Madrid.
Moya Luzuriaga, A. de. 1989. *Catecismo de Doctrina Civil* (Cádiz, 1810), in *Catecismos políticos españoles: arreglados a las constituciones del siglo XIX.* Madrid: Comunidad de Madrid.

Ochoa, E. de. 1861. *París, Londres y Madrid*. Paris: Baudry.
Ortega y Gasset, J. 2004. 'Vieja y nueva política' (1914), in *Obras Completas*, vol. I (1902–15). Madrid: Taurus–Fundación José Ortega y Gasset, 707–37.
Pérez-Díaz, V.M. 1993. *The Return of Civil Society: The Emergence of Democratic Spain*. Cambridge, MA: Harvard University Press.
Rodríguez, G. 1860–61. 'La democracia y el socialismo', *La Razón* I–V.
Rodríguez Alonso, M. 1985. 'La correspondencia privada de Jorge Villiers referente a España (1833–1839)', *Revista de historia contemporánea* 4, 51–72.
Rosales, J.M. 2016. 'Parliamentarism in Spanish Politics in the Nineteenth and Twentieth Centuries: From Constitutional Liberalism to Democratic Parliamentarism', in P. Ihalainen, C. Ilie and K. Palonen (eds), *Parliaments and Parliamentarism*. New York: Berghahn Books, 277–91.
Rubio, C. 1865. *Progresistas y demócratas. Cómo y por qué se han unido. ¿Pueden constituir una comunión en el futuro?* Madrid: Imprenta de La Iberia.
San Francisco, A. 2014. 'Chile', in *Democracia*, G. Caetano (ed.) in J. Fernández-Sebastián (dir.), *Diccionario político y social del mundo iberoamericano. Conceptos políticos fundamentales, 1770–1870*. Madrid: Centro de Estudios Políticos y Constitucionales, 101–15.
Santiago Guervós, J. de. 1992. *El léxico político de la transición española*. Salamanca: Universidad de Salamanca.
Santirso, M. 2012. *España en la Europa liberal (1830–1870)*. Barcelona: Ariel.
Thomson, G. 2009. *The Birth of Modern Politics in Spain: Democracy, Association and Revolution, 1854–75*. Basingstoke: Palgrave Macmillan.

Chapter 7

The First World War, the Russian Revolution and Varieties of Democracy in Northwest European Debates

Pasi Ihalainen

The First World War constituted a catalytic transnational experience that inspired new discourses referring to democracy. The impact of the war on individuals and societies, revolutions in Russia and Germany, suffrage reforms and constitutional changes seemed to make it essential for any modern polity to embody political democracy – in the sense of the will of the people being considered through universal suffrage and parliamentary representation[1] or through alternative direct forms of participation. 'Democracy' was moving to the centre of the political debate, becoming a procedural as well as a normative and increasingly future-oriented ideological term with which to identify. The concept became subject to constant disputes over its meanings, applications and implications. Debates on democracy were also at times exceptionally transnational in the period 1917–19, even though they mostly concerned nation states.

By 1917, leaders on both sides understood that the war was leading to an entirely new kind of society. The German Chancellor, Theobald von Bethmann Hollweg, conceded that the war had fostered the emergence of 'a new era with a regenerated people' and that this might imply reconsidering the right way to ascertain the will of that people, particularly vis-à-vis the unequal Prussian suffrage system.[2] The British War Cabinet led by David Lloyd George concluded that it had become impossible to exclude from suffrage men *and women* who had participated in the war and thereby 'made the new Britain possible'.³ Unlike in previous revolutionary eras, the term 'democracy' was used by most ideological groups.⁴ Optimism about democracy became prevalent on the left and mostly in the centre, but to a lesser extent on the right.

This chapter analyses the ways in which the war, as a challenge to the legitimacy of the states and previous conceptions about politics and international relations, internationalized and transnationalized debates on democracy.⁵ It explores similarities and differences in debates on democracy in two great powers, Britain and Germany, and two smaller states, Sweden and Finland. These mostly remained nation state-centred, ideologically motivated and related to the party-political calculations of the day, but also had interconnections. The analysis is based on the uses of 'democracy' in parliamentary and press debates on constitutional reform during the cycle of discourse that followed the Russian February Revolution and the entry of the United States into the war. In parliaments, political elites debated future democracy in comparable institutional circumstances, making comparisons with other countries and thereby opening up possibilities for discursive transfers. The wartime press, too, was highly dependent on parliaments as forums for national discussion. Crossnational scholarly debates were also linked to parliaments through contributions by representatives who were academics.

How and why did conservatives oppose, doubt or redescribe parliamentary democracy in a period of total war, and how were some able to adapt to universal suffrage? Why were liberals, despite their reformism, cautious and divided? How did revisionist social democrats view parliamentary democracy while the far left called for direct action? To what extent were these debates affected by the state of international affairs or transnationally linked through the press and the activities of individual politicians? Examples from plenary debates, related press coverage and pamphlets from four European countries representing different paths to democratization allow for a degree of European-level generalization on these questions.⁶ 'Democratization' is used here in the contemporary Weberian sense of a process of transformation during which the masses enter politics; this process embodies at least the introduction of universal suffrage.⁷

Britain had an established parliamentary government, but lacked universal suffrage and had experienced a wartime decrease in parliamentary vis-à-vis executive power. Germany had a constitutional monarchy and universal male suffrage for the Reichstag, but its political system, dominated by Prussian political culture, was far from the kind of parliamentary democracy that the domestic opposition or the Entente was calling for. Sweden remained a monarchical polity within which pro-German and pro-Entente factions competed and that extended suffrage only after Germany lost the war. Finland, an autonomous grand duchy within the Russian Empire, had introduced democratic suffrage, but had a nearly powerless parliament and a constitutional question to solve after the fall of Tsarist power, a crisis of parliamentary government, disputes on the proper nature of democracy, a declaration of independence and a civil war. Whereas Britain tended to be increasingly viewed as a model for rarely defined 'Western' democracy, the German polity was presented in Allied war propaganda as constituting its counter-concept. Sweden and Finland were moving from German ideals of constitutional monarchy towards parliamentary democracy of the Western type – one in relative calm and the other in circumstances where ideological interpretations of democracy clashed in a civil war.

The Great War that Turned into a Battle over Democracy

German war propaganda had been mobilizing the nation to fight against 'the West' and its 'democracy' since 1914. By 1917, both sides in the war were abusing these concepts in simplifying descriptions of the confrontation.[8] The term 'Western democracy' was used in British discourse partly to persuade the Americans to enter the war, partly as a result of the impact of the American rhetoric of democracy; in Germany, it was cited as a reaction to claims about 'Prussianism'; and in Sweden and Finland, it was employed when their political elites needed to choose between national, Anglo-American, German or Russian democracy – or no democracy at all. The concept divided Europe by including some political cultures and excluding others, the dividing line running between the Entente and the Central Powers. On both sides, some oppositional forces were also questioning the democracy of their own country as opposed to that of the enemy.[9]

In German discourse on the so-called 'democracy' of the West, much criticism had been based on the classical notion of democratic systems tending to be subverted by demagogy and public opinion. Many Germans concluded that Western propaganda merely defended pseudo-democratic systems since not even all Western commentators believed in democracy.[10] This dispute entered a new phase when the Entente began to emphasize opposition to Prussianism as their war goal: in propaganda, and gradually also in the broader political debate, the war turned into a global battle over democracy as a universal form of government. 'Western democracy' united the Allied powers despite different understandings of this ambiguous concept and turned into a normative concept, affecting the self-understandings of the political elites, though still defined in a variety of ways to serve particular political goals. David Lloyd George, the British Prime Minister, started to define democracy in the domestic political context only once he had secured an election victory after the war.[11] Despite contrary claims in war propaganda, he was hostile to the emerging German democracy.[12] This had the transnational effect of discrediting democracy in Germany.

The fall of the Romanovs on 15 March 1917 provoked international interest in the democratic future of Russia, with socialist leaders such as Arthur Henderson of Britain, Hjalmar Branting of Sweden and many of the leaders of the Finnish Social Democratic Party finding their way to Petrograd to observe the course of events. Two weeks later, the British War Cabinet introduced its previously prepared electoral reform proposal, which suggested that suffrage in the oldest of parliamentary governments would be democratized. Once the United States entered the war and declared on 2 April that '[t]he world must be made safe for democracy', the German and Continental European debates were forced to take a stand on the Western understanding of democracy.[13] From a German rightist perspective, such propagation of 'democracy' was an attempt to alienate the German government and people from each other. The critics of this authoritarian state, on the other hand, saw democracy as challenging Prussian notions of the state.[14] However, the kind of democracy they proposed was not uncritically Western; they spoke for a more organic German democracy.

Democracy was extensively debated at the Reichstag in the spring and summer of 1917 and again in October 1918, when the Prussian system was falling. In Britain, discourse on democracy emerged in the late spring of 1917, but remained modest until the left began in 1918 to call for the advancement of domestic democracy through reforms. The question of democracy was no less acute for the Swedish and Finnish politicians, whose ways of thinking were moulded by the evolving war. As long as the German war effort seemed to be successful, the right preferred the German monarchical model to 'Western' democracy, or then they referred to traditional native 'democratic' traditions.[15] They would be forced to rethink their relationship to democracy more as a result of the victory of the Entente than as a response to demands for reform at home.

After the war, there was enthusiasm for the construction of a specifically German version of a popular state among the left and some liberals, but a revolution in November 1918 left all sides dissatisfied. Accusations that the war had been lost because of a betrayal by the Social Democrats, the abuses of the leftist councils, the state of latent civil war, the limited economic benefits of the transition to parliamentary democracy[16] and especially the feeling that the Western democracies had not honoured their promises to the new democratic Germany in the peace negotiations all made democracy appear a suspect party-political (essentially Social Democratic) and unpatriotic concept.

In Sweden, the suffrage reform was obstructed by the right, frightened by the Finnish Civil War and still believing in a German victory. By contrast, the Social Democratic leader Hjalmar Branting profiled himself internationally as a pro-Entente spokesman for parliamentary democracy.[17] In Finland, the Social Democrats and the non-socialist coalition fundamentally disagreed on the proper ways to realize democracy. When German academic traditions suspicious of unlimited democracy met radically Marxist notions of democracy as the rule of the proletariat, supported by transnational links with Bolshevist revolutionaries and isolation from alternative socialist discussion, the debates on democracy became exceptionally confrontational. Only after the crushing of the Reds in the Civil War, the German defeat and a general realization that Finland needed the recognition of its independence by the Anglo-American great powers was the monarchist right ready for a compromise on a parliamentary democracy limited by presidential power.

Anti-democratic Conservatism

A compromise on democracy was sought in all four polities. In Britain, the Conservative opposition to extended suffrage did not explicitly question democracy, but used rhetorical redescriptions and proposed postponements and amendments in order to mould it to their liking.[18] The majority of the Conservatives recognized the inevitability of the transition to universal suffrage and accepted it partly out of party-political calculations, expecting the patriotic atmosphere of wartime to give them an election victory.[19]

In Germany, Sweden and Finland, democracy was widespread in mainstream discourse, but right-wing opposition to democracy consisting of high-ranking civil servants, officers and leading academics spoke out on behalf of the old elites, who feared the loss of their privileged status.[20] Kuno von Westarp and Albrect von Graefe, representatives of the Prussian bureaucratic elite, rejected the democratization of the German Constitution[21] once the left suggested that Russia had joined the 'democratically governed, liberally administrated countries'[22] and that Germany was surrounded by democracies.[23] In the Weimar National Assembly, the right protested against the proposed democratic constitution, and the rightist press continued to hope for the restoration of an autocratic system.[24]

The determination of the German right to defend the established 'constitutional monarchy' encouraged their counterparts in Sweden and Finland to stick to similar views. Ultra-conservatives in Britain, Sweden and Finland engaged in debates on the nature of democracy, which perhaps made it easier for them to reconcile the new political order with conservatism. However, the sceptics of the Swedish right continued to protest even when the reform was about to be confirmed. Hugo Hammarskjöld, a former minister for ecclesiastical affairs, rejected 'the rule by the masses' and questioned the ability of democracy to make people any happier.[25] Indeed, a considerable degree of principled opposition to democracy continued to exist until the early 1930s.[26] In Finland, though there were proposals to qualify it, no actual attacks on democracy were heard from the right in 1917 – the conservative but emancipatory Finnish Party being in principle on the side of 'the people'. The Civil War, however, demonstrated to many conservatives the pernicious consequences of universal suffrage. R.A. Wrede, a former professor of law and MP for the Swedish People's Party, maintained that the Finnish case, in which the unicameral parliament elected by universal suffrage had jeopardized the entire society, demonstrated the global decline of democracy.[27] A strong anti-democratic reaction followed in autumn 1918. Even after Finland had gained independence, some of the academic and economic elite questioned the ability of the nation to form a democracy, using arguments based on classical political theory and the adverse experience of Social Democratic dominance in the unicameral parliament.

Academic Scepticism of Democracy

A slightly more moderate version of conservative scepticism was presented by other transnationally linked professors. James Bryce, 1st Viscount Bryce and a leading Liberal who had made a distinguished career both as an academic in law and history (he had written a well-known book on U.S. institutions and was currently President of the British Academy) and as a high-level civil servant (including the post of Ambassador to the United States), saw it as a mistake to adopt suffrage reform in wartime.[28] Bryce reflected on international developments in a functionalist comparative analysis entitled *Modern Democracies* (1921) as well.[29]

In Sweden, Carl Hallendorff, a historian and the Rector of Stockholm School of Economics, warned about plutocracy taking over in the name of democracy,[30] just as it had done in America. In the spring of 1918, the Swedish right still had good reasons to doubt claims about any pan-European breakthrough of democracy after both the Russian and German attempts of 1917 had failed and the Finnish Civil War had demonstrated what universal suffrage implied.[31] Even after its introduction seemed unavoidable in late 1918, Karl Hildebrand found evidence of the double-edged nature of democracy in the United States, France and Germany.[32] It was not 'the mature will of the people based on understanding but the primitive and immature one that makes an unjustified use of the name of the will of the people' that was being mobilized.[33] Harald Hjärne, a professor of history, insisted that appeals to the will of the people were as unreal as appeals to divine providence under autocracy, since that will was a result of manipulation in elections.[34] The leading ideologists of the Swedish right clearly had not revised their political theory by the time of the transition to democratic suffrage. Such hardliners also included Hugo Suolahti, the Chairman of the Finnish National Coalition Party and Vice-Rector of the University of Helsinki, who viewed 'the class hatred which the Social Democratic Party has used as its weapon in a fight against the so-called bourgeoisie' as a manifestation of democracy at its worst.[35] Most Finnish conservatives would adapt themselves to parliamentary democracy only by the early 1930s.[36]

Conservative Rhetorical Redescriptions of Democracy

A unifying feature of the right was the use of rhetorical redescription to defend the continuity or the slow evolutionary change of the prevailing constitution. It was the favourite argument of the British Unionist minority – similar to their anti-Parliament Act arguments of the early 1910s[37] – to claim that Britain already possessed 'democracy' and that they themselves championed it against innovations introduced with 'Prussian' methods. William Burdett-Coutts, an American by background, suggested that the proposed extension of suffrage struck 'at the foundations of a democratic Government based on the representative principle'.[38] It could be argued that Britain was already progressing towards democracy within its gradually evolving political system and thus that no reform was needed. Besides, France, another 'democracy', was not implementing such a reform either.[39] After all, as it was held, the Western powers were democratic in principle.

In the Weimar Assembly, Konrad Beyerle, a professor of law representing the Catholic Centre, saw the revolution in autumn 1918 as having already led to a sufficient extension of 'a democratic-parliamentary form of government' and opposed any 'socialist' additions in the name of democracy.[40] The rightist leader Clemens von Delbrück talked about a sufficiently 'democratic monarchy' being created already with the reforms of October 1918.[41]

The Swedish right was equally keen on using such rhetorical ploys to obstruct reform. According to Carl Hallendorf, 'the democracy which we have' should be allowed to develop towards 'as extensive a capability of judgment and true maturity as possible' without sudden reforms.[42] In the view of Karl Hildebrand, the Swedish Constitution and societal spirit were 'far more democratic than in most other countries'.[43] Both were experiencing a 'democratizing development'; the Constitution could be changed once the evolutionary transformation had gone far enough.[44]

Among Finnish conservatives, the existing political order and the government's proposals for a constitution were viewed in 1917 as 'democratic' thanks to 'one of the most democratic assemblies of representatives in the world'.[45] After the Civil War, the monarchists insisted that their constitutional proposal was more 'democratic' than any of the republican proposals.[46] It seemed necessary to call any future political order – even a Germanic monarchy – a 'democracy': 'Demands for a king represent the most mature expression of democratic notions at the present moment. The people know and acknowledge that they need a royal head of their democratic constitution. Therefore they want to establish a royal democracy.'[47] Prime Minister J.K. Paasikivi considered all criticism of the monarchical proposal to be unfounded unless 'democracy' was 'understood to stand for an ultra-socialist people's commissariat',[48] which is illustrative of the will to take over 'democracy' from the socialists. While the need to counter Bolshevism caused conservatives to talk about democracy, it also persuaded some of them to make concessions to appease the left and accept a less pernicious system. In Finland, the right successfully used similar redescriptions to force through a presidential republic after being defeated in an attempt to establish a monarchy.

Conservative Adaptations to Democracy

The adaptation of the majority of the right to parliamentary democracy would be decisive for a successful transition to it. This adaptation was happening most clearly in Britain and would start among the Swedish and Finnish right, but no signs of it can be found in the speeches of the German right. After a decision by the Conservative Party to support reform, Lord Henry Cavendish-Bentinck advised his party to 'cultivate friendly relations with the great forces of democracy'. Once conservatism allied with democracy and set out to promote the welfare of the people, it would win 'a great and glorious future'.[49] The party was, quite rightly, counting on electoral support from the patriotic women and soldiers, and even most of the reform opponents refrained from delaying it.

In the Swedish First Chamber, Rudolf Kjellén, a professor of political science, expressed some understanding of the inevitability of democratization in June 1917,[50] at a time when reform was expected in Germany. However, even in late 1918, Carl Swartz, a former prime minister and university chancellor, was the only major rightist leader to openly concede that 'the time for the change of our constitution in a purely democratic direction has come' as 'the Swedish people are just as capable as many other peoples of taking care of their affairs on the basis of a democratic constitution'.[51] Nevertheless, the

Swedish right continued to play a double hand and reserved the chance to appeal to their argumentative opposition should the reform fail.

In Finland, many members of the Finnish Party, the conservative party of the Finnish-speakers, sympathetic to social reform were not fundamentally anti-democratic. In December 1917, the liberal minister Onni Talas, who later became a conservative, argued that the constitution should be based on 'the most democratic principles' as 'the Finnish people are democratic' in their entire essence[52] – the obvious comparison being with Russian autocracy. The particular connotation of the Finnish vernacular translation of democracy (*kansanvalta*) as 'rule by the people' also in an ethnic sense, suggesting the engagement of the educated Finnish-speaking people in running the state as opposed to the Swedish-speaking elite,[53] opened up a way for Finnish-speaking conservatives to accept democracy provided that a clear division of power and hence limits on majority parliamentarism were maintained.

Liberal, Progressivist and Agrarian Views on Democracy

Liberal parties had played major roles in the advocacy of constitutional reforms, but their contributions to defining 'democracy' in debates were rather modest, emphasizing the parliamentarization of the government and hiding concern for the party-political consequences of mass suffrage. Liberals in Britain and Sweden were generally pro-democracy, while their German and Finnish brethren tended to distance themselves from 'pure' democracy.

Cautiousness is characteristic of the British Liberal rhetoric of democracy. In the Commons, Willoughby Dickinson was the only MP 'flying the flag of democracy' in March 1917.[54] In May, Herbert Samuel, a former cabinet minister, characterized the major institutions of Britain as 'democratic'.[55] The British Liberals feared a takeover by the Labour Party and were cautious about calling for any democratic reforms until Lloyd George ensured the continuity of his mandate. The Liberal press nevertheless distinguished itself from the Conservative press in its openness to the idea of democratizing the British Empire in the sense of giving Indians a say in their government,[56] an example of the rising global dimension of democracy.

The German National Liberals were far from enthusiastic about adopting political models from the West in 1917, though their spokesman Gustav Stresemann recognized the dynamism of democracy.[57] The party would continue to hold a critical attitude towards democratization, rejecting the Weimar Constitution as being based on 'the spirit of an extreme democracy'.[58] The left-liberal Progressivists spoke more openly for 'the development of the state in a democratic direction' during the war[59] and characterized themselves as democrats and the new Germany as a 'democracy' after it, but even they did this with more hesitation than liberals elsewhere;⁶⁰ this reluctance reflects the prevailing reservations about the concept in German political discourse. Hugo Preuß, who planned the Weimar Constitution, did not use democracy as a programmatic concept and preferred to talk about a 'state of the people' (*Volksstaat*) instead.⁶¹

Swedish Liberals allied with the Social Democrats much more clearly than their German counterparts in challenging the right. They viewed democracy as a procedural concept for opposing rightist policies rather than spelling out any concrete objects of democratic reforms. The Minister of Justice, Eliel Löfgren, aimed at 'ensuring the undisturbed development of society by giving the right to, and share of, responsibility to the many, not only to the few'.⁶² For Axel Schotte, the Minister of Public Administration, democratization was not so much a goal as a medium for further transformation, 'which has everywhere and in all times been essential for a society that wishes to live'.⁶³ Liberal democracy remained regulated, focusing on procedures and explicitly rejecting 'the pure line' of democratization of the far left in favour of 'bourgeois democracy'.⁶⁴ This stood essentially for favouring representative over direct democracy.

Finnish liberals were divided over the desirable degree of parliamentarization and democratization. Among the Progressivists, Bruno Sarlin presented bourgeois democracy as the very force with which the Civil War had been won and Bolshevism crushed.⁶⁵ The Civil War had been fought by various social groups 'for democracy, for democratic equal rights in the state and society and the liberty of the people/nation'.⁶⁶ Here, the notions of political democracy within a polity, ethnicity and national self-determination merged in a way typical of Finnish discourse.⁶⁷ Sarlin described how very different notions of democracy had clashed in the Finnish Civil War more dramatically than elsewhere. Sarlin's liberal definition contributed to an understanding of the confrontation that brought the victorious bourgeois groups together, persuading the conservatives, too, to accept bourgeois democracy while continuing to exclude any far-left versions.

A feature particular to Finland was derived from the exceptional early modern Swedish-Finnish tradition of the representation of the Peasant Estate in the Diet. This discourse resembled contemporary Danish and Norwegian discourses on peasant democracy (see also the chapters by Beurle, and Kurunmäki and Herrmann in this volume). The nonsocialist and anti-capitalist Agrarian League built its radical programme of democracy (or rather 'rule by the people') on this tradition and played a key role in constitutional disputes, opposing both Bolshevist and reactionary bourgeois definitions of democracy.⁶⁸ Speaking against the monarchical majority of the Rump Parliament of 1918, the leader of the party, Santeri Alkio, insisted that it was 'a natural law' that 'the development of all humankind proceeds towards democracy'.[69] The Finns, too, should trust in 'the development of the people, the inner power of the people, the education of the people and a constitution that enables the realization of rule by the people'.[70] Alkio asserted that democracy would, despite all its acknowledged shortcomings, inevitably prevail and that the old elites had simply better recognize that in time.[71] Alkio's unreservedly optimistic and future-oriented, nonsocialist and antielitist description of democracy was exceptional in the post-Civil-War context. The availability of this variety of Nordic peasant democracy, as a middle way between conservative and radical socialist conceptions, provides one explanation as to why the majority of Finns opted for parliamentary democracy as opposed to the Russian or German alternatives.

Moderate Social Democratic Definitions of Parliamentary Democracy

Various branches of socialist thought advocated different concepts of democracy, ranging from the process-like concept of the revisionist majority Social Democrats to radical leftist understandings of democracy as the rule of the working class and the Bolshevist replacement of parliamentary democracy with a dictatorship of the proletariat.

In the case of the British Labour Party, the reformist implications of democracy were raised more distinctly only during the election campaign of 1918. In the reform debates of 1917, few Labour MPs used democracy as a programmatic concept, which differed from the contemporary Social Democratic discourses in Germany, Sweden and Finland. The Labour Party was careful not to associate itself with 'Russian democracy', the future direction of which was not yet known. Democracy was used rhetorically either to oppose or to defend proportional representation.[72] In the opinion of the British far left, Britain lacked democracy, even in comparison with Germany, and preparations for direct action were thus considered necessary.[73] As the Labour Party set out to demand democratic reforms at home and support for democracy in Europe in 1918,[74] Lloyd George responded with insinuations of Bolshevism.[75] Despite a poor election result, the Labour Party continued to prioritize representative democracy over direct action,[76] distancing itself from council democracy – though its leading theorist, James Ramsay MacDonald, continued to emphasize weaknesses in parliamentary democracy and called for a British combination of democracy and socialism.[77]

The German Social Democrats openly challenged the Prussian order from late 1916 onwards with calls for political democracy in the sense of extended suffrage and the parliamentarization of the government. From the autumn of

1918 onwards, they competed with the far left by making cautious promises of economic and social democracy in addition to political democracy. A German version of democracy was their goal both during the war and after it: the Western democracies had their institutional deficiencies, whereas Germany had progressed in most areas of life and needed a revision of the political system to strengthen the state.[78] While the German Social Democrats and their centrist allies failed to force through a reform in Germany in 1917 and became associated by the right with plotting on behalf of the enemy, their calls for democratization, which were reported in the press, encouraged the Swedish and Finnish left (and even the British far left) to call for related reforms at home.

The political situation in Germany had changed completely by the time of the Weimar National Assembly in the spring of 1919. The polity had been preliminarily parliamentarized in October 1918, with some calling for the democratization of the constitution and others supporting changes mainly to please the Entente in the hope of more favourable peace terms. The monarchy had fallen, and leftist experiments with direct council democracy had provided an alternative to parliamentary democracy, albeit one that the majority Social Democrats rejected as Bolshevism. In Weimar, the discourse on democracy was dominated by Social Democratic leaders who tried to find a middle way, playing down rightist accusations of betraying the nation by importing Western notions of democracy, on the one hand, and countering far-left criticism that they were not advancing the interests of the workers to a sufficient extent, on the other. One solution was to vernacularize democracy every now and then to underscore its national character as 'rule by the people' (*Volksherrschaft*),[79] which was not so far away from the organic concept of a 'people's community' (*Volksgemeinschaft*) favoured by practically all political groups.[80] Eduard David, the minister responsible for the preparation of the new constitution, presented the proposal as 'the most democratic constitution in the world'[81] and the future Germany as a 'democratic republic, a republic in which the supreme state power rests in the people, in which the representation of the people is the source of political power'.[82] Social Democrats spoke about 'the democratic construction of our country' in 'the spirit of democracy',[83] but failed to win support for this discourse from the other parties. In Germany, democratic discourse remained distinctly party-political; it was overwhelmingly Social Democratic. Furthermore, disappointment with the Western powers resulting from the Treaty of Versailles gave democracy a questionable reputation.

The rhetoric of democracy and calls for suffrage reform (and other reforms that would follow in due course) were particularly strong among the Swedish Social Democrats. Their discourse was also the most internationalist, in that it viewed Swedish democratization as part of an irresistible pan-European, if not a global, process.[84] In the aftermath of the Russian February Revolution, the Social Democrats emphasized the breakthrough of 'democratism' (a term that the right loathed) in every neighbouring country, a development that forced Sweden into introducing a reform.[85] Democratization would create opportunities for the talents of the people to develop and would lead to an increase in rational thinking among the masses; it would not lead to any upheavals.[86] The Swedish right was presented as allying itself with the 'antidemocratic ideals' of the past and with contemporary Germany by opposing the will of the Swedish people.[87]

The Liberal–Social Democratic coalition managed to force through the reform only after the fall of the German monarchy. The Social Democrats emphasized external pressures – the victory of Western democracy in the war and the German Revolution – in addition to the demands of the Swedish people, as forcing Sweden to change. To persuade the right, Hjalmar Branting described the future democracy as 'mature' and 'informed', and promised that it would proceed with caution when changing society:[88] an essentially 'Swedish democracy' would solve future problems in accordance with the will of the people,[89] a choice of words that reflects the general tendency to nationalize democracy after the war, which added to earlier national historiographies of democracy. On the other hand, in order to please the left, Branting promised that the democratization would take place in the spirit of 'our socialistic and democratic ideals' and bring the rule of the privileged to an end.[90] Swedish Social Democrats were positively optimistic about their future victory once majority parliamentarism was strengthened through universal suffrage, and they did not hesitate to identify the goals of democracy with their own ideology.

In Finland, the Social Democrats followed Kautskyist teachings about the priority of parliamentary activity in the expectation of a peaceful revolution in principle, but in practice their discourse on democracy had been more radical and was further radicalized under the influence of the Russian Bolsheviks. The lack of a split among the socialists, unlike what happened in Sweden and Germany, meant that the moderates moved closer to the radicals. In July 1917, the possibility of a Bolshevik takeover in Petrograd (and expected constitutional changes in Berlin) encouraged the Social Democratic parliamentary majority to aim at full parliamentary sovereignty on the basis of a Marxist concept of democracy as the rule of the working classes. After the Russian October Revolution, the party adopted an openly revolutionary concept of democracy, one that the bourgeois parties associated with Bolshevism. Also after the Civil War, most Social Democratic speakers maintained their opposition to 'bourgeois' democracy, although some members aimed at building a bridge between the party and the centre by giving up the class-based exclusion of nonsocialist groups from the democratic forces. The aim of the revisionist moderates was to create 'such a constitution that the democratic majority of the people can act within it and advance social development'. They recognized the potential of the republican constitution as a compromise,[91] and in the interwar years they joined the bourgeois republicans in constructing a democratic Finland based on majority parliamentarism.

Radical Leftist Definitions of Democracy

In Britain, the far left remained on the fringes of political discourse, propagating their views mainly through the press. The German and Swedish Social Democratic Parties, unlike the Finnish Social Democratic Party, were divided into revisionist majorities and radical Marxist minorities during the spring of 1917. Among the minorities, examples from Russia supported more radical conceptions of democracy: criticisms of parliamentary representation as a realization of democracy were heard and 'direct democracy' idealized. The Swiss political system, in which there was no division between legislative and executive power, was presented as an alternative to Western parliamentarism, which was 'the opposite of democracy'.[92]

In Germany, many radical leftists were active in the council revolution, aiming at direct democracy. In Weimar, they wished to extend the concept of democracy: Oskar Cohn called for the democratization of all aspects of national life and the abolition of distinctions between the governing and the governed.[93] Despite trying to avoid associations with Bolshevism, the Independent Social Democrats rejected 'bourgeois' compromises on democracy and parliamentarism. For Alfred Henke, the proposed system constituted no more than a 'democracy of a minority' that legitimated the continuation of capitalist rule.[94] Though marginalized, the leftists forced the Majority Social Democrats to recognize that, in addition to political democracy, economic democracy and social justice should also be advanced.[95]

The Swedish leftists initially defined democracy in more inclusive terms than German or Finnish radicals, speaking for a democratic bloc that excluded only the 'anti-democratism' of the right.[96] They called for social and economic as well as political democracy, echoing the German far left and forcing the Majority Social Democrats to make promises on related reforms. They demanded *both* democracy and parliamentarism,[97] although appeals to the masses remained in their arsenal. Many leftists also sympathized with the uprising of the Finnish Reds, with whom they shared the notion of an ancient Swedish democratic tradition that needed to be restored.[98]

Bolshevik Democracy?

On the far left, a rejection of parliamentary democracy in favour of a dictatorship of the proletariat was arising. This concept tended to supplant alternative understandings of democracy in Russian discourse and was actively imported to other countries, the first of which was Finland. In Britain, Germany and Sweden, the sympathizers of the Bolsheviks never managed to take over.

The disappointment of the Finnish Social Democrats with parliamentary means of reform after 1907 was exacerbated in 1917 by a gradually radicalizing revolutionary discourse that contributed to their armed rising against parliamentary government in January 1918. In July 1917, Yrjö Mäkelin, Chairman of the Constitutional Committee, accused the bourgeoisie of 'a fear of the people's power', i.e. the rule of the working classes.[99] Under transnational influence from Russia, with Finnish MPs attending revolutionary assemblies in Petrograd, revolutionary Russian soldiers present and Bolshevik leaders visiting Helsinki, Kautskyist notions of parliamentarism and democracy were supplanted by Russian revolutionary discourse, in which contrasts between the educated classes and the workers as constituting the 'people' proper were emphasized (see the chapter by Beuerle in this volume). The bourgeois parties were excluded from cooperation in the construction of democracy; only the socialist majority represented true democrats. After the October Revolution, Social Democratic definitions of democracy were radicalized further, and the bourgeois parties, which now held a majority in parliament, were accused of being 'hungry for violence and illegality in the fear of democracy'.[100] The bourgeoisie lacked 'a democratic conscience' and were ready to make use of Russian counter-revolutionary forces 'against the democratic parliament of Finland, against Finnish democracy', referring to the dissolved former parliament with its Social Democratic majority.[101] The Bolshevik power in Russia, by contrast, represented 'true democracy'.[102]

In the eyes of the Finnish bourgeois parties, this uncompromising discourse became associated with the Bolshevik rejection of parliamentarism and democracy in favour of terror.[103] They responded with a republican constitutional proposal based on the principles of democracy as they understood it.[104] A violent confrontation on the proper form of democracy was approaching as Otto Wille Kuusinen challenged this proposal as mere 'bourgeois democracy', the parliamentary model of which did not represent true democracy at all.[105] He claimed that Joseph Stalin, the commissar responsible for national questions, had instead recently shown in Helsinki the way to 'the democratic self-determination of Finland'.[106] Internationally, the Finnish Civil War constituted an example of a Bolshevik threat to representative democracy that made even conservative circles more ready to try regulated forms of democracy. The communist parties founded in this period, for their part, customarily denounced democracy and parliamentarism in their 'bourgeois' forms.

Conclusion

The collective experiences and propagandistic discourses of the First World War and the Russian Revolution brought democracy to the centre of political debate around Europe and among all ideological groups. Democracy was becoming an increasingly normative and future-oriented programmatic and procedural concept concerning the organization and functioning of political systems. It was becoming a concept of identification for most political groups as well as an object of dispute about its proper meanings, applications and implications. The political rhetoric of democracy – if not always democracy as a functioning system of government enjoying legitimacy in the eyes of the majority of the people – was making progress.

The discourse on democracy was greatly influenced by the international situation, especially after U.S. President Woodrow Wilson had given the concept normative and goal-oriented content. The prospective result of the war also affected understandings of democracy in smaller countries, the Swedish and Finnish right providing the most obvious examples of wartime opportunism and the far left being equally inspired by the Russian Revolution. In Britain, the democratization of Germany, though demanded in war propaganda, was viewed with suspicion for domestic party-political reasons, which, in turn, decreased German respect for democracy. Debates on democracy were affected by international comparisons and transnational transfers carried out in particular by internationalist socialists and conservative academics.

Even if catalysed by the transnational moment of early 1917, the debates on democracy remained overwhelmingly nation state-centred and were nationalized everywhere again in 1918 and 1919, giving the impression that transitions to democratic suffrage had been national processes. Whereas in Britain democracy was becoming a concept used by most political groups to characterize the established or future political order, and in Germany and Sweden it was mainly only the right who remained doubtful of democracy as a Western import or outdated idea, in Finland a violent confrontation on the understandings of democracy between socialists and nonsocialists emerged, which was reflective of the challenge of the Bolshevik ideal of the dictatorship of the proletariat to regulated 'bourgeois' parliamentary democracy.

Typical of the debates was an emphasis on equal voting rights and the parliamentary representation of the people as constitutive of democracy as a process leading to reforms; this definition also became increasingly accepted by Social Democrats, while the far left spoke for revolutionary council models and the immediate implementation of social and economic democracy. The German and Finnish left and some centrists associated democracy with the republican form of government, whereas the right continued to prefer monarchical and organic conceptions of the political system and mere revisions of the mixed constitution.

After revisionist Social Democrats prioritized parliamentary democracy in nation states, the readiness of the right to adapt to extended participation by the people would be decisive. A common strategy of obstruction among conservatives had been to rhetorically redescribe the established order as 'democratic'. Now the even less palatable scenario of a takeover by Bolshevism contributed to their adaptation to democracy. The British Conservatives reconsidered their stance under exceptional wartime circumstances. In Sweden and Finland, the right deferred reluctantly to a constitutional compromise after the fall of the Prussian model. In Germany, the right shunned such compromises and maintained their anti-democratic attitudes.

Pasi Ihalainen is Professor of Comparative European History at the University of Jyväskylä, Finland. His authored and coedited books include *Protestant Nations Redefined* (2005), *Agents of the People: Democracy and Popular Sovereignty in British and Swedish Parliamentary and Public Debates, 1734–1800* (2010), *Scandinavia in the Age of Revolution: Nordic Political Cultures, 1740–1820* (2011), *Language Policies in Finland and Sweden: Interdisciplinary and Multi-sited Comparisons* (2015) and *The Springs of Democracy: National and Transnational Debates on Constitutional Reform in the British, German, Swedish and Finnish Parliaments, 1917–1919* (2017).

Notes

1. For further background, see P. Ihalainen, C. Ilie and K. Palonen (eds), *Parliament and Parliamentarism: A Comparative History of a European Concept* (New York: Berghahn Books, 2016).
2. Speech (27 February 1917). *Stenographische Berichte* (Berlin, 1917–19). *Verhandlungen des Reichstags* (VdR), http://www.reichstagsprotokolle.de/index.html, 2374–75.
3. Speech (28 March 1917). Hansard Online, http://hansard.millbanksystems.com, c. 489.
4. Search Google Books Ngram Viewer for 'democracy' between 1700 and 2014 to see a distinct peak in British and American English references and a considerable rise in German ones in 1917–19. A rise in Russian references started in 1914, but peaked only in 1922.

5. J. Leonhard, *Die Büchse der Pandora. Geschichte des Ersten Weltkriegs* (Munich: C.H. Beck, 2014), 11, 14; R. Bessel, 'Revolution', in J. Winter (ed.), *The Cambridge History of the First World War, Vol. 2: The State* (Cambridge: Cambridge University Press, 2014), 126–27, 144.
6. See P. Ihalainen, *The Springs of Democracy: National and Transnational Debates on Constitutional Reform in the British, German, Swedish and Finnish Parliaments 1917–1919* (Helsinki: Finnish Literature Society, 2017), https://doi.org/10.21435/sfh.24, for extended national contexts. The intention here is to focus on how various ideological groups discursively constructed democracy.
7. M. Weber, *Gesammelte politische Schriften*, ed. Johannes Winckelmann (Tübingen, 1988 [1918]), 405. The term 'democratization' was in use in the other studied languages, but only to a very limited extent in English, in which it mainly referred to what should or was claimed to be happening in Germany. Its later social scientific meanings are not discussed here.
8. R. Bavaj and M. Steber, 'Germany and "the West": The Vagaries of a Modern Relationship', in R. Bavaj and M. Steber (eds), *Germany and 'the West': The History of a Modern Concept* (New York: Berghahn Books, 2015), 17–18; M. Llanque, 'The First World War and the Invention of "Western Democracy"', in Bavaj and Steber, *Germany and 'the West'*, 70–71.
9. Gustav Noske, VdR, 29 March 1917, 2841; *The Herald*, 'The Prussian Reform Bill', 15 December 1917; 'Appeal to the Congress', 29 December 1917.
10. M. Llanque, *Demokratisches Denken im Krieg. Die deutsche Debatte im Ersten Weltkrieg* (Berlin: Academie Verlag, 2000), 102; Llanque, 'The First World War', 74–75.
11. *Manchester Guardian*, 'Trade Unionism and Democracy', 2 September 1918; *The Times*, 'Towards a Programme', 14 November 1918, 'The Voter's Choice', 12 December 1918; *Manchester Guardian*, 'Premier & Government Promises', 2 January 1919.
12. D. Newton, *British Policy and the Weimar Republic, 1918–1919* (Oxford: Clarendon Press, 1997), 1, 10–11, 415, 417, 424–25.
13. Llanque, *Demokratisches Denken*, 102–4, 106, 111–12.
14. Llanque, *Demokratisches Denken*, 12–13, 214, 307.
15. P. Ihalainen, 'The 18th-Century Traditions of Representation in a New Age of Revolution: History Politics in the Swedish and Finnish Parliaments, 1917–1919', *Scandinavian Journal of History* 40(1) (2015), 70–96.
16. C. Gusy, 'Einleitung: Demokratisches Denken in der Weimarer Republik – Entstehungsbedingungen und Vorfragen', in C. Gusy (ed.), *Demokratisches Denken in der Weimarer Republik* (Baden-Baden: Nomos, 2000), 11–36, 27.
17. *The Times*, 'M. Branting's Tribute to British Army', 22 July 1918; *Manchester Guardian*, 'M. Branting's Visit', 28 July 1918, 'Socialist Appeal to Mr. Henderson', 17 November 1918.
18. N.R. McCrillis, *The British Conservative Party in the Age of Universal Suffrage: Popular Conservatism, 1918–1929* (Columbus: Ohio State University Press, 1998), 16.

19. J. Garrard, *Democratization in Britain: Elites, Civil Society and Reform since 1800* (Basingstoke: Palgrave Macmillan, 2001), 4.
20. For Germany, see T. Mergel, *Parlamentarische Kultur in Weimarer Republik. Politische Kommunikation, symbolische Politik und Öffentlichkeit im Reichstag* (Düsseldorf: Droste, 2007), 38–39.
21. VdR, 27 February 1917, 2404.
22. VdR, 29 March 1917, 2859.
23. Von Graefe, VdR, 30 March 1917, 2919.
24. *Neue Preußische Zeitung*, 1 August 1919; Mergel, *Parlamentarische Kultur*, 38–39.
25. *Riksdagens protokoll vid ... riksmötet år ... Första kammaren* (FK) (Stockholm: Riksdagen, 1867–1948), 17 December 1918, 10:68–69.
26. T. Nilsson, *Mellan arv och utopi. Moderata vägval under hundra år, 1904–2004* (Stockholm: Santérus, 2004), 81, 145.
27. *Valtiopäiväasiakirjat* (VP), *Pöytäkirjat* (Helsinki: Eduskunta, 1907–75), 12 June 1918, 1253, 1651.
28. Viscount Bryce, House of Lords Hansard, House of Commons Parliamentary Papers Database, 17 December 1917, c. 176.
29. J. Bryce, *Modern Democracies*, 2 vols (New York: Macmillan, 1921).
30. *Riksdagens protokoll vid ... riksmötet ... Andra kammaren* (AK) (Stockholm: Riksdagen, 1867–1948), 5 June 1917, 72:65.
31. Arvid Lindman, AK, 27 April 1918, 44:42–43.
32. AK, 26 November 1918, 9:2632.
33. AK, 17 December 1918, 18:44.
34. FK, 17 December 1918, 11:9–10.
35. VP, 21 June 1919, 1021.
36. J. Kurunmäki and J. Strang (eds), *Rhetorics of Nordic Democracy* (Helsinki: Finnish Literature Society, 2010).
37. R. Saunders, 'Democracy', in D. Craig and J. Thompson (eds), *Languages of Politics in Nineteenth-Century Britain* (Basingstoke: Palgrave Macmillan, 2013), 142–67.
38. Hansard, 22 May 1917, c. 2173–76.
39. Henry Craik, Hansard, 22 May 1917, c. 2237.
40. Beyerle, VdR, 28 February 1919, 464–65.
41. VdR, 28 February 1919, 383.
42. AK, 21 March 1917, 33:60.
43. AK, 14 April 1917, 41:38.
44. AK, 14 April 1917, 41:69.
45. Eirik Hornborg, VP, 8 November 1917, 28.
46. R.A. Wrede, VP, 12 July 1918, 1652.
47. Paavo Virkkunen, VP, 7 August 1918, 1824.
48. VP, 8 October 1918, 53.
49. Hansard, 23 May 1917, c. 2409.
50. FK, 9 June 1917, 56:45–46.
51. FK, 26 November 1918, 5:30.

52. VP, 6 December 1917, 368.
53. M. Hyvärinen, 'Valta', in M. Hyvärinen et al., *Käsitteet liikkeessä. Suomen poliittisen kulttuurin käsitehistoria* (Tampere: Vastapaino, 2003), 83.
54. Hansard, 23 March 1917, 2395.
55. Hansard, 23 May 1917, cc. 2343, 2346.
56. *Manchester Guardian*, 'The Government of India', 6 July 1918, 'A New Epoch in India', 7 July 1918, 'Indian Reforms', 12 July 1918, 'The New Era in India', 18 August 1918.
57. VdR, 29 March 1917, 2854.
58. Rudolf Heinze, VdR, 30 July 1919, 2093.
59. Otto Wiemer, VdR, 27 February 1917, 2400.
60. Friedrich von Payer, VdR, 10 February 1919, 20; *Berliner Tageblatt*, 11 February 1919.
61. VdR, 8 February 1919, 13.
62. AK, 27 April 1918, 44:21–22; FK, 27 April 1918, 27:32.
63. AK, 17 December 1918, 17:8.
64. Carl Gustaf Ekman, FK, 17 December 1918, 11:13.
65. VP, 14 June 1919, 884.
66. VP, 14 June 1919, 884.
67. In the Finnish language, there is no such clear distinction between the political people (*kansa*), the ethnic nation (*kansakunta*) or even a person with the rights of a citizen (*kansalainen*).
68. Santeri Alkio, VP, 12 June 1917, 511.
69. VP, 12 June 1918, 1254.
70. VP, 12 July 1918, 1659–60.
71. VP, 24 May 1919, 513.
72. Ramsay MacDonald, Hansard, 22 May 1917, c. 2227; Charles Cripps, House of Lords Hansard, 17 December 1917, c. 193.
73. *The Herald*, 'The New Germany', 12 October 1918, and 'The Dud Parliament', 21 December 1918.
74. *Manchester Guardian*, 'The Labour Appeal', 28 November 1918, 'Mr. Arthur Henderson', 2 December 1918.
75. C. Wrigley, *Lloyd George and the Challenge of Labour: The Post-War Coalition 1918–1922* (Hemel Hempstead: Harvester Wheatsheaf, 1990), 1–2.
76. *Manchester Guardian*, 'Labour in the New Parliament', 1 January 1919.
77. J.R. MacDonald, *Parliament and Revolution* (S.l., s.n. [1919]), 64–65, 103–4.
78. Gustav Noske, VdR, 29 March 1917, 2839; Eduard David, VdR, 30 March 1917, 2902; Friedrich Ebert in July 1917 as cited in Llanque, *Demokratisches Denken*, 200.
79. VdR, 4 March 1919, 500.
80. See Llanque, *Demokratisches Denken*, 322; Mergel, *Parlamentarische Kultur*, 54.
81. VdR, 7 February 1919, 8.
82. VdR, 4 March 1919, 498.
83. See for instance Paul Löbe, VdR, 10 February 1919, 20.

84. AK, 27 April 1917, 50:22; AK, 5 June 1917, 72:5.
85. AK, 14 April 1917, 41:27.
86. Gunnar Löwegren, AK, 14 April 1917, 41:26–27.
87. Harald Hallén, AK, 27 April 1918, 44:37.
88. AK, 26 November 1918, 9:22; AK, 17 December 1918, 17:22.
89. AK, 26 November 1918, 9:24.
90. AK, 17 December 1918, 17:24; AK, 17 December 1918, 17:32.
91. Hannes Ryömä, VP, 24 May 1919, 510; 14 June 1919, 927.
92. Carl Lindhagen, AK, 21 March 1917, 33:37, 64.
93. T. Pohl, *Demokratisches Denken in der Weimarer Nationalversammlung* (Hamburg: Kovac, 2002), 125.
94. Pohl, *Demokratisches Denken*, 137.
95. Pohl, *Demokratisches Denken*, 140; Eduard David, VdR, 7 February 1919, 9; 4 March 1919, 500–1.
96. Ivar Vennerström, AK, 27 April 1917, 50:24.
97. Ivar Vennerström, AK, 5 June 1917, 72:11–12, 67; 26 November 1918, 9:15; Fredrik Ström, FK, 26 November 1918, 5:35, 17 December 1918, 10:42, 45; Ivar Vennerström, AK, 17 December 1918, 17:61, 71; 17 December 1918, 18:36, 24 May 1919, 54:16; A. Friberg, *Demokrati bortom politiken: en begreppshistorisk analys av demokratibegreppet inom Sveriges socialdemokratiska arbetareparti 1919–1939* (Stockholm: Atlantis, 2013).
98. AK, 5 June 1917, 72:50; Ihalainen, 'The 18th-Century Traditions of Representation'.
99. VP, 2 July 1917, 687, 689.
100. Jaakko Mäki, VP, 8 November 1917, 15.
101. Edvard Hänninen-Walpas, VP, 10 November 1917, 62–63.
102. Yrjö Sirola, VP, 8 November 1917, 25–26; 26 November 1917, 221–23; 7 December 1917, 411.
103. Paavo Virkkunen, VP, 26 November 1917, 206, 244.
104. VP, 24 November 1917, 182.
105. Otto Wille Kuusinen, VP, 5 December 1917, 350.
106. Yrjö Sirola, VP, 7 December 1917, 412, 416.

Bibliography

Bavaj, R., and M. Steber. 2015. 'Germany and "the West": The Vagaries of a Modern Relationship', in R. Bavaj and M. Steber (eds), *Germany and 'the West': The History of a Modern Concept*. New York: Berghahn Books, 1–37.

Bessel, R. 2014. 'Revolution', in J. Winter (ed.), *The Cambridge History of the First World War, Vol. 2: The State*. Cambridge: Cambridge University Press, 2014, 126–44.

Bryce, J. 1921. *Modern Democracies*, 2 vols. New York: Macmillan.

Friberg, A. 2013. *Demokrati bortom politiken: en begreppshistorisk analys av demokratibegreppet inom Sveriges socialdemokratiska arbetareparti 1919–1939.* Stockholm: Atlantis.

Garrard, J. 2001. *Democratization in Britain: Elites, Civil Society and Reform since 1800.* Basingstoke: Palgrave Macmillan.

Gusy, C. 2000. 'Einleitung: Demokratisches Denken in der Weimarer Republik – Entstehungsbedingungen und Vorfragen', in C. Gusy (ed.), *Demokratisches Denken in der Weimarer Republik.* Baden-Baden: Nomos, 11–36.

Hyvärinen, M. 2003. 'Valta', in M. Hyvärinen et al., *Käsitteet liikkeessä. Suomen poliittisen kulttuurin käsitehistoria.* Tampere: Vastapaino, 63–113.

Ihalainen, P. 2015. 'The 18th-Century Traditions of Representation in a New Age of Revolution: History Politics in the Swedish and Finnish Parliaments, 1917−1919', *Scandinavian Journal of History* 40(1), 70–96.

———. 2017. *The Springs of Democracy: National and Transnational Debates on Constitutional Reform in the British, German, Swedish and Finnish Parliaments, 1917–1919.* Helsinki: Finnish Literature Society. https://doi.org/10.21435/sfh.24.

Ihalainen, P., C. Ilie and K. Palonen (eds). 2016. *Parliament and Parliamentarism: A Comparative History of a European Concept.* Oxford: Berghahn Books.

Kurunmäki, J., and J. Strang (eds). 2010. *Rhetorics of Nordic Democracy.* Helsinki: Finnish Literature Society.

Leonhard, J. 2014. *Die Büchse der Pandora. Geschichte des Ersten Weltkriegs.* Munich: C.H. Beck.

Llanque, M. 2000. *Demokratisches Denken im Krieg. Die deutsche Debatte im Ersten Weltkrieg.* Berlin: Academie Verlag.

———. 2015. 'The First World War and the Invention of "Western Democracy"', in Bavaj and Steber, *Germany and 'the West'*, 69–80.

MacDonald, J.R. [1919]. *Parliament and Revolution.* S.l., s.n.

McCrillis, N.R. 1998. *The British Conservative Party in the Age of Universal Suffrage: Popular Conservatism, 1918–1929.* Columbus: Ohio State University Press.

Mergel, T. 2007. *Parlamentarische Kultur in Weimarer Republik. Politische Kommunikation, symbolische Politik und Öffentlichkeit im Reichstag.* Düsseldorf: Droste.

Newton, D. 1997. *British Policy and the Weimar Republic, 1918–1919.* Oxford: Clarendon Press.

Nilsson, T. 2004. *Mellan arv och utopi. Moderata vägval under hundra år, 1904–2004.* Stockholm: Santérus.

Pohl, T. 2002. *Demokratisches Denken in der Weimarer Nationalversammlung.* Hamburg: Kovac.

Saunders, R. 2013. 'Democracy', in D. Craig and J. Thompson (eds), *Languages of Politics in Nineteenth-Century Britain.* Basingstoke: Palgrave Macmillan, 142–67.

Weber, M. 1988. *Gesammelte politische Schriften* (1918), Johannes Winckelmann (ed.). Tübingen: Mohr Siebeck,.

Wrigley, C. 1990. *Lloyd George and the Challenge of Labour: The Post-War Coalition 1918–1922.* Hemel Hempstead: Harvester Wheatsheaf.

Chapter 8

The Edges of Democracy

German, British and American Debates on the Dictatorial Challenges to Democracy in the Interwar Years

Marcus Llanque

The interwar years have been described retrospectively as a 'high noon of dictators'.[1] But these years started as the heyday of democracy. To 'make the world safe for democracy' had been the battle cry of the United States when it entered the war on the side of the Entente, joining the allies against Germany and Habsburg Austria only after Tsarist Russia had left the alliance. The idea of 'Western democracy' as opposed to German militarism was an invention of the First World War's propaganda battles.[2] In 1917 and 1918 monarchies disappeared, to be followed by democratization. The victorious powers of the West themselves had to face democratic demands and in reaction broadened the suffrage extensively: Great Britain enacted the Representation of the People Act of 1918 extending the suffrage to all males, while in the United States, the Nineteenth Amendment granted all female citizens the right to vote in 1920.

Nothing seemed more certain than a bright future for democracy. Its idea could claim a hegemonic position in political thinking. James Bryce was no exception in talking about the 'universal acceptance of democracy as the normal and natural form of government' in 1921.[3] Nevertheless, if democracy was the 'temple' of political thinking, it soon found itself deserted, as Mazower puts it in the opening chapter 'Rise and Fall of Democracy' in his *The Dark Continent*.[4] But this position is misleading. From Bryce to Mazower, the standard or 'normal' interpretation of democracy is understood as 'liberal' democracy, which immediately after the First World War turned out to be contested. Democracy did prevail, and it dominated all political debates. Not democracy as such but the liberal interpretation of democracy was what was challenged. Keystones of liberal thinking, such as parliament, legislation, an individualistic understanding of liberty and the rule of law, were losing their powers of persuasion. Paths of democratic thinking beyond liberalism were taken, among them dictatorship. To explore whether or not dictatorship could take the place of parliament without abandoning democracy itself was one of the major issues of the interwar years. The purpose of this chapter is to show that the idea of liberal democracy was indeed contested[5] not only by the enemies of democracy, but also by its supporters.

In retrospect, democratic theorists after the Second World War created an antagonistic opposition between the ideas of democracy and dictatorship,[6] and criticized interwar theories for not having taken a firm stance against dictatorship right from the beginning. The liberal interpretation of democracy succeeded and established a hegemonic place in the constellation of political ideas only after 1945. In analysing the interwar discourse from within, we find a much more complex situation. First, there were many interpretations of democracy beyond the liberal one claiming to be modern. Moreover, we find liberal thinkers relinquishing the conviction that liberalism provided an adequate understanding of politics. Many of them tended to accept what fascism kept repeating, namely, that liberalism was over and in decline everywhere. But liberalism was shaken not only in Germany or Italy, as we also find such discussions in the United States and in Great Britain. Many liberals were expressing their doubts about whether or not there was a specific democratic weakness responsible for the rise of dictatorial regimes. Many democrats considered liberalism to be a major weakness of modern democracies. In the end, not all critiques of liberalism were motivated by the intention to take sides against democracy and for dictatorship. Staunch supporters of democracy found themselves forced to discuss the extent to which democracies should reconsider their liberal roots and the extent to which democracies should adopt dictatorial features in order to overcome this democratic weakness. There was a rising uncertainty in the camp of democrats as to whether or not a liberal interpretation of democracy was up to the task of coping with the socioeconomic problems of the time that triggered the debate: integration of the masses into a functioning social body, meeting their needs in terms of both material resources and ideological identification, and above all providing society with a political system that was able to organize collective action. The interpretation to understand democracy as the opposing idea to dictatorship was the result of the interwar years' debate, not its starting point.

Political actions are framed by the ideas that guide them. The debate on democracy was shaped by different kinds of authors, from political philosophers to institutional reformers. The former sometimes tended towards metaphysical speculation, while the latter sometimes lost themselves in detail. The group of authors discussed here was not without political experience, most of them were members of personal networks close to political practitioners. Many of them had been active party members such as Karl Löwenstein and Theodor Heuss, who were both members of the DDP (German Democratic Party); Heuss was also a member of parliament, as was Karl Kautsky, a prominent party leader of the Social Democrats. James Bryce was a member of parliament on the liberal side. Alexander Dunlop Lindsay stood for parliament in 1938 campaigning against the Munich Agreement (and losing to the conservative candidate). Carlo Sforza was an Italian ambassador in Paris before he resigned when Mussolini took over power.

In this chapter, the case of Germany is the obvious starting point because democracy failed and dictatorship prevailed there. We find in the Weimar Republic the most ardent debate about the affinity between democracy and dictatorship. Great Britain was able to deal with modernity on the basis of traditional institutions; in particular, the British Parliament had a respected standing in the public regard that the German parliament was unable to achieve. The United States may have been far from Europe, especially after Wilsonian politics proved to be a failure and, as a result, the United States did not become a member of the League of Nations, but in terms of democratic thinking and the efforts to learn from other countries' experiences, the United States was very much involved.

Democracy in the Interwar Years: Between 'Welfare State' and 'Mass Democracy'

The motivation to debate the proximity between democracy and dictatorship stemmed from the perception of modernity. Was liberal democracy able to deal with modern challenges, especially with the protection of the masses in times of economic and social crises? Many contemporary observers concluded that liberal democracy was elevating the intensity of these challenges rather than dealing with them efficiently. Facing the social and political struggles after 1918, democracy was less often perceived as 'Western democracy', which had won the First World War, than as 'mass democracy',[7] a term that designated the tendency of modernity to uproot people, challenging all traditional forms of bonds (including parliament) and nurturing the willingness to look beyond traditional institutions and beliefs. Discussions on mass democracy had begun before the First World War[8] and dominated the debate in the 1920s.[9] 'Mass democracy' was also a sociological term, widely used by leading sociologists such as Max Weber. Although Weber died early in 1920, his ideas dominated the German debate on democracy during the 1920s.[10] He did not invent the concept of 'mass democracy', but he used it extensively in his analysis of modern society and its political regime. The advantage of the concept of 'mass democracy' was its abandonment of any essentialist thinking of the 'people' or the 'Volk' as the collective subject of democracy. In a way, mass democracy was a step ahead in political theory, since it was asking which bonds and ties were holding groups of individuals together rather than assuming that there were or should be such bonds due to the nature of the nation, the people or the state as such. To discuss democracy under the auspices of modern society was the major gain of the sociological turn in the general field of political theory. Not just Weber but also German sociological research, as well as American and British sociology, discussed the structure of modern society and its impact on the political system.[11] To speak of the masses suggests a vision of a disengaged society asking how to integrate the masses into a people able to govern themselves rather than being governed by elites or even singular leaders.

One way to integrate the 'masses' was to satisfy their material needs. Probably the major achievement of the interwar years was the rapid expansion of the welfare state. Throughout Europe, 'social democracy' became the notion entailing many ingredients that we customarily call the democratic welfare state today.[12] In retrospect, it even makes sense to speak of 'social democratic momentum'.[13] What today is known as the 'modern welfare state' was not fully established until after the Second World War, but the term 'welfare state' had been discussed well before the First World War. At least in Germany, 'Wohlfahrtsstaat' was a common phrase, used by Ferdinand Tönnies and Max Weber, covering the paternalistic efforts of the German state since Bismarck to serve the interests of the population through policies of healthcare, social security and/or education. In part, these policies were aimed at deflecting demands for further democratization. In Weimar Republic governments led by Social Democrats, these welfare policies were continued and now included areas such as housing and unemployment insurance.

Seen through the lens of our times, welfare policies can be understood as the keystone of modern democracy, whereas no political idea seems to be more opposed to democracy than dictatorship. But totalitarian countries were keen to establish a welfare system in order to prove that dictatorship had the interests of the common people in mind. There is no doubt that fascism and above all National Socialism tried to buy the support of the masses by feeding them.[14]

What then were the bonds between the population and democracy? Was the welfare provided by the democratic state or liberalism regarded as the appropriate institutional setting? Whereas liberalism cared for individual liberty, democracy could be seen as having the liberty of the people in mind, meaning a more collective approach to politics. And if liberalism organized political representation in terms of parliament, was it not also possible to represent the people by strong executive institutions or persons of the executive, for instance, 'leaders'? Was a dictator a person who could act on behalf of the people because there could be no opposition from the elite establishment? The proximity of democracy to leadership in order to protect the people from the ruling classes was already an established interpretation in the history of political ideas.

Dictatorial systems such as Fascism in Italy or National Socialism in Germany claimed to be democratic in substance while avoiding liberal forms. Giovanni Gentile saw the 'Fascist State' as the 'people's state, and, as such, the democratic state par excellence'.[15] Adolf Hitler in *Mein Kampf* even claimed to lay the groundwork for democracy, although of the 'German' kind. In the editions he published during the Weimar years, the term 'democracy' was prominent, whereas it was omitted in all editions after 1933 as it was no longer necessary to argue that National Socialist ideas were truly democratic.[16] Liberals could not tolerate these claims. From the liberal perspective, dictatorship was perceived as the intensification or even escalation of authoritarianism, especially in the view of those who personally experienced this kind of illiberal dictatorship. Contemporary observers like the exile Carlo Sforza, an Italian diplomat before being forced into exile in 1928, called it an 'epidemic' that was spreading across Europe as a result of the experience of the First World War.[17] But this seemed to be true only for countries in the European periphery, including Russia under Bolshevik rule, which was also called dictatorial. The Bolshevik Revolution caused a debate among leading socialists about the political nature of the Russian revolutionary experiment in a country of the industrialized periphery. Karl Kautsky strongly asserted that parliamentary democracy rather than dictatorship was the universal road to socialism. On that issue, fierce debate between Kautsky, on the one hand, and Lenin and Trotsky, on the other, began between 1918 and 1920,[18] with the Russians calling Kautsky a traitor of the socialist cause and Kautsky denouncing Bolshevism as an imitation of Tsarist authoritarian rule. At least before the electoral successes of the Nazis in 1932, dictatorship seemed to belong to the political periphery of Europe. But the debate among democrats was different from the start. Regardless of Italian Fascism and long before the Nazis became a significant political power, the theoretical debate about the prospects of democracy and its modern features had started, calling into question the ability of democracy to adjust to the challenges of modernity and mass society.

The Case of the United States in the mid 1920s

Winning the First World War for the democratic cause provided a major push for the democratic idea in the United States. Doubts about the value of democracy, expressed during the decades before the war, now seemed to come to an end. Corrupt urban democracy (Tammany Hall) as well as the problems of integrating the huge masses of more or less uneducated immigrants into what native authors believed to be Americanism had given rise to complaints about the 'unforeseen tendencies of democracy'. Political science, a relatively new discipline at American universities, had begun to discuss the impact of social diversity on the republican polity of the United States Constitution, which had been implemented by its framers under very different circumstances.[19] Progressivism was an attempt to provide democracy with expert knowledge in order to advise the government independently of public opinion. It was the significant impact of governmental propaganda on shaping and managing public opinion during the First World War that triggered reflections about the modernity of democracy. Regardless of the aim of such propaganda and the fact that it seemed justified in view of the democratic goals of the war, its methods and success in achieving more or less unanimous support from the public now alarmed many experts. Walter Lippmann was a Progressivist thinker who had played a major role in managing that propaganda during the war. Afterwards, he was terrified by his own success.[20] He worried about the amount of manipulative power in modern society long before fascism learned to instrumentalize these techniques for its own, anti-democratic goals.

The success of democratic propaganda during the war challenged the classical view that it was the free and independent mind of the common citizen and a free public sphere that secured progressive ideals in the end. In a famous controversy, Walter Lippmann and John Dewey sought to re-adjust the relationship between democracy and public opinion.[21] This controversy was not one between a leading democratic thinker and his anti-democratic counterpart, but a debate between two leading thinkers of Progressivism who believed in democratic ideals. In reaction to the Tennessee state law prohibiting the teaching of Darwinist evolutionary theory in state schools in the 1920s, Lippmann distanced himself from the position that majority rule was an absolute ingredient of democracy; if atavistic and regressive politics was the outcome, absolute majority rule should be questioned.[22] Dewey himself articulated concerns about majority rule, stating that it was not the institutional design that provided democracy in the end, but the minds of the citizens, therefore he proposed to invest more in education.[23] It was the contingent outcome of formal democratic procedures that troubled the supporters of the idea of democracy.

The German Case in the 1920s

In a speech given at the Reichstag on 31 July 1919, Eduard David, the German Social Democratic Minister of the Interior, proudly announced that the Weimar Constitution was the most democratic constitution in the world. With its many democratic components, both parliamentarian and plebiscitarian, the newly founded Weimar Republic surpassed any other democratic regime in terms of popular participation. The emergence of fascism in Italy did not directly impinge on the German debate at first. Many believed fascism to be a specifically Italian event. Political movements that tried to imitate Italian fascism like National Socialism were defeated after the failure of the attempt to copy the 1922 march on Rome in Munich in November 1923. As late as June 1927, liberal authors like Theodor Heuss were convinced that National Socialism was only a remnant of the era of inflation in the early 1920s. He came to the conclusion that the movement was losing vigour and momentum.[24] He was not the only one to be surprised by the rapid rise of National Socialism in terms of voter approval starting in 1930. Most analysts tended to ascribe the fascist triumphs in the early 1930s to failures and malpractices of liberal democracy and the parliamentary republic. But there was also a rising amount of background analysis of whether or not the structure of modern society was compatible with political practices of the bourgeois era.

In the Weimar debate, dictatorship already seemed to be seen as an integral part of the political system, since the emergency powers of the president were called the 'dictatorship of the President of the Republic' without any reluctance. Hence, dictatorship was an established juridical term in the debate on the balance of powers between the president and the parliament. Although we find such constitutional provisions for emergencies as well as the tendency of a gradual shift from constitutional dictatorship to totalitarian dictatorship in many European countries,[25] it was in Germany that the semantics of dictatorship seemed acceptable. Even such liberal interpreters of the Weimar Constitution as Hugo Preuss or Richard Thoma did not call that semantic practice into question.[26]

The most prominent contribution to the idea of dictatorship as a political idea was provided by Carl Schmitt, probably the most controversial author of the interwar years. As a lawyer, Schmitt was familiar with the concept of constitutional dictatorship, but he had already developed his interest in dictatorship during the First World War, when he was preparing a study of the history of dictatorship as a political idea.[27] The broad scope of that study was its unique value, dealing with many aspects of dictatorship, from constitutional provisions to the concept of the dictatorship of the proletariat.[28] Schmitt discussed dictatorship as a proper political framework for the far right as well as the far left. In his view, liberalism was not just squeezed between the extremes, but was ultimately left behind by modern political developments. Liberalism, he stated, was an anachronistic way of political thinking that belonged to the bourgeois epoch. The interesting question was now, in the early and mid 1920s, whether or not democracy would be able to cut its ideological bonds to liberalism. He contended that democracy would fare better without liberal obstacles in order to launch its core project, that is, to establish equality for all. He held liberalism to be responsible for a paralysis of dynamic political actions and proposed thinking beyond liberalism; in his view, it was – at least conceptually – no contradiction to combine democracy with dictatorship.[29] It was Schmitt who inspired his liberal counterparts among the leading jurists to integrate dictatorial measures into the model of democratic government, at least in times of emergency.[30]

For many authors, support for a liberal parliamentary democracy was not only in decline, but was already in the process of dissolution. Shortly before the Nazis took power, Gerhard Leibholz, who later became a Supreme Court judge in the Federal Republic, asked what would become of democracy after the dissolution of liberal democracy. Leibholz demanded reform in the direction of more authoritarian rule in order not to become totalitarian like Italy. The advantage of authoritarianism was, at least in Leibholz's eyes, that it would respect fundamental individual rights, whereas totalitarian rule would not only revoke the parliamentary system but would also ignore core liberal values.[31] He was just one voice in a liberal chorus singing the swan song of liberalism in the last years of the Weimar Republic. As their belief in individualism vanished, its replacement by collectivism seemed inexorable.[32]

The German case is important because of the variety of discussions on democracy in general and its relationship to dictatorship in particular, but the decline of liberalism was perceived by many as inevitable, even in established democracies such as the United States and Britain, where the challenge of totalitarian politics was discussed in terms of the limits, weaknesses and self-induced dangers of democracy.

Great Britain in the 1920s

The idea of democracy was flourishing in Great Britain in the 1920s. Conservative thinkers had already started to include democratic ideas into their political thinking even before the First World War and continued to do so in order to compete with socialist parties after 1918, sometimes highly successfully.³³ But not everybody was delighted by the prospect of democratization as the general tendency of European countries after the First World War. Former Prime Minister Herbert Asquith was quoted as saying that giving women the vote would lead to constant changes in public opinion because women are prone to be led by sentiments.³⁴ This kind of thinking may reflect the misogynistic tradition in general as well as the long opposition to women's political participation in particular, but it was also the articulation of fears that Parliament could not work properly if it were to be democratized too much.

Democracy could work only as parliamentary democracy, according to James Bryce. In his magisterial study on modern democracies, a systematic comparison of democratic regimes before the First World War, Bryce declared effective parliaments to be more important for self-government of the people than a democratically modelled scheme of broadening political participation.³⁵ Like other liberals, he was concerned about the rapid extension of the suffrage and favoured a step-by-step approach that would enable a corresponding expansion of political judgment and experience in order to promote the responsible exercise of the franchise.

Only a few authors questioned democracy immediately after 1918. Among them was Ivor Brown in his *The Meaning of Democracy* (1920).³⁶ Brown worked in the Home Office before writing mostly in the *Manchester Guardian* and becoming editor of *The Observer* in the 1940s. After the First World War, democratic idealism seemed to rule the hour. This 'New Jerusalem' of political thinking did not gain his support. Sceptics of democracy like W.H. Mallock welcomed developments towards dictatorship as a way to dampen democratic enthusiasm. He believed that he was proven right by the dictatorial phenomena in the interwar years.³⁷

Alexander Dunlop Lindsay, fellow of Balliol College and later an opponent of appeasement politics, discussed the relationship between democracy and dictatorship in 1929. In his opinion, democracy rested on the idea of consent and unanimity. But the only political regime that seemed to achieve complete consensus was dictatorship.³⁸ To Lindsay, democracy found its fulfilment in dictatorship. Like Carl Schmitt three years earlier, he saw no fundamental opposition between democracy and dictatorship. Lindsay tried to reconstruct the Anglo-Saxon roots of fascist thinking and drew an interesting connection between the Levellers in the seventeenth century, the Puritans on both sides of the Atlantic, and the modern fascists, all of whom opposed and defeated parliamentary rule. According to him: 'The attempt to get complete democracy ends in tyranny.'³⁹

In Lindsay's view, the battleground for fighting fascism was not the political system, but society. A democratic regime needs to be built on a democratic society. Therefore, 'non-political associations' with a democratic structure that could turn out to be 'schools of citizenship' should be promoted.[40] It is unclear to what extent Lindsay was influenced by the American debate between Lippmann and Dewey. His focus on the subpolitical dimension of democratic society resembles what was later advocated by neo-Tocquevillians in the 1960s, when political science in the United States established the new discipline of studying political culture.

The United States in the 1930s

Developments in Europe – and especially the transformation of German democracy into a totalitarian dictatorship – led to political as well as sociological efforts to better understand modern dictatorship and to put it into context with the general course of history and the development of society. From the moment when scientists could not attribute dictatorship to the specifics of a particular nation, its history and culture, that is, the moment when the impression was deepening that dictatorship was spreading around the world and might even flourish in well-established democracies, comparative analyses of dictatorship started as a serious business.

The Foreign Policy Association, based in New York, published an anthology on European dictatorships in 1934, which was reprinted the following year,[41] and published again in revised and enlarged form in 1937. The introductory contribution by Vera Micheles Dean called dictatorship an 'attack on democracy'.[42] The focus on Europe was understandable since Fascism in Italy and its German version were always seen as the paradigmatic examples of a modern dictatorship. But the focus broadened significantly as soon as dictatorship turned into a worldwide phenomenon. Guy Stanton Ford initiated a couple of conferences dealing with this. The first publication of one of these conferences in 1935[43] was significantly expanded into a second edition in 1939. Besides Europe, the new edition also analysed Turkey, Japan, several Latin American countries and the Soviet Union.

Since dictatorship could not be isolated as a development particularly linked to Europe, the focus widened dramatically and the relationship between modern society and fascism came under scrutiny.[44] Could fascism be seen as a specific result of social factors like mass society or was it even the foreseeable consequence of the general trend of social development?

Although totalitarian dictatorship was no option for American democratic theorists, the constitutional aspect of dictatorship was not foreign to American debates. As early as 1897, Abraham Lincoln's presidency had been discussed as a kind of dictatorship, a debate renewed by European events during the 1930s and also by the presidency of Franklin D. Roosevelt, who attempted to tackle the Great Depression by claiming emergency measures as a prerogative of the executive branch.[45]

In order to legitimize Roosevelt's stand against adherents of a more traditional view of American democracy, many political scientists argued that the idea of democracy had changed and distanced itself from liberalism. In his presidential address to the American Political Science Association in 1935, Walter Shepard claimed that economic individualism was now discredited, and that the notion of sovereignty of the people or the will of the people was no longer acceptable and proved only to be a constraint on modern democratic politics, which he wanted to overcome. Therefore, he prepared his audience by claiming that in the course of further developments and in order to adjust democracy to modern society, reform politics may even entail elements already practised in fascism and communism. Among them were economic planning and the strategy of relying more on intelligence than on the majority of the people and its contingent wishes.[46] In May 1935, the U.S. Supreme Court declared the National Recovery Administration, Roosevelt's key instrument in fighting the effects of the Great Depression, to be unconstitutional. However, Roosevelt did not shy away from a major political battle in which he threatened to expand the number of seats on the court and to select judges more favourable to his policies. This strategy for overcoming the Supreme Court's resistance to the government's legislative agenda in social and economic politics provoked particular criticism. The government was accused of exercising quasi-dictatorial means. But these were desperate times and there were also some voices who wished for Roosevelt to become some kind of 'genial and lighthearted dictator' in order to circumvent the resistance of the courts as well as Congress against his economic and social measures.[47]

Once again, the initial question concerned the extent to which the liberal idea of democracy could solve modern problems. A 'drift to dictatorship' seemed inevitable for many.[48] Totalitarian dictatorship of the European kind in itself was not seen as a threat to American democracy, but it raised the suspicion that the adjustment of democracy to modern problems was not finished yet.

Even stern adherents of the democratic idea such as John Dewey were forced to react to the growing uncertainty over whether or not and in what ways democracy was still a modern and adequate political idea. Dewey wrote a series of publications in the 1930s in which he considered democracy to be the opposite of dictatorship and the only possible reaction to the totalitarian challenge at the same time. The main task was to disentangle democracy from liberalism. The latter rather than the former seemed to be in serious crisis.[49] It was possible to practise democracy using genuinely democratic methods.[50] Instead of standing in the tradition of liberalism, democracy belonged to human nature as its ultimate project.⁵¹ In this context, Dewey developed his famous idea of democracy as a 'way of life'.⁵² He initially coined this phrase to include education within the scope of democratic thinking, this idea going back to his 'Democracy and Education' from 1916. In 1937, and facing Nazism, it was also an attempt to counter the educational efforts of a totalitarian regime aimed at controlling its subjects rather than emancipating them. Furthermore, Dewey implied that democracy was not just a form of government but was also an ethical goal in itself, a worthy focus of one's loyalty even if the democratic institutions may have seem temporarily to be in trouble.⁵³ Critics of Dewey were doubting whether his ideas had been motivated only by concerns for the future of democracy, or were also intended to delegitimize liberalism, parliamentary rule and the constitutional state as such.⁵⁴

The outbreak of the Second World War cleared the range of alternatives. In the United States, the struggle began over whether or not to enter the war, and on which side. Regardless of his efforts to define what democracy really meant and what its historical task was apart from liberalism, Dewey did not hesitate to contribute to a volume by transatlantic scientists and intellectuals in which freedom was marked as the opposite of fascism.⁵⁵ Besides Dewey, we find such other distinguished contributors as Charles Beard, Henri Bergson, Benedetto Croce, Albert Einstein, J.B.S. Haldane, Harold Laski, Thomas Mann, Jacques Maritain, Bertrand Russell and A.N. Whitehead.

Great Britain in the 1930s

Apart from the perception that fascism had something to do with modern society, in Britain the major problem with fascism was believed to be political in nature: how to respond to the emergence of fascist tendencies within democracies and from outside. Among contributors to this debate in the 1930s were Harold Laski, John A. Hobson, Ernest E. Kellett, Ernest Barker and Alfred Cobban with his study on dictatorship.

Harold Laski, teaching political science at the London School of Economics and Political Science and advising Labour,⁵⁶ gave a series of talks at the University of North Carolina in 1931, published as *Democracy in Crisis* in 1933. He still believed his older conviction to be true: that there is a connection between liberalism and capitalism, and he maintained his criticism of the 'atomic conception of social life' in capitalist democracy'.⁵⁷ But at that moment, he found it more urgent to address the modernity of liberalism rather than to criticize it. In his view, parliamentarism was the counterpart to dictatorship, preventing what the latter promoted most: action without discussion.⁵⁸ Nevertheless, a worldwide crisis of 'authority and discipline' in capitalist democracies was undeniable. Democracies were having difficulties in finding sufficient support for democratic principles among the people.[59] Laski did not find the grounds for that crisis in a taste for anarchy or dictatorship, but in the disorientation of the public and the general uncertainty caused by the Great Depression.[60] People were not sure if democracy would be able to solve these problems. However, mere calls for 'strong government' ran the risk of turning democracy into dictatorship.[61]

In order to deepen support for democracy, the Association for Education in Citizenship initiated a volume on 'Constructive Democracy'. The Association addressed itself to the task of implementing democracy as a kind of positive ideology and aimed at rooting this belief in the wider population.[62] The contributors were politicians such as Lord Halifax and Clement Attlee, as well as scientists and lawyers like the German emigrant Moritz Julius Bonn. The liberal economist Ernest Simon edited the volume and provided its opening chapter, 'The Faith of a Democrat'.[63] But the impression still prevailed that a certain 'appeal of dictatorship' should be taken into account when considering the future of democracy.[64]

Alfred Cobban was teaching history at University College London when he published his study on dictatorship in 1939.[65] In his view, the First World War had been the decisive watershed: before 1914, dictatorial tendencies could have been interpreted as mere atavistic reactions to an otherwise inevitable progress of modernity. But after 1918, a model of political regime was spreading that found its paradigm in Napoleon I, a regime of personal rule only formally legitimized by democratic means, but able to modernize society and not merely to defend its conservative features. As a historian, Cobban preferred the term 'tyranny', but he did not want to confuse it with the contemporary usage of the word. In order to make a distinction compared to republican forms of dictatorship, he coined the term 'totalitarian dictatorship'.[66] He also discussed Carl Schmitt's work on dictatorship, but he rejected Schmitt's differentiation between commissary and sovereign dictatorship as an effort to undertake politics by semantic means.[67] For Cobban, it was not democracy itself but the amalgamation of democracy with nationalism that had to take the blame for fascism. Nationalism provided dictatorship with the outlook of a spiritual concept – only now, the totalitarian dictator could claim to be both 'emperor' and 'pope' in one person.[68]

As was the case in the United States later on, it was the outbreak of the Second World War that ended these debates and the uncertainties of the public. The British people seemed unbroken by military defeat after defeat even before the United States joined the war. The concerns about whether or not the people would resist the appeal of dictatorship proved to be unfounded. A new idea entered the debate in order to provide a boundary between the ways of political thinking of the major opponents in that war: human rights. If totalitarian regimes could claim any democratic support at all or suggest that they were the more modern way to realize democracy, respect for individual human rights could now be emphazised to be the main distinction between the Western allies and the enemy.

Germany in the 1930s: German Exiles and the Concept of Militant Democracy

Even before the Nazis seized power in Germany, a flow of intellectuals had begun to emigrate. After March 1933, German jurists, historians, political thinkers and all kinds of intellectuals travelled to countries in Europe that were still free and later on crossed the Atlantic. Many emigrants provided the remaining democracies with firsthand information and advice on how to respond to fascism. The experiences with the failure of the Weimar Republic were transformed into political theory very differently, in general as well as in terms of democracy. Some intellectuals were motivated to include fascism as part of a broader picture of social development and present civilization. Members of the Frankfurt School, dispersed in different places of exile, drew a very dark picture of the present and the future. Modern civilization turned out not to be the result of progress, but was showing signs of regress into barbarism, of which fascism was only one facet, albeit not the least important one. Fascism could have been judged as a disruption of the irresistible process of civilization or its exception; now it turned out to be the rule and the main direction of history as such.[69]

Other German exiles did not lose their faith in democracy and started to campaign against coping with fascism by imitating its political features. Hans Kelsen, for instance, warned against replacing parliamentary rule with party dictatorship, notwithstanding the temptation that only an authoritarian regime could solve the economic and social problems of the present.[70]

But the lasting and probably most important contribution to the debate on the current standing and prospects of democracy at that time was the theory of 'militant democracy'.[71] Again, it was a German emigrant who started the debate: Karl Löwenstein, a former constitutional lawyer with a deep interest in the history of political ideas.[72]

Löwenstein discussed how to make democratic regimes immune to the spread of dictatorship, thus trying to provide a counter-strategy.[73] In his view, contemporary times were dominated by the struggle between democracies and nondemocracies, regardless of the difference between autocratic and dictatorial politics, which he considered to be only a matter of degree. The battleground was not only between established democracies and newly installed dictatorships, but also lay within the borders of old democracies. Löwenstein observed the appeal of dictatorships in long-established democracies like Great Britain (mentioning Mosley) and France (Croix de feu), as well as the Netherlands, Finland, the other Scandinavian countries, Czechoslovakia and even Switzerland. In his view, facism is able to abuse democracy's most likeable weakness: 'democratic tolerance'.[74]

The usual protections and constitutional grants that democracies traditionally offered even to the critics of democracy should not be given to dictators and their supporters. Democracies were under attack throughout Europe: 'A virtual state of siege confronts European democracies.'[75] Adherents of dictatorship should be treated as traitors or enemies of the constitution. But Löwenstein was convinced that a mere institutional counter-strategy was bound to fail. Although he offered a couple of such constitutional and legislative devices to oppose dictatorial movements, he also pointed out that most of these devices had been legally in effect in Weimar Germany, but did not prevent the downfall of democracy there.[76] In the end, all devices depended on individuals who could handle them correctly, firmly and with perseverance.

Therefore, Löwenstein demanded a spirit of 'militant democracy'.[77] Democrats have to strike fascists by imitating the way they fight. One potential tool he discussed was the establishment of a 'political police' in order to infiltrate and oppress enemies of democracy. He wanted to deprive the members of parliament elected on fascist lists of immunity or indemnity. For him, the real power basis of fascism was its sense of technicity and the artistic management of mass demagoguery. These means were modern aspects of contemporary society and should be integrated into the traditional concept of democracy. Facing such an enemy, democracies should overcome liberal restraints. Liberalism, Löwenstein stated, is for 'aristocratic'-minded citizens only.[78]

Any defence of liberalism and the dignity of the individual needed to be adjusted to the scope of threats embodied in modern dictatorship. At least for a transitional period, the situation required liberal-minded politicians in democracies to establish a rule of discipline and even authoritarianism in order to prevent losing everything that liberalism and democracy cherished. The goal was still a liberal one – to protect and develop individual fundamental rights – but the rights of individuals who used these privileges in order to turn democracies into the opposite should no longer be respected.[79]

Löwenstein's concept of militant democracy was a theoretical reflection of democratic practices that were already taking place in different countries. In Germany, politicians had reacted to political assassinations and military formations of extreme political parties by enacting legislation for the protection of the republic (*Republikschutzgesetz*), but ultimately it was not applied. Many European countries reacted to the rise of extremist parties and movements.[80]

In Britain, the Public Order Act was established as late as 1936, an instrument in fighting extremism.[81] But all these cases followed the tradition of defining extremism in terms of rebellion and seditious acts, and they protected the state in general rather than democracy in particular. Löwenstein drew attention to the necessity to mark a line between democrats and nondemocrats, and to deal with the paradox that democracy as the form of government for the whole people had to exclude those people who prevented democracy from governing.

It is obvious that Löwenstein proposed a very thin line between necessary adjustments of democracies to combat adherents of dictatorship and changes that would produce a dictatorial regime. Which parts of dictatorial rule modern democracies should adopt in order to steer clear of dictatorship at all was the central question. Was it enough to prohibit paramilitary formations, was it necessary to ban political parties or was it necessary to deprive individuals of some of their rights?

Conclusion and Outlook

The interwar years can be interpreted as a laboratory of discussing a wide variety of models of polity and the democratic idea. The task had been to adjust the idea of democracy to meet its contemporary challenges. One path that was intensely debated was the possibility or even necessity of finding a democratic way besides its liberal interpretation. One major impact of the interwar years debate was to draw lessons from dictatorship by inventing the theory of 'militant democracy'. This solution consists in the inclusion of means and tools practised in a more unchecked way in dictatorial regimes. Militant democracy was meant to defend democracy against its enemies even when it drove democracy nearer to dictatorship. As a result, democracy and dictatorship came to be seen as opposite ideas in principle. The process of learning was a transnational one, linking debates on democracy in German with British and American discourse. Emigrants from Germany made British and American debates aware of the danger of totalitarian dictatorship, but the debate had already started before the first emigrants arrived in exile.

It was not only the radical critics of liberalism such as Carl Schmitt who saw an affinity between democracy and dictatorship, and who asserted the alleged artificial and contingent nature of the combination of democracy with liberalism or parliamentarianism respectively. What is bewildering for the present-day observer is not so much the number of anti-liberal positions to be found in the interwar years, but rather the vanishing support for liberal democracy by those who were supposed to defend it. Maybe democracy was overwhelmed by anti-liberal forces. In some places the citadel had already been abandoned before the final storm, while in others a firm conviction would have been needed to hold it.

Britain and the United States experienced a democratic expansion of the electorate after the First World War, but maintained their traditional institutional frameworks. Nonetheless, the public debate in both countries struggled over whether the challenges of modernity should lead to major changes in the practice of democracy. It was not that authoritarian or even dictatorial preferences emerged on a significant scale, but doubts arose about the capability of liberal democracy to deal with modern challenges of integrating the masses.

Only the outbreak of the Second World War ended the debate on the future of liberal democracy. It became clear that the authoritarian way of interpreting modern democracy was not just a path alongside the path of liberal and social democracy, but was seen as being in clear contradiction to democracy and therefore had to be defeated in order to help democracy survive.

It should be noted that the terminology changed after 1945. What had been referred to as dictatorship before was increasingly called totalitarianism (as a political system) and extremism (as a political position within democracies). At the same time, the strategy to defend democracy against interior dangers by constitutional and governmental means was supplemented by educational means in order to spread the attitude that democracy was also a 'way of life' that had to be secured in hearts and minds as well. In the struggle with international communism, this Deweyian position of thinking about democracy was narrowed down to the argument that democracy and capitalism were to be considered twin concepts. Since 1990, and with a view to the transformation of the former communist countries in Eastern Europe into democracies, the argument over the way of life was transformed into the idea that a democratic government rests on a civil society and that democracy is about social practice on all levels of society. At the same time, the idea that democracy should be able to defend itself against enemies from within endured in many different forms. Democratic debates after 1945 tried to learn the lessons of the interwar years.

Marcus Llanque is Professor of Political Theory at Augsburg University. He has published extensively on the history of political ideas. His authored and coedited books include *Souveräne Demokratie und soziale Homogenität: Das politische Denken Hermann Hellers* (2010), *Verfassungsidee und Verfassungspolitik* (2015) and *Geschichte der politischen Ideen. Von der Antike bis zur Gegenwart* (2016).

Notes

1. Conan Fischer, *Europe between Democracy and Dictatorship, 1900–1945* (Oxford: Blackwell, 2011), 199–270.
2. Marcus Llanque, 'Massendemokratie zwischen Kaiserreich und westlicher Demokratie', in Christoph Gusy (ed.), *Demokratisches Denken in der Weimarer Republik* (Baden-Baden: Nomos, 2000), 38–70; Marcus Llanque, 'Der Einfluß von Max Weber auf die Entstehung der Politikwissenschaft in der Weimarer Republik', in Manfred Gangl (ed.), *Das Politische. Zur Entstehung der Politikwissenschaft während der Weimarer Republik* (Frankfurt am Main: Peter Lang, 2008), 193–215; Marcus Llanque, 'The First World War and the Invention of "Western Democracy"', in Riccardo Bavaj and Martina Steber (eds), *Germany and 'the West': The History of a Modern Concept* (Oxford: Berghahn Books), 69–80.
3. James Bryce, *Modern Democracies*, 2 vols (New York: Macmillan, 1921), vol. 1, 4.
4. Mark Mazower, *Dark Continent: Europe's 20th Century* (London: Penguin, 1998), 1–39.
5. Jan-Werner Müller, *Contesting Democracy: Political Ideas in 20th Century Europe* (New Haven / London: Yale University Press, 2011).
6. Giovanni Sartori, *Demokratietheorie* (Darmstadt: Wissenschaftliche Buchgesellschaft, 1992), 183–211; Ernst Fraenkel, 'Die repräsentative und die plebiszitäre Komponente im demokratischen Verfassungsstaat' (1958), in Ernst Fraenkel, *Deutschland und die westlichen Demokratien* (Frankfurt am Main: Suhrkamp, 1990), 153–203; Ernst Fraenkel, 'Strukturdefekte der Demokratie und deren Überwindung (1964)', in Fraenkel, *Deutschland und die westlichen Demokratien.* (Frankfurt am Main: Suhrkamp, 1990), 68–94.
7. Llanque, 'Massendemokratie'.
8. Daria Frezza, 'Masses, Crowds, Mobs: Collective Identities and Democratic Citizenship in American Social Sciences, 1890–1915', in Cornelis A. van Minnen and Sylvia L. Hilton (eds), *Federalism, Citizenship and Collective Identites in U.S. History* (Amsterdam: VU University Press, 2000), 141–64.
9. Daria Frezza, *The Leader and the Crowd: Democracy in American Public Discourse 1880–1941* (Athens, GA: University of Georgia Press, 2006); see also Stefan Jonsson, *Crowds and Democracy: The Idea and Image of the Masses from Revolution to Fascism* (New York: Columbia University Press, 2013).
10. Llanque, 'Der Einfluß von Max Weber'.
11. Dirk Berg-Schlosser and Jeremy Mitchell (eds), *Conditions of Democracy in Europe, 1919–1939* (Basingstoke: Palgrave, 2000); Dirk Berg-Schlosser and Jeremy Mitchell (eds), *Authoritarianism and Democracy in Europe, 1919–1939: Comparative Analysis* (Basingstoke: Palgrave, 2002).
12. Anselm Doering-Manteuffel, 'Soziale Demokratie als transnationales Ordnungsmodell im 20. Jahrhundert', in Jost Dülffer and Wilfried Loth (eds), *Dimensionen internationaler Geschichte* (Munich: Oldenbourg 2012), 313–33; Tim B. Müller, *Nach dem Ersten Weltkrieg. Lebensversuche moderner Demokratien* (Hamburg: Hamburger Edition 2014).

13. Sheri Berman, *The Social Democratic Moment: Ideas and Politics in the Making of Interwar Europe* (Cambridge, MA: Harvard University Press, 1998).
14. Götz Aly, *Hitler's Beneficiaries: Plunder, Racial War, and the Nazi Welfare State* (New York: Metropolitan Books, 2007).
15. Giovanni Gentile, 'The Philosophic Basis of Fascism', *Foreign Affairs* 6 (1928), 290–304, at 302.
16. Hermann Hammer, 'Die deutschen Ausgaben von Hitlers *Mein Kampf*', *Vierteljahreshefte für Zeitgeschichte*, 4 (1956), 161–78.
17. Carlo Sforza, *European Dictatorships* (New York: Brentano's, 1931 [London, 1932; German edition: Europäische Diktaturen, Berlin 1932]), Preface.
18. Karl Kautsky, *Demokratie oder Diktatur? Ein Katechismus der Sozialdemokratie* (Berlin: Cassirer, 1918); Vladimir Lenin, *Die proletarische Revolution und der Renegat Kautsky* (Bern: Promachos, 1918); Karl Kautsky, *Terrorismus und Kommunismus. Ein Beitrag zur Naturgeschichte der Revolution* (Berlin: Neues Vaterland, 1919); Leon Trotsky, *Terrorismus und Kommunismus: Anti-Kautsky* (Hamburg: Hoym, 1920); Karl Kautsky, *Von der Demokratie zur Staatssklaverei. Eine Auseinandersetzung mit Trotzki* (Berlin: Genossenschaft Freiheit, 1921).
19. John G. Gunnell, *Political Theory: Tradition and Interpretation* (Cambridge, MA: Winthrop 1979). John G. Gunnell, *The Descent of Political Theory: The Genealogy of an American Vocation* (Chicago: University of Chicago Press, 1993); Dennis J. Mahoney, *Politics and Progress: The Emergence of American Political Science* (Lanham, MD: Lexington, 2004).
20. Walter Lippmann, *Public Opinion* (London: Allen & Unwin, 1922).
21. Christopher Lasch, *The Revolt of the Elites and the Betrayal of Democracy* (New York: Norton, 1995), 161–75; Marcus Llanque, *Politische Ideengeschichte. Ein Gewebe politischer Diskurse* (Vienna: Oldenbourg-Verlag, 2008), 406–10.
22. Walter Lippmann, 'Why should the Majority rule?' (1926) in *The Essential Lippmann. A Political Philosophy for Liberal Democracy*, Clinton Rossiter and James Lare (eds) (New York: Random House, 1963), 7–8.
23. John Dewey, *The Public and its Problems* (London: Allen & Unwin, 1927).
24. Theodor Heuss, *Politik. Ein Nachschlagebuch für Theorie und Geschichte* (Halberstedt: Meyer, 1928), 138.
25. Gerhard Besier, *Das Europa der Diktaturen. Eine neue Geschichte des 20. Jahrhunderts* (Munich: DVA, 2006), 23–30.
26. Hugo Preuß, 'Reichsverfassungsmäßige Diktatur', in: *Zeitschrift für Politik*, 13 (1924), 97–113; Richard Thoma, 'Die Regelung der Diktaturgewalt', *Deutsche Juristenzeitung* 29 (1924), 654–60.
27. Carl Schmitt, *Die Diktatur. Von den Anfängen des modernen Souveränitätsgedankens bis zum proletarischen Klassenkampf* (Munich/Leipzig: Duncker and Humblot, 1921; 2nd ed, 1928).
28. Cf. John P. McCormick, 'From Constitutional Technique to Caesarist Ploy: Carl Schmitt on Dictatorship, Liberalism, and Emergency Powers', in Peter Baehr and Melvin Richter (eds), *Dictatorship in History and Theory. Bonapartism, Cae-*

sarism, and Totalitarianism (Cambridge: Cambridge University Press, 1999), 197–219.
29. Carl Schmitt, 'Der Begriff der modernen Demokratie', *Archiv für Sozialwissenschaft und Sozialpolitik* 51 (1923), 817–23.
30. Richard Thoma, 'Zur Ideologie des Parlamentarismus und der Diktatur', *Archiv für Sozialwissenschaft und Sozialpolitik* 53 (1925), 212–17; Carl Schmitt, *Die geistesgeschichliche Lage des heutigen Parlamentarismus* (Munich, Leipzig: Duncker and Humblot, 1923, 2nd ed. 1926).
31. Gerhard Leibholz, *Die Auflösung der liberalen Demokratie in Deutschland und das autoritäre Staatsbild* (Munich/Leipzig: Duncker and Humblot, 1933), 70–71.
32. Marcus Llanque, 'Der Untergang des liberalen Individuums. Zum Fin de siècle des liberalen Denkens in Weimar', in Karsten Fischer (ed.), *Neustart des Weltlaufs? Fiktion und Faszination der Zeitenwende* (Frankfurt am Main: Suhrkamp, 1999), 164–83.
33. Helen McCarthy, 'Whose Democracy? Histories of British Political Culture between the Wars', *Historical Journal* 55 (2012), 221–38.
34. Edmund S. Morgan, *Inventing the People: The Rise of Popular Sovereignty in England and America* (New York: Norton, 1988), 139.
35. James Bryce, *Modern Democracies*, 2 vols (New York: Macmillan, 1921).
36. Ivor Brown, *The Meaning of Democracy* (London: R. Cobden-Sanderson, 1920).
37. W.H. Mallock, *The Limits of Pure Democracy* (London: Chapman & Hall, 1918). W.H. Mallock, *Democracy*, an abridged edition of *The Limits of Pure Democracy* (London: Chapman & Hall, 1924).
38. A. D. Lindsay, *The Essentials of Democracy* (London: Oxford University Press, 1929, 2nd. ed. 1935), 33; cf. Norman Wintrop, *Democratic Theory as Public Philosophy: Alternative to Ideology and Utopia* (Aldershot: Ashgate, 2000), 149–66.
39. Lindsay, *The Essentials of Democracy*, 33.
40. Ibid., 80–81.
41. Vera Micheles Dean (ed.), *New Governments in Europe*, with an introduction by Raymond Leslie Buell (New York: Nelson, 1935).
42. Vera Micheles Dean, 'Attack on Democracy', in Dean, *New Governments in Europe*, 15–35.
43. Guy Stanton Ford (ed.), *Dictatorship in the Modern World* (Minneapolis: University of Minnesota Press, 1935).
44. Robert C. Bannister, 'Principle, Politics, Profession: American Sociologists and Fascism, 1930–1950', in Stephen P. Turner and Dirk Käsler (eds), *Sociology Responds to Fascism* (London: Routledge, 1992), 172–213.
45. W.E. Binkley, *The Powers of the President. Problems of American Democracy* (Garden City, NJ: Doubleday Doran, 1937); cf. Clinton Rossiter, *Constitutional Dictatorship: Crisis Government in Modern Democracies* (Princeton: Princeton University Press, 1948).
46. Walter J. Shepard, 'Democracy in Transition', *American Political Science Review* 29 (1935), 1–20, at 2–4; cf. John G. Gunnell, *Imagining American Polity: Political*

Science and the Discourse of Democracy (University Park, PA: Penn State University Press, 2004), 188–89.
47. Cited in Benjamin L. Alpers, *Dictators, Democracy, and American Public Culture: Envisioning the Totalitarian Enemy 1920s–1950s* (Chapel Hill: University of North Carolina Press, 2003), 26.
48. Tompkins McIlvain, 'The Drift to Dictatorship', *North American Review* 246 (1938), 10–34.
49. John Dewey, 'Renascent Liberalism', in *Later Works*, Jo Ann Boydston (ed.) (Carbondale: Southern Illinois University Press, 1988), vol. 11, 41–65.
50. John Dewey, 'Democratic Ends Need Democratic Methods for Their Realization' (1939), in *Later Works*, Boydston (ed.), vol. 14, 367–69.
51. John Dewey, 'Democracy and Human Nature', in *Later Works*, Boydston (ed.), vol. 13, 136–55. John Dewey, 'Creative Democracy: The Task before Us', in *Later Works*, Boydston (ed.), vol. 14, 224–30.
52. John Dewey, 'Democracy and Educational Administration', in *Later Works*, Boydston (ed.), vol. 11, 222.
53. John Dewey, 'The Basic Values and Loyalties of Democracy', in *Later Works*, Boydston (ed.), vol. 14, 275–77.
54. William Yandell Elliott, *The Pragmatic Revolt in Politics: Syndicalism, Fascism, and the Constitutional State* (New York: Macmillan, 1928); cf. Gunnell, *Imagining American Polity*, 167.
55. Ruth Nanda Anshen (ed.), *Freedom: Its Meaning* (London: George Allen & Unwin, 1940).
56. Peter Lamb, *Harold Laski: Problems of Democracy, the Sovereign State, and International Society* (Basingstoke: Palgrave Macmillan, 2004).
57. Harold J. Laski, *Democracy in Crisis* (London: Allen & Unwin, 1933), 61.
58. Ibid., 80–81.
59. Ibid., 147–232.
60. Ibid., 216.
61. Ibid., 167–69.
62. Ernest Simon (ed.), *Constructive Democracy* (London: Allen & Unwin, 1938).
63. Ibid., 13–36.
64. Maurice Alderton Pink, *The Defence of Freedom* (London: Macmillan, 1935).
65. Alfred Cobban, *Dictatorship in History and Theory* (London: Jonathan Cape, 1939).
66. Ibid., 9.
67. Ibid., 335–46.
68. Ibid., 283.
69. Max Horkheimer, 'Egoismus und Freiheitsbewegung', *Zeitschrift für Sozialforschung* 6 (1936), 161–233.
70. Hans Kelsen, 'The Party-Dictatorship', *Politica*, vol. 2 (1936), 19–32.
71. See Giovanni Capoccia, *Defending Democracy. Reactions to Extremism in Interwar Europe* (Baltimore: Johns Hopkins University Press, 2005); Marcus Llanque, 'Die Diktatur im Horizont der Demokratieidee. Zur verfassungspolitischen

Diskussion der Zwischenkriegszeit', in Christoph Gusy (ed.), *Demokratie in der Krise. Europa in der Zwischenkriegszeit* (Baden-Baden: Nomos, 2008), 52–87; Jan-Werner Müller, 'Militant Democracy', in Michael Rosenfeld and András Sajó (eds), *The Oxford Handbook of Comparative Constitutional Law* (Oxford: Oxford University Press, 2012), 1253–69.
72. See Robert van Ooyen, 'Ein moderner Klassiker der Verfassungstheorie: Karl Löwenstein. Eine Skizze', *Zeitschrift für Politik* 51 (2004), 68–86; Markus Lang, *Karl Löwenstein. Transatlantischer Denker der Politik* (Stuttgart: Franz Steiner Verlag, 2007).
73. Karl Löwenstein, 'Militant Democracy and Fundamental Rights', *American Political Science Review* 31 (1937), part I: 591–622 and part II: 725–74.
74. Löwenstein, 'Militant Democracy and Fundamental Rights', 423.
75. Ibid., 432.
76. See also Frederick Mundell Watkins, *The Failure of Constitutional Emergency Powers under the German Republic* (Cambridge, MA: Harvard University Press, 1939).
77. Löwenstein, 'Militant Democracy and Fundamental Rights', 430–31.
78. Ibid., 657.
79. Ibid., 658.
80. See Capoccia, *Defending Democracy*, 204–5.
81. Cf. Christina Bussfeld, *'Democracy versus Dictatorship'. Die Herausforderung des Faschismus und Kommunismus in Großbritannien, 1932–1937* (Paderborn: Schöningh, 2001).

Bibliography

Alpers, B.L. 2003. *Dictators, Democracy, and American Public Culture: Envisioning the Totalitarian Enemy 1920s–1950s*. Chapel Hill: University of North Carolina Press.
Aly, G. 2007. *Hitler's Beneficiaries: Plunder, Racial War, and the Nazi Welfare State*. New York: Metropolitan Books.
Anshen, R.N. (ed.). 1940. *Freedom: Its Meaning*. London: George Allen & Unwin.
Bannister, R.C. 1992. 'Principle, Politics, Profession: American Sociologists and Fascism, 1930–1950', in S.P. Turner and D. Käsler (eds), *Sociology Responds to Fascism*. London: Routledge, 172–213.
Berg-Schlosser, D. and J. Mitchell (eds). 2000. *Conditions of Democracy in Europe, 1919–1939*. Basingstoke: Palgrave.
――――. (eds). 2002. *Authoritarianism and Democracy in Europe, 1919–1939: Comparative Analysis*. Basingstoke: Palgrave.
Berman, S. 1998. *The Social Democratic Moment. Ideas and Politics in the Making of Interwar Europe*. Cambridge, MA: Harvard University Press.
Besier, G. 2006. *Das Europa der Diktaturen. Eine neue Geschichte des 20. Jahrhunderts*. Munich: DVA.
Binkley, W.E. 1937. *The Powers of the President: Problems of American Democracy*. Garden City, NJ: Doubleday Doran.
Brown, I. 1920. *The Meaning of Democracy*. London: R. Cobden-Sanderson.

Bryce, J. 1921. *Modern Democracies*, 2 vols. New York: Macmillan.
Bussfeld, C. 2001. *'Democracy versus Dictatorship'. Die Herausforderung des Faschismus und Kommunismus in Großbritannien, 1932–1937*. Paderborn: Schöningh.
Capoccia, G. 2005. *Defending Democracy. Reactions to Extremism in Interwar Europe*. Baltimore: Johns Hopkins University Press.
Cobban, A. 1939. *Dictatorship in History and Theory*. London: Jonathan Cape.
Dean, V.M. 1935. 'Attack on Democracy', in Dean, *New Governments in Europe*, 15–35.
———. (ed.). 1935. *New Governments in Europe*. New York: Nelson.
Dewey, J. 1927. *The Public and its Problems*. London: Allen & Unwin.
———. 1988a. 'The Basic Values and Loyalties of Democracy', in *Later Works*, J.A. Boydston (ed.). Carbondale: Southern Illinois University Press, vol. 14, 275–77.
———. 1988b. 'Democratic Ends Need Democratic Methods for Their Realization' (1939), in in *Later Works*, Boydston (ed.), 367–69.
———. 1988c. 'Renascent Liberalism', in *Late Later Works*, Boydston (ed.), vol. 11, 41–65.
Doering-Manteuffel, A. 2012. 'Soziale Demokratie als transnationales Ordnungsmodell im 20. Jahrhundert', in J. Dülffer amd W. Loth (eds), *Dimensionen internationaler Geschichte*. Munich: Oldenbourg, 313–33.
Elliott, W.Y. 1928. *The Pragmatic Revolt in Politics. Syndicalism, Fascism, and the Constitutional State*. New York: Macmillan.
Fischer, C. 2011. *Europe between Democracy and Dictatorship, 1900–1945*. Oxford: Blackwell.
Ford, G.S. (ed.). 1935. *Dictatorship in the Modern World*. Minneapolis: University of Minnesota Press.
Fraenkel, E. 1990. 'Die repräsentative und die plebiszitäre Komponente im demokratischen Verfassungsstaat' (Tübingen 1958), in *Deutschland und die westlichen Demokratien*. Frankfurt am Main: Suhrkamp, 153–203.
———. 'Strukturdefekte der Demokratie und deren Überwindung (1964)' in *Deutschland und die westlichen Demokratien*. Frankfurt am Main: Suhrkamp, 68–94.
Frezza, D. 2000. 'Masses, Crowds, Mobs: Collective identities and democratic citizenship in American social sciences, 1890–1915', in C.A. van Minnen and S.L. Hilton (eds), *Federalism, Citizenship and Collective Identites in U.S. History*. Amsterdam: VU University Press, 141–64.
———. 2006. *The Leader and the Crowd. Democracy in American Public Discourse 1880–1941*. Athens, GA: University of Georgia Press.
Gentile, G. 1928. 'The Philosophic Basis of Fascism', *Foreign Affairs* 6, 290–304.
Gunnell, J.G. 1979. *Political Theory: Tradition and Interpretation*. Cambridge, MA: Winthrop.
———. 1993. *The Descent of Political Theory: The Genealogy of an American Vocation*. Chicago: University of Chicago Press.
———. 2004. *Imagining American Polity. Political Science and the Discourse of Democracy*. University Park, PA: Penn State University Press.

Hammer, H. 1956. 'Die deutschen Ausgaben von Hitlers *Mein Kampf*', *Vierteljahreshefte für Zeitgeschichte* 4, 161–78.

Heuss, T. 1928. *Politik. Ein Nachschlagebuch für Theorie und Geschichte.* Halberstedt: Meyer.

Horkheimer, M. 1936. 'Egoismus und Freiheitsbewegung', *Zeitschrift für Sozialforschung* 6, 161–233.

Jonsson, S. 2013. *Crowds and Democracy: The Idea and Image of the Masses from Revolution to Fascism.* New York: Columbia University Press.

Kautsky, K. 1918. *Demokratie oder Diktatur? Ein Katechismus der Sozialdemokratie.* Berlin: Cassirer.

———. 1919. *Terrorismus und Kommunismus. Ein Beitrag zur Naturgeschichte der Revolution.* Berlin: Neues Vaterland.

———. 1921. *Von der Demokratie zur Staatssklaverei. Eine Auseinandersetzung mit Trotzki.* Berlin: Genossenschaft Freiheit.

Kelsen, H. 1936. 'The Party-Dictatorship', *Politica*, vol. 2, 19–32.

Lamb, P. 2004. *Harold Laski. Problems of Democracy, the Sovereign State, and International Society.* Basingstoke: Palgrave Macmillan.

Lang, M. 2007. *Karl Löwenstein. Transatlantischer Denker der Politik.* Stuttgart: Franz Steiner Verlag.

Lasch, C. 1995. *The Revolt of the Elites and the Betrayal of Democracy.* New York: Norton.

Laski, H.J. 1933. *Democracy in Crisis.* London: Allen & Unwin.

Leibholz, G. 1933. *Die Auflösung der liberalen Demokratie in Deutschland und das autoritäre Staatsbild.* Munich/Leipzig: Duncker and Humblot.

Lenin, V. 1918. *Die proletarische Revolution und der Renegat Kautsky.* Bern: Promachos.

Lindsay, A.D. 1929. *The Essentials of Democracy.* London: Oxford University Press, 1929.

Lippmann, W. 1922. *Public Opinion.* London: Allen & Unwin.

———. 1963. 'Why should the Majority rule?' (1926), in *The Essential Lippmann: A Political Philosophy for Liberal Democracy*, C. Rossiter and J. Lare (eds). New York: Random House, 6–14.

Llanque, M. 1999. 'Der Untergang des liberalen Individuums. Zum Fin de siècle des liberalen Denkens in Weimar', in K Fischer (ed.), *Neustart des Weltlaufs? Fiktion und Faszination der Zeitenwende.* Frankfurt am Main: Suhrkamp, 164–83.

———. 2000. 'Massendemokratie zwischen Kaiserreich und westlicher Demokratie', in C. Gusy (ed.), *Demokratisches Denken in der Weimarer Republik.* Baden-Baden: Nomos, 2000, 38–70.

———. 2008a. 'Der Einfluß von Max Weber auf die Entstehung der Politikwissenschaft in der Weimarer Republik', in M. Gangl (ed.), *Das Politische. Zur Entstehung der Politikwissenschaft während der Weimarer Republik*, Frankfurt am Main: Peter Lang, 193–215.

———. 2008b. *Politische Ideengeschichte. Ein Gewebe politischer Diskurse.* Vienna: Oldenbourg-Verlag.

———. 2008c. 'Die Diktatur im Horizont der Demokratieidee. Zur verfassungspolitischen Diskussion der Zwischenkriegszeit', in C. Gusy (ed.), *Demokratie in der Krise. Europa in der Zwischenkriegszeit*, Baden-Baden: Nomos, 52–87.

———. 2015. 'The First World War and the Invention of "Western Democracy"', in R. Bavaj and M. Steber (eds), *Germany and 'the West': The History of a Modern Concept*. Oxford: Berghahn Books, 69–80.

Löwenstein, K. 1937. 'Militant Democracy and Fundamental Rights', *American Political Science Review* 31, part I: 591–622 and part II: 725–74.

Mahoney, D.J. 2004. *Politics and Progress: The Emergence of American Political Science*. Lanham, MD: Lexington.

Mallock, W.H. 1918. *The Limits of Pure Democracy*. London: Chapman & Hall.

Mazower, M. 1998. *Dark Continent: Europe's 20th Century*. London: Penguin.

McCarthy, H. 2012. 'Whose Democracy? Histories of British Political Culture between the Wars', *Historical Journal* 55, 221–38.

McCormick, J.P. 1999. 'From Constitutional Technique to Caesarist Ploy: Carl Schmitt on Dictatorship, Liberalism, and Emergency Powers', in P. Baehr and M. Richter (eds), *Dictatorship in History and Theory: Bonapartism, Caesarism, and Totalitarianism*. Cambridge: Cambridge University Press, 197–219.

McIlvain, T. 1938. 'The Drift to Dictatorship', *North American Review* 246, 10–34.

Morgan, E.S. 1988. *Inventing the People: The Rise of Popular Sovereignty in England and America*. New York: Norton.

Müller, J-W. 2011. *Contesting Democracy. Political Ideas in 20th Century Europe*. New Haven: Yale University Press.

———. 2012. 'Militant Democracy', in M. Rosenfeld and A. Sajó (eds), *The Oxford Handbook of Comparative Constitutional Law*, Oxford: Oxford University Press, 1253–69.

Müller, T.B. 2014. *Nach dem Ersten Weltkrieg. Lebensversuche moderner Demokratien*, Hamburg: Hamburger Edition.

Ooyen, R. van. 2004. 'Ein moderner Klassiker der Verfassungstheorie: Karl Löwenstein. Eine Skizze', *Zeitschrift für Politik* 51, 68–86.

Pink, M.A. 1935. *The Defence of Freedom*. London: Macmillan.

Preuß, H. 1924. 'Reichsverfassungsmäßige Diktatur', *Zeitschrift für Politik* 13, 97–113.

Rossiter, C. 1948. *Constitutional Dictatorship: Crisis Government in Modern Democracies*. Princeton: Princeton University Press.

Sartori, G. 1992. *Demokratietheorie*. Darmstadt: Wissenschaftliche Buchgesellschaft.

Schmitt, C. 1921. *Die Diktatur. Von den Anfängen des modernen Souveränitätsgedankens bis zum proletarischen Klassenkampf*. Munich/Leipzig: Duncker and Humblot.

———.1923a. 'Der Begriff der modernen Demokratie', *Archiv für Sozialwissenschaft und Sozialpolitik* 51, 817–23.

———. 1923b. *Die geistesgeschichtliche Lage des heutigen Parlamentarismus*. Munich/Leipzig: Duncker and Humblot.

Sforza, C. 1931. *European Dictatorships*. New York: Brentano's.

Shepard, W.J. 1935. 'Democracy in Transition', *American Political Science Review* 29, 1–20.

Simon, E. (ed.). 1938. *Constructive Democracy.* London: Allen & Unwin.
Thoma, R. 1924. 'Die Regelung der Diktaturgewalt', *Deutsche Juristenzeitung* 29, 654–60.
———. 1925. 'Zur Ideologie des Parlamentarismus und der Diktatur', *Archiv für Sozialwissenschaft und Sozialpolitik* 53, 212–17.
Trotsky, L. 1920. *Terrorismus und Kommunismus: Anti-Kautsky.* Hamburg: Hoym.
Watkins, F.M. 1939. *The Failure of Constitutional Emergency Powers under the German Republic.* Cambridge, MA: Harvard University Press.
Wintrop, N. 2000. *Democratic Theory as Public Philosophy: Alternative to Ideology and Utopia.* Aldershot: Ashgate.

Chapter 9

A Nation Allied with History

Czech Ideas of Democracy, 1890–1948

Peter Bugge

Towards the end of the First World War, the Wilsonian slogans of a 'world safe for democracy' and 'national self-determination' swept across Europe, and inspired leaders of national movements and popular masses alike. Whether they interpreted Woodrow Wilson's ideas and intentions accurately or not, these political leaders tended to regard the two ideas as inseparable. National independence, they held, was a necessary expression of the democratic principle among civilized nations, while the new independent nation states had to be democratic. In practice this typically meant the introduction of a republican state form with constitutions modelled after French or American paragons and parliamentary systems based on universal suffrage for men and women.[1]

Eight new nation states emerged from the ruins of the Russian, German and Austro-Hungarian empires, and all but one defined themselves as democratic republics.[2] As in Southern Europe, nearly all these new democracies collapsed during the interwar years and were replaced with a range of autocratic or dictatorial regimes.[3] The one exception in East Central Europe was Czechoslovakia, whose democracy fell only after the dismantling of the country with the Munich Agreement of 29 September 1938. Whatever the actual quality of Czechoslovak interwar democracy, Czechoslovak political leaders remained committed to the idea until the end. As Karel Čapek, an eminent writer and close associate of the country's first president, T.G. Masaryk, wrote in an English-language anthology published in 1938 to mobilize international support for the threatened state:

> By depriving it after the Thirty Years' War of its nobility and its bourgeoisie, and by placing all public offices, all property, all dignities, all privileges and

all economic power in alien hands, [the Habsburg Empire] made our people a democratic nation to the very core . . . Its democracy is hereditary and inborn as the democracy of the American nation; it lacked only liberty in order to be able to express its democracy in laws, institutions and political life.[4]

Freedom came, he held, with the creation of Czechoslovakia on 28 October 1918. While Čapek's explanation of the intense national commitment to democracy was essentially a piece of historical sociology, he praised the enlightened governance of Czechoslovakia's two presidents, T.G. Masaryk and Edvard Beneš, for keeping the country committed to 'the great European tradition of spiritual and intellectual liberty, of civic equality and of social rights'.[5]

Čapek's argument highlights three core themes of the present chapter: the idea that democracy is an essential attribute of Czech national identity; the association of democracy with spiritual liberty, equality and social rights; and finally the pivotal role of Presidents Masaryk and Beneš. By analysing the use of the concept of democracy in the writings of Masaryk and Beneš and other Czech and Slovak intellectuals from the late nineteenth century to 1939 and beyond,[6] the chapter seeks to demonstrate how the potentially universalist idea of democracy could become symbiotically tied to a specific vision of Czech national interests; it will also identify the core meanings associated with the concept in these discourses, and it will discuss the political consequences of these particular definitions of democracy. It is a case study of how the concept of democracy was mobilized for nation-building and state-building in Europe in the first half of the twentieth century.

Czechs and Slovaks in the Habsburg Empire

Čapek's portrayal of the Czechoslovak condition under Habsburg rule may have reflected popular stereotypes more than historical reality, but since the mid nineteenth century, Czech leaders had in fact sought to justify the nation's existence and development by associating it with democracy. This embedding of national aspirations in general narratives of democratization and progress gained extraordinary political potency after 1918.

In 1914, the Habsburg Empire was the third-biggest country by population in Europe. It was also a modern constitutional monarchy, which for decades had developed its political system to integrate ever larger groups of citizens into central, regional and local decision-making while respecting liberal principles of the rule of law. After a failed attempt in 1848–49 to replace absolutism with constitutional rule and a period of constitutional experiments starting in 1860, the Empire settled in 1867 on an arrangement that was to last until its collapse in 1918: that of a dual monarchy, Austria-Hungary, in which foreign policy and the military remained centrally governed, while each half of the state enjoyed autonomy in most other matters.[7]

In December 1867, the Parliament (*Reichsrat*) of the Austrian half of the monarchy passed a liberal constitution with a broad catalogue of civic rights. Article 19 recognized the equal rights of all nationalities (*Volksstämme*), including the right to preserve and cultivate their nationality and language. This liberal political framework served the Czech national movement well. The crownlands of Bohemia and Moravia, where Czechs formed the majority, became the most industrialized parts of the Empire, and by the turn of the twentieth century, illiteracy was largely eradicated. Education in Czech was possible at all levels from 1882, and Czechs controlled numerous town halls and much of the crownland administration of Bohemia. There were Czech banks, insurance companies and media, a rich associational life and a diverse set-up of political parties, the core structure of which was to last until 1938. In short, Czechs were and mostly also felt at home in the Habsburg Empire.[8]

Developments took a different path in Hungary. The largely aristocratic Hungarian elites oscillated between conservatism and liberalism, and the Hungarian Parliament never passed an equivalent to the Austrian Constitution of 1867. A Nationalities Law of 1868 proclaimed that 'all Hungarian citizens constitute a nation in the political sense, the one and indivisible Hungarian nation', thus denying collective rights to the nearly 50 per cent of the population that belonged to ethnic minorities, and the Hungarian elites pursued an increasingly vigorous policy of 'Magyarisation'.[9] These policies severely hampered the development of a Slovak national movement, and until 1918 Slovak national activism remained limited. A largely Catholic conservative faction was loyal to the Hungarian crown and hoped for concessions from Budapest, whereas a mostly Protestant progressive minority looked to Prague for inspiration and support, though without challenging the territorial integrity of Hungary.[10]

Ideas of Democracy in the Habsburg Empire

Democracy first became a broadly discussed topic in the Habsburg Empire in the revolutionary year of 1848–49.[11] The collapse of the old regime and the sudden promise of free elections to a constitutional assembly resulted in numerous writings that sought to explain the meaning of 'democracy', 'constitution' and other political terms.[12] By the end of 1848, the term 'democrat' – or 'radical democrat' – had become firmly associated with factions that went further than the liberals in demanding political rights for the lower social strata.[13] Meanwhile, political and social radicalism across the Empire had become a pretext for counter-revolution and the dispersion of the constitutional assembly in March 1849 introduced a decade of 'neo-absolutism'.

In 1860, Emperor Franz Joseph cautiously reintroduced constitutional rule and convened a *Reichsrat*. Struggles over its mandate and over centralism or regional autonomy characterized the 1860s, and the introduction of the Constitution of 1867 stimulated further debate about democracy. The first parties with 'democratic' in their names appeared and, as in 1848, they positioned themselves to the left of the Liberals as they sought to address the needs of the lower middle classes and the emerging working class. In 1873 a Vienna-based Democratic Party won five seats in the Reichsrat, and around 1879 a left-liberal faction labelled itself 'Democrats' in Polish Galicia. No Czech party used the label, since the more reform-oriented liberals preferred to call themselves 'progressive' or 'freethinking'.

An All-Austrian Social Democratic Party was founded in 1874, followed by a 'Czechoslav Social Democratic Workers' Party' in 1878. Initially the Social Democrats were heavily persecuted, but by the end of the 1880s, the Austrian government recognized that calls for workers' representation would not disappear. As the Social Democrats integrated into Austrian political life, debates about democracy centred on questions of franchise extension – including the issue of women's voting rights – and on political versus social or economic democracy.

Democracy in Czech National ideology

Early nineteenth-century Czech 'national awakeners' held that the Czechs – as Slavs in general – were innately democratic, but the term had no political implications. Democratic stood for egalitarian and nonfeudal, qualities serving to separate Slavs from the feudal Germans. In 1848, František Palacký – an influential historian and for decades the undisputed leader of the Czech national movement – developed this idea into an elaborate philosophy of Czech history, which he defined as determined by the 'continual association and conflict' between the Slavic and the German elements in Bohemia and Moravia, i.e. between democratic and autocratic, decentralizing and centralizing forces.[14] Politically, Palacký belonged to the liberal camp and he did not translate his identification of ancient democratic traits in the Czech national character into a political programme carrying that name. But from the 1870s onwards, the idea was appropriated by more radical segments of the Czech national movement, including the Social Democrats.

In the late 1880s, in a context of social and political ferment, three young intellectuals, Josef Kaizl, Karel Kramář and T.G. Masaryk, questioned the policies of the dominant liberal parties. In 1890 they presented a 'Draft of a People's ['lidového'] Programme', in which they boldly declared: 'We are *lidovci* [approximately, men of the people], we are no longer democrats.' The noun *lid* means 'the common people' as opposed to the upper classes, and the word and its derivations have a clear social accent missing in *národ*, the Czech approximate equivalent of the German *Volk*. *Lid* also appears in the phrase 'people's democracy', which after 1945 came to denote the hybrid form of rule preceding the full communist seizure of power in 1948. According to the Czech-German historian Eva Schmidt-Hartmann, this is no coincidence. The intellectual roots of the postwar sell-out of liberal democratic principles, she argues, date back to the 1890 draft programme and the thinking of T.G. Masaryk.[15]

We will return to Masaryk, but there is hardly a direct thread from the 1890 programme to post–1945 notions of democracy. The draft programme's talk of extending 'the narrower democratism to a popular standpoint' or declaration that 'we do not speak about liberty in general, but about where liberty can and should manifest itself' were not calls for the exclusion of the nobility or the bourgeoisie from politics, but for an extension of liberal freedoms and for universal manhood suffrage. In short, it advocated a broader understanding of democracy than the one offered by mainstream liberals.[16]

Eventually, the three were elected to the Reichsrat in 1891 for the liberal National Freethinking Party, but Masaryk soon withdrew from politics to develop a national philosophy, arguing that good politics depended on a culturally, morally, intellectually and socially healthy national community, and not the other way round. In a series of books written in the mid 1890s, he sought to demonstrate that the raison d'être of the Czech nation had always been the 'ideal of humanity'. First expressed in the Czech Reformation of the fifteenth century, it reappeared in the early nineteenth-century national revival, and any present crisis of Czech politics and society was due to the neglect of this ideal. Masaryk criticized Czech politics for its petty nationalism, but he saw nations as organic communities given by nature, and rejected Catholicism and religiously indifferent Western European liberalism as 'un-Czech'.[17] He demanded a 'socialization' of politics, i.e. an extension of political and social rights to the whole population, and a daily, intensive 'petty work' ('drobná práce') to nurture the self-emancipation of the people.

Masaryk did not refer to democracy here, and his calls for a unifying idea for a nation led by an 'invisible party' of philosophers-awakeners were evidently anti-liberal. They were also controversial, and his former ally Kaizl responded in 1895 with a book, *Czech Thoughts*. Masaryk, he held, was mistaken in seeing in the Czech national revival a continuation of the Reformation. In reality, and fortunately so, the Czechs had found inspiration in those Western liberal ideas that Masaryk rejected as un-Czech. Nor did Kaizl see any crisis in Czech politics. The National Freethinking Party remained committed to the progressive tradition in Western civilization and combined core principles of liberalism with new and socialising trends. For Kaizl, pluralism was a virtue, and he rejected the call for almighty, omniscient leaders.[18]

Masaryk's Turn to Democracy

While Masaryk's philosophy of Czech history found limited support, his thoughts on petty work made a bigger impact. They also provoked him to take a stance on socialism in the 1898 monograph *The Social Question: The Philosophical and Sociological Foundations of Marxism*.[19] As a Protestant, Masaryk rejected the materialism of Marxism, but he declared himself a supporter of many of its goals. Now discussing parliamentary government and political systems at length, he made positive references to 'democracy' or, more frequently, to 'democratism'. The latter term, also found in the 1890 'People's Programme', appears regularly in Masaryk's prewar writings. He never defined the concept or explained how it differed semantically from 'democracy', but a context analysis suggests that parallel to other '-isms', democratism signifies a democratic stance or ideology, as in the request that 'democratism must grow into a general view of life and of the world'.[20]

Masaryk advocated universal suffrage for men and women, along with proportional voting and minority representation. He criticized contemporary Marxists for overrating the parliament as a seat of politics not because he – unlike syndicalists or anarchists – wished to eliminate parliaments, but because he wanted them to focus more on political content, on regional and local institutions of self-government, production cooperatives and supply associations, and on education in the broadest sense of the word:

> Modern politics is not exhausted with the democratization of the state. It also has another and no less important task – to make out of politics a practical science and a practical art based on science, to organize and secure through democracy the social influence of professional and political education.[21]

Masaryk was preoccupied with how the right people could come to rule. He acknowledged that mass access to politics would result in the discovery of more political talent, but he persisted in his elitist critique of the 'democratic superstition' that the majority, the mass, was automatically right. This has made the U.S. professor of history Roman Szporluk argue that what Masaryk 'seems to have wanted to justify and to call democratic was the rule by a minority, free from responsibility to, or control by, the whole body of citizens ("all")'.[22] Though exaggerating and overlooking inner contradictions in Masaryk's reasoning, Szporluk has a point, since Masaryk showed little interest in the need for control mechanisms against the abuse of power within democratic systems. This was to become an issue after the First World War.

Masaryk soon became a vigorous preacher of democracy. Whatever the reason for his change of terminology, his 1905 declaration that 'the programme of the Czech people was and is always essentially progressive and democratic'[23] was certainly closer to mainstream national rhetoric than his 1890s writings on 'humanity'. From the 1890s, Czech parties had become leading advocates in Austria of universal suffrage and democratic reform, policies often justified with reference to the Czech national character and history.[24] As before, Masaryk identified democracy with an ethos of work, individual and collective self-administration, respect for knowledge and morality, freedom from old or new oligarchies (including those identified within parties by Robert Michels and Moisey Ostrogorsky), democratization of the army, state administration and schools, and a 'democratizing and socializing' revision of the liberalism of John Stuart Mill and others.[25] There was, however, a significant new development.

In 1898, Masaryk had rejected Marx's ideas of revolution as romantic and as 'an aristocratic political sport' incompatible with the ethics of work otherwise present in Marxism.[26] But after the 1905 events in Russia, he acknowledged that circumstances might give a people the right to resort to revolution.[27] In 1912, Masaryk again defended the right to self-defence against oppression, but he insisted that the most important revolution was philosophical and educational: 'Revolution in the right sense of the word, as a modern democrat wishes it, is that the people ["lid"] are prepared to take over the reins of administration; a constitution and parliamentary government are only the beginning of this uncompleted revolt.'[28]

In 1913, Masaryk published a monumental study, *Russia and Europe*, in which he sharpened his views on revolution:

> Experience has shown that theocratic aristocracy in its absolutist form is essentially coercive, and it is prone to the use of force; hence the resistance offered by the democracy is fully justified. Revolution may be a right and necessary means of resistance, and it is then ethically justified. It may even become a moral duty.[29]

In Masaryk's view, responsible individuals with the proper motives had the right to 'recognise and declare that the revolution is necessary' if they could 'adduce proof that the revolution is actually in conformity with the true interests of the people, that it represents a real progress in democratic evolution, and that it is indispensable'.[30] The proximity in diction to the Leninist position is evident.

The phrase 'theocratic aristocracy' was significant. In the chapter 'Democracy versus Theocracy', Masaryk argued that the struggle between the two had determined European history since the Middle Ages. Like Max Weber (to whom he made a passing reference), Masaryk held that organized religion had a decisive influence on the process. Protestantism was better equipped than Catholicism or Orthodoxy to replace theocratic and aristocratic rule with a democratic order expressed in the slogan of liberty, equality and fraternity, and based on an ethics of science and respect for honest work. This explained why democracy was most advanced in the United Kingdom, the United States and in Scandinavia, while revolutions tended to be more radical and violent and less philosophically mature in Catholic or Orthodox countries.[31] Masaryk did not explicitly put the Czechs in the Protestant camp here, but his old opposition between authentic Czech and false Western humanity had given way to a model that firmly placed his nation on the progressive side in a world-historical process.

The First World War and the Making of Czechoslovakia

In August 1914, Austria-Hungary entered into war with Serbia and Russia. German-Austrian nationalists were quick to interpret the conflict as a general strife between Germans and Slavs, a view shared by influential circles at court and in the army. As Slavs, the Czechs were put under collective suspicion of sympathizing with their Serbian and Russian kin. Although mobilization proceeded without major incidents, Vienna introduced repressive measures against Czech nationalist organizations. These developments were disastrous for Czech aspirations since a victory for Austria and Germany would also be a triumph for German nationalists, threatening to undo decades of Czech political achievements. Most Czech parties chose to keep the lowest possible profile, but for Masaryk, circumstances now justified a revolutionary act. He went into exile to work for the destruction of the Habsburg Empire and the creation of an independent Czechoslovak nation state.[32]

Masaryk was convinced that Slovaks constituted a branch of the larger Czech (or, as it was increasingly called, Czechoslovak) nation. But their inclusion also served the strategic purpose of increasing the Slavic element in the new state, which faced a substantial German minority in Bohemia and Moravia. By 1918, Czechs overwhelmingly supported the merger, and all factions in the Slovak national movement had come to see joint statehood as the only viable road to national development. They were right. From an official interwar point of view – a view shared by most Czechs and many Slovaks – Slovaks were not a national minority, but an integral part of the titular Czechoslovak nation. However, a new Slovak school system soon produced local elites critical of Czech political and economic dominance and of the lack of recognition of Slovaks as a separate nation. The Munich Agreement helped Slovak autonomists gain the upper hand, and in 1945 Czechoslovakia was resurrected in the name of two equal nations.[33]

For Paris and London, the decision to dismember Austria-Hungary and create a number of new nation states was as much a product of *realpolitik* as of any conviction about the superiority of Wilson's ideas. Masaryk, however, held that the war confirmed his interpretation of European history and that an Allied victory also had to be a victory of national self-determination. Strongly inspired by Wilsonian idealism and the general turn to the left at the end of the war, Masaryk's 1918 definition of democracy was quite radical:

> Democracy is a society resting on labor. In a democracy there are no men and classes exploiting the labor of others; a democratic state does not admit of militarism or secret diplomacy; its internal and external policy is subject to the judgment and direction of Parliament.[34]

This turned out to be more than what Masaryk's new republic could live up to.

Democracy in Czechoslovakia

Before 1914, Masaryk had been one Czech intellectual among others. By November 1918, he had become the 'President-Liberator', a man proven right, the eminent leader of his nation. His authority was enormous, and the Czechoslovak Constitution of 29 February 1920 exempted him from the general provision that a person could be elected president only twice in succession.

The Constitution defined Czechoslovakia as a democratic republic with a president at its head, a bicameral parliament elected by proportional vote, with equal, secret and universal suffrage for men and women, the separation of powers and a rich catalogue of civil and political rights. While a chapter guaranteed the 'Protection of national, religious and racial minorities', the Constitution's preamble defined the law-making subject as: 'We, the Czechoslovak nation, [which] in the spirit of our history . . . desire to take our place in the Family of Nations as a member at once cultured, peace-loving, democratic and progressive.'[35] History, the wording suggests, was on the side of democracy and hence of the Czechs.

Czechoslovakia did treat its numerous minorities quite well by interwar standards. But in the eyes of Czech decision-makers, this benevolence was a gift that testified to Czechoslovak progressiveness. The U.S. historian Tara Zahra has succinctly described the situation: 'As Czech nationalists assumed state power in 1918, they knit democratic principles, national self-determination, and ethnic character into a tightly woven tautology.'[36] Consequently, any critique of state policies could be dismissed as anti-democratic by definition.[37]

Masaryk's insistence that national self-determination was a democratic right did not lead him to recommend large-scale revisions of historical borders (or, alternatively, population transfers) to make the ethnic and the political unit congruent. Once a nation had obtained its state, he argued, its minorities had to accept their fate as long as their cultural and language rights were fully respected.[38] This was certainly the case in Czechoslovakia, professor of law Jiří Hoetzel asserted in 1920. He admitted that 'conditions resulting from the War' had prevented the 'non-Czech citizens of the Republic [i.e., Germans and Magyars]' from participating in the drafting of the Constitution, but their absence had only motivated the Czechs to secure that it was 'just and impartial'. Hoetzel summed up:

> [T]he definitive Constitution of the Czechoslovak Republic aims at being the democratic and just basis of public life in our State. It is a matter then, especially for our minorities, racial and religious, loyally to acknowledge these good traits and aims of our Constitution and to act accordingly.[39]

In 1930, the Slovak historian Daniel Rapant applied a similar logic to justify how the 1920 Treaty of Trianon had given Czechoslovakia territories in southern Slovakia with a Hungarian majority population. The new border, he argued, respected the democratic principle of collective self-determination by giving the Czechoslovak nation the territory needed to secure its national existence. If, however, the Hungarian state and Hungarian national mentality someday came to fully embrace the educating force of global democracy, it would be undemocratic to refuse to discuss border revisions: 'In this sense it would be possible – somewhat paradoxically – to say that the Hungarians will never come closer to a revision of Trianon than when they sincerely and definitively relinquish it.'[40]

National minority representatives criticized this monopolizing of a democratic ethos for the Czechoslovak nation. But as Zahra has shown in her study of how the rights of children became a nationalist battlefield in the Czech lands, 'Czech and German nationalists alike promoted a vision of national democracy after 1918 that was focused more on protecting the nation's collective claims on children than on the preservation of individual rights'.[41] This widespread collectivist understanding of democracy found a fierce Czech critic in the biologist and philosopher Emanuel Rádl.

In his 1928 book *The War of the Czechs with the Germans*, Rádl attacked Czech minority policies. He distinguished between three types of democracy: organic, majoritarian and contractual. The organic concept of democracy understands the people ('lid') as a natural force and the state as its organ. The 'rule of the people' therefore means the rule of this mythical collective, not of a collective of autonomous individuals. Organic democracy had its roots in Herder, Hegel and Fichte, but it had become part of Pan-Slavism and Czech national thinking before finding its newest formulation in Italian fascism. Fascism (and communism too with its mix of organic and majoritarian ideas) therefore had more in common with popular Czech understandings of democracy, Rádl maliciously remarked, than most Czechs were willing to acknowledge. This was because the Czechs understood 'nation' in cultural and ethnic terms, and saw the Czechoslovak state as the property and instrument of their own nation. Rádl instead advocated a political definition of 'nation' as the sum of all citizens of a given state, united by loyalty to its constitutional order.[42]

Majority democracy sees the people as a sum of largely atomistic individuals of equal value, who make binding decisions for all by a simple majority. This conception, Rádl found, was superior to the organic model, but it lacked a mechanism to prevent the majority from abusing its power. Anglo-Saxon contractual democracy, by contrast, sees the state and the rule of the people as instruments to secure justice and to protect individuals and groups. It stemmed from post-Reformation struggles for the autonomy of small nonconformist Churches, and although it was later associated with economic liberalism, the latter was democratically insufficient. People were to be morally and spiritually free from state control, not just economically. A truly democratic constitutional order had to incorporate a full catalogue of human rights as 'fruits of the conviction of the sovereignty of the individual over the state'.[43] Czechoslovak democracy, in Rádl's view, had little in common with this ideal:

> The theory of Germans and Magyars as minority nationalities of our state is based on a combination of the organic and the majoritarian understanding of democracy. In the spirit of the organic conceptualization, the Czechs are the only ruling tribe in the land, fulfilling its historical mission. In the spirit of the majoritarian conceptualization there are more of them (that is, if we count Czechs and Slovaks together) and so as a majority they can pass into law everything against the Germans who are just a minority.[44]

Rádl considered Masaryk to be far more committed to universal democratic values than the average Czech nationalist. Although his thinking on democracy oscillated between the majority principle (and an organic view of nations) and the contractual view, Rádl believed that the latter was closer to Masaryk's general ideals. But 'instead of limiting the absolute power of the majority with a contract, with inalienable rights, natural law or good customs (as it is done in the West) [Masaryk] limits it with humanitarianism', Rádl found, and Masaryk's humanitarian democracy therefore shared with enlightened absolutism the fact that in principle neither of them abolished the relationship of ruler and ruled: 'in the end [it] leaves power in the hands of those who de facto have it and just appeals to their conscience to use it humanely'.[45] The affinity to Szporluk's critique is evident.

Rádl's argument was largely ignored or rejected by his contemporaries, and Masaryk and Beneš continued to praise the virtues of democracy – and their Czechoslovak version of it – throughout the interwar years.[46] In times of crisis, the President and the government frequently violated the letter of the Constitution to protect the state, which in the dominant political rhetoric had become synonymous with democracy. 'First is democracy, and only then comes the freedom of the press', a politician from the National Socialist Party argued in 1933 in support of a law that sharpened political censorship.[47] The year 1933 also brought with it the so-called 'Authorizing Bill', which gave the government legislative functions at the expense of the parliament.[48] In part, these legislative measures in 'protection of democracy' were responses to genuine threats to the political order from extremist forces to the left and the right.[49] But Masaryk's notion of democracy as a specific ethos and an everyday practice removed focus from the formal dimensions of democracy, a trend reinforced by his emphasis on political leadership as an art and a science, and by his view of politics as a form of administration rather than a procedure for the legitimate handling of conflicts of interest.[50]

Beneš on Democracy: Hope Springs Eternal

In 1938, one could easily think that history had deserted both democracy and Czechoslovakia. In Munich in September, the United Kingdom and France forced Czechoslovakia to cede large parts of its territory to Hitler. Without the Sudeten Germans, and with Slovakia enforcing autonomy, the Czechs were left alone to draft the political system of their part of rump Czecho-Slovakia. Their response was to dismantle the parliamentary system, introduce an authoritarian regime with one ruling party, and suspend many basic political and civic rights. According to the Czech historian Jan Rataj, this transformation towards fascism, which met with little resistance, had firm domestic roots, and the events seemed to show that democracy was less innate to the Czech national character than Masaryk and his many post–1918 proselytes had argued.[51] In 1933, the politician Emil Franke had indicated that the value of democracy depended on other factors: 'Our democracy is suitable for normal conditions, quiet times and relative wealth. If conditions are extraordinary one cannot exclude equally extraordinary measures.'[52] Once Munich put the nexus 'democracy – national interest' under severe duress, many Czechs opted for the abandonment of the former in the name of the latter.

The most prominent victim of the fall of Czechoslovak democracy was Edvard Beneš, who was forced to resign as president. In October 1938, he went into exile in London, which he left in February 1939 for a chair in Sociology at the University of Chicago. There he was asked to give lectures on the development of democracy in Europe since the eighteenth century. The lecture series appeared in book form in the autumn of 1939 as *Democracy Today and Tomorrow*.[53]

Beneš' analysis of European history largely followed Masaryk, and he insisted that the creation of nation states in Central and Eastern Europe after the First World War was a positive development, despite the difficult conditions for democracy in most of these states. Soon they were faced with threats from communism, fascism and exaggerated nationalism, and from conservative bourgeois forces fearing a spillover from political democracy into the social and economic spheres. Inevitably the new democracies made mistakes, but, Beneš insisted, that did not 'condemn democracy as a regime; it shows only that democracy is a benefit always in danger and always to be defended, cultivated, guarded, and improved'.[54]

The March 1939 news that Hitler had occupied the rest of Bohemia and Moravia convinced Beneš that a new world war was inevitable and that democracy (and with it Czechoslovakia) would again prove victorious. No compromise was possible between authoritarianism and democracy, he argued, since the former was built on 'a brutally and materialistically aristocratic conception of public and social life' and on an anti-individualistic cult of the party, the nation or the state, whereas the latter was spiritual, moral and individualistic. Individuals had to organize, but only in a political democracy could humans justly and reasonably negotiate the balance between collectivity and individual freedom.[55] Beneš analysed Nazism, fascism and communism at length, and talked about 'totalitarian states' and 'totalitarianism'. He saw numerous similarities between the three, but noticed that communist theory – unlike the others – defined its dictatorship and restrictions on individual freedoms as temporary:

> In theory, communism is nearer to democracy. In certain sections of its political practice it uses in a large degree the methods and means which the other authoritarian régimes use, and is, therefore, nearer to fascism and national socialism. But also in theory, there are certain communistic theses which are identical with the theses of authoritarian systems and philosophies. In principle, therefore, my criticism as to the question of the relation between communism and democracy is the same as that of fascism and national socialism.[56]

Beneš was profoundly optimistic about the future of democracy. He called it a 'sociological law' that every revolution was prone to early exaggerations and therefore encountered a reaction, but that in the longer run, 'a new wave, a higher wave of evolution of human civilisation comes'. Democratic theory and practice would have to learn from sociology, and postwar democracies would have to accept an increase in the role of the state and the executive. This could remedy weaknesses of existing party and voting systems, bring evolutionary solutions to social problems, and create a balance between patriotism, nationalism and internationalism based on a system of collective security. A tall order, but as Beneš ended his book: 'It is worth being a democrat.'[57]

Epilogue: Ever-Triumphant Democracy!?

Beneš was an astute observer of international politics. He correctly foresaw the war and predicted that the alliance between Hitler and Stalin would not last, and that the Soviet Union and the United States would eventually join forces with the United Kingdom until Nazi Germany was defeated. He also soon figured out that his country would be liberated from the east and that its security would depend on good relations with the Soviet Union. As he in 1942 prepared a Czech version of his book on democracy, he therefore made some significant adjustments.

Beneš now explicitly rejected the idea that the Soviet system was as 'totalitarian' as Nazism and fascism, but his main novelty was a convergence theory. He now argued elaborately that postwar democracy and Soviet socialism would move closer to each other and possibly even converge. The Soviet system would have to abandon its temporary dictatorship of the proletariat, while the political democracies had to 'socialise', that is, to restrict capitalism and introduce scientific economic planning. Also, the number of political parties should be reduced. Once the old vertical, class-based stratification of society was replaced by a horizontal stratification of complementary social groups, the mutual control exercised by a limited number of parties would suffice to guarantee political liberty and freedom of conviction. All this would take democracy to a higher level than before, Beneš declared.[58]

In 1945, history again seemed to be on the side of democracy and of Beneš, who returned home in triumph as President of a restored Czechoslovakia. The Soviet Union was declared the country's greatest friend, the Communists joined a united 'National Front' as a legitimate partner, and the country immediately set out to create a truly popular ('lidová') 'socialising democracy'. Right-wing parties were forbidden, banks and big industry were nationalized, and 'national committees' were introduced to democratize local civil service. Few asked about the end goal of these transformations. Masaryk too had, after all, spoken about the need to socialize democracy.

The Communists did have clear ideas about goals, and in February 1948 the non-Communist parties learned that popular democracy could also turn against them. Within weeks, all remains of the old, 'bourgeois' democracy were eliminated. The fate of the country's neighbours suggests that Communist rule would have been introduced no matter what, but nowhere did it happen as smoothly and with so much public support as in Czechoslovakia. Unintentionally, Beneš and other non-Communist politicians and intellectuals had paved the way for the Communists to take discursive control of the meaning of democracy. Who, after all, were better equipped to socialize it and lead the democratic potential in the Czech and Slovak nations to its fullest bloom!?[59]

It is as wrong to see a linear inevitability from Masaryk's early critique of liberal understandings of democracy to the postwar embrace of socializing democracy as it is to deny that elements in his and Beneš' thinking facilitated this embrace. Their writings reveal a genuine, if at times lopsided, commitment to human emancipation in the name of democracy, and they were not alone in Europe in holding that democratic institutions were of little worth without a shared democratic ethos among people and leaders alike. Nor were they the only democrats to underestimate the importance of legal and political instruments in protecting democracy not just from its enemies, but also from its friends. Even the exceptionalism expressed in the idea that the Czechs had a special historical tie to democracy is unexceptional in a European or global context. We meet it in republican form in the nationalist universalisms of France and the United States, and as ethnohistorical myth in Greece, Scandinavia or Switzerland. In the latter cases, as among the Czechs, the identification of 'demos' with 'ethnos' proved to be a powerful tool in the promotion of democracy, but at a price: as seen in interwar Czechoslovakia, the term could turn into an almost empty signifier or it could stand for something not quite the same: ethnocracy.

Peter Bugge is Associate Professor of Czech and European Studies at Aarhus University. Since his 1994 dissertation, 'Czech Nation Building: National Self-Perception, and Politics, 1780–1914', he has published extensively on Czech and Czechoslovak political and cultural history of the nineteenth and twentieth centuries, and on the history of the concepts of Central and Eastern Europe. He is a member of the executive board of *Collegium Carolinum – Forschungsinstitut für die Geschichte Tschechiens und der Slowakei*, Munich, and of the Academic Council of the *Institute for the Study of Totalitarian Regimes*, Prague.

Notes

1. A. Sharp, 'The Genie That Would Not Go Back into the Bottle: National Self-Determination and the Legacy of the First World War and the Peace Settlement', in S. Dunn and T.G. Fraser (eds), *Europe and Ethnicity: World War I and*

Contemporary Ethnic Conflict (London: Routledge, 1996), 10–23. T. Throntveit, 'The Fable of the Fourteen Points: Woodrow Wilson and National Self-Determination', *Diplomatic History* 35(3) (2011), 445–81; J-W. Muller, *Contesting Democracy: Political Ideas in Twentieth Century Europe* (New Haven: Yale University Press, 2011), 18.

2. The exception was Hungary, which never established a constitutional democracy. A short-lived Communist Soviet Republic was replaced in late 1919 by the autocratic right-wing rule of Miklós Horthy. The other states were Finland, Estonia, Latvia, Lithuania, Poland, Czechoslovakia and Yugoslavia. Austria, which only reluctantly accepted independent statehood, also became a democratic republic. Nation-state formation in South-East Europe had progressed throughout the nineteenth and early twentieth centuries as the Ottoman Empire crumbled.

3. Democracy collapsed in Italy in 1922, in Bulgaria and Spain in 1923 (with Spain experiencing a democratic interlude from 1930 to 1936), in Albania in 1925, in Poland and Portugal in 1926, in Yugoslavia and Lithuania in 1929, in Romania in 1930, in Germany and Austria in 1933, in Estonia and Latvia in 1934 and in Greece in 1935. N. Davies, *Europe: A History* (Oxford: Oxford University Press, 1996), 943 and 1320. Finland was the great exception in North-East Europe. See A. Siaroff, 'Democratic Breakdown and Democratic Stability: A Comparison of Interwar Estonia and Finland', *Canadian Journal of Political Science/Revue Canadienne de science politique* 32(1) (1999), 103–24.

4. K. Čapek, 'Introduction', in K. Čapek et al., *At the Cross-Roads of Europe: A Historical Outline of the Democratic Idea in Czechoslovakia* (Prague: PEN Club, 1938), 17.

5. Ibid., 17–18. T.G. Masaryk, President from 1918 to 1935, died in 1937 at the venerable age of eighty-seven, while Edvard Beneš, his successor, had the ill fortune to preside over the collapse of Czechoslovak democracy twice, in 1938 and again in 1948. Masaryk in particular enjoyed considerable international prestige as a democratic leader. E. Ludwig, *Defender of Democracy: Masaryk of Czechoslovakia* (New York: R.M. McBride, 1935 [German original: *Gespräche mit Masaryk, Denker und Staatsmann* (Amsterdam: Querido, 1935)]); W. Preston Warren, *Masaryk's Democracy: A Philosophy of Scientific and Moral Culture* (London: George Allen & Unwin, 1941); H. Hanak, 'British Attitudes to Masaryk', in H. Hanak (ed.), *T.G. Masaryk (1850–1937). Volume 3: Statesman and Political Force* (London: Macmillan, 1989), 125–48.

6. The focus on Masaryk and Beneš is, I believe, justified by their towering political influence (far stronger than envisioned for the office of the president in the Czechoslovak Constitution) and by the fact that both men – one a professor of philosophy, the other with a degree in political science – wrote extensively on democracy.

7. Inevitably, the Habsburg Empire had a bad press in its successor states, an image that has spilled over into scholarship. In recent years, historians have presented a far more nuanced picture of the Empire, highlighting its ability to develop economically and politically, and to secure the loyalty of the overwhelming majority of its citizens. See P.M. Judson, *The Habsburg Empire: A New History* (Cambridge, MA: Harvard University Press, 2016); J. Deak, *Forging a Multinational*

State: Stake Making in Imperial Austria from the Enlightenment to the First World War (Palo Alto, CA: Stanford University Press, 2015); G.B. Cohen, 'Nationalist Politics and the Dynamics of State and Civil Society in the Habsburg Monarchy, 1867–1914', *Central European History* 40(2) (2007), 241–78.
8. P. Bugge, 'Czech Nation-Building, National Self-Perception and Politics 1780–1914'. Ph.D. dissertation, Aarhus University, 1994; J. Křen, *Die Konfliktgemeinschaft. Tschechen und Deutsche 1780–1918* (Munich: Oldenbourg, 1996).
9. L. Kontler, *Millenium in Central Europe: A History of Hungary* (Budapest: Atlantisz Publishing House, 1999), 279–300 (quotation at 282).
10. The Slovak national movement faced far more difficult starting conditions than its Czech counterpart. Whereas Czech patriots could point to the medieval Kingdom of Bohemia and to the prominence of Czech as its official language, the territories inhabited by Slovaks had since the tenth century been an integral part of the Kingdom of Hungary. A standard for written Slovak was only established in the 1840s. See E. Mannová (ed.), *A Concise History of Slovakia* (Bratislava: Academic Electronic Press, 2000), 185–234; A. Maxwell, *Choosing Slovakia: Slavic Hungary, the Czechoslovak Language and Accidental Nationalism* (London: I.B. Tauris, 2009).
11. The following survey is based on H. Rebhan, *Entwicklung zur Demokratie in Österreich: Verfassung, Kampf um Gleichstellung und Demokratiedebatten in der Habsburgermonarchie (1867–1918)* (Marburg: Tectum Verlag, 2014); H. Rumpler and P. Urbanitsch (eds), *Die Habsburgermonarchie 1848–1918 Vol. VIII/1+2: Politische Öffentlichkeit und Zivilgesellschaft* (Vienna: Verlag der Österreichischen Akademie der Wissenschaften, 2006); P.M. Judson, *Exclusive Revolutionaries: Liberal Politics, Social Experience, and National Identity in the Austrian Empire* (Ann Arbor: University of Michigan Press, 1996) and on extensive searches in the catalogues of the Austrian National Library, the National Library of the Czech Republic and the Bavarian State Library.
12. A. Likawetz-Oberhauser, *Die Demokratie in Oestreich* (Prague: F. Ehrlich, 1849); G. Wolf, *Democratie und der Socialismus; das allgemeine Wahlrecht und die Gleichberechtigung aller Nationalitäten in Oesterreich* (Vienna: Sommer, 1849). Among the Czechs, the liberal journalist and writer Karel Havlíček Borovský was indefatigable in his efforts to enlighten his countrymen politically.
13. Rumpler and Urbanitsch, *Die Habsburgermonarchie*, 24–26, 135–40; Judson, *Exclusive Revolutionaries*, 38–49.
14. Bugge, *Czech Nation-Building*, 51–53, 111–12; J.F. Zacek, *Palacký: The Historian as Scholar and Nationalist* (The Hague: Mouton, 1970).
15. E. Schmidt-Hartmann, 'People's Democracy: The Emergence of a Czech Political Concept in the Late Nineteenth Century', in S.J. Kirschbaum (ed.), *East European History: Selected Papers of the Third World Congress for Soviet and East European Studies* (Columbus, OH: Slavica Publishers, 1988), 125–40 (quotation at 129). See also E. Schmidt-Hartmann, 'T.G. Masaryk und die Volksdemokratie', *Bohemia* 23(2) (1982), 370–87.
16. Quotations from J. Křížek, *T.G. Masaryk a česká politika: Politické vystoupení českých 'realistů' v letech 1887–1893* (Prague: SNPL, 1959), 148.

17. Bugge, *Czech Nation-Building*, 241–45.
18. J. Kaizl, *České myšlénky* (Prague: Edvard Beaufort, 1896).
19. T.G. Masaryk, *Otázka sociální: Základy marxismu sociologické a filosofické, Vol. I+II*. (Prague: Čin, 1946). Originally published in Czech in 1898, the book was translated into German in 1899 and into Russian in 1900.
20. Masaryk, *Otázka sociální*, vol. II, 349. Masaryk may have borrowed the term from German, where it was used with similar meanings from the late eighteenth century. The German term could also have negative connotations, expressing an exaggeration of democratic principles. This was not the case in Masaryk's usage. *Deutsches Fremdwörterbuch, 2. edition, Vol. 4: da Capo – Dynastie* (Berlin: Walter de Gruyter, 1999), 251.
21. Masaryk, *Otázka sociální*, vol. II, 340.
22. R. Szporluk, 'Masaryk's Idea of Democracy', *Slavonic and East European Review* 41(1) (1962), 35.
23. Quotation from R. Hoffmann, *T.G. Masaryk und die tschechische Frage* (Munich: Oldenbourg, 1988), 279.
24. Křen, *Konfliktgemeinschaft*, 196.
25. Masaryk summed up these points in his 1912 lecture 'Demokratism v politice', printed in T.G. Masaryk, *Ideály humanitní* (Prague: Melantrich, 1990), 97–113.
26. Masaryk, *Otázka sociální*, vol. I, 407.
27. T.G. Masaryk, 'Politika vědou a uměním', in Z.V. Tobolka (ed.), *Česká politika, Vol. I* (Prague: Jan Laichter, 1906), 6–7.
28. Masaryk, 'Demokratism v politice', 109.
29. The book was originally published in German as T.G. Masaryk, *Russland und Europa. Studien über die geistigen Strömungen in Russland*. 2 vols (Jena: Diederichs, 1913). Quotation from the English edition: T.G. Masaryk, *The Spirit of Russia: Studies in History, Literature and Philosophy*, 2nd ed., 3 vols (London: George Allen & Unwin, 1955), vol. 2, 535.
30. Ibid., 539.
31. Ibid., Chapter 25.
32. Masaryk was followed by the young Edvard Beneš, who shared his worldviews and loyally implemented his politics. The two cooperated closely with M.R. Štefánik, a Slovak with French citizenship and good political connections. Štefánik, an army pilot, died in a plane crash in May 1919.
33. E. Bakke, *Doomed to Failure? The Czechoslovak Nation Project and the Slovak Autonomist Reaction 1918–38* (Oslo: Department of Political Science, University of Oslo, 1998); C.S. Leff, *The Czech and Slovak Republics: Nation versus State* (Boulder: Westview Press, 1997), 19–45.
34. T.G. Masaryk, *The New Europe (The Slav Standpoint)* (Lewisburg, PA: Bucknell University Press, 1972), 176–77. The pamphlet was written in 1918 and appeared in English and French in the fall of that year, and in Czech in 1920.
35. Quotations from a semi-official English version of the text: J. Hoetzl and V Joachim (eds), *The Constitution of the Czechoslovak Republic* (Prague: Édition de la Société L'Effort de la Tchéchoslovaquie, 1920), 45 and 19.

36. T. Zahra, *Kidnapped Souls: National Indifference and the Battle for Children in the Bohemian Lands 1900–1948* (Ithaca, NY: Cornell University Press, 2008), 106.
37. P. Bugge, 'Czech Democracy 1918–1938 – Paragon or Parody?', *Bohemia* 47(1) (2006–7), 3–4, 24.
38. Masaryk, *The New Europe*, 84–86, 177; T.G. Masaryk, *The Making of a State: Memories and Observations, 1914–1918* (London: G. Allen & Unwin, 1927), 429–35. Czech original: T.G. Masaryk, *Světová revoluce* (Prague: Orbis-Čin, 1925), 524–32.
39. J. Hoetzel, 'Introduction', in *The Constitution of the Czechoslovak Republic*, 12, 18. Masaryk made a similar argument in 1925. See Masaryk, *Světová revoluce*, 527.
40. D. Rapant, 'Maďarizácia, Trianon, revízia a demokracia', in R. Chmel (ed.), *Slovenská otázka v 20. storočí* (Bratislava: Kalligram, 1997), 113. The essay was originally printed in the journal *Prúdy* in 1930.
41. Zahra, *Kidnapped Souls*, 10.
42. E. Rádl, *Válka Čechů s Němci* (Prague: Melantrich, 1993), 114–28. Rádl's book was immediately translated into German as *Der Kampf der Tschechen mit den Deutschen* (Reichenberg/Liberec: Stiepel, 1928).
43. Ibid., 128–57 (quotation at 140).
44. Ibid., 130. Rádl recognized collective as well as individual human rights and argued that the more autonomy Czechoslovakia granted to national communities, the closer it would come to contractual democracy and lasting peace with the country's Germans.
45. Ibid., 260, 268.
46. Masaryk's collected presidential speeches were published in several volumes as 'The Way of Democracy'. T.G. Masaryk, *Cesta demokracie*, vols 1–2 (Prague: Čin, 1933–34). Later volumes could appear only after 1989. T.G. Masaryk, *Cesta demokracie*, vols 3–4 (Prague: Ústav T.G. Masaryka, 1993, 1997). Masaryk also presented his thoughts on democracy in a memoir narrated to Karel Čapek: K. Čapek, *Hovory s T.G. Masarykem* (Prague: Československý spisovatel, 1990), 327–33. The book was first published in 1935 and appeared in English and German translations the following year. Beneš was also a prolific writer of books and articles about democracy, foreign policy and other political issues.
47. Quoted from H. Slapnicka, 'Die Grundrechte des geistigen Lebens und die Zensur', in K. Bosl and F. Seibt (eds), *Kultur und Gesellschaft in der Ersten Tschechoslowakischen Republik* (Munich: Oldenbourg, 1982), 161. The National Socialist Party had the support of Edvard Beneš and was a near-permanent part of interwar government coalitions. Unlike its German namesake, it advocated democracy and parliamentary rule.
48. These measures have led the German historian Peter Heumos to argue that interwar Czechoslovak parliamentary democracy owed much of its stability to its never having been exposed to the burden of true responsibility. P. Heumos, 'Konfliktregelung und soziale Integration: Zur Struktur der Ersten Tschechoslowakischen Republik', *Bohemia* 30(1) (1989), 68.

49. G. Capoccia, 'Legislative Responses against Extremism: The "Protection of Democracy" in the First Czechoslovak Republic (1920–1938)', *East European Politics and Societies* 16(3) (2002), 691–738. Compare with Bugge, 'Czech Democracy', 8–13.
50. I do not argue that Masaryk was indifferent to democratic control, only that it was a marginal concern of his. In Čapek's conversation with Masaryk we read: 'I am not afraid of words and will say that without a certain degree of dictatorship there is no democracy either; when Parliament is not in session, the government and the President of the Republic decide without limitations; but they are bound by laws and exposed to the future critique and control of parliament, the critique of newspapers and meetings. This is after all also a foundation of democracy: free critique and public control.' Čapek, *Hovory*, 332–33.
51. J. Rataj, *O autoritativní národní stát: Ideologické proměny české politiky v druhé republice 1938–1939* (Prague: Karolinum, 1997), 234. See also Bugge, 'Czech Democracy', 5–7.
52. Quoted from Z. Hradilák, 'Československá sociální demokracie a zmocňovací zákon v roce 1933', *Příspěvky k dějinám KSČ* 7, (1967), 42. Franke was a leading member of the Czechoslovak National Socialist Party.
53. E. Beneš, *Democracy Today and Tomorrow* (London: Macmillan, 1939). On Beneš' activities in 1938–39, see Z. Zeman and A. Klimek, *The Life of Edvard Beneš 1884–1948* (Oxford: Oxford University Press, 1997), 142–48.
54. Beneš, *Democracy Today and Tomorrow*, 58.
55. Ibid., 140–41.
56. Ibid., 182–83. Emphasis in original removed. On totalitarianism, see also 69–70.
57. Ibid., 184–220, quotations at 189 and 220. Like Masaryk, Beneš devoted far more space to a description of the qualities needed by political leaders than to mechanisms of public democratic control.
58. The book was first published in Czech in London in 1942. I refer to a later edition: E. Beneš, *Demokracie dnes a zítra* (Prague: Společnost Edvarda Beneše, 1999). On communism vs. Nazism and fascism, see 231–32; on convergence, see 219–43; on socializing democracy, see 274–90.
59. B.F. Abrams, *The Struggle for the Soul of the Nation: Czech Culture and the Rise of Communism* (Lanham, MD: Rowman & Littlefield, 2004); C. Brenner, *'Zwischen Ost und West': Tschechische politische Diskurse 1945–1948* (Munich: Oldenbourg, 2009).

Bibliography

Abrams, B.F. 2004. *The Struggle for the Soul of the Nation: Czech Culture and the Rise of Communism.* Lanham, MD: Rowman & Littlefield.

Bakke, E. 1998. *Doomed to Failure? The Czechoslovak Nation Project and the Slovak Autonomist Reaction 1918–38.* Oslo: Department of Political Science, University of Oslo.

Beneš, E. 1939. *Democracy Today and Tomorrow.* London: Macmillan.
———. 1999. *Demokracie dnes a zítra.* Prague: Společnost Edvarda Beneše.
Brenner, C. 2009. *'Zwischen Ost und West': Tschechische politische Diskurse 1945–1948.* Munich: Oldenbourg.
Bugge, P. 1994. 'Czech Nation-Building, National Self-Perception and Politics 1780–1914'. Ph.D. dissertation, Aarhus University.
———. 2006–7. 'Czech Democracy 1918–1938 – Paragon or Parody?' *Bohemia* 47(1), 3–28.
Čapek, K. 1990. *Hovory s T.G. Masarykem.* Prague: Československý spisovatel.
Čapek, K. et al. 1938. *At the Cross-Roads of Europe: A Historical Outline of the Democratic Idea in Czechoslovakia.* Prague: PEN Club.
Capoccia, G. 2002. 'Legislative Responses against Extremism: The "Protection of Democracy" in the First Czechoslovak Republic (1920–1938)', *East European Politics and Societies* 16(3), 691–738.
Cohen, G.B. 2007. 'Nationalist Politics and the Dynamics of State and Civil Society in the Habsburg Monarchy, 1867–1914', *Central European History* 40(2), 241–78.
Davies, N. 1996. *Europe: A History.* Oxford: Oxford University Press
Deak, J. 2015. *Forging a Multinational State: Stake Making in Imperial Austria from the Enlightenment to the First World War.* Stanford, California: Stanford University Press.
Deutsches Fremdwörterbuch, 2. edition, Vol. 4: da Capo – Dynastie. 1999. Berlin: Walter de Gruyter.
Hanak, H. 1989. 'British Attitudes to Masaryk', in H. Hanak (ed.), *T.G. Masaryk (1850–1937). Volume 3: Statesman and Political Force.* London: Macmillan, 125–48.
Heumos, P. 1989. 'Konfliktregelung und soziale Integration: Zur Struktur der Ersten Tschechoslowakischen Republik', *Bohemia* 30(1), 52–70.
Hoetzl, J., and V Joachim (eds). 1920. *The Constitution of the Czechoslovak Republic.* Prague: Édition de la Société L'Effort de la Tchéchoslovaquie.
Hoffmann, R. 1988. *T.G. Masaryk und die tschechische Frage.* Munich: Oldenbourg
Hradilák, Z. 1967. 'Československá sociální demokracie a zmocňovací zákon v roce 1933', *Příspěvky k dějinám KSČ* 7, 29–51.
Judson, P.M. 1996. *Exclusive Revolutionaries: Liberal Politics, Social Experience, and National Identity in the Austrian Empire.* Ann Arbor: University of Michigan Press.
———. 2016. *The Habsburg Empire: A New History,* Cambridge, MA: Harvard University Press.
Kaizl, J. 1896. *České myšlénky.* Prague: Edvard Beaufort.
Kontler, L. 1999. *Millenium in Central Europe: A History of Hungary.* Budapest: Atlantisz Publishing House.
Křen, J. 1996. *Die Konfliktgemeinschaft. Tschechen und Deutsche 1780–1918.* Munich: Oldenbourg.
Křížek, J. 1959. *T.G. Masaryk a česká politika: Politické vystoupení českých 'realistů' v letech 1887–1893.* Prague: SNPL.
Leff, C.S. 1997. *The Czech and Slovak Republics: Nation versus State.* Boulder: Westview Press.
Likawetz-Oberhauser, A. 1849. *Die Demokratie in Oestreich.* Prague: F. Ehrlich

Ludwig, E. 1936. *Defender of Democracy: Masaryk of Czechoslovakia*. New York: R.M. McBride.
Mannová, E. (ed.). 2000. *A Concise History of Slovakia*. Bratislava: Academic Electronic Press.
Masaryk, T.G. 1906. 'Politika vědou a uměním', in Z.V. Tobolka (ed.), *Česká politika, Vol. I*. Prague: Jan Laichter, 1–31.
———. 1927. *The Making of a State: Memories and Observations, 1914–1918*. London: G. Allen & Unwin.
———. 1933. *Cesta demokracie, Vol. I*. Prague: Čin.
———. 1934. *Cesta demokracie, Vol. II*. Prague: Čin.
———. 1946. *Otázka sociální: Základy marxismu sociologické a filosofické, Vol. I+II*. Prague: Čin.
———. 1955. *The Spirit of Russia: Studies in History, Literature and Philosophy, Vol. I–III*, 2nd ed. London: George Allen & Unwin.
———. 1972. *The New Europe (The Slav Standpoint)*. Lewisburg, PA: Bucknell University Press.
———. 1990. *Ideály humanitní*. Prague: Melantrich.
———. 1993. *Cesta demokracie, Vol. III*. Prague: Ústav T.G. Masaryka.
———. 1997. *Cesta demokracie, Vol. IV*. Prague: Ústav T.G. Masaryka.
Maxwell, A. 2009. *Choosing Slovakia: Slavic Hungary, the Czechoslovak Language and Accidental Nationalism*. London: I.B. Tauris.
Muller, J-W. 2011. *Contesting Democracy: Political Ideas in Twentieth Century Europe*. New Haven: Yale University Press.
Rádl, E. 1928. *Der Kampf der Tschechen mit den Deutschen*. Reichenberg/Liberec: Stiepel.
———. 1993. *Válka Čechů s Němci*. Prague: Melantrich.
Rapant, D. 1997. 'Maďarizácia, Trianon, revízia a demokracia', in R. Chmel (ed.), *Slovenská otázka v 20. storočí*. Bratislava: Kalligram, 98–113.
Rataj, J. 1997. *O autoritativní národní stát: Ideologické proměny české politiky v druhé republice 1938–1939*. Prague: Karolinum.
Rebhan, H. 2014. *Entwicklung zur Demokratie in Österreich: Verfassung, Kampf um Gleichstellung und Demokratiedebatten in der Habsburgermonarchie (1867–1918)*. Marburg: Tectum Verlag.
Rumpler, H., and P. Urbanitsch (eds). 2006. *Die Habsburgermonarchie 1848–1918 Vol. VIII/1+2: Politische Öffentlichkeit und Zivilgesellschaft*. Vienna: Verlag der Österreichischen Akademie der Wissenschaften.
Schmidt-Hartmann, E. 1982. 'T.G. Masaryk und die Volksdemokratie', *Bohemia* 23(2), 370–87.
———. 1988. 'People's Democracy: The Emergence of a Czech Political Concept in the Late Nineteenth Century', in S.J. Kirschbaum (ed.), *East European History: Selected Papers of the Third World Congress for Soviet and East European Studies*, Columbus, OH: Slavica Publishers, 125–40.
Sharp, A. 'The Genie That Would Not Go Back into the Bottle: National Self-Determination and the Legacy of the First World War and the Peace Settlement',

in S. Dunn and T.G. Fraser (eds), *Europe and Ethnicity: World War I and Contemporary Ethnic Conflict*. London: Routledge, 1996, 10–29.

Siaroff, A. 1999. 'Democratic Breakdown and Democratic Stability: A Comparison of Interwar Estonia and Finland', *Canadian Journal of Political Science / Revue Canadienne de science politique* 32(1), 103–24.

Slapnicka, H. 1982. 'Die Grundrechte des geistigen Lebens und die Zensur', in K. Bosl and F. Seibt (eds), *Kultur und Gesellschaft in der Ersten Tschechoslowakischen Republik*, Munich: Oldenbourg, 151–62.

Szporluk, R. 1962. 'Masaryk's Idea of Democracy', *Slavonic and East European Review* 41(1), 31–49.

Throntveit, T. 2011. 'The Fable of the Fourteen Points: Woodrow Wilson and National Self-Determination', *Diplomatic History* 35(3), 445–81.

Warren, W. Preston. 1941. *Masaryk's Democracy: A Philosophy of Scientific and Moral Culture*. London: George Allen & Unwin.

Wolf, G. 1849. *Democratie und der Socialismus; das allgemeine Wahlrecht und die Gleichberechtigung aller Nationalitäten in Oesterreich*. Vienna: Sommer.

Zacek, J.F. 1970. *Palacký: The Historian as Scholar and Nationalist*. The Hague: Mouton.

Zahra, T. 2008. *Kidnapped Souls: National Indifference and the Battle for Children in the Bohemian Lands 1900–1948*. Ithaca, NY: Cornell University Press.

Zeman, Z., and A. Klimek. 1997. *The Life of Edvard Beneš 1884–1948*. Oxford: Oxford University Press.

Chapter 10

Democracy in Western Europe after 1945

Martin Conway

In 1960, the political scientist Herman Finer published a weighty textbook, clearly intended for the burgeoning range of undergraduate courses in politics in universities in the United States and elsewhere, entitled *The Major Governments of Modern Europe*.[1] It is a work very much of its time, and one that has long been relegated to the distant storage stacks of most university libraries. However, it provides a convenient encapsulation of the political attitudes of its age, both in North America and in Western Europe. Finer was a very appropriate figure to give expression to those views. He was, at the time of the book's publication, a professor at the University of Chicago, but he had been born into a Jewish family in Bessarabia on the borders of Imperial Russia and Romania in 1898 before migrating at an early age to Britain, where, along with his younger brother Samuel Finer, he became part of what was effectively the first generation of British university-based political scientists. He was active in the Fabian movement in Britain, and wrote a number of books during the 1930s and 1940s, including a well-received critical account of Mussolini's Italy and, while at Harvard in 1945, *Road to Reaction* – a polemical denunciation of Friedrich Hayek and the message of resurgent liberalism that Hayek had expounded in *The Road to Serfdom* – before he took up his chair at Chicago in 1946.[2]

Finer's textbook provides comprehensive parallel accounts of what he regarded as the major states (excluding the United States) of the time: the Soviet Union, Britain, Germany and France. However, in a brief introduction, he sought to outline the political assumptions of the postwar age. Central to this was the power of government, which he stated was 'the tremendous fact' of the twentieth century. Government had extended the range and depth of its activities in all modern states to such a degree that it had acquired an unprecedented ability to subordinate its citizens and all of the associations of civil society – such as the churches – to its purposes: 'government is the single most potent force that molds [sic] all the phases of living, economic, social, and moral, in these modern political societies called nations or states'.[3] If there were echoes here of the denunciations of the power of totalitarian states that characterized the liberal politics of the early Cold War,[4] Finer was at pains to emphasize that government was, for him, primarily a force for good. Given the ever-increasing complexity of modern society, he argued that there was a functional necessity for government to take on the role of the super-manager, by providing a mechanism for rational decision-making, but also by delivering the benefits that only the guiding hand of the state could provide, foremost among which were social and economic justice. The expansion of government was therefore, to his mind, principally demand-led: 'Every individual, every group in the community, cries out, organizes, presses, propagandizes for a function of government at some time or another.'[5]

However, not all of the regimes were the same. His book was ahead of its time in the way in which it recognized the similarities of purpose and of mentality within the Soviet bureaucracy and the ruling elites of the West. But, while state rule in the Soviet Union took the form of a dictatorship that subordinated civil society and its citizens to its exclusive will, in the West it took the form of democracy. But what then was that democracy? For Finer, as for many other analysts of his era, the answer was above all institutional. Democracy was a structural framework by which the legislative juggernaut of modern government could be directed towards an ethos of responsibility towards its citizens. This certainly did not mean that it should be the executor of the direct will of the people; nor did it even seem to have much to do with consulting the people, either through elections or, still less, through the unpredictable and dangerous tool of referenda. In common with many political-science books of the 1960s, his study paid little attention to elections, seeing them as simple *intermezzi* in the serious business of the preparation and enactment of legislation, and the problem-solving tasks of modern government.[6] What mattered more than the people in a democracy were therefore organizations. Parties, socioeconomic interest groups such as trade unions, and a wide variety of other associations all had an essential role. They gave voice to sectional interests and ensured that the process of government did indeed work for the benefit of all, or at least to the advantage of the most significant sections of the population. The danger, however, as Finer was aware, was that the ever more entangled interplay of these parties and pressure groups would result in legislative and executive immobilism. The ghost of the recent collapse of the Fourth Republic in France in 1958, under the pressure of the consistent failure of short-lived governments to implement an effective policy in Algeria, hung heavy over Finer's work, leading him to define the other essential ingredient of modern democracy as leadership. With the model of de Gaulle clearly in his mind, Finer argued that modern democracy required political leaders capable of grasping the overall shape of complex problems and identifying the needs of the national community. Democratic leaders therefore needed to demonstrate what he presented as a strikingly alliterative list of qualities: consciousness, coherence, constancy, conviction, creativeness, conscientiousness, courage, captivation (by which he meant a certain charisma) and ultimately cleverness.[7]

For the student of democracy, both then and more especially now, Finer's book with its rather obsessive empiricism, organizational charts of bureaucratic hierarchies and half-digested analyses of the still-nascent structure of the French Fifth Republic has all too evident shortcomings. However, through what he argued, and more broadly perhaps through the way in which he conceived of its subject, Finer's study has an obvious value for a conceptual history of democracy. The purpose of this chapter is therefore to use Finer's analysis as a window through which to explore the wider assumptions concerning democracy in the era from the Second World War to the 1970s. That era – which I have termed elsewhere Western Europe's democratic age – was in many ways remarkable.[8] For the first time, all of Europe west of the Iron Curtain and north of the Pyrenees was ruled by democratic political regimes. Each had its own particular nuances, which reflected the influence of history, both recent and more long-lasting. Some were emphatically republican in spirit, while others retained the trappings of monarchy; the majority were centralized, but some were more federal; and while some had state-directed welfare structures, others devolved responsibility for welfare to social organizations that remained largely independent of the state. As we shall see, these differences mattered, but they remained variations on a theme, and that theme was a particular and widely shared understanding of democracy.

A Western and Modern Democracy

Finer's personal trajectory from Bessarabia to Britain, to Harvard and ultimately to Chicago was a personal demonstration of the new Western world that had come into existence over the course of his lifetime. It is therefore perhaps not surprising that his presentation of democracy was bounded by that world. Whatever might have been happening in the democratic politics of newly independent states such as India and Indonesia or in Africa, democracy was, for Finer, an emphatically Western and more especially European phenomenon. Moreover, it was one firmly anchored in the present day. His own life as a Jewish-born émigré from his homeland and ultimately from Europe had been deeply marked by the collective traumas of Europe during the first half of the twentieth century, but in his textbook, he provided his student readers with almost no sense of historical evolution. Instead, the Western democratic state was presented emphatically as a present-day phenomenon – a regime that was adapted to the needs of the modern world with its industrial technology, complex and largely urban societies, and social welfare structures. Between this regime and the violent past of the first half of the twentieth century, there lay tacitly a gulf, which made that past irrelevant to his pedagogic purpose.

This was a widely held attitude. One of the most striking features of how democracy was conceived of and discussed in Western Europe after 1945, at least up until the end of the 1960s, was its present-mindedness. References to the past were rare and democracy was presented, along with the new roads and hydroelectric power plants, as the reflection of the new form of society generated by the rapid economic growth that followed 1945. This silence about Europe's democratic past was not accidental. Democracy did not possess much sense of a usable past in most of the states of postwar Western Europe. There were of course national, often patriotic, narratives of emancipation and liberation that, in the case of the states of Scandinavia or the Low Countries, carried a certain historical content of democratic self-government. Thus, in the Netherlands and Belgium, for example, postwar democracy was celebrated as the expression of the historic commitment of their peoples to freedom, just as in Scandinavia the development of structures of welfare democracy from the 1930s onwards was presented as the continuation of long-standing traditions of democratic egalitarianism.[9]

Elsewhere, however, history was less easy to mobilize for these democratic purposes. In Austria and Germany, a democratic past had to be excavated at the margins of a much darker recent history, in evocations of a medieval past or in the local narratives of *Heimat*.[10] Much more problematic were the more immediate examples of the Austrian First and German Weimar Republics. One might have anticipated that these recent experiences of pluralist democracy would have been celebrated as expressions of a democratic past that had fallen victim (just as the Spanish Second Republic had done) to fascist, and perhaps some communist, subversion. But in fact these republics were widely regarded in strongly negative terms as warnings of the dangers inherent within modern democracy. By granting excessive liberty to the people, the Austrian and German parliamentary regimes of the 1920s had permitted social conflicts and popular passions to develop, which in turn were encouraged and exploited by the political radicals of the extreme left and right. Seen in this way, the antecedents of the Third Reich came to seem alarmingly democratic: Nazi success had resulted not from an anti-democratic coup, but from too unstructured a form of democracy, which had led the German people to cast their votes for unscrupulous opportunists.[11] Much of the same negative perception of past democratic experiences was evident in France and Italy. The effective surrender of parliamentary democracy to its opponents in Italy after 1922 and in France in 1940 served to underscore what was regarded as the weakness of prewar democratic structures, which had been undermined by the fickle nature of public opinion, the self-interested corruption of parliamentarians and the impotence of state structures governed by ineffective coalitions of ministers.[12]

If democracy were to succeed in the post–1945 world, it therefore had to learn from the negative experiences of the recent past. Democracy, it was widely assumed, was a political system that did not work on its own, and the people would have to undergo an apprenticeship in democratic procedures before they could be authorized to operate it.[13] This defensive mentality was in large part the consequence of the circumstances generated by the Cold War. The western territories of Europe derived their unity within NATO and the many other institutions of postwar European cooperation from the pervasive sense of a communist threat, that was both internal and external, and against which they were almost obliged to present themselves as true democracies, committed to individual and collective freedom.[14] The espousal of democracy was, however, much more than a convenient flag around which the Western states could rally; it was also a response to the energy with which the communist-led states in Central and Eastern Europe adopted the trappings of 'people's democracies', which had grafted goals of social justice onto more longstanding notions of popular sovereignty. This made the Cold War into a war about democracy, or indeed between democracies. When a Commission established by UNESCO published its substantial report on contemporary understandings of democracy at the height of the Cold War in 1951, it noted that democracy enjoyed unprecedented universal assent. 'For the first time in the history of the world, no doctrines are advanced as antidemocratic', the report declared; however, it went on to observe that opinions about the meaning of democracy had become polarized to such an extent that 'both sides profess good reasons to believe that the conditions essential to democracy in the one sense are incompatible with democracy in the other'.[15]

Much of the postwar nervousness about democracy therefore derived from the fear that it would fall into the wrong hands or (remembering the experience of the Weimar Republic) that democracy would itself become the means by which the enemy would triumph. Especially in the years of almost continuous emergency from the Prague coup of February 1948 to the building of the

Berlin Wall in 1961, Western European rulers were preoccupied by the need to constrain democratic freedoms as part of the wider mobilization against communism. The Nazi demagogues of the recent past had been replaced by the communist militants of the present, who through their manipulation of democratic structures and of the grievances of the people, were subverting the spaces provided by democracy – elections, mass meetings, marches and peace campaigns – to serve their inherently anti-democratic purposes.[16] Thus, not only the communist parties of Western Europe, but a much wider range of social and civil organizations, as well as individuals, thought to be sympathetic to communism were discriminated against, spied on and infiltrated by police and security institutions, the actions of which were legitimized by the necessary defence of freedom and democracy.

However, the pervasive sense of constraint that characterized democracy in Western Europe from the 1940s to the 1960s had origins that went deeper than the circumstantial imperatives imposed by the Cold War. It also reflected the much wider distrust of mass participation, and to some extent of the people themselves, which characterized many of the postwar discourses of democracy. The social and political violence of the interwar years, as well as the military and paramilitary violence of the war years and its aftermath, had left a durable sense of how easily political structures could be overthrown and the norms of civilized behaviour inverted.[17] Pessimistic definitions of the capacity of the people to commit evil lay at the heart of much post-Holocaust writing by conservative-minded liberals, such as Hannah Arendt,[18] and, especially in Central Europe, there was a palpable nervousness about the role that the people should play in democracy. Popular sovereignty remained the ultimate source of legitimation of democratic regimes, both at the national and the local levels, but its practical application needed to be treated with some caution. Thus, in designing the political systems of the postwar era, there was a desire to avoid simple majoritarian votes. Direct elections of heads of state were generally avoided, and though a number of referenda were held in the immediate postwar years – notably concerning the French Constitution and the future of the monarchy in Italy and Belgium – these were consciously defined as exceptional events, which occurred outside of the normal procedures of elections and parliamentary government.

Underlying these hesitations was a broader sense of the simple difficulty of democracy – what Finer had already characterized in 1946 as 'the most difficult and delicate form of government'.[19] Caught between lessons of the recent past and the model of the people's democracies of the Communist Bloc, democracy in Western Europe was always seen as something of a balancing act, in which carefully calibrated doses of popular participation needed to be offset by effective executive authority and judicial oversight. Of course, that nervousness was most marked in Germany and Austria, where there was an understandable awareness, on both the political right and left, of how easily mass democracy could lead to authoritarian rule or the victory of demagogic forces. The solution, in the words of Karl von Loewenstein, lay in 'a disciplined democracy'. Loewenstein was a German exile from Nazism, who had spent the war years in North America, where he had reflected on the difficult task of building a stable and enduring democracy on German soil.[20] As an official in the American military administration in occupied Germany from 1945, Loewenstein had the opportunity to put his ideas into operation by helping to draft the Basic Law that sought to set a defining framework for the operation of the Federal Republic and that was subsequently used by the judges of the Constitutional Court to ban the German Communist Party in 1956.[21]

The context of Lowenstein's comments was specifically German, but the mentality to which he gave expression was widely shared. The democracy that was introduced into Western Europe after the final defeat of the Third Reich was indeed a liberation, which inaugurated a new politics based on universal rights, male and female suffrage, and enhanced provision of social welfare. However, what was remarkable was the lack of euphoria that accompanied this most dramatic of democratic victories. The resonant phrases of the Italian Constitution of 1948 apart, there was little air of celebration.[22] The people were free, but the uncertainties, both external and more especially internal, were too pressing for the victory of democracy to be regarded as anything more than provisional. The dominant mood was one of caution and of the need to control the potential for democratic excess.[23] If democracy was to prove to be a durable solution to the problem of Europe's modern politics, it had to be constrained both by the pragmatic need to restore effective governance and also by the need to establish a regime of essential human rights, within which modern democratic freedoms could operate securely.[24]

The Necessary Architecture of Democracy

The project of postwar democracy was therefore from the outset inseparable from that of order. In 1945, Europe was indeed – especially in the case of many of its major cities – in ruins, but, more importantly, many of its populations and rulers also believed themselves to be living amidst ruins. Once again, the strength of this feeling did, of course, vary across the different regions of Europe, but few regimes (outside of Britain and Scandinavia perhaps) emerged with the sense of their legitimacy having been reinforced. Elsewhere, the war had demonstrated the failings of the old order, out of which a new regime of legitimate government could only be gradually and incrementally constructed.²⁵ This explains why the construction of new or renovated democratic structures in Europe was presented as a medium-term project of rescue and reconstruction. In contrast to previous moments of democratic breakthrough such as 1789, 1848 or even 1918, little attention was paid to the rhetorical and symbolic trappings of freedom. Liberation from oppressive rule might have been achieved, but the task of building a durable democratic regime was recognized to be one that would require time, effort and skill.

Central to this challenge was the reconstruction of a viable and stable structure of representation. The age when citizens might have gathered in a town square to settle their affairs in a Rousseauian manner or have voted to send one of their notables on a train to the national parliament to voice their interests and play his part in the government of the nation was emphatically at an end. Central to the new form of democracy were therefore, as Finer recognized, political parties. Modern well-organized parties, he wrote, 'are the vital link between mass populations and the vast apparatus of omnicompetent government'.²⁶ Each of the major political traditions in postwar Western Europe – Christian democrats, social democrats, liberals and agrarians – had their own ideological and political heritages, but at a more profound level, they were now all participants in a common process of government. The role of parties was to aggregate and articulate opinions and grievances, ensuring that the necessary distance between ruler and ruled did not become a gulf within which resentment could develop. Central to this purpose was the need for parties to be disciplined and effective organizations that, in contrast to the opportunist coalitions that had proliferated in interwar Europe, would act as effective transmission belts between their voters and the arenas of governmental decision-making. Ideology therefore mattered less than consistency and coherence. The role of parties was not to sweep up broad coalitions of voters behind a populist message of opposition to those in power. Instead, parties should act as voices for the complex economic and social constituencies that were recognized as being the defining characteristic of modern European societies. In this way, parties were the way by which the people found their home in democracy, but also by which democracy became rooted within society. The systems of proportional representation adopted in many Western European states after the Second World War encouraged this process of democratic consolidation. By minimizing the impact of transient swings in electoral fortune, proportional representation promoted a continuity of the principal political parties in parliament and therefore in government.

Representation, rather than election, was therefore at the heart of this modern ethos of democratic governance. Winning and losing were replaced by coexistence, whereby each of the major constituencies of modern society felt themselves to be represented within a continuous process of political and social negotiation. This changed the temper of democratic politics. Exceptions did of course arise, most strikingly in France, where de Gaulle's emphasis on a personal bond between ruler and people served as a consistent contrast to the more collective, almost anonymous, ethos of the governments of the Fourth Republic.[27] But, understandably enough, the cult of individual leaders had largely gone out of fashion in postwar Europe. The need was no longer for national saviours, but for quiet men (and a very small number of women) who had the technical skills to guide the affairs of the state and whose 'ordinary' character as family men possessed of common-sense values served as a reassuring demonstration of their democratic character.[28]

In place of the polarization towards the extremes that had often occurred during previous eras of mass politics, parliamentary politics in Europe after 1945 was therefore characterized by what the Dutch-born political sociologist Arend Lijphart termed 'the politics of accommodation'. Lijphart used the term to describe the peaceful coexistence in the Netherlands (and to a lesser extent in Belgium) of distinct Catholic, Protestant, socialist and liberal 'pillars' of socioeconomic organizations, each of which was represented in parliament by a distinct political party.[29] But the world he described, and the socioeconomic landscape it reflected, was also true of many other areas of Western Europe. Particularly in predominantly Catholic regions of Europe, such as western Germany, Austria and northern Italy, the divisions of political life reflected the historical faultline that had long developed between confessional and secular social organizations, while in much of Northern Europe, notably in the states of Scandinavia, the frontiers between the socialist, liberal and agrarian parties were not simply political, but reflected wider differences of socioeconomic interest and of social milieu. There were of course exceptions, notably the existence of influential communist parties in Italy and France, but they too adapted to the more predictable pattern of politics in the 1950s and 1960s by retreating into the defence of their bastions of municipal and trade union power.[30] Only in France did politics retain the ability to surprise, first with the emergence of the Poujadist protest movement in the mid 1950s and, at the end of that decade, the collapse of effective government under the pressure of events in Algeria, and the emergence of de Gaulle as the dominant and highly personal leader of the new Fifth Republic.[31]

The more settled character of democratic politics was reflected in election campaigns. In a system of plural parties and of proportional representation, landslides in terms of votes and more especially in numbers of elected representatives were all but impossible. Success was therefore measured in the more modest currency of incremental shifts in the number of representatives that each party had in parliament and, more especially, by their success in maximizing the turnout of voters within their own milieu. This was particularly so at the frontier between the socialist and Christian democrat parties. With the decline in electoral support for communist parties that occurred in much of Western Europe during the 1950s, socialists and Christian democrats had become the two principal political groupings in much of Western Europe from the Low Countries to the Alps. Through their control of governmental power, either jointly or in opposition to each other, at both the national and the local levels, these two political traditions were able to impose their imprint on the wider society. That impact, moreover, went beyond the political. Both parties were essentially the political wing of much wider coalitions of affiliated trade unions, women's organizations and educational structures that shaped individual and collective identities.

The twin logics of electoral competition and of coalition government drew both of these camps towards a political centre ground and the practice of incremental reforms within the existing democratic system. However, their attitudes to that democracy did differ in significant ways. The Christian democrat parties of the post–1945 era accepted a pluralist politics of democracy, as well as a concomitant regime of rights and freedoms, but, for them, the principal concern was always more social than political. Drawing on longstanding Catholic and papal social teachings, Christian democrats sought to decentre an overly mighty state through encouraging the role of subsidiary organizations that would foster a honeycomb of interlinked communities, both professional and social.[32] This was very different from socialist understandings of democracy. With the exception of the Italian Socialist Party, all of the major Western European socialist parties had defined themselves against communism in the immediate post–1945 period, adopting instead a Western and democratic definition of their identity. This encouraged, too, a gradual abandonment by socialist parties of the Marxist teleology whereby democracy was simply a staging post on the road to socialism; instead, in a phrase adopted with modest variations by many socialist parties during the postwar years, socialism would be achieved within democracy.[33] This new stance reached ideological definition in the new programmes of social-democratic principles that were endorsed by many of the principal socialist parties in the 1950s and early 1960s, which embraced not only a political regime of democracy, but also individual freedoms and an economy of predominantly private ownership.[34] However, this socialist commitment to democracy went hand in hand with a continued commitment to secular values and more especially with a belief in the liberating role of the state. In contrast to Christian democrats, socialists argued that it was through the use of the instruments of state power that they would create what Tage Erlander, the long-serving Swedish Prime Minister of the postwar decades, termed 'the strong society'.[35]

These differences in their understanding of democracy were significant and would remain so, but they also allowed for important points of overlap, most notably the shared belief that the political and constitutional framework of democracy was of less importance than its wider social structures. Thus, for both political traditions, democracy became in the decades following 1945 a project – a *chantier* – which would be brought to fruition through medium-term projects of social reform, welfare provision and education, which would ultimately create a participatory democratic society.

The Project of a Democratic Society

To proclaim democracy, Finer and others agreed, was therefore not enough. Freedom could be declared, as had indeed frequently been the case, in much of Europe since the end of the eighteenth century. But, as the UNESCO Commission of 1951 warned, 'democracy can only operate insofar as the people understand and are committed to its institutions'.[36] The more substantial goal was to root that democracy within society and make it what the Danish writer Alf Ross termed 'a way of life'.[37] The central focus of the project of democracy-building from the 1940s to the 1960s concerned not so much institutions or even democratic freedoms, but rather the need to take democracy out into society. With the completion of mass enfranchisement, the new frontier of democracy appeared to lie outside of the political realm, and most notably in the socioeconomic sphere. This was especially so in industry. For those who had experienced the upheavals of the previous decade, the most important goal after 1945 was to create a new economic order, which by destroying the untrammelled sovereignty of the employer class would create the basis of a more rational, and democratic, structure of control.[38]

One obvious means of doing so would be to bring the principal industries under the control of the state. But, after an initial series of nationalisations in the 1940s, prompted by the wartime crimes of individual industrialists or the urgent dictates of postwar reconstruction, enthusiasm for direct state control of industry waned. Instead, the new priority appeared to be planning, and corporatist institutions, which by bringing together the representatives of industry, of labour and of other interest groups in a common structure of decision-making would subordinate the arbitrary logics of market forces to more collective control. Such corporatism was not new; it had long been advocated by many Catholic thinkers, and corporatist chambers of various kinds had been a prominent element of many of the authoritarian regimes of the interwar years. But in its post–1945 incarnation, such corporatism was inseparable from a wider project of democracy. By bringing together all of the principal economic groups (including white-collar workers and the self-employed such as shopkeepers and farmers) within a framework of socioeconomic democracy, it was hoped that the new councils and chambers created after the war would provide the means to replace the bitter material conflicts of the previous decades with a new ethos of negotiation and incremental reform.[39] In many ways, these corporatist institutions failed to achieve their principal goals. With the unexpected resurgence of rapid capitalist growth during the postwar decades, they were often ineffective in constraining the power of international corporations or in assuaging the material grievances of the workers.[40] However, in other ways, they changed the shape of democracy. By devolving responsibility for issues of socioeconomic policy from the state and national parliaments to these corporatist institutions, the postwar reforms created a third arena of democracy, outside of legislatures and the structures of national and local government, which tied the associations of society into the new regime of democracy.

This, however, was only one part of the wider project of building the structures of a society that would be more prosperous, more just and also more democratic. Especially viewed in hindsight, the large projects of state reform that were carried through in the postwar decades appear to represent the apogee of a mentality of technocratic planning. The massive programmes of apartment building, of urban planning and of welfare reform contained few opportunities for citizens to question the logics of state action. However, at the time, these were very much perceived as forming an integral element of how the modern democratic society would be created. By sweeping away, often quite literally, the rubble of the past, such projects would provide the people with the means to become democratic citizens. At the heart of this vision lay the family. The central position that the nuclear family acquired in postwar democracy reflected the priorities of state officials, and more especially of Catholic politicians and social activists, who were concerned to counter the individualist ills of modern society. But it also demonstrated how democracy was intended as a means whereby Western European societies would recover a certain imagined normality and personal wellbeing in the aftermath of the traumas, both large-scale and more intimate, of war. Above all, this manifested itself in the emotional centrality accorded to children. By ensuring a better future for children through the provision of new housing, welfare structures and expanded educational opportunities, the rulers of postwar Europe were also creating the basis of the democratic society of the future.[41]

The concern with family was of course inseparable from issues of gender. As a consequence of the losses sustained in war, men were a distinct minority in postwar democracy, not only in society as a whole, but also, as the consequence of the final equal enfranchisement of women in Italy, France and Belgium, in the polling stations. That this enfranchisement did not lead to a wider emancipation of women in postwar European society is of course an indisputable fact: women remained, most notably as a consequence of the gendered structures of education, the law and employment, very much second-class citizens.[42] But the politics of gender in postwar democracy were more complex than a simple reassertion of male power. Men occupied the positions of power, but women were also present and visible: as activists in political parties, at the national and more obviously local levels; and as energetic and assertive leaders of pressure groups in domains such as housing, health and education, where women's voices had, according to the gendered standards of the age, an incontestable legitimacy. This was also reflected in the character of democracy. Prior to the Second World War, democracy had had a predominantly male definition, as expressed through both its personnel and its broader mores in parliament, in mass meetings and in public rallies. In contrast, the democracy of the post–1945 era was much more consciously inclusive of women. This was evident in the iconographic representation of the serious-minded female voter, consciously weighing up the relative merits of different party programmes and, more substantially, in the priority that political parties and governments accorded to those issues, such as welfare and housing, that had a direct relevance to women's material lives.[43] The democracy of the postwar decades was therefore one that recognized and included women not as equal citizens, but as gendered participants with a distinct role to play in the processes of debate and decision-making.

However, at the centre of this new democracy was the state. As Finer's book well illustrated, the institutions, personnel and resources of the state acquired an unprecedented centrality in postwar Western Europe. Whatever the hesitations of some Christian democrats and liberals at this apparently inexorable rise of the state, the functional requirements of a complex modern society appeared to dictate that the state in its national and local manifestations must act as the rational arbiter of daily life. The nature of that state also changed. From the building of motorways to the provision of healthcare, and from the operation of nuclear power stations to the new Keynesian tools of economic management, the major dossiers of postwar politics were on the whole matters that were indisputably best left to experts. The essentially amateur governance of elected representatives and local notables, which had characterized the parliamentary regimes of Europe in the early decades of the twentieth century, was replaced by a more professional bureaucracy, composed of a new caste of technocrats, notably economists and engineers, who had the qualifications required to staff and direct the complex business of modern government.[44]

The nature of political decision-making therefore changed over the course of the postwar decades. Much of the process of government passed from elected office-holders, and the citizens who had chosen them, to the ranks of professional experts embedded in the institutions of the state and its closely affiliated institutions. What Finer evocatively termed the 'omnicompetence' of government created a new elite of state officials who, as Pierre Mendès-France had warned in the mid 1950s, tended to regard the ill-informed views of citizens as simply an obstacle to effective decision-making.[45] This changed the relations of power within democracy. Confronted by the formidable complexity of state decision-making, as well as its much more effective tools of policing and social control, citizens might campaign and protest, but they could rarely hope to challenge governmental policy. In many ways, the awareness of this relative impotence encouraged the popular demobilization, which characterized the more settled democratic politics of Europe in the 1950s and the early 1960s. As contemporary commentators often remarked, there was an air of anti-climax to many postwar elections, as if citizens were conscious that they were accomplishing a legal duty as citizens rather than taking power into their own hands. But such attitudes were also the consequence of painful experience. Too many Europeans had ended up on the losing side over the course of previous years to throw themselves without caution into political action. Dreams of societal change therefore gave way to a more cautious and sectional politics, in which individuals and groups sought to find (and protect) their means of influence within the new political and social world. In some respects, this reflected the way in which the rapid changes of the postwar years had appeared to render obsolete the divisions of the past, creating a post-ideological politics in which the fundamental clashes of worldviews of the left and right no longer appeared to have the same relevance.[46] But it was also the consequence of the emergence of a new and more tactical sense of citizenship whereby individuals, socioeconomic groups and communities negotiated their relations with the all-powerful state. As the influence of the state reached ever further into the lives of many West Europeans, the focus of political involvement moved away from direct forms of political engagement to means of influencing the actions of the state. Everywhere from the Mezzogiorno to the Ruhr, citizens had become lobbyists of the state, seeking both as individuals and as members of communities and socioeconomic interest groups to influence the decisions of the state over issues such as welfare payments, the location of infrastructure projects or forms of economic protection that could have a substantial impact on their lives.[47]

The Discontents of Democracy

How far the people were ever content with this democracy that emerged in Western Europe after 1945 is of course difficult to assess. Not everybody had wished for democracy in 1945, and many had certainly not wanted it in the particular shape that it acquired in Western Europe over the subsequent decades. Indeed, in many areas of Western Europe – perhaps most tangibly in northern Italy – the democratic politics of the postwar years never fully escaped from the sense of disappointment that the expectations generated by the Resistance movements and by the volatile politics of the liberation era had not led to more radical changes in the structure of politics and of society.[48] Moreover, the resilient oppositional culture of the communists, as well as the more short-lived surges in support for the protest politics of the right, such as the *Uomo Qualunque* movement in Italy in the 1940s and Pierre Poujade's campaigns in France in the 1950s, demonstrated the persistence both of other democratic languages and of a strong undercurrent of material resentments.[49] As the large number of strikes and other labour disputes in postwar Western Europe well indicated, not everybody was content with the material terms of the postwar settlement. That was especially so for the industrial working class, who often found themselves marginalized in the postwar years, as they struggled to make their grievances heard in a political system that often seemed to be more attentive to the interests of other groups, such as farmers or the middle class.[50]

Yet, compared with the often violent crowd politics of the interwar years, the character of democracy in postwar Europe was indisputably relatively quiescent. Some campaigns – notably over issues such as nuclear weapons in West Germany and Britain, or the Algerian War in France – did have the ability to bring large crowds onto the streets,[51] but on the whole, the militant people had left the political stage. After the mobilizations and traumas of the war years, it seemed that the Western European public were content to retreat into the individualist pleasures of the private domain, to rebuild their personal and professional lives, but also to enjoy the new distractions and possessions that came with postwar economic growth. Relative affluence, and the individualism it encouraged, was an unexpected, and very welcome, element of the new society that came into existence after 1945, creating a sense of an expanding personal frontier of freedom, within which political freedom was no longer perhaps the most important component.[52] There was, however, no simple connection between such relative prosperity – which for many only arrived slowly – and political quiescence. More significant was the way in which most postwar Western Europeans appear to have felt that they had more to gain from working within the established structures of democratic politics than from protesting from the outside. Whatever their private scepticism about their rulers, the rapid expansion in forms of state provision – in everything from education and welfare to housing and transport connections – made possible by relatively buoyant state finances encouraged many Western Europeans to explore what might be in democracy for them.[53]

The question of course was what would happen when material progress failed to keep pace with this revolution in rising expectations, or when the balance sheet of personal and collective interests moved from positive to negative. In an aside in the introduction to his book, Finer allowed himself a moment of doubt about the apparent solidity of the democratic systems when he asked rhetorically 'at what point in the increase of governmental functions will the machinery of the state fail to give back to the people, in values of all kinds, at least as much as it has taken from them?'[54] It was a timely question to pose in 1960, and one that would become more apposite over the decade following the publication of his book. From the early 1960s onwards, there was a tangible shift in the mood of democratic politics. A surge in forms of protest was accompanied by an awareness of the inequalities of class, of gender and, with the arrival of immigrant populations from outside of Europe, of race that endured within the democratic societies of Western Europe. The reasons for this change were part material and part ideological. In particular, new generations of citizens who had come of age in the postwar years voiced critiques of the limits of democratic participation, as manifested in the young Jurgen Habermas' trenchant criticism of the German Federal Republic in 1961 as an electoral monarchy: a *Wahlmonarchie*.[55] Rather than being passive actors in an electoral politics that rarely changed anything, these critics wanted a more participatory and, to their mind, more meaningful role in public debate.

Perhaps the most profound impact of this change was to change the way in which postwar populations perceived their democracy. For Finer, democracy had been inherently static – a plateau created by the modernization of Western societies that it was impossible to go beyond, except through catastrophe or revolution. Now, however, radical groups of different ideological hues began to demand a different democracy: one that was more authentic, more local and, above all, more empowering. As the rather chaotic language and actions that found expression around the year 1968 would demonstrate, such protests were more effective in identifying the shortcomings of the established order than in articulating an alternative. But this familiar critique of 1968 that, in the intemperate words of Raymond Aron, the student demonstrators were seeking to overthrow the bases of a free society without any idea as to what they wanted to put in its place[56] serves to disguise the wider destabilization of the postwar definition of democracy that took place from the early 1960s to the mid 1970s. The radical activism, street demonstrations and protests against distant wars that captured the attention of the omnipresent television cameras of the late 1960s were in this respect less important than the more profound ways in which the democracy created after 1945 no longer seemed to provide an adequate framework for the new form of society brought into existence by postwar economic and social change.

Ideologies, Richard Toye has recently stimulatingly argued, are not so much fixed body of ideas, but constellations, united by a shared state of mind.[57] Seen in those terms, democracy in the postwar era had come close to being a self-sufficient ideology. It had many variants, ranging from democratic socialism to Christian democracy as well as a consistent undercurrent of liberal values, but common to the different elements of this constellation was a democratic mindset – one that feared the alternatives that lay outside democracy, but that also recognized the positive affinity that lay in working within, and for, the project of democracy. By the late 1960s, however, it was evident that the coherence of that constellation was breaking down. Dissatisfaction with the existing structures took many different forms, but at its heart lay a critique of the way in which democracy had been subsumed by the state, and the narrowing of the political spectrum that this had encouraged. For those neoliberals of the right who drew their inspiration from the ideas of Finer's one-time adversary, Friedrich von Hayek, the overmighty state was the enemy of personal and economic freedom;[58] for others, notably on the libertarian left, the bureaucratic structures of the state, and more especially its policies of social welfare, served to crush the self-government that ought to be at the heart of true democracy. As the French left socialist André Gorz wrote in the mid 1960s, 'Representative democracy in every industrially advanced country is in a state of profound crisis' as the consequence of the remorseless development of what he termed 'the modern authoritarian regime'.[59] Indeed, for some, the state became the enemy, not only in words but also in action, as demonstrated by the violent direct action groups of the 1970s and the various regional nationalist movements, such as those in Northern Ireland or Corsica, which sought freedom from their democratic nation state. All of these were of course minority currents, but especially during the economic crises of the mid 1970s, their criticisms of the state merged with wider currents of economically motivated protest, fostering something of a return to an authoritarian mentality among the embattled agents of the democratic state.[60] The democratically elected rulers of Western Europe, it seemed, could no longer be entirely confident that the people were on their side.

None of this implied that the postwar ascendancy of democracy was at an end; indeed, perhaps the greatest achievement of the postwar democratic order was that almost all of those who opposed it in the late 1960s and the 1970s did so in the name of a more true or wider democracy. Moreover, little of this contestation was fundamentally new; in many respects, the renewed conflicts around the content and practice of democracy in the 1970s recalled the conflicts of the interwar years between different political forces, each concerned to advance its particular understanding of democracy. But it did indicate that democracy had lost the sense of convergence around a common core that it had seemed to possess in the immediate post–1945 decades. The virtuous wheel of election, representation, negotiation and government no longer turned so smoothly, prompting coalitions of the discontented to look elsewhere – to the new liberalism of the United States or to the democracies of Asia and Africa – for inspiration. Finer, who died rather prematurely in 1969, did not live to digest these renewed conflicts, but, had he done so, one suspects that the second edition of his textbook would have been rather different.

Martin Conway is Professor of Contemporary European History at the University of Oxford and a fellow of Balliol College. He is the author of *Collaboration in Belgium: Léon Degrelle and the Rexist Movement 1940–44* (1993) and *The Sorrows of Belgium: Liberation and Political Reconstruction* (2012), as well as the coauthor of *The War for Legitimacy in Europe 1936–46* (2008) and *Europeanization in the Twentieth Century* (2010).

Notes

1. H. Finer, *The Major Governments of Modern Europe* (London: Methuen & Co., 1960).
2. H. Finer, *Mussolini's Italy* (London: Victor Gollancz, 1934); H. Finer, *Road to Reaction* (London: D. Dobson, 1946). Regarding Samuel Finer, see the excellent portrait by P. Pulzer, 'Samuel Finer', *Oxford Dictionary of National Biography*, www.odnb.com.
3. Finer, *Major Governments of Modern Europe*, 1.
4. C. Friedrich and Z. Brzezinski, *Totalitarian Dictatorship and Autocracy* (Cambridge, MA: Harvard University Press, 1956).
5. Finer, *Major Governments of Modern Europe*, 2.
6. See, for example, A. Lijphart, 'Typologies of Democratic Systems', in A. Lijphart (ed.), *Politics in Europe: Comparisons and Interpretations* (Englewood Cliffs, NJ: Prentice Hall, 1969), 46–80.
7. Finer, *Major Governments of Modern Europe*, 15–16.
8. M. Conway, 'The Rise and Fall of Western Europe's Democratic Age, 1945–1973', *Contemporary European History* 13 (2004), 67–88. See also M. Conway, 'Democracy in Post-War Western Europe', *European History Quarterly* 32 (2002), 59–84.
9. M. Conway, *The Sorrows of Belgium. Liberation and Political Reconstruction 1944–47* (Oxford: Oxford University Press, 2012), 249–52; W.P.J. Pompe, *Bevrijding. Bezetting – Herstel – Vernieuwing* (Amsterdam: Vrij Nederland, 1945), 9, 85–130; J.A. Lauwerys (ed.), *Scandinavian Democracy. Development of Democratic Thought*

and Institutions in Denmark, Norway and Sweden (Copenhagen: Danish Institute, Norwegian Office of Cultural Relations, Swedish Institute, American-Scandinavian Foundation, 1958); J. Kurunmäki and J. Strang (eds), *Rhetorics of Nordic Democracy* (Helsinki: Finnish Literature Society, 2010).

10. C. Applegate, *A Nation of Provincials: The German Idea of Heimat* (Berkeley: University of California Press, 1990), 242–43.
11. S. Ullrich, *Der Weimar-Komplex. Das Scheitern der ersten deutschen Demokratie und die politische Kultur der frühen Bundesrepublik 1945–1959* (Göttingen: Wallstein, 2009); V. Depkat, *Lebenswenden und Zeitenwenden: deutsche Politiker und die Erfahrungen des 20. Jahrhunderts* (Munich: Oldenbourg, 2007), 370–94.
12. F. Chabod, *L'Italie contemporaine. Conférences données à l'Institut d'Etudes Politiques de l'Université de Paris* (Paris: Éditions Domat-Montchrestien, 1950), 52–58; F. Goguel, *La politique des partis sous la IIIe République*, 2 vols (Paris: Éditions du Seuil, 1946), vol. 2, 330–44.
13. G. Hoyois, 'La réponse des peuples à la Démocratie', in *Les lignes de faite de la démocratie. XXVIIIe Semaine Sociale Wallonne, 1946* (Namur: 1946), 237.
14. L. Risso, 'Propaganda on Wheels: The NATO Travelling Exhibitions in the 1950s and 1960s', *Cold War History* 11 (2011), 9–25.
15. R. McKeon and S. Rokkan (eds), *Democracy in a World of Tensions* (Paris: United Nations Educational, Scientific and Cultural Organization, 1951), 522–23.
16. The image of the communists as anti-democratic demagogues was a frequent element of postwar rhetoric: G. Saragat, *Socialismo democratico e socialismo totalitario. Per l'autonomia del Partito Socialista* (Milan: Critica Sociale, 1946); R. Aron, *Le grand schisme* (Paris: Gallimard, 1948).
17. S. Ranulf, *On the Survival Chances of Democracy* (Copenhagen: Munksgaard, 1948).
18. H. Arendt, *Men in Dark Times* (London: Jonathan Cape, 1970), vii–x. See also J. Talmon, *The Origins of Totalitarian Democracy* (London: Secker & Warburg, 1952); and M.H. Hacohen, *Karl Popper – The Formative Years 1902–1945: Politics and Philosophy in Interwar Vienna* (Cambridge: Cambridge University Press, 2000), 506–10.
19. H. Finer, *The Future of Government* (London: Methuen & Co., 1946), 140.
20. K. Loewenstein, *Political Reconstruction* (New York: Macmillan, 1946), 126–29; M. Lang, *Karl Lowenstein. Transatlantischer Denker der Politik* (Stuttgart: Steiner Press, 2007), 238–45.
21. P. Major, *The Death of the KPD: Communism and Anti-communism in West Germany 1945–1956* (Oxford: Clarendon Press, 1997), 283–93.
22. Regarding the language of the Italian Constitution, see R.A. Ventresca, *From Fascism to Democracy: Culture and Politics in the Italian Election of 1948* (Toronto: University of Toronto Press, 2004).
23. A. Kasamas, *Programm Österreich. Die Grundsätze und Ziele der Österreichischen Volkspartei* (Vienna: Österreichischer Verlag, 1949), 92–100.
24. J-W. Müller, *Contesting Democracy. Political Ideas in Twentieth-Century Europe* (New Haven: Yale University Press, 2011), 146–50. Regarding the language of

human rights in postwar European politics, see notably the essays in S-L. Hoffmann (ed.), *Human Rights in the Twentieth Century* (Cambridge: Cambridge University Press, 2011).
25. Regarding legitimacy, see M. Conway and P. Romijn et al., *The War for Legitimacy in Politics and Culture 1936–1946* (Oxford: Berg, 2008).
26. Finer, *Major Governments of Modern Europe*, 8–9.
27. C. de Gaulle, *Discours et messages*, 5 vols (Paris: Plon, 1970), vol. 2, 417–18, 422–23, 503–4. Regarding de Gaulle's distinctive understanding of democracy, see also J. Touchard, *Le gaullisme 1940–1969* (Paris: Éditions du Seuil, 1978).
28. H. te Velde, *Stijlen van leiderschap. Persoon en politiek van Thorbecke tot Den Uyl* (Amsterdam: Wereldbibliotheek, 2002), 158–63, 179–86; J. Vercleyen, *Témoignage sur Achille Van Acker* (Brussels: Éditions Labor, 1967), 79–88.
29. A. Lijphart, *The Politics of Accommodation: Pluralism and Democracy in the Netherlands* (Berkeley: University of California Press, 1968).
30. G. Ross, *Workers and Communists in France: From Popular Front to Eurocommunism* (Berkeley: University of California Press, 1982); M-P. Dhaille-Hervieu, *Communistes au Havre. Histoire sociale, culturelle et politique, 1930–1983* (Mont Saint-Aignan: Publications des Universités de Rouen et du Havre, 2009).
31. R. Rémond, *Le retour de de Gaulle: 1958*, 2nd ed. (Brussels: Éditions Complexe, 1987).
32. See also M.F. Herz, 'Compendium of Austrian Politics, 2 December 1948', in R. Wagnleitner (ed.), *Understanding Austria* (Salzburg: Wolfgang Negebauer, 1984), 580–81. See also P. Misner, *Catholic Labor Movements in Europe, 1914–1965* (Washington DC: Catholic University of America Press, 2015); M. Mitchell, *The Origins of Christian Democracy: Politics and Confession in Modern Germany* (Ann Arbor, MI: University of Michigan Press, 2012).
33. See the very similar formulations in Herz, 'Compendium', 587–88; Conway, *Sorrows of Belgium*, 179–86; M.R. Myant, *Socialism and Democracy in Czechoslovakia, 1945–1948* (Cambridge: Cambridge University Press, 1981), 122. See also J. Bank, 'De theorie van de vernieuwing en de praktijk van de wederopbouw. Het Nederlandse socialisme in de tweede helft van de jaren veertig', in J. Bank et al., *In dienst van het gehele volk. De Westeuropese social-democratie tussen aanpassing en vernieuwing 1945–1950* (Amsterdam: Bakker, 1987), 98–121.
34. D.L. Parness, *The SPD and the Challenge of Mass Politics: The Dilemma of the German Volkspartei* (Boulder: Westview Press, 1991); R. Kreichbaumer, *Parteiprogramme im Widerstreit der Interessen* (Vienna: Verlag für Geschichte und Politik; Münich: Oldenbourg, 1990), 330–34; Parti Socialiste Belge, *Programme pour les élections législatives de 1965* (Liège: Biblio, 1965), 33–34. For a general overview of postwar socialism, see D. Sassoon, *One Hundred Years of Socialism: The West European Left in the Twentieth Century* (London: I.B. Tauris, 1996), 131–91.
35. O. Ruin, *Tage Erlander: Serving the Welfare State, 1946–1969* (Pittsburgh, PA: University of Pittsburgh Press, 1990), 214–21. Regarding Scandinavian social democracy, see more generally F. Sejersted, *The Age of Social Democracy: Norway and Sweden in the Twentieth Century* (Princeton: Princeton University Press, 2011).

36. McKeon and Rokkan, *Democracy in a World of Tensions*, vii.
37. A. Ross, 'What is Democracy?', in Lauwerys, *Scandinavian Democracy*, 55–57.
38. For a characteristic example of such rhetoric, see 'The Resistance Charter', in D. Thomson, *Democracy in France: The Third and Fourth Republics*, 2nd ed. (Oxford: Oxford University Press, 1952), 277.
39. A. Steinhouse, *Workers' Participation in Post-Liberation France* (Lanham, MD: Lexington Books, 2001); D. Luyten, *Sociaal-economisch overleg in België sedert 1918* (Brussels: VUBpress, 1995).
40. R. Mencherini, *Guerre froide, grèves rouges* (Paris: Syllepse, 1998); J. Lewis, *Workers and Politics in Occupied Austria, 1945–55* (Manchester: Manchester University Press, 2007), 110, 116, 129, 144–47; J. Neuville and J. Yerna, *Le choc de l'hiver '60–'61. Les grèves contre la loi unique* (Brussels: De Boeck POL-HIS, 1990).
41. T. Zahra, *The Lost Children: Reconstructing Europe's Families after World War II* (Cambridge, MA: Harvard University Press, 2011).
42. See, for example, R. Moeller, *Protecting Motherhood: Women and the Family in the Politics of Postwar West Germany* (Berkeley: University of California Press, 1993).
43. M. Tambor, *The Lost Wave: Women and Democracy in Postwar Italy* (Oxford: Oxford University Press, 2014); E. Carter, *How German is She? Postwar West German Reconstruction and the Consuming Woman* (Ann Arbor, MI: University of Michigan Press, 1997).
44. J. Meynaud, *La technocratie. Mythe ou réalité?* (Paris: Payot, 1964). See, for a wider discussion of the professionalization of the state, P. Nord, *France's New Deal: From the Thirties to the Post-War Era* (Princeton: Princeton University Press, 2010).
45. P. Mendès-France, 'La crise de la démocratie', in *Oeuvres Complètes*, 6 vols (Paris: Gallimard, 1986), vol. 3, 82.
46. D. Bell, *The End of Ideology: On the Exhaustion of Political Ideas in the Fifties* (Glencoe, IL: The Free Press of Glencoe, 1960). See also G. Scott-Smith, 'The Congress for Cultural Freedom, the End of Ideology and the 1955 Milan Conference: "Defining the Parameters of Discourse"', *Journal of Contemporary History* 37 (2002), 437–55.
47. R. Forienza, 'A Party for the Mezzogiorno: The Christian Democratic Party, Agrarian Reform and the Government of Italy', *Contemporary European History* 19 (2010), 335–43.
48. T. Behan, *The Long-Awaited Moment: The Working Class and the Italian Communist Party in Milan, 1943–1948* (New York: Peter Lang, 1997); G. Faravelli, *Per l'autonomia del Partito Socialista. Marxismo ed utopismo* (n.p.: Tipi dell'Industria d'Arti Grafiche, 1946), 3–4.
49. P. Corduwener, 'Challenging Parties and Anti-fascism in the Name of Democracy: The *Fronte dell'Uomo Qualunque* and its Impact on Italy's Republic', *Contemporary European History* 26 (2017), 69–84; D. Borne, *Petits-bourgeois en révolte? Le movement poujade* (Paris: Flammarion, 1977).
50. R. Vinen, *Bourgeois Politics in France 1945–1951* (Cambridge: Cambridge University Press, 1995).

51. H. Nehring, 'The British and West German Protests against Nuclear Weapons and the Culture of the Cold War, 1957–1964', *Contemporary British History* 19 (2005), 224–30; J. House and N. Macmaster, *Paris 1961: Algerians, State Terror and Memory* (Oxford: Oxford University Press, 2006).
52. Regarding affluence, see notably the classic text: J.K. Galbraith, *The Affluent Society* (London: Hamish Hamilton, 1958). For an intelligent discussion of the political impact of affluence, see Carter, *How German is She?*, 51–59.
53. The 'us' and 'them' mentality of many postwar Europeans towards their rulers is well expressed in L. Wylie, *Village in the Vaucluse*, 3rd ed. (Cambridge, MA: Harvard University Press, 1974), 206–10; P. Allum, *Politics and Society in Post-War Naples* (Cambridge: Cambridge University Press, 1973). 93–100.
54. Finer, *Major Governments of Modern Europe*, 12.
55. M. Specter, *Habermas: An Intellectual Biography* (Cambridge: Cambridge University Press, 2010), 62–63.
56. R. Aron, *La révolution introuvable* (Paris: Fayard, 1968), 141–53. See also J-W. Müller, 'What Did They Think They were Doing? The Political Thought of (the West European) 1968 Revisited', in V. Tismaneau (ed.), *Promises of 1968: Crisis, Illusion and Utopia* (Budapest: Central European University Press, 2011), 73–102.
57. R. Toye, 'Keynes, Liberalism and 'the Emancipation of the Mind'', *English Historical Review* 130 (2015), 1162–91.
58. Müller, *Contesting Democracy*, 220–27; P. Mirowski and D. Plehwe (eds), *The Road from Mont Pèlerin: The Making of the Neoliberal Thought Collective* (Cambridge, MA: Harvard University Press, 2009).
59. A. Gorz, *Socialism and Revolution* (London, Allen Lane, 1975), 73. Many of the same ideas are found in H. Marcuse, *One Dimensional Man: Studies in the Ideology of Advanced Industrial Society* (London: Routledge & Kegan Paul, 1964).
60. T. Judt, *Postwar: A History of Europe since 1945* (London: Penguin, 2005), 484–503.

Bibliography

Allum, P. 1973. *Politics and Society in Post-War Naples*. Cambridge: Cambridge University Press.
Applegate, C. 1990. *A Nation of Provincials: The German Idea of Heimat*. Berkeley: University of California Press.
Arendt, H. 1970. *Men in Dark Times*. London: Jonathan Cape.
Aron, R. 1948. *Le grand schisme*. Paris: Gallimard.
———. 1968. *La révolution introuvable*. Paris: Fayard.
Bank, J. 1987. 'De theorie van de vernieuwing en de praktijk van de wederopbouw. Het Nederlandse socialisme in de tweede helft van de jaren veertig', in J. Bank et al., *In dienst van het gehele volk. De Westeuropese social-democratie tussen aanpassing en vernieuwing 1945–1950*. Amsterdam: Bakker, 1987, 98–121.

Behan, T. 1997. *The Long-Awaited Moment. The Working Class and the Italian Communist Party in Milan, 1943–1948.* New York: Peter Lang.
Bell, D. 1960. *The End of Ideology: On the Exhaustion of Political Ideas in the Fifties.* Glencoe, IL: The Free Press of Glencoe.
Borne, D. 1977. *Petits-bourgeois en révolte? Le movement poujade.* Paris: Flammarion.
Carter, E. 1997. *How German is She? Postwar West German Reconstruction and the Consuming Woman.* Ann Arbor, MI: University of Michigan Press.
Chabod, F. 1950. *L'Italie contemporaine. Conférences données à l'Institut d'Etudes Politiques de l'Université de Paris.* Paris: Éditions Domat-Montchrestien.
Conway, M. 2002. 'Democracy in Post-war Western Europe', *European History Quarterly* 32, 59–84.
———. 2004. 'The Rise and Fall of Western Europe's Democratic Age, 1945–1973', *Contemporary European History* 13, 67–88.
———. 2012. *The Sorrows of Belgium. Liberation and Political Reconstruction 1944–47.* Oxford: Oxford University Press.
Conway, M., P. Romijn et al. 2008. *The War for Legitimacy in Politics and Culture 1936–1946.* Oxford: Berg.
Corduwener, P. 2017. 'Challenging Parties and Anti-fascism in the Name of Democracy: The *Fronte dell'Uomo Qualunque* and its Impact on Italy's Republic', *Contemporary European History* 26, 69–84.
Depkat, V. 2007. *Lebenswenden und Zeitenwenden: deutsche Politiker und die Erfahrungen des 20. Jahrhunderts.* Munich: Oldenbourg.
Dhaille-Hervieu, M-P. 2009. *Communistes au Havre. Histoire sociale, culturelle et politique, 1930–1983.* Mont Saint-Aignan: Publications des Universités de Rouen et du Havre.
Faravelli, G. 1946. *Per l'autonomia del Partito Socialista. Marxismo ed utopismo.* n.p.: Tipi dell'Industria d'Arti Grafiche.
Finer, H. 1934. *Mussolini's Italy.* London: Victor Gollancz.
———. 1946a. *Road to Reaction.* London: D. Dobson.
———. 1946b. *The Future of Government.* London: Methuen & Co.
———. 1960. *The Major Governments of Modern Europe.* London: Methuen & Co.
Forienza, R. 2010. 'A Party for the Mezzogiorno: The Christian Democratic Party, Agrarian Reform and the Government of Italy', *Contemporary European History* 19, 335–43.
Friedrich, C., and Z. Brzezinski. 1956. *Totalitarian Dictatorship and Autocracy.* Cambridge, MA: Harvard University Press.
Galbraith, J.K. 1958. *The Affluent Society.* London: Hamish Hamilton.
Gaulle C. de. 1970. *Discours et messages,* 5 vols. Paris: Plon.
Goguel, F. 1946. *La politique des partis sous la IIIe République,* 2 vols. Paris: Éditions du Seuil.
Gorz, A. 1975. *Socialism and Revolution.* London: Allen Lane.
Hacohen, M.H. 2000. *Karl Popper – The Formative Years 1902–1945: Politics and Philosophy in Interwar Vienna.* Cambridge: Cambridge University Press.

Herz, M.F. 1984. 'Compendium of Austrian Politics, 2 December 1948', in R. Wagnleitner (ed.), *Understanding Austria*, Salzburg: Wolfgang Negebauer, 580–81.

Hoffmann S-L. (ed.). 2011. *Human Rights in the Twentieth Century*. Cambridge: Cambridge University Press.

House, J., and N. Macmaster. 2006. *Paris 1961: Algerians, State Terror and Memory*. Oxford: Oxford University Press.

Hoyois, G. 1946. 'La réponse des peuples à la Démocratie', in *Les lignes de faite de la démocratie. XXVIIIe Semaine Sociale Wallonne, 1946*. Namur, 237.

Judt, T. 2005. *Postwar: A History of Europe since 1945*. London: Penguin.

Kasamas, A. 1949. *Programm Österreich. Die Grundsätze und Ziele der Österreichischen Volkspartei*. Vienna: Österreichischer Verlag.

Kreichbaumer, R. 1990. *Parteiprogramme im Widerstreit der Interessen*. Vienna: Verlag für Geschichte und Politik; Münich: Oldenbourg.

Kurunmäki, J., and J. Strang (eds). 2010. *Rhetorics of Nordic Democracy*. Helsinki: Finnish Literature Society.

Lang, M. 2007. *Karl Lowenstein. Transatlantischer Denker der Politik*. Stuttgart: Steiner Press.

Lauwerys, J.A. (ed.). 1958. *Scandinavian Democracy. Development of Democratic Thought and Institutions in Denmark, Norway and Sweden*. Copenhagen: Danish Institute, Norwegian Office of Cultural Relations, Swedish Institute, American-Scandinavian Foundation.

Lewis, J. 2007. *Workers and Politics in Occupied Austria, 1945–55*. Manchester: Manchester University Press.

Lijphart, A. 1968. *The Politics of Accommodation: Pluralism and Democracy in the Netherlands*. Berkeley: University of California Press.

———. 1969. 'Typologies of Democratic Systems', in A. Lijphart (ed.), *Politics in Europe. Comparisons and Interpretations*. Englewood Cliffs, NJ: Prentice Hall, 46–80.

Loewenstein, K. 1946. *Political Reconstruction*. New York: Macmillan.

Luyten, D. 1995. *Sociaal-economisch overleg in België sedert 1918*. Brussels: VUBpress.

Major, P. 1997. *The Death of the KPD: Communism and Anti-communism in West Germany 1945–1956*. Oxford: Clarendon Press.

Marcuse, H. 1964. *One Dimensional Man: Studies in the Ideology of Advanced Industrial Society*. London: Routledge & Kegan Paul.

McKeon R., and S. Rokkan (eds). 1951. *Democracy in a World of Tensions*. Paris: United Nations Educational, Scientific and Cultural Organization.

Mencherini, R. 1998. *Guerre froide, grèves rouges*. Paris: Syllepse.

Mendès-France, P. 1986. 'La crise de la démocratie', in *Oeuvres Complètes*, 6 vols. vol. 3. Paris: Gallimard, 82.

Meynaud, J. 1964. *La technocratie. Mythe ou réalité?* Paris: Payot.

Mirowski, P., and D. Plehwe (eds). 2009. *The Road from Mont Pèlerin: The Making of the Neoliberal Thought Collective*. Cambridge, MA: Harvard University Press.

Misner, P. 2015. *Catholic Labor Movements in Europe, 1914–1965*. Washington DC: Catholic University of America Press.

Mitchell, M. 2012. *The Origins of Christian Democracy: Politics and Confession in Modern Germany.* Ann Arbor, MI: University of Michigan Press.

Moeller, R. 1993. *Protecting Motherhood. Women and the Family in the Politics of Postwar West Germany.* Berkeley: University of California Press.

Müller, J-W. 2011a. *Contesting Democracy. Political Ideas in Twentieth-Century Europe.* New Haven: Yale University Press.

———. 2011b. 'What Did They Think They were Doing? The Political Thought of (the West European) 1968 Revisited', in V. Tismaneau (ed.), *Promises of 1968: Crisis, Illusion and Utopia.* Budapest: Central European University Press, 73–102.

Myant, M.R. 1981. *Socialism and Democracy in Czechoslovakia, 1945–1948.* Cambridge: Cambridge University Press.

Nehring, H. 2005. 'The British and West German Protests against Nuclear Weapons and the Culture of the Cold War, 1957–1964', *Contemporary British History* 19, 224–30.

Neuville, N., and J. Yerna. 1990. *Le choc de l'hiver '60–'61. Les grèves contre la loi unique.* Brussels: De Boeck POL-HIS.

Nord, P. 2010. *France's New Deal: From the Thirties to the Post-War Era.* Princeton: Princeton University Press.

Parness, D.L. 1991. *The SPD and the Challenge of Mass Politics: The Dilemma of the German Volkspartei.* Boulder: Westview Press.

Parti Socialiste Belge. 1965. *Programme pour les élections législatives de 1965.* Liège: Biblio.

Pompe, W.P.J. 1945. *Bevrijding. Bezetting – Herstel – Verniewing.* Amsterdam: Vrij Nederland.

Pulzer, P. n.d. 'Samuel Finer', *Oxford Dictionary of National Biography,* www.odnb.com.

Ranulf, S. 1948. *On the Survival Chances of Democracy.* Copenhagen: Munksgaard.

Rémond, R. 1987. *Le retour de de Gaulle: 1958,* 2nd edn. Brussels: Éditions Complexe.

Risso, L. 2011. 'Propaganda on Wheels: The NATO Travelling Exhibitions in the 1950s and 1960s', *Cold War History* 11, 9–25.

Ross, G. 1982. *Workers and Communists in France: From Popular Front to Eurocommunism.* Berkeley: University of California Press.

Ruin, O. 1990. *Tage Erlander: Serving the Welfare State, 1946–1969.* Pittsburgh, PA: University of Pittsburgh Press.

Saragat, G. 1946. *Socialismo democratico e socialismo totalitario. Per l'autonomia del Partito Socialista.* Milan: Critica Sociale.

Sassoon, D. 1996. *One Hundred Years of Socialism. The West European Left in the Twentieth Century.* London: I.B. Tauris.

Scott-Smith, G. 2002. 'The Congress for Cultural Freedom, the End of Ideology and the 1955 Milan Conference: "Defining the Parameters of Discourse"', *Journal of Contemporary History* 37, 437–55.

Sejersted, F. 2011. *The Age of Social Democracy: Norway and Sweden in the Twentieth Century.* Princeton: Princeton University Press.

Specter, M. 2010. *Habermas: An Intellectual Biography*. Cambridge: Cambridge University Press.
Steinhouse, A. 2001. *Workers' Participation in Post-Liberation France*. Lanham, MD: Lexington Books.
Talmon, J. 1952. *The Origins of Totalitarian Democracy*. London: Secker & Warburg.
Tambor, M. 2014. *The Lost Wave: Women and Democracy in Postwar Italy*. Oxford: Oxford University Press.
Thomson, D. 1952. *Democracy in France: The Third and Fourth Republics*, 2nd ed. Oxford: Oxford University Press.
Touchard, J. 1978. *Le gaullisme 1940–1969*. Paris: Éditions du Seuil.
Toye, R. 2015. 'Keynes, Liberalism and "the Emancipation of the Mind"', *English Historical Review* 130, 1162–91.
Ullrich, S. 2009. *Der Weimar-Komplex. Das Scheitern der ersten deutschen Demokratie und die politische Kultur der frühen Bundesrepublik 1945–1959*. Göttingen: Wallstein.
Velde, H. te. 2002. *Stijlen van leiderschap. Persoon en politiek van Thorbecke tot Den Uyl*. Amsterdam: Wereldbibliotheek.
Ventresca, R.A. 2004. *From Fascism to Democracy: Culture and Politics in the Italian Election of 1948*. Toronto: University of Toronto Press.
Vercleyen, J. 1967. *Témoignage sur Achille Van Acker*. Brussels: Éditions Labor.
Vinen, R. 1995. *Bourgeois Politics in France 1945–1951*. Cambridge: Cambridge University Press.
Wylie, L. 1974. *Village in the Vaucluse*, 3rd edn. Cambridge, MA: Harvard University Press.
Zahra, T. 2011. *The Lost Children: Reconstructing Europe's Families after World War II*. Cambridge, MA: Harvard University Press.

Chapter 11

Political Participation and Democratization in the 1960s

The Concept of Participatory Democracy
and its Repercussions

Ingrid Gilcher-Holtey

The 1960s saw emerging criticism of Western liberal democracies. Protest movements challenged the leading values and the institutional order of the parliamentary democracies. What did they criticize about the democratic systems established after the Second World War? What did democracy mean to them? What expectations did they project onto a 'different' democratic basic order? Did their critique change the theory and practice of democracy? Identifying the consequences of social movements for the political culture of a country presents methodological challenges.[1] With an intention to sketch the development of the concept of democracy in the 1960s, my deliberations focus on the critique of democracy in the context of the 68-movements. Ten observations about the term 'democracy' in the 1960s are subsequently described. The political – which is the premise of the following analysis – starts when protagonists call into question dominant schemes of perception and classification, and set examples through expressive and subversive discourses, proclaiming the cancellation of the clandestine assent to the prevailing order, redefining situations and events, and formulating alternative referential values or leading ideas, thereby confronting the established order with an alternative concept or order.[2] The history of concepts shows that the critique of established democratic institutions in the 1960s was accompanied by a widening of the definition of 'democracy'.

Demand for a 'Participatory Democracy'

The critique of the student New Left, which ignited the mobilization process of the 68-movements, aimed at the prevailing notion of democracy as a political system confined only to regular elections. This restricted notion of democracy as a form of state and government was contrasted with an understanding of democracy that called for participation in all social areas. The concept of democracy was broadened: now democracy also included a distinctive form of society. The American student group Students for a Democratic Society (SDS), which had separated from the League for Industrial Democracy in the early 1960s, used the term 'participatory democracy' for this broader perception of democracy. It first appeared in its 1962 programme, the Port Huron Statement, which carried the subtitle 'Agenda for a Generation' and endeavoured to search for a 'true democratic alternative' for humankind in the second half of the twentieth century.[3] The term 'participatory democracy' had been coined by the German-Jewish philosopher Walter Arnold Kaufmann. Kaufmann had immigrated to the United States in 1939. He taught at the University of Michigan in Ann Arbor at the beginning of the 1960s, where he happened to be the academic supervisor of the main author of *The Port Huron Statement*, Tom Hayden. Hayden became the leading and symbolic figure of the 68-protest movements in the United States.[4] Kaufmann had borrowed the concept of a 'participatory democracy' from John Dewey, who had differentiated between democracy as a form of government and as a form of societal living as early as the 1930s.[5] *The Port Huron Statement* defines 'participatory democracy' as a 'social system of a democracy of individual participation, governed by two central aims; that the individual share in those social decisions determining the quality and direction of his life; that society be organized to encourage independence in men and provide the media for their common participation'.[6]

This concept changes the relationship between citizens and institutions. It implies that common grievances are not disposed of by simply directing them into established political channels. Instead, decision-making of a basic social scope should be carried out by public groupings. In this way, politics becomes 'the art of collectively creating an acceptable pattern of social relations'. Participatory democracy extends democracy to the economic and social sphere, and calls for the establishment of democratic structures in the workplace, the neighbourhood and even the family.[7]

Extracts of *The Port Huron Statement* were published for the first time in German in 1969 as part of documentation about *Die Neue Linke in den USA*. 'Participatory democracy' was translated as 'partizipierende Demokratie'.[8] One year later, Hannah Arendt also translated it into German. She had closely observed the protest movements in the United States, Germany and France, and saw the concept of 'participatory democracy' as the 'only positive password of the new movement'. She considered it an example of the revolutionary tradition of the council democracy, whose origins she traced back to the revolutionary societies and municipal councils of the French Revolution. She chose the term 'Mitbestimmungsdemokratie' as an adequate translation.[9] In the Federal Republic of Germany, more participation within the democratic system had been demanded since the beginning of the 1960s. The Sozialistische Deutsche Studentenbund (SDS), which was, just like the American SDS, a part of the worldwide New Left, took up this idea by propagating the term 'social democracy'. With this term, the German SDS defined democratization of all areas of society in its memorandum *Hochschule in der Demokratie* (1961), which started with the academic sector.[10] The SDS saw its concept of democracy in the tradition of the German-Jewish political scientist Franz Neumann, who had emigrated in 1933. Neumann had written in his book *The Democratic and the Authoritarian State* (1957): 'Democracy is not a form of state as any other. Its essence consists of the execution of large-scale social change, which enhances and maybe even completes the liberties of the citizens. Democracy is based on the autonomy of mankind, and only when this has become real, the former is truly achieved.'[11]

The adoption of Neumann's perception of democracy paralleled the publication of a study of the Institut für Sozialforschung in Frankfurt, which had surveyed German students' political awareness. Its conclusion showed that not even 10 per cent of the students would support the democratic system in case of political crisis, while 16 per cent openly opposed it. Confronted with the 'historical alternative of the extension of liberal democracy towards social democracy or its transformation in plebiscitary-hierarchical forms of authoritarian democracy', Jürgen Habermas, coeditor of the study, referred to Neumann as well. He defined 'political participation' as a means to achieve the transformation from formal to material, liberal to social democracy.[12] The German SDS, supported by Habermas, went from theory to practice. It demanded participation in the decision-making processes of the autonomous institutions of the German universities. In 1968, it extended its demand for participation from a third parity to a half parity.[13]

In Germany, Ralf Dahrendorf rejected the claim that political theory would presuppose the 'total democratization' of society. Equating democracy with parliamentary democracy, he characterized the latter with recourse to Josef Schumpeter as 'that certain institutional arrangement for the production of political decisions, in which individuals acquire the power to decide with the help of a competition for the votes of the people'. In *Gesellschaft und Demokratie in Deutschland* (1965), he concluded that this 'ominous procedure could, strictly speaking, only be appropriate for the political polity'. 'All other institutions have', he opined, 'social structural traits, which either exclude the political procedure right away or use it metaphorically, thereby changing its effect.'[14] With this stance he stood in opposition to the revised university memorandum of the SDS, which was published under the title *Hochschule in der Demokratie* with a preface by Jürgen Habermas in 1965. It deplored that democracy as a concept to organize diverse areas of societal life was not mentioned anywhere in the Federal Republic of Germany.[15] Thus, the conflict about the very nature of the term 'democracy', which had already been fought in Germany in 1848,[16] became apparent again shortly before the formation of the 68-movement.

Changing the Institutions of Society

'Participatory democracy' or 'social democracy' implies a structural transformation of society through a change of its institutions. A part of the New Left believed that the established political system itself could not bring about such structural change.

'If there is to be a politics of the new Left, what needs to be analyzed is the structure of institutions, the foundations of policies', C. Wright Mills, who influenced the student movements in the United States as much as in Germany, declared in his 'Letter to the New Left!' (1960).[17] With this statement, he pointed out a weak point in the political theory of the old left. 'Under social democratic leadership parties tend to become simply electoral machines', Charles Taylor had already stated in the *New Left Review* shortly before.[18] The German SDS, which had been expelled by the Social Democratic Party 1960, accused the party of 'curtail[ing] the internal democracy by authoritarian attempts of manipulating party members and voters, thereby showing, how far the authoritarian tendencies, which we have verified for the GDR, have already progressed into the SPD'.[19] Daniel Cohn-Bendit, the leading figure of the Movement of the 22nd of March, which triggered the mobilization process of the 68-movement in France, also directed his critique against the political parties, primarily against the Communist Party of France. In his book *Linksradikalismus. Gewaltkur gegen die Alterskrankheit des Kommunismus*, he wrote: 'Democracy is not perverted by bad organizational directives, but by the mere existence of the party. Democracy cannot be effected intentionally, because the party in itself is not a democratic organism. It doesn't represent the classes it purports to.'[20]

Apart from the critique of the political parties, the critique of the parliamentary system also accompanied the demands for an extension of the concept of democracy. In 1969, Herbert Marcuse noticed in his *Essay on*

Liberation 'an alienation of the radical opposition from the existing democratic process and its institutions'. Differentiating between 'democracy' and 'pseudo-democracy', he wrote: 'a strong revulsion against traditional politics prevails: against the whole network of parties, committees and pressure groups on all levels; against working within this network and with its methods'.[21]

For the rebels, Marcuse continues, 'nothing that any of these politicians, representatives, or candidates declares is of any relevance'.[22] His view is reflected in the texts of the American and German New Left movements. *The Port Huron Statement* explains: 'The American political system is not the democratic model which its glorifiers speak of. In actuality it frustrates democracy by confusing the individual citizen, paralyzing policy discussion, and consolidating the irresponsible power of military and business interests.'[23] The *neue kritik*, the periodical of the German SDS, observed 'an erosion of the parliamentary democracy',[24] the 'destruction of the democratic public',[25] a process of 'dedemocratization' and an 'involution of the parliamentary governmental system'.[26] Rudi Dutschke, the symbolic figure of the German extraparliamentary opposition (APO), presented this stance in a December 1967 TV interview: to 'consider the present parliamentary system as useless'.[27] Answering a question about how the society he imagined should be organized, administrated and governed, Dutschke sketched organizational structures that differed fundamentally from the present ones. He outlined the basic differences with these words: 'we have started to build organizations, which differ from the structure of a political party by the way they lack professional politicians, where no apparatus can develop and where the interests and needs of those, who participate in the institutions, are represented'.[28] What was supposed to replace the established democratic institutions?

Self-Organization, Counter-Institutions and 'Autogestion' as Leading Ideas

In 1960, E.P. Thompson had proclaimed in the *New Left Review* 'democratic self-activity' in order to fight against apathy in society.[29] 'Self-organization' became a basic structural element of the new, alternative society, and was at the same time considered a *conditio sine qua non* of the radical opposition on its way to that goal. Hans Magnus Enzensberger wrote in his *Kursbuch*, the forum of the extraparliamentary opposition, under the headline 'Berliner Gemeinplätze': 'Real democracy, decentralization of decisions, cooperation instead of subordination: these elementary demands, which the opposition wants to realize in future societies, must first of all be fulfilled in the forms of its own organization.'[30]

How could this idea of self-organization be put into practice? How should it be defined? Where should its realization start? Herbert Marcuse concluded: 'If democracy means self-government of free people with justice for all, the realization of democracy would presuppose the abolition of the existing pseudo-democracy.'[31] Marcuse's diagnosis was confirmed by the conduct of the demonstrators in Paris in May 1968. Daniel Guérin reported that the demonstrators nonchalantly passed by parliament. No one took notice of the building.[32] The New Left did not aspire to conquer the political power, but to alter it through the formation of counter-power, counter-institutions and counter-public.[33]

Counter-institutions are directed against something, but they do not intend to be mere opposition. They are seen as models for the future. Counter-institutions transfer the future into the present, and attempt to establish alternative cultural values and new relational structures within micro-milieus. For this concept, Wini Breines developed the term 'prefigurative politics' in order to point out 'an essentially anti-organizational politics characteristic of the movement as well as parts of the new left leadership'.[34] The idea of constituting counter-institutions quickly caught on with the 68-movements and found manifold ways of expression beyond them. Models of direct democracy, basic democracy or council democracy shaped the counter-institutions of the New Left.

The American SDS was the first to put this idea of self-organization into practice. It was first carried out by their Economic Research and Action Project (ERAP). In order to strengthen 'community organization' in slums and poverty-stricken neighbourhoods in big cities, project members offered to promote self-help without claiming leading positions. The underlying premise was that working in a collective would alter the individual. Attempting to wake the poor from their unconsciousness, their objective was to create an 'interracial movement of the poor'.[35]

In Germany, plans to leave the campus to get into contact with the poor in their neighbourhoods and with workers in their factories were either not carried out or failed. Taking up the theory on the manipulation of consciousness through the consciousness industry (newspapers, publishing houses, radio, television and films) as the key industry of the twentieth century (Enzensberger),[36] the New Left launched a campaign against the monopolization of the press (the Anti-Springer-Kampagne) and initiated attempts to establish a counter-public through the self-organization of alternative newspapers (Extrablatt), alternative publishing houses (Verlag der Autoren) as well as through the democratization of literary production (democratization of publishing houses).

In France, the May 1968 student demonstrations led to a wave of public support among the French workers. During the general strike, which covered the whole of France, a new form of self-organization was developed for the factory workers. When the spark of protest ignited the factories, the workers' union CFDT, which sympathized with the New Left, gave out the maxim: 'The liberty in the universities should correspond to the liberties in the corporations, since the students' fight is the same fight the workers have led since the birth of the workers' movement. Industrial and administrative monarchy must be replaced by democratic structures on the basis of autogestion.'[37]

The term 'autogestion' (self-management) symbolized a strategy of transformation that differed from that of the Old Left since it led the mobilization processes of the students and the workers to a new horizon. In place of possession and property, autogestion shifted the focus to power-making and decision-making relationships. 'Art-critique' 'superposed' social critique. This is Luc Boltanski's und Ève Chiapello's thesis about May 1968 in France. It was directed against alienation, not against exploitation. It brought into focus the misery of daily life, the dehumanization of the world under the influence of technologization and technocracy, the loss of autonomy and lack of creativity.[38] From the 'art-critique' followed critique against the hierarchy-principle, against power-making and decision-making structures, against authoritarianism and paternalism within the institutions and organizations of society.[39] Authority became a key term, whose multidimensionality was considered to be an advantage as it could reflect various societal phenomena: applying this term, one could focus on a character trait of a person as well as relationships between people or on the structure of institutions. The idea of liberating the consciousness as a productive power to revolutionize society gained momentum. It reflected a reinterpretation and revision of Marxist theory. In France, West Germany and the United States, the rise of an intellectual Nouvelle Gauche, Neue Linke or New Left preceded the mobilization process of the 1968 movements.

Cognitive Orientation of the New Left

The New Left distinguished itself from the Old Left, from the reformism of the social democratic and socialist parties as well as from the perversion of communism by Stalinism. The New Left was anti-capitalistic and anti-communistic. The intellectual Nouvelle Gauche, Neue Linke or New Left grew out of discussion forums, which, since the late 1950s, grouped themselves around magazines: *New Left Review, Arguments, Socialisme ou Barbarie, Internationale Situationniste, Quaderni Rossi* or *Quaderni Piacentini*, to name only a few of them. The cognitive orientation with which the free-floating intellectuals of the New Left confronted the traditional Left consisted of the following five elements.

First, the new orientation centred on a reinterpretation of Marxist theory. Referring to the early writings of Marx, the New Left accentuated the aspect of alienation rather than exploitation. It attempted to open the theoretical interpretation by combining Marxism with existentialism and psychoanalysis to free the former from its sclerotic paralysis and identification with institutionalized Marxism. Second, the New Left envisioned a new model of society that would not be restricted to political and social revolution, seizure of power and nationalization of the means of production. Rather, it should eliminate the alienation felt by the individuals in everyday life, recreation and family, as well as in sexual and societal relationships. Third, partisans of the New Left embraced a new transformation strategy. They believed that the individual should be freed from subordination to the collective. The premise was that changes in the cultural sphere must precede social and political transformation. New lifestyles and modes of communication had to be anticipated and developed on an experimental basis by creating new cultural ideals, applying them in subcultures and testing them as alternatives within existing institutions. Fourth, the new cognitive orientation required a new organizational concept. The New Left understood itself as a movement, not a party. It sought to generate awareness through action to change the individuals taking part in it. Finally, the New Left also called for the redefinition of the historical subject of social change. The proletariat was no longer seen as the leader of social and cultural change. Instead, the New Left believed that the impetus for social transformation would come from other groups: the new (skilled) working class, the young intelligentsia and the social fringe groups.[40]

Redefinition of 'the Political' (by the New Left)

The New Left's strategy of transformation is based on a redefinition of 'the political', a detachment of the political from the state and its institutions. 'The political' shifts to public spaces, to streets and squares.

When in the middle of the 1960s the student movement occupied university halls, lecture rooms, theatres, streets and squares, Hannah Arendt noted about these events: 'This generation has experienced what the 18th century has called "public happiness". This means: When the citizens act in public, they open up a certain dimension of human existence, which is otherwise closed for them and somehow forms part of the complete human happiness.'[41]

The atmosphere in the plenary meetings in Berkeley, Berlin or Paris confirmed Arendt's assessment: 'L'avenir est à prendre' was the slogan on the walls of the Odéon theatre in May 1968, 'car l'avenir est perdu par un Gouvernement vieillard'. 'Inventer, c'est prendre le pouvoir de demain.' Thousands rushed to the theatre each day to watch the process of creating a new future.⁴² Later no one was able to reconstruct the discussion. But what was spoken was not important; its importance lay in the fact that it had been spoken. Michel de Certeau observed that the seizure of the word symbolized the upcoming cultural upheaval.⁴³ Michael Rossmann characterized the birth of the Free Speech Movement in Berkeley as a similar liberation: 'It's almost enough to make you believe that if it had a chance, the democratic process might work. It just might work. People quoted books as if books were relevant. They talked about Greeks, and they talked about theories of politics, as if it all meant something. And listening to them, I almost believed for the first time in years that it did mean something.'⁴⁴

The self-awareness and self-formation through collective discussion was linked to one premise: the occupation of a room, in which the written and unwritten rules would be suspended temporarily, autonomy would be established and hierarchical structures would be reversed.⁴⁵

New spaces of communication were created through go-ins, sit-ins, teach-ins, the disruption of lectures or the occupation of university buildings. Asked by a journalist, what they wanted to achieve by occupying the Sorbonne, the occupiers answered: 'On verra. C'est dans la discussion que nous nous définirons.'⁴⁶ 'Discussion' and 'to discuss' became buzzwords. 'Democracy is discussion' was the slogan of the 68-movement in Germany as well.⁴⁷

The symbolic practice of discussion in autonomous, liberated spaces, which characterized the 68-movement, overlapped with Hannah Arendt's concept of politics. In *Vita activa* (1960), she defined 'political action' as 'thinking out of talking', 'the finding of the right word at the right moment', which in itself is 'already acting'.⁴⁸ For Arendt, the political was linked with deliberation in public space, which necessitates freedom and plurality. Politics grows, according to her, in the space between human beings.⁴⁹ And exactly here, the student New Left applied their theory. They focused on power relations beyond the Leviathan. Special emphasis was placed on the revelation of authoritarian structures, which permeated the established institution. Provocation was considered to be one of the methods to unveil them. The occupation of a lecture room or an institute could create space for unconventional topics, allowing themes to be put on the agenda that were thus far untouched and made negotiable. The strategy of controlled rule-violation through provocative action went one step further. It managed 'to force the representative democracy to openly show its class-character, its hierarchy-character, to unmask itself as dictatorship of power'.⁵⁰

The anti-authoritarian New Left, which criticized the established democratic institutions, followed a dual strategy of transformation: autonomy through self-administration and alteration of the individual in and through provocative direct action. It thereby tied in with the action strategies of the black civil rights movement in the United States, but also with the strategies of the artistic vanguard of the twentieth century. They rediscovered what the historical vanguard had accentuated: the relevance of schemes of perception for the maintenance or alteration of the existing order.

It is possible to call experimenting with different kinds of perception, as the New Left students did, 'politics of perception', which aims 'at maintaining or subverting the order of things by transforming or conserving the categories through which it is conceived, the words in which it is expressed'.[51] So Marcuse wrote in the spring of 1968, while observing the protests: 'Today's rebels want to see, hear and feel new things in a new way. They connect liberation with the dissolution of the usual and regulated way of perception.' He concluded: 'The revolution must, simultaneously, be a revolution of perception, which accompanies the material and mental reconstruction of society and produces the new environment.'[52] The politics of perception, triggered by self-proclaimed, spontaneous and locally acting 'revolutionary awareness groups' or 'small minorities', led to tensions and conflicts within the 68-movements in the United States, France and Germany. The Old Left returned.

Subversion of Participatory Democracy by a New Old Left

In the process of the demobilization of the 68-movements, the new Old Left prevailed over the student New Left. Together with the Maoist, Trotskyist and Leninist cadre groups, the seemingly dead concept of democracy celebrated a comeback in the political arena: 'Government and control from above' (the top-down approach) returned.

The deficiencies of participatory democracy had already been articulated within the American SDS in the autumn of 1967, when the national management level became increasingly unable to exert influence over the various local groups. 'The basic problem with participatory democracy', Creg Calvert, national spokesman of the organization, explained, 'lies not in its analysis or vision, but in its basic inadequacy as a style of work for a serious radical organization.' What the SDS lacked, in his view, was 'responsible collective leadership' or a 'steering committee . . . responsible for the development of long-range organizing strategies and programs which can be intelligently discussed and criticized by members'.[53]

Who would win in teach-ins was a question that vexed many members. At the first plenary assembly in the occupied Sorbonne, a council of occupiers was elected as an executive organ. It consisted of fifteen members and was elected each evening anew in an 'en bloc' procedure, which would hide the drain of participants. In the debates, a fight for the control of the microphone and the loudspeakers soon developed in order to fortify or suppress speeches and statements. The supervisors of the technical services – the printing machines for the flyers and articles included – wielded the real power in the Sorbonne.[54] Informal, unclear power structures occurred within the German SDS as well and contributed to the anti-anti-authoritarian turn. The spontaneity of the basic and ad hoc groups destroyed the indirect internal will-formation of student associations in both Germany and the United States. Therefore, the founding of political parties was perceived as a liberating development after a phase of direct democracy because it led to clear relationships and order.[55] The former anti-authoritarian wing of the German students' movement joined forces with the diverse communist groups. With the rise of new parties, the organizational principle of 'democratic centralism' celebrated its renaissance. The turn to organization implied the return of hierarchy within the new organizations.

After 1968, discussions shifted back to closed rooms, to which only those who were registered were admitted. Basic democracy and ideas of self-government were abandoned. Factory, basic and apprenticeship groups, which had sprung up spontaneously in the context of the extraparliamentary opposition, lost ground. After 1970, the top-down approach prevailed. The basic groups were used only as instruments of power.[56] With the new self-concept, the question of power was also brought up again. The concept of the council democracy, rediscovered by the anti-authoritarian New Left and propagated in 1968 by leading SDS representatives who considered the Paris Commune as a role model for a new decentralized order in Berlin, was tossed into the dustbin of history. Autonomy and council democracy were considered an 'ideology of ultra-democratism' by the KPD/AO (Communist Party of Germany/Construction Organization)[57] and were blown away by the new wind of the cadre groups. The new definition of politics as well as democracy shrank with the demise of these ideas and concepts. Power was again identified as something related to political parties and the state. The acquisition of political power was back as the leading idea. The new parties oriented themselves towards the 'people's democracies' in China, North Korea or Vietnam and once again differentiated between 'social democracy' and 'bourgeois democracy'.

The Renaissance of Participatory Democracy within the New Social Movements

As the 68-protest movement collapsed, successor movements sprouted that were classified as new social movements.[58] These tied in with the concept of 'participatory democracy', but altered it simultaneously. The agenda of these new movements did not list material social problems or conflicts in the sphere of production, but problems of everyday life: quality of life, gender equality, individual self-realization, political participation and human rights.[59] The private and the personal were considered 'the political' and thus they came into focus. Tying in with the leading idea of participatory democracy, the new social movements also articulated 'problems of collective goods';[60] however, they did not refer to a 'historical subject', which would accelerate the societal transformation process. They intersected the ideological tie to the labour movement. In contrast to the New Left, they did not develop an alternative model to the existing order that comprised society as a whole. Instead, they questioned the utopian contents of previous models of societies. They were not led by visions of the future. Their search for a collective identity became apparent 'in the here and now of an individual identity'.[61] 'Participation in collective action', as Alberto Melucci put it, 'was considered worthless as long as it didn't contribute directly to the fulfilment of personal needs.'[62] What motivated the new social movements was the idea of self-determination. The protagonists looked at the social order as a product of the will; structural changes would therefore be declared consequences of changes in individual attitudes and behaviour.[63] Their attitude towards welfare-state capitalism remained ambivalent. Their positions ranged from outright rejection to reform concepts.[64]

Support for the new social movements in West Germany was supplied by a 'left-alternative milieu', which grew out of the dissolution of the 68-movement. Contemporary social science research in around 1980 estimated that about 2.7 million people, aged fourteen to fifty-four, belonged to this milieu.[65] Leading values of this milieu were participatory democracy and anti-hierarchy. Organizationally, this left-alternative milieu was without a firm structure, anti-institutional, set against political parties and the state, and organized along basic democratic principles. The communicative coherence was ensured 'not the least, by the alternative press', which was triggered by the mobilizing processes of the 68-movement.[66]

The milieu consisted of a multitude of decentralized networks, which acted autonomously and on a local level.[67] Democratization, humanization and authentic self-determination were the political slogans of this left-alternative milieu.[68] The democratization started in everyday life and in its individual conduct. This milieu was comprised of agricultural collectives and self-governing firms that claimed to avoid labour conditions that estranged the workers. Decisions of the firm were supposed to be taken through procedures that were basic-democratic, collective and consensual.[69] Relations in the areas of housing, labour, family, education and gender were identified as in need of democratization. In France and the United States, new models of labour and living were also experimentally tested in the 1970s.[70]

Transfers of Participatory Democracy in the 1970s

In the 1970s, participatory democracy was tested not only in the left-alternative milieu, but also in the well-established institutions of the field of cultural production (theatres and universities),[71] as well as in the business sector. The transfer showed the limits as well as the adaptability of the concept. Here, I concentrate on the theatre and the business sectors.

For the students of the New Left, the only chance to change the apparatus of the theatre was to break with its hierarchies and its authoritarian spirit. The ensemble of the Berliner Schaubühne, which had emanated from a student theatre, adopted this perspective. They called for:

> a reduction of bureaucracy to a minimum, abolition of the theatre director's feudal autocratic rule, instead, [they called for] a collective leadership, appointed not by the financial backers, but by the producers in the theatre, which can be voted out of office, participation of all members of the ensemble in planning the programme, and disclosure of all artistic and commercial decisions to be transparent.[72]

For the actors, belonging to a theatre collective that worked on the basis of direct democracy meant fourteen- to sixteen-hour days, as making decisions jointly took up inordinate amounts of time. Minutes were taken of all meetings – of actors, technicians, management and plenary sessions – with the aim of rendering the decision-making process within the theatre transparent. These minutes represent a unique record of an attempt to break down hierarchies and authoritarian structures within the theatre.[73] At the same time, they demonstrate ambivalence towards democratizing the theatre. The central question was whether artistic issues could be subjected to majority decision-making. In the internal debates, director Peter Stein vehemently resisted having his assessment of an actor's abilities and limitations put to the vote. Yet in 1971, he declared that he was ready to have the casting put to a general vote. He directed *Peer Gynt* with five different principal actors. In the ballot, all the actors had claimed the role of Peer Gynt for themselves.

The endeavours to democratize the theatre thereby found their limits, as director Stein saw it. 'The attribution of roles' was not wholly 'democratizationable [i.e. suitable for democratization]'. 'Democratization was only possible', he declared, 'with regard to the utterance of opinions. If he would be outvoted in a question of cast, he would be ready to accept the vote and still give his best as director . . . but what the outcome would be, would be a completely different story.'[74] The Berliner Schaubühne was not a unique case. A survey of 120 West German theatres at the end of the theatre season 1968/1969 revealed that the struggle for more participation and the experiments with codetermination were being conducted everywhere.[75] In most cases actual changes were limited to improvement in the communication and information structures of the theatre or to strengthening the rights of the staff representatives. The stage hands' trade union had reservations against autogestion.

Entrepreneurs and managers in France reacted differently. The business sector adopted the idea of self-administration and self-responsibility in the 1970s, fitted it into their system and subordinated them to their interest. Confronted with a refusal to obey orders and a refusal to work, as well as with strikes and sabotage in their firms, French businessmen looked for new ways to re-establish the undisturbed functioning of their factories. Since they interpreted the protest that had been carried out mostly by young and skilled labourers as directed against estranged labour, they offered new forms of cooperation in some model plants for a start. These then spread out quickly, propagated by the mainstream management literature in the 1980s. This 'New Spirit of Capitalism' featured the de-hierarchization of structures of leading and deciding, and thereby the adoption of one of the central demands of the May 1968 movement. This started with the establishment of small, autonomous work teams, which were granted autonomy, but, according to the research of Luc Boltanski and Ève Chiapello, at the price of the reduction of labour protection guarantees and social standards in the factories. The creation of autonomous working teams was accompanied by the weakening of the labour unions.[76] So actually, self-determination served the goals of a transition to a flexible internal structure, the mobility and adaptability of the firms.

In West Germany, codetermination in the area of business firms was blocked by the then Liberal Party (FDP), when it became part of the sociliberal coalition in 1969. This agreement stipulated that there would be no discussion of codetermination on the basis of parity.[77]

The Development of a 'Deliberative Democracy' in the 1980s

As a version or submodel of participatory democracy, the concept of 'deliberative democracy' developed in political theory. Joshua Cohen, who shaped the debate in the United States in 1989, defined 'deliberative democracy' as 'an association whose affairs are governed by the public deliberation of its members'. He emphasized 'public reasoning among equal citizens' as characteristic for this association. Public reasoning provides the basis for democratic legitimacy, according to Cohen. His notion of the ideal type of deliberative democracy was based on the assumption 'that a direct democracy with citizens gathering in legislative assemblies is the only way to institutionalize a deliberative procedure'. But since he believed that direct democracy under modern conditions would be impossible, he aimed for the strengthening of democratic legitimacy by establishing 'arenas', 'in which citizens can propose issues for the political agenda and participate in debate about those issues'.[78] He sketched an ideal scheme of deliberation, in which – and he quotes Habermas – '"no force except that of better argument is exercised"'.

This quotation by Habermas on which Cohen rests his argument stemmed from the former's book *Legitimationsprobleme im Spätkapitalismus* (1973), which had been published in English in 1975 under the title *Legitimation Crisis*. It had been written while Habermas and Carl Friedrich von Weizsäcker were co-directors of the Max-Planck-Institut für die Erforschung der Lebensbedingungen der wissenschaftlich-technischen Welt (research about the living conditions of the scientific-technical world) in Starnberg. This institute was administered on the principles of direct (or basic) democracy. Drawing on concepts from the 68-movement, the members of the institute had introduced structures of self-determination. They had founded an institute-council and stipulated that the plenary meeting of the members should have the competence of deciding basic issues. This basic-democratic claim of the members of the institute had contributed to its dissolution in 1980.

The institute had also been influenced by the 68-movement with regard to the determination of its research focus. In *Legitimationsprobleme im Spätkapitalismus*, which served as a concept paper for the institutional agenda, Habermas referred to the experience with the mobilization process of the 68-movement. He attributed the central conflicts of late capitalist society not to the phenomenon of economic deprivation, but to political legitimacy: to the clash of systemic demands and new normative structures. The protests of students and the youth had shown, as he saw it, that a new level of moral learning had been reached. Observing the young protesters and students, he saw 'agents of motivation, who would not be integrated anymore. They are not adapted and weaken the legitimacy of the political system'.[79] With his category of 'interaction conveyed by symbols', he provided a theoretical framework to interpret group and class consciousness as a cooperative learning process of subjects.[80] With the discursive establishment of norms of behaviour, he paved the way for a concept of 'procedural legitimacy'[81] that was as distinct from the decisionism of Carl Schmitt as from an ethic of material values and that also formed the basis of the 'deliberative procedure' of Joshua Cohen.

Habermas reimported the term 'deliberative democracy' as well as the American debate that had been triggered by his own discourse theory and integrated both into his own theory. He introduced the term as politics resulting from institutionalised, discursively structured deliberation- and decision-procedures within a political rule-of-law system'.[82] Deliberative politics is not a procedure for the government of society as a whole, but a 'network of discourses and bargaining processes that is supposed to facilitate the rational solution of pragmatic, moral, and ethical questions – the very problems that accumulate with the failure of the functional, moral, and ethical integration of society elsewhere'.[83] Deliberative politics, as Habermas sees it, is a means for coping with conflicts by communication. It rests on the interplay of the democratically composed formation of the will and the informal formation of opinion. It thereby supplements democratic procedure, but does not replace it.

Participatory Democracy within the Alter-Globalization Movements

Presently, a look beyond the 1960s shows that the concept of participatory democracy outlived the demobilization process of the 68-movement and influenced the alter-globalization movements – from the Occupy Movement[84] to the Climate Justice Movement.[85]

The start of the alter-globalization movement in the Western industrialized countries was marked by the protests against the World Trade Organization (WTO) conference in Seattle in 1999. It is not the process of globalization itself that the 'altermondialistes' oppose, but the ideology of neoliberalism, which has painted the picture of a self-regulating economy and that has propagated for its enforcement three leading maxims: radical free trade, deregulation and privatization.[86] Often defined as a 'new New Social Movement', the alter-globalization movement is based on individual movements as well as on affinity groups that work together on an ad hoc basis and through consensus decision-making. Many of the members call themselves the 'New Anarchists'. 'Anarchism is the heart of the movement, its soul, the source of most of what's new and hopeful about it', writes David Graeber, who considers himself a new anarchist. The movement is anti-state, anti-hierarchic, basic democratic and consensus-oriented. It does not want to conquer political power. It is rather, as Graeber writes, 'a movement about reinventing democracy ... creating and enacting horizontal networks instead of top-down structures like states, parties or corporations, by exposing, delegitimising and dismantling mechanisms of rule, while winning ever-larger spaces of autonomy from it'.[87] In order to alter the rules behind the rules, the movement relies on direct actions and the creation of platforms of criticism of today's society, the enabling of alternative ways of thinking and behaviour and structures of relationships and communication. The principle of communication and decision-making is the consensus-oriented exchange among equals. Autonomy, self-determination and self-administration are tested in local and transnational fora. They distinguish themselves from the anarchists of the nineteenth century by their general renunciation of violence, their rejection of the historical subject as agent of societal transformation and, finally, by their abandonment of political vanguard concepts of any kind. Their leading idea, changing the world without taking political power, remains a democratic challenge in a globalized world.

Ingrid Gilcher-Holtey is Professor of Contemporary History at Bielefeld University and Associate Member of the Centre de Sociologie Européenne (CSE/EHESS-Paris). She was Visiting Professor at Sciences Po, Paris (1999–2000) and at St Antony's College, Oxford (2008–9). Her main publications include *1968: Eine Zeitreise* (2008); *Eingreifendes Denken: Die Wirkungschancen von Intellektuellen* (2007); *Die 68er Bewegung: Deutschland – Westeuropa – United States* (5th edn., 2017); *Die Phantasie an die Macht: Mai 68 in Frankreich* (2nd edn., 2001); and *1968 – Vom Ereignis zum Gegenstand der Geschichtswissenschaft* (1999).

Notes

1. See M. Guigni and L. Bosi, 'The Impact of Protest Movements on the Establishment: Dimensions, Models, and Approaches', in K. Fahlenbach, M. Klimke, J. Scharloth and L. Wong (eds), *The Establishment Responds: Power, Politics, and Protest since 1945* (New York: Palgrave Macmillan, 2012), 17–28.
2. P. Bourdieu, *Language and Symbolic Power* (Oxford: Polity Press, 1991), 127–28, 234; P. Bourdieu, *Das politische Feld. Zur Kritik der politischen Vernunft* (Konstanz: UVK, 2001), 93f; P. Bourdieu, 'La représentation politique. Éléments pour une théorie du champ politique', *Actes de la recherche en sciences sociales* 7(36/37) (1981), 3–24, at 8.
3. T. Hayden, *The Port Huron Statement: The Visionary Call of the 1960s Revolution. With a New Introduction of the Author* (New York: Thunder's Mouth Press, 2005), 48.
4. T. Hayden, *Reunion: A Memoir* (New York: Random House, 1988), 42, 86.
5. R. Flacks, 'Ursprünge der amerikanischen New Left', in I. Gilcher-Holtey (ed.), *1968. Vom Ereignis zum Mythos* (Frankfurt am Main: Suhrkamp, 2008), 201–21.
6. Hayden, *Port Huron Statement*, 53.
7. T. Hayden, 'The Dream of Port Huron', in T. Hayden (ed.), *Inspiring Participatory Democracy: Student Movements from Port Huron to Today* (Boulder: Paradigm, 2012), 1–32, at 6.
8. P. Jacobs and S. Landau, *Die Neue Linke in den USA: Analyse und Dokumentation*. Translated by H. Zischler and G. Wagner ((Munich: Hanser, 1969), 151.
9. H. Arendt, *Macht und Gewalt* (Munich: Pieper, 1970), 25; H. Arendt, *On Revolution* (New York: Viking Press, 1963), 259, 265.

10. Sozialistischer Deutscher Studentenbund, *Hochschule in der Demokratie Denkschrift des Sozialistischen Deutschen Studentenbundes zur Hochschulreform* (Frankfurt am Main: Sozialistischer Deutscher Studentenbund, Bundesvorstand, 1961), 2, 147.
11. Franz Neumann's *The Democratic and the Authoritarian State* (1957) is referred to in: Sozialistischer Deutscher Studentenbund, *Hochschule in der Demokratie Denkschrift des Sozialistischen Deutschen Studentenbundes zur Hochschulreform*, 89, 90.
12. J. Habermas, 'Reflexionen über den Begriff der politischen Beteiligung', in J. Habermas, L. von Friedeburg, C. Fehler, F. Welt et al., *Student und Politik, Eine soziologische Untersuchung zum Bewußtsein Frankfurter Studenten* (Neuwied: Luchterhand, 1961), 11–56, at 55.
13. 'Kampf gegen die technokratische Hochschulreform für die Befreiung der Universitäten', in W. Kraushaar (ed.), *Frankfurter Schule und Studentenbewegung. Von der Flaschenpost zum Molotowcocktail. 1946–1995. Band 2: Dokumente* (Hamburg: Rogner & Bernhard, 1998), 528.
14. R. Dahrendorf, *Gesellschaft und Demokratie in Deutschland* (Munich: Pieper, 1965), 169.
15. W. Nitzsch, U. Gerhardt, C. Offe and U.K. Preuß (eds), *Hochschule in der Demokratie* (Darmstadt: Luchterhand, 1965), 5.
16. C. Meier et al. [W. Conze], 'Demokratie', in O. Brunner, W. Conze and R. Koselleck (eds), *Geschichtliche Grundbegriffe. Historisches Lexikon zur politisch-sozialen Sprache in Deutschland,* Band 1 A-D (Stuttgart: Klett-Cotta 1972), 873–84, 884.
17. C. Wright Mills, 'Letter to the New Left!', *New Left Review* 1(5) (1960), 21.
18. C. Taylor, 'Changes in Quality', *New Left Review* 1(4) (1960), 5.
19. T. von der Vring, 'Ein Jahr Neue Linke', *neue kritik* 4 (14) (1963), 15.
20. G. Cohn-Bendit and D. Cohn-Bendit, *Linksradikalismus. Gewaltkur gegen die Alterskrankheit des Kommunismus* (Reinbek: Rowohlt, 1968), 266.
21. H. Marcuse, *Essay on Liberation* (Boston: Beacon Press, 1969), 63, 65.
22. Ibid., 65.
23. Hayden, *Port Huron Statement*, 67.
24. G. Wegeleben, 'Staatsbankrott', *neue kritik* 7(38/39) (1966), 3.
25. 'Resolution zum Kampf gegen Manipulation und für die Demokratisierung der Öffentlichkeit', *neue kritik* 8(44) (1967), 28–34, at 30.
26. J. Agnoli, 'Thesen zur Transformation der Demokratie und zur außerparlamentarischen Opposition', *neue kritik* 9(47) (1968), 29, 31.
27. R. Dutschke, 'Zu Protokoll, Fernsehinterview von Günter Gaus', in *Mein langer Marsch. Reden, Schriften und Tagebücher aus zwanzig Jahren,* G. Dutschke-Klotz, H. Gollwitzer and J. Miermeister (eds) (Reinbek: Rowohlt, 1980), 42–57, at 43.
28. Ibid., 44.
29. S. Hall, 'Editorial. Introducing NLR', *New Left Review* 1(1) (1960), 1–3, at 1.
30. H.M. Enzensberger, 'Berliner Gemeinplätze', *Kursbuch* 4(11) (1968), 151–69.
31. Marcuse, *Essay on Liberation*, 65.

32. D. Guérin, 'Nachbemerkung des Autors zur dritten Auflage', in *Anarchismus. Begriff und Praxis* (Frankfurt am Main: Suhrkamp, 1975), 157–61.
33. See for the variety of counter-cultural activities and projects: M. Schmidtke, *Der Aufbruch der jungen Intelligenz. Die 68er Jahre in der Bundesrepublik und den USA* (Frankfurt am Main: Campus, 2003), 97ff.
34. W. Breines, *Community and Organization in the New Left. 1962–1968: The Great Refusal* (New York: Praeger, 1989), 6.
35. Hayden, *Reunion*, 125.
36. H.M. Enzensberger, 'Bewußtseins-Industrie', in *Einzelheiten I* (Frankfurt am Main: Suhrkamp, 1962), 7–17, at 10.
37. Published in A. Detraz et les militants de la CFDT, 'Positions et action de la CFDT', *Syndicalisme*, Numéro spécial, 53f.
38. L. Boltanski, È. Chiapello, *Der neue Geist des Kapitalismus* (Konstanz: UVK, 1999), 216–17.
39. Ibid., 226–27.
40. See I. Gilcher-Holtey, *'Die Phantasie an die Macht'. Mai 68 in Frankreich* (Frankfurt am Main: Suhrkamp, 2001), 94–104.
41. A. Reif, 'Interview mit Hannah Arendt', in Arendt, *Macht und Gewalt*, 107–33, at 109.
42. C. Bouyer, *Odéon est ouvert. Tribune libre* (Paris: Debresse, 1968), 7.
43. M. de Certeau, *La prise de parole. Pour une nouvelle culture* (Paris: Seuil, 1968).
44. M. Rossman, *The Birth of FSM* qtd. in Breines, *Community*, 46.
45. C. Donolo, 'Theorie und Praxis der Studentenbewegung in Italien', *Kursbuch* 4(13) (1968), 48–66.
46. See *Le Figaro*, 15 May 1968, 5.
47. See J. Scharloth, *1968. Eine Kommunikationsgeschichte* (Munich: Fink 2011), 211ff.
48. H. Arendt, *The Human Condition* (Chicago: University of Chicago Press, 1958), 25–26..
49. H. Arendt, 'Kultur und Politik' (1958), in *Zwischen Vergangenheit und Zukunft. Übungen im politischen Denken I* (Munich: Pieper, 1994), 277–304, at 300; H. Arendt, *Was ist Politik? Fragmente aus dem Nachlass* (Munich: Pieper, 1993), 11.
50. R. Dutschke, 'Wir fordern die Enteignung Axel Springers'. *Spiegel*-Gespräch mit dem Berliner FU-Studenten Rudi Dutschke, *Der Spiegel* 21(29), 29–33, at 32.
51. P. Bourdieu, *Pascalien Meditations* (Oxford: Polity Press 2000), 186; I. Gilcher-Holtey, *A Revolution of Perception? Consequences and Echoes of 1968* (New York: Berghahn, 2014).
52. Ibid., 61.
53. C. Calvert, quoted in K. Sale, *The Rise and Development of the Students for Democratic Society* (New York: Random House, 1973), 393.
54. Gilcher-Holtey, *Revolution*, 450.
55. Statements by Joscha Schmierer and Christian Semler, quoted in G. Hinck, *Wir waren wie Maschinen: Die bundesdeutsche Linke in den 70er Jahren* (Berlin: Rotbuch, 2012), 110, 144.

56. Ibid., 146.
57. Ibid., 143.
58. Compare the empirical study by D. Rucht, *Modernisierung und neue soziale Bewegungen. Deutschland, Frankreich und USA im Vergleich* (Frankfurt am Main: Campus 1994), 191.
59. T. Kern, *Soziale Bewegungen. Ursachen, Wirkungen, Mechanismen* (Wiesbaden: Verlag für Sozialwissenschaften, 2008), 57.
60. K. Eder, *Kulturelle Identität zwischen Tradition und Utopie. Soziale Bewegungen als Ort gesellschaftlicher Lernprozesse* (Frankfurt am Main: Campus, 2000), 21.
61. Ibid., 71.
62. A. Melucci, *Nomads of the Present: Social Movements and Individual Needs in Contemporary Society* (London: Hutchinson, 1989); A. Melucci, 'Soziale Bewegungen in komplexen Gesellschaften', in A. Klein, H.J. Legard and T. Leif (eds), *Neue soziale Bewegungen – Impulse, Bilanzen und Perspektiven* (Opladen: Westdeutscher Verlag, 1999), 114–30.
63. Rucht, *Neue Soziale Bewegungen*, 84.
64. Ibid., 153.
65. S. Reichardt, *Authentizität und Gemeinschaft. Linksalternatives Leben in den siebziger und achtziger Jahren* (Berlin: Suhrkamp, 2014), 42.
66. Ibid., 17, 55.
67. Ibid., 874.
68. Ibid., 888.
69. Ibid., 878. The focus of the alternative economy lay in the service sector. About 18,000 projects were founded.
70. B. Lacroix, *L'utopie communautaire. L'histoire d'une révolte* (Paris: PUF, 2006); P. Artières and M. Zancarini-Fournel (eds), *68. Une histoire collective (1962–1981)* (Paris: Découverte, 2008); Hayden, *Inspiring Participatory Democracy*.
71. Concerning the democratization of the universities, see A. Rohstock, *Von der 'Ordinarienuniversität' zur 'Revolutionszentrale'? Hochschulreform und Hochschulrevolte in Bayern und Hessen. 1957–1976* (Munich: Oldenburg, 2010).
72. W.M. Schwiedrzik and P. Stein, 'Demokratie ist auch Aktion' *Theater heute*, 9 (September 1968), 3.
73. F.P. Steckel, 'Was ist politisches Theater? Eine Debatte mit Zeitzeugen', in I. Gilcher-Holtey, D. Kraus and F. Schößler (eds), *Politisches Theater nach 1968. Regie Dramatik und Organisation* (Frankfurt am Main: Suhrkamp, 2006), 19–124, at 77–78.
74. Ibid., 83. The limits of democratization of theatres and museums are also stressed by M. Kittel, 'Das Frankfurter Modell kommunaler Kulturpolitik. Anspruch und Wirklichkeit einer "Demokratisierung der Gesellschaft"', in U. Wengst (ed.), *Reform und Revolte. Politischer und gesellschaftlicher Wandel in der Bundesrepublik Deutschland vor und nach 1968* (Munich: Oldenburg, 2011), 62–74.
75. See D. Kraus, 'Selbst- und Mitbestimmung: Demokratisierungskonzepte im westdeutschen Theater der frühen siebziger Jahre', in Gilcher-Holtey et al., *Politisches Theater*, 125–52.

76. Boltanski and Chiapello, *Geist des Kapitalismus*, 254ff.
77. A. Baring, *Machtwechsel. Die Ära Brandt-Scheel* (Stuttgart: DVA, 1982), 184.
78. J. Cohen, 'Deliberation and Democratic Legitimacy' (1989), retrieved 31 January 2018 from http://philosophyfaculty.ucsd.edu/faculty/rarneson/JCOHEN DELIBERATIVE%20DEM.pdf. The term 'deliberative democracy' was coined by Joseph M. Bessette in his essay 'Deliberative Democracy: The Majority Principle in Republican Government', in R.A. Goldwin (ed.), *How Democratic is the Constitution?* (Washington DC: AEI Press, 1980), 102–16.
79. F. Nullmeier, 'Spätkapitalismus und Legitimation', in H. Brunkhorst, R. Kreide and C. Lafont (eds), *Habermas-Handbuch* (Stuttgart: Metzler, 2009), 188–99, at 195; see J. Habermas, *Legitimationsprobleme im Spätkapitalismus* (Frankfurt am Main: Suhrkamp, 1975), 126–28.
80. A. Honneth, 'Von Adorno zu Habermas. Zum Gestaltwandel kritischer Gesellschaftstheorie', in W. Bonß and A. Honneth (eds), *Sozialforschung als Kritik. Zum sozialwissenschaftlichen Potential der Kritischen Theorie* (Frankfurt am Main: Suhrkamp, 1982), 87–126, at 116.
81. See R. Nickel, 'Legalität, Legitimität und Legitimation', in Brunkhorst et al., *Habermas-Handbuch*, 345–47, 346; J. Habermas, *Rekonstruktion des Historischen Materialismus* (Frankfurt am Main: Suhrkamp, 1976), 277–79.
82. See J. Habermas, *Between Facts and Norms: Contributions to a Discourse Theory of Law and Democracy* (Cambridge: Polity Press, 1996), 287ff; N. Deitelhoff, 'Deliberation', in Brunkhorst et al., *Habermas-Handbuch*, 301–3, at 301.
83. Habermas, *Between Facts and Norms*, 287ff.
84. D. Graeber, *Inside Occupy* (Frankfurt am Main: Campus, 2012); N. Chomsky, *Occupy!* (Münster: Unrast, 2012).
85. See N. Klein, *This Changes Everything: Capitalism vs. Climate* (New York: Simon & Schuster, 2014).
86. G. Pleyers, A. Touraine, *Alter-Globalization: Becoming Actors in the Global Age* (Cambridge: Polity Press, 2011), 17.
87. D. Graeber, 'The New Anarchists', *New Left Review* 53(13) (2012), 70.

Bibliography

Agnoli, J. 1968. 'Thesen zur Transformation der Demokratie und zur außerparlamentarischen Opposition', *neue kritik* 9(47), 24–33.
Arendt, H. 1958. *The Human Condition*. Chicago: University of Chicago Press.
———. 1963. *On Revolution*. New York: Viking Press.
———. 1970. *Macht und Gewalt*. Munich: Pieper.
———. 1993. *Was ist Politik? Fragmente aus dem Nachlass*. Munich: Pieper.
———. 1994. 'Kultur und Politik', in *Zwischen Vergangenheit und Zukunft. Übungen im politischen Denken I*. Munich: Pieper, 277–304.
Artières, P., and M. Zancarini-Fournel (eds). 2008. *68. Une histoire collective (1962–1981)*. Paris: Découverte.
Baring, A. 1982. *Machtwechsel. Die Ära Brandt-Scheel*. Stuttgart: DVA.

Bessette, J.M. 1980. 'Deliberative Democracy: The Majority Principle in Republican Government', in R. A. Goldwin (ed.), *How Democratic is the Constitution?* Washington DC: AEI Press, 102–16.

Boltanski, L., and È. Chiapello. 1999. *Der neue Geist des Kapitalismus.* Konstanz: UVK.

Bourdieu, P. 1981. 'La représentation politique. Éléments pour une théorie du champ politique', *Actes de la recherche en sciences sociales* 7(36/37), 3–24.

———. 1991. *Language and Symbolic Power.* Oxford: Polity Press.

———. 2000. *Pascalien Meditations.* Oxford: Polity Press.

———. 2001. *Das politische Feld. Zur Kritik der politischen Vernunft.* Konstanz: UVK.

Bouyer, C. 1968. *Odéon est ouvert. Tribune libre.* Paris: Debresse.

Breines, W. 1989. *Community and Organization in the New Left. 1962–1968. The Great Refusal.* New York: Praeger.

Certeau, M. de. 1968. *La prise de parole. Pour une nouvelle culture.* Paris: Seuil.

Chomsky, N. 2012. *Occupy!* Münster: Unrast.

Cohen, J. 1989. 'Deliberation and Democratic Legitimacy', retrieved 31 January 2018 from http://philosophyfaculty.ucsd.edu/faculty/rarneson/JCOHENDELIBERATIVE%20DEM.pdf.

Cohn-Bendit, G., and D. Cohn-Bendit. 1968. *Linksradikalismus: Gewaltkur gegen die Alterskrankheit des Kommunismus.* Reinbek: Rowohlt.

Dahrendorf, R. 1965. *Gesellschaft und Demokratie in Deutschland.* Munich: Pieper.

Deitelhoff, N. 2009. 'Deliberation', in H. Brunkhorst, R. Kreide and C. Lafont (eds), *Habermas-Handbuch.* Stuttgart: Metzler, 301–3.

Detraz, A. et les militants de la CFDT. 1968. 'Positions et action de la CFDT', *Syndicalisme,* Numéro spécial, 53f.

Donolo, C. 1968. 'Theorie und Praxis der Studentenbewegung in Italien', *Kursbuch* 4(13), 48–66.

Dutschke, R. 1967. 'Wir fordern die Enteignung Axel Springers'. *Spiegel*-Gespräch mit dem Berliner FU-Studenten Rudi Dutschke, *Der Spiegel* 21, 29–33,

———. 1980. 'Zu Protokoll, Fernsehinterview mit Günter Gaus', in *Mein langer Marsch. Reden, Schriften und Tagebücher aus zwanzig Jahren,* G. Dutschke-Klotz, H. Gollwitzer and J. Miermeister (eds). Reinbek: Rowohlt, 1980, 42–57.

Eder, K. 2000. *Kulturelle Identität zwischen Tradition und Utopie. Soziale Bewegungen als Ort gesellschaftlicher Lernprozesse.* Frankfurt am Main: Campus.

Enzensberger, H.M. 1962. 'Bewußtseins-Industrie', in *Einzelheiten I.* Frankfurt am Main: Suhrkamp, 1962, 7–17.

———. 1968. 'Berliner Gemeinplätze', *Kursbuch* 4(11), 151–69.

Flacks, R. 2008. 'Ursprünge der amerikanischen New Left', in I. Gilcher-Holtey (ed.), *Vom Ereignis zum Mythos.* Frankfurt am Main: Suhrkamp, 2008, 201–21.

Gilcher-Holtey, I. 2001. *'Die Phantasie an die Macht'. Mai 68 in Frankreich.* Frankfurt am Main: Suhrkamp.

———. 2014. *A Revolution of Perception? Consequences and Echoes of 1968.* New York: Berghahn Books.

Graeber, D. 2012a. *Inside Occupy.* Frankfurt am Main: Campus.

———. 2012b. 'The New Anarchists', *New Left Review* 53(13), 61–73.

Guérin, D. 1975. 'Nachbemerkung des Autors zur dritten Auflage' (1969), in *Anarchismus. Begriff und Praxis*. Frankfurt am Main: Suhrkamp, 157–61.

Guigni, M., and L. Bosi. 2012. 'The Impact of Protest Movements on the Establishment: Dimensions, Models, and Approaches', in K. Fahlenbach, M. Klimke, J. Scharloth and L. Wong (eds), *The Establishment Responds: Power, Politics, and Protest since 1945*. New York: Palgrave Macmillan, 17–28.

Habermas, J. 1961. 'Über den Begriff der politischen Beteiligung', in J. Habermas, L. von Friedeburg, C. Fehler, F. Welt et al., *Student und Politik, Eine soziologische Untersuchung zum Bewußtsein Frankfurter Studenten*. Neuwied: Luchterhand, 11–56.

———. 1975. *Legitimationsprobleme im Spätkapitalismus*. Frankfurt am Main: Suhrkamp.

———. 1976. *Rekonstruktion des Historischen Materialismus*. Frankfurt am Main: Suhrkamp.

———. 1996. *Between Facts and Norms. Contributions to a Discourse Theory of Law and Democracy*. Cambridge: Polity Press.

Hall, S. 1960. 'Editorial. Introducing NLR', *New Left Review* 1(1), 1–3.

Hayden, T. 1988. *Reunion: A Memoir*. New York: Random House.

———. 2005. *The Port Huron Statement. The Visionary Call of the 1960s Revolution. With a New Introduction of the Author*. New York: Thunder's Mouth Press.

———. 2012. 'The Dream of Port Huron', in T. Hayden (ed.), *Inspiring Participatory Democracy: Student Movements from Port Huron to Today*. Boulder: Paradigm, 1–32.

Hinck, G. 2012. *Wir waren wie Maschinen: Die bundesdeutsche Linke in den 70er Jahren*. Berlin: Rotbuch.

Honneth, A. 1982. 'Von Adorno zu Habermas. Zum Gestaltwandel kritischer Gesellschaftstheorie', in W. Bonß and A. Honneth (eds), *Sozialforschung als Kritik. Zum sozialwissenschaftlichen Potential der Kritischen Theorie*. Frankfurt am Main: Suhrkamp, 87–126.

Jacobs, P., and S. Landau. 1969. *Die Neue Linke in den USA: Analyse und Dokumentation*. Translated by H. Zischler and G. Wagner. Munich: Hanser.

Kern, T. 2008. *Soziale Bewegungen. Ursachen, Wirkungen, Mechanismen*. Wiesbaden: Verlag für Sozialwissenschaften.

Kittel, M. 2011. 'Das Frankfurter Modell kommunaler Kulturpolitik. Anspruch und Wirklichkeit einer "Demokratisierung der Gesellschaft"' in U. Wengst (ed.), *Reform und Revolte. Politischer und gesellschaftlicher Wandel in der Bundesrepublik Deutschland vor und nach 1968*. Munich: Oldenburg, 62–74.

Klein, N. 2014. *This Changes Everything: Capitalism vs. Climate*. New York: Simon & Schuster.

Kraus, D. 2006. 'Selbst- und Mitbestimmung: Demokratisierungskonzepte im westdeutschen Theater der frühen siebziger Jahre', in I. Gilcher-Holtey, D. Kraus and F. Schößler (eds), *Politisches Theater nach 1968. Regie Dramatik und Organisation*. Frankfurt am Main: Suhrkamp, 125–52.

Kraushaar, W. (ed.). 1998. *Frankfurter Schule und Studentenbewegung. Von der Flaschenpost zum Molotowcocktail. 1946–1995. Band 2: Dokumente*. Hamburg: Rogner & Bernhard.

Lacroix, B. 2006. *L'utopie communautaire. L'histoire d'une révolte*. Paris: PUF.
Marcuse, H. 1969. *Essay on Liberation*. Boston: Beacon Press.
Meier, C. et al. 1972. 'Demokratie', in O. Brunner, W. Conze and R. Koselleck (eds), *Geschichtliche Grundbegriffe. Historisches Lexikon zur politisch-sozialen Sprache in Deutschland*, Band 1 A–D. Stuttgart: Klett-Cotta, 821–99.
Melucci, A. 1989. *Nomads of the Present: Social Movements and Individual Needs in Contemporary Society*. London: Hutchinson.
———. 1999. 'Soziale Bewegungen in komplexen Gesellschaften' in A. Klein, H.J. Legard and T. Leif (eds), *Neue soziale Bewegungen – Impulse, Bilanzen und Perspektiven*. Opladen: Westdeutscher Verlag, 114–30.
Nickel, R. 2009. 'Legalität, Legitimität und Legitimation', in Brunkhorst, Kreide and Lafont, *Habermas-Handbuch*, 345–47.
Nitzsch, W., U. Gerhardt, C. Offe and U.K. Preuß (eds). 1965. *Hochschule in der Demokratie*. Darmstadt: Luchterhand.
Nullmeier, F. 2009. 'Spätkapitalismus und Legitimation', in Brunkhorst, Kreide and Lafont, *Habermas-Handbuch*, 188–99.
Pleyers, G., and A. Touraine. 2011. *Alter-Globalization: Becoming Actors in the Global Age*. Cambridge: Polity Press.
Reichardt, S. 2014. *Authentizität und Gemeinschaft. Linksalternatives Leben in den siebziger und achtziger Jahren*. Berlin: Suhrkamp.
Reif, A. 1970. 'Interview mit Hannah Arendt', in Arendt, *Macht und Gewalt*, 107–33.
'Resolution zum Kampf gegen Manipulation und für die Demokratisierung der Öffentlichkeit' (1967), *Neue kritik* 8(44), 28–34.
Rohstock, A. 2010. *Von der 'Ordinarienuniversität' zur 'Revolutionszentrale'? Hochschulreform und Hochschulrevolte in Bayern und Hessen. 1957–1976*. Munich: Oldenburg.
Rucht, D. 1994. *Modernisierung und neue soziale Bewegungen. Deutschland, Frankreich und USA im Vergleich*. Frankfurt am Main: Campus.
Sale, K. 1973. *The Rise and Development of the Students for Democratic Society*. New York: Random House.
Scharloth, J. 2011. *1968. Eine Kommunikationsgeschichte*. Munich: Fink.
Schmidtke, M. 2003. *Der Aufbruch der jungen Intelligenz. Die 68er Jahre in der Bundesrepublik und den USA*. Frankfurt am Main: Campus.
Schwiedrzik, W.M., and P. Stein. 1968. 'Demokratie ist auch Aktion' *Theater heute*, H. 9 (September 1968), 3.
Sozialistischer Deutscher Studentenbund. 1961. *Hochschule in der Demokratie Denkschrift des Sozialistischen Deutschen Studentenbundes zur Hochschulreform*. Frankfurt am Main: Sozialistischer Deutscher Studentenbund, Bundesvorstand.
Steckel, F.P. 'Was ist politisches Theater? Eine Debatte mit Zeitzeugen', in Gilcher-Holtey et al., *Politisches Theater*, 19–124.
Taylor, C. 1960. 'Changes in Quality', *New Left Review* 1(4), 3–5.
Vring, T. von der. 1963. 'Ein Jahr Neue Linke', *Neue kritik* 4(14), 13–16.
Wegeleben, G. 1966. 'Staatsbankrott', *Neue kritik* 7(38/39), 3.
Wright Mills, C. 1960. 'Letter to the New Left!', *New Left Review* 1(5), 18–23.

Chapter 12

Democracy and European Integration
A Transnational History of the Danish Debate

Jeppe Nevers

In the history of democracy in modern Europe, the creation of the European Union (EU) is certainly one of the most important developments in the last half-century. This chapter examines the impact of European integration on the concept of democracy: how have debates about European integration challenged and changed how democracy is conceived?

There is an old tradition, not least among European federalists, of linking the concept of democracy to visions of a united Europe. As early as 1948, one of the objectives of the European Union of Federalists was as follows: 'United Europe will not be simply a new "nationality" or a centralized state: we wish to be as far as possible decentralized, both regionally and functionally; not a super state but a real democracy, built up of self-governing basic communities.'[1]

But if we turn to the treatises of the EU, we get a different picture. In the Treaty of Rome (1957), in which the Member States agreed on the famous formula of 'an ever-closer union among the peoples of Europe', one searches in vain for any use of the term. Even three decades later, in the Single European Act (1986), the Member States agreed only that they were determined to work together 'to promote democracy on the basis of the fundamental rights recognized in the constitutions and laws of the member states'. In the Treaty of Maastricht (1992), the Member States confirmed their 'attachment to the principles of liberty, democracy and respect for human rights', and the treaty also stated that: 'The Union shall respect the national identities of the Member States, whose systems of government are founded on the principles of democracy.' In other words, even in the Treaty of Maastricht, the formulations about democracy were not about the EU as such, but about a principle and the system of government in the member states.

This picture changed with the Treaty of Amsterdam (1997), in which a passage mentions democracy as a 'core value' of the union itself, and this passage is repeated in the current Treaty of Lisbon (2007), in which Article 2 states that: 'The Union is founded on the values of respect for human dignity, freedom, democracy, equality, the rule of law and respect for human rights, including the rights of persons belonging to minorities.' Article 10 of the Treaty further states that 'The functioning of the Union shall be founded on representative democracy', and ideas of federal bicameralism embodied in the European Parliament and the Council of Ministers are related to this idea of representative democracy: 'Citizens are directly represented at Union level in the European Parliament' and 'Member States are represented in the European Council by their Heads of State or government and in the Council by their governments, themselves democratically accountable either to their national Parliaments, or to their citizens'. In other words, since 2007 the EU has in its own words been a representative democracy, a significant difference from how it was depicted in the Treaty of Rome and an important change in how democracy is conceptualized.[2]

Over the years, the EU has indeed become more and more like a representative democracy, and therefore it is perhaps not so strange that the treaties now state that this is the case. In this perspective, the identification of the EU as a democracy is probably the most significant example in the world of an attempt at creating a political democracy beyond or above the nation state, a 'post-national democracy'.[3] But, as we shall see in this chapter, the relationship between 'democracy' and European integration is much more complicated and multilayered if we include debates at the national level.

The case examined in this chapter is Denmark, a country that joined the European Economic Community (EEC) in 1973 and that since then has attracted attention for its many referenda on European affairs, not least for its important rejection of the Treaty of Maastricht in 1992. Therefore, the Danish case is well-suited to test what happened to 'democracy' in the context of debating European integration. It is the main argument of this chapter that shifting to this national level unveils a strong and persistent link between the concept of democracy and the nation state. As we shall see, 'democracy' has since the 1970s been widely cherished as the name of the political system at the national level, and European integration has typically been seen either as a threat to such national democracy or defensively described as something supplementary to national democracy. Thus, in the relation to the European history of the concept of democracy, this chapter argues that although European integration in the last half-century has been a significant challenge to the link between democracy and the nation state, the history of debating this challenge tells us that so far this link has not really been broken.

The Danish Context: Referenda and Popular Sovereignty

On 2 October 1972, the Danes voted on membership in the EEC. Of the votes cast, 63.4 per cent were in favour of membership and on 1 January 1973, Denmark joined the EEC together with Great Britain and Ireland in the first expansion of the community since the Treaty of Rome. Since then, the Danes have had seven referenda on European affairs: in 1986, 56.2 per cent of the votes were in favour of the Single European Act; in 1992, 50.7 per cent rejected the Treaty of Maastricht; in 1993, 56.7 per cent of the votes were in favour of the Edinburgh Agreement, according to which Denmark joined the Treaty of Maastricht, but with four exceptions (single currency, EU citizenship, defence and legal affairs); in 1998, 55.5 per cent voted yes to the Treaty of Amsterdam; in 2000, 53.2 per cent rejected the single currency; in 2014, 62.5 per cent agreed to joining the Unified Patent Court; and in 2015, 53.1 per cent rejected a proposal to reform the exception on legal affairs. The most significant of the referenda was that on the Treaty of Maastricht. The Danish 'no' echoed throughout Europe and together with the 'petit oui' in France, also in 1992, it ended the age of consensus on European integration and established the reputation of Denmark as a Eurosceptic country.

The reason for all the referenda is constitutional. According to Article 20 of the Danish Constitution of 1953, the Danish government can hand over sovereignty to a foreign jurisdiction only if it has a five-sixths majority in the Danish Parliament. Since there has never been such a majority, shifting governments have been obliged to hold referenda if the Ministry of Legal Affairs has determined that a treaty is diminishing Danish sovereignty. If the jurists determine that this is not the case (as was, for instance, determined with the Treaty of Lisbon), the government may join on the basis of a simple majority, but Danish citizens may file a lawsuit against the prime minister. This has been done twice, and both times the citizens have lost in the Supreme Court. The only referendum that stands out is that on the Single European Act in 1986. At that time, the government led by the conservatives even had a majority in Parliament against joining, but it won support for having a 'guiding referendum' that showed popular support, and hence Denmark joined the European Single Market.

Behind Article 20 lies an idea of democracy that might be described as a peculiar version of a European postwar democracy. As argued by historians such as Martin Conway and Jan-Werner Müller, there was a Central European postwar consensus on the need for having democratic constitutions able to guard against sudden changes and unreasonable decisions by majorities at any given time, hence the strong executive offices, the constitutional courts, the bureaucracies and the bicameralism in the constitutions of the postwar European democracies.[4] According to Müller, this postwar settlement, which was basically about avoiding the weaknesses of the interwar years, later became the basis for European integration 'with its inbuilt distrust of popular sovereignty, and the delegation of bureaucratic tasks to agencies which remained under the close supervision of national governments'.[5]

But Danish democracy was never seriously challenged in the interwar years. Nazis and communists never gained momentum. The political system rested on the Constitution of 1915, which was a political compromise between the victorious democratic forces from the late nineteenth century. These democrats – agrarian and urban liberals as well as social democrats – disagreed on many issues, but they agreed on the sovereignty of the people. A leading voice in the agrarian liberal party (Venstre) famously said that there should be nothing besides or above the Folketing (the lower chamber of Parliament).[6] Thus, in the Danish experience, the proponents of checks and balances, bicameralism and the rule of law were the conservative jurists behind the conservative governments in the late nineteenth century. After 1901, those ideas had no strong proponents in Danish politics (and the upper chamber mostly survived because liberals and conservatives were afraid of the social democrats). This led, for instance, to a rather strong separation of politics and the judiciary, and only in 1999 did the Supreme Court rule against a law passed in the Parliament. Thus, when the concept of democracy had its wider breakthrough in Danish political discourse in the late nineteenth and early twentieth centuries, it was closely tied to the concept of the people. Indeed, the most common expression of the concept in the late nineteenth century was in the definite form, 'the democracy' (*Demokratiet*), which was a group label for the democratic forces representing the ordinary people.[7]

Therefore, when the upper chamber (Landstinget) was abolished in the Constitution of 1953, its role was not replaced by a constitutional court or some bureaucratic arrangement; it was replaced by the institution of referenda. The people were to check that politicians did not make hasty or undemocratic decisions. This tendency is also reflected in the widespread popularity of the term *folkestyre*, the vernacular synonym to democracy that typically connotes an organic and participatory vision of democracy. This term was developed by agrarian liberals in the late nineteenth century (drawing inspiration from Norway) as a more harmonic alternative to confrontation-led 'democracy', and from the 1920s it circulated across the political spectrum, often keeping its more romantic connotations.[8] Even today, *folkestyre* is often used as a synonym for democracy, and this tradition is tightly linked to a continuously strong position of the concept of the people in Danish political language; *folkestyre* even more than 'democracy' invokes the power of the people. Several Danish political parties are, or have been, labelled 'people's parties' (for instance, the Conservative People's Party, the Danish People's Party, the Socialist People's Party, and in the early 1960s some liberals even wanted the liberal party to be the liberal people's party). The historical background is first and foremost that the two big parties in Danish politics, the liberal party (Venstre) and the Social Democratic Party, are built on democratic and popular movements from the late nineteenth century, and this has had a lasting influence on the status of popular sovereignty. For example, the opposition to membership of the EEC joined in a People's Movement against the EEC in 1971. In other words, there was a strong tradition for connecting democracy not only to the Danish political system, but perhaps even more to the sovereignty of the Danish people.

The Debate on Membership of the EEC

In the Danish debate about membership of the EEC, which began in the late 1950s and continued through the 1960s, the most common framework for debating the EEC was articulated in terms of a market. Most often, the EEC was simply referred to as 'the common market' (*fællesmarkedet*). The debate on Danish membership was generally referred to as 'the market debate' (*markedsdebatten*), and the minister responsible for questions concerning the EEC was the Minister of Economy and Market.

Therefore, it is not surprising to learn that membership of the EEC was first and foremost argued in economic terms. For instance, famous posters in the yes campaign even had 'yes' and 'no' price tags on a selection of ordinary goods. A prominent example of a politician who employed mostly economically oriented arguments would be Poul Nyboe Andersen, an acclaimed economist who was Member of Parliament for the liberal party Venstre and who served as Minister of Economy and Market from 1968 to 1971. Venstre comes out of an agrarian tradition and was at this point the most enthusiastic party regarding the EEC, not least for reasons connected to the agricultural sector's economic interests.[9] As 'market Minister' for Venstre between 1968 and 1971, Nyboe Andersen repeatedly and in various contexts presented what we might call the mainstream liberal view, stressing that the EEC was not 'a kind of federal state, but on the contrary *a cooperation between independent, sovereign nations* on practical matters concerning commerce and production'.[10] In other words, the EEC was first of all about creating 'a common market, meaning an area in which one can exchange goods freely across borders without custom duty and restrictions'.[11]

Although the Danish debate about the EEC was not primarily about political visions or matters of more or less democracy, the concept of democracy did surface in the debate, and many of the typical arguments that later came to dominate were present. Nyboe Andersen, for instance, addressed the question of democracy in the institutions of the EEC and stressed that '*the democratic control* with decision-making procedure is maintained. A Danish minister will not in an expanded EEC be able to support any action that a majority in the Danish parliament opposes'.[12] On this ground, he also criticized those who believed that the Danish Parliament was to be reduced to a kind of municipal council. He also addressed the position that the EEC was not 'democratic enough' and agreed that there was no directly elected parliament, but this he regarded as a proof of the sovereignty of each individual country. In other words, the EEC posed no threat to (Danish) democracy.

One of those arguing that the EEC was a threat to Danish democracy was Frode Jakobsen, a prominent social democrat and former resistant during the German occupation. As an MP, he participated in the parliamentary debate on the EEC in late 1971, in which he refused to support the common market: 'In my opinion there is no other democracy than "near democracy" (*nærdemokrati*). We often hear that Christiansborg [the Danish Parliament] is too far away. The road to Brussels is considerably longer. We are dwarfed by the giant. I don't believe that it will be compatible with true democracy.'[13] The concept of 'near democracy' was introduced into Danish political debate in 1969, taking inspiration from Sweden, and during the 1970s it was used in many different debates and exercised a lasting influence on how many Danes think of democracy,[14] not far from positions in classical political thought (Montesquieu or Rousseau, for instance): that democracy functions best in rather small political organizations. Hal Koch, a Danish theologian who more than anyone shaped Danish debates on democracy in the postwar period with his ideas of democracy as a culture of deliberation and compromise, had also held the position that democratic processes should have a limited number of participants in order for true deliberation to take place.[15] Jakobsen addressed the question of democracy in the institutions of the EEC on that basis. He agreed on the need to strengthen the role of the parliament in the EEC, but at the same time he argued that this would still be a reduction of actual democracy from the Danish perspective: 'In a truly democratically and popular elected parliament Denmark will seriously drown. We will probably not even reach the two per cent representation that is our own cutoff.'[16]

Jakobsen was certainly not alone in his criticism of the EEC as a threat to Danish democracy. In 1971, the People's Movement against Membership in the EEC was formed, an organization that even today has a representative in the European Parliament. Although the People's Movement was intended to be pan-political, a real 'people's movement', its rhetoric was primarily left wing and anti-authoritarian (the EEC as capitalist, hierarchical, etc.). Democracy was not a key concept in the early phase, but there was certainly a widespread feeling that the magnitude and the top-down structure of the EEC would lead to less and not more democracy.[17] As an example, the introduction of direct representation in the European Parliament was not regarded as democratic progress.[18] A recurring theme in the anti-EEC rhetoric, a theme that was already apparent in the 1960s, argued that the EEC would pull Denmark away from the Nordic countries, which were conceived as having a much stronger democratic tradition.[19] In Norway and Sweden the feeling of democratic superiority was even stronger than in Denmark, and in Norway the image of the EEC as a threat to Norwegian democracy was an important factor behind its rejection of membership in the 1972 referendum.[20]

The anti-EEC movement followed international developments closely, with the British debate as an especially important comparison, and, just as in Britain, the political base of the anti-EEC movement was on the left wing and among social democrats and some social liberals. In contrast to Britain, Euroscepticism had only a small base among liberals and conservatives, with the national conservative pastor and writer Søren Krarup as one of the notable exceptions, and he also made the argument that the EEC was incompatible with true *folkestyre*.[21]

In the parliamentary debate, Nyboe Andersen responded to the argument that the EEC would mean a decrease in democratic quality, arguing that Danish representatives could simply join forces with likeminded representatives from other countries. He stressed especially – and this was typical for the debate in the early 1970s – that Danish ideas about democracy and politics were close to British ideas: 'I think that British democracy has had a decisive influence on Denmark's democratic development, and here I am referring both in the development of political democracy and what Mr. Frode Jakobsen and I would understand by the popular (*folkelige*) Danish democracy.'[22] Along the same lines, the Social Democratic minister of economic affairs in 1971 stressed that an expansion of the EEC with Great Britain, Ireland, Norway and Denmark would also 'strengthen the democratic forces in the EEC'.[23]

Frode Jakobsen was not the only Social Democrat to be in doubt or even against the EEC.[24] In contrast to Venstre, the Social Democratic Party was deeply divided on the question of the EEC, and it remained so until the early 1990s. Another prominent Social Democrat who was against membership was Svend Auken, later a chairman of the party (from 1987 to 1992). In 1972 he criticized, among other things, the bureaucratic nature of the EEC: 'The institutions of the common market are supranational, and the democratic control with their dispositions is limited. This does not create problems for a country such as France, where democratic control of the administration is limited. But what about a country such as Denmark where we support democratic control?'[25] According to Auken, it was the very idea of the common market that 'government officials and experts and technocrats' should be the leading forces, and therefore he was glad that some supporters of the common market acknowledged that the EEC 'is not a simple commercial arrangement with a few advantages for the farmers, but that it is a new type of political union with far-reaching political perspectives'.[26]

The leader of the Social Democratic Party and the Prime Minister of Denmark at the time of the referendum, Jens Otto Krag, was one of these firm believers in European cooperation. Just like Nyboe Andersen, Krag, who was also trained as an economist, stressed the economic advantages of membership, but he also had a more political interpretation of the EEC alongside the focus on economic advantages. He was of the opinion that international actors and trends would come to assume increasing importance and therefore 'the need to secure a democratic control of the development will be felt more and more strongly'.[27] In other words, the purpose of European cooperation, and of Danish membership, was:

> to secure the conditions for production and employment, for a high standard of living and social justice, for a cooperation regarding culture and technology, for governing and controlling the mighty economic forces that in so many ways are affecting the everyday of individual human beings, for a continuation of the democratic development of society and for a securing of human and natural environment.[28]

In the parliamentary debate on the EEC in 1971, the same line of argument was also presented by a member of the left-liberal party, Det radikale Venstre: 'The general development of society will always be ahead of the political decision-making. We should watch out that it does not run away from us, therefore I appeal that we do not reject this opportunity for the *folkestyre* to continue having the power to solve the important problems of society.'[29] Thus, it certainly goes back to the 1970s that European integration could be interpreted as a necessary development of democracy, but in the bigger picture, not least among the sceptics, the dominant pattern was to argue that the EEC was either a threat to democracy or something compatible with the existing form of national democracy.

The Spectre of 'the Democratic Deficit'

As shown above, the opponents of the EEC already argued in the 1970s that membership of the EEC would lead to less democracy. This pattern certainly continued in the 1980s and in the early 1990s, in the period before the referendum on the Treaty of Maastricht, culminating in the breakthrough of the idea of a 'democratic deficit' in the EU.

In the debate on European cooperation, the identification of a 'democratic deficit' in the EEC goes back at least to the early 1970s and, most importantly, to people arguing in favour of a stronger role for the European Parliament. In early federalist writings from the 1950s and the 1960s, the Parliament (or the assembly as it was called in the early phase) was identified as the 'democratic' institution in the workings of the common market,[30] and the reforms of the Parliament in the 1970s and the introduction of direct elections were connected to a widely perceived 'need to strengthen democratic controls of the European Commission and the Council of Ministers'.[31] The precise origins of the concept of the 'democratic deficit' are difficult to determine, but in January 1974, the British Labour MP Peter Shore, an opponent of Britain's entry to the EEC, talked in the House of Commons about the 'vast democratic deficit in the institutions, of the EEC'.[32] Against this background, the concept of 'the democratic deficit' was occasionally used in the 1970s, without a real international breakthrough. A manifesto by the Young European Federalists from 1977 famously used this expression in their call for a more democratic European community, and in 1979 the British pro-Europe Labour MP David Marquand also used the expression. In his famous book *Parliament for Europe*, he wrote, in a section headed 'The Democratic Deficit': 'There can be no democracy without accountability . . . In the Community system, no one is unambiguously answerable for anything. The buck is never seen to stop; it is hidden from view, in an endless scrimmage of consultation and bargaining.'[33] For Marquand, there was no doubt of the result: 'The resulting "democratic deficit" would not be acceptable in a Community committed to democratic principles. Yet such a deficit would be inevitable unless the gap were somehow to be filled by the European Parliament.'[34] The same argument was repeated by Bill Newton Dunn, a pro-Europe Conservative MEP, later a Liberal, in several writings in the late 1980s.[35] The mid and late 1980s also seems to be the period in which the term had its wider breakthrough, both in Britain and beyond.[36] The mid 1980s in general saw a political and scholarly discussion of democracy in relation to the future of the Community. In 1986, for instance, the British constitutional scholar Vernon Bogdanor published an article on two different models of democracy for the Community as a whole,[37] and in 1988 the European Parliament's Committee on Institutional Affairs published a report on the democratic deficit.[38]

In the Danish case, the rhetoric of a 'democratic deficit' seems to have arisen only in the late 1980s and the early 1990s, although the wider idea of a lack of democratic legitimacy was present from the very beginning of the debates. But from around 1990, the rhetoric of a democratic deficit began to catch on in the Danish debate. In December 1990, for instance, an article in *Århus Stiftstidende* argued that in the EEC, there is 'to a much larger degree than in Denmark a rule of government officials. This is the reason for all the talk in Denmark about a "democratic deficit" in the EEC'.[39] A year later, in November 1991, a rather neutral article in the newspaper *Jyllands-Posten* similarly stated:

> Almost everyone acknowledges that the EEC has a democratic deficit in its decision-making processes that separates the EEC from parliamentary democracies in a very profound way. After the ratification of the Single European Act this lack of democracy was only made even more apparent since unanimity was replaced by majority decisions in the Council of Ministers in a number of areas. This change of procedure means that countries can now be forced to implement laws that are against a will of a majority in the individual country.[40]

Hence, when the Danish debate on the Treaty of Maastricht took place in 1992, the concept of a 'democratic deficit' in the EU was an important part of the debate. Although the variety of voices increased in the debate in 1992,[41] the People's Movement was still the dominant force, led by MEP Jens-Peter Bonde, who was elected to the European Parliament in 1979. Bonde authored many books on the EEC and later the EU, almost all of them with a strong emphasis on the lack of democratic legitimacy and from around 1990 on the 'democratic deficit' in the EU. In 1989, Bonde wrote against the Single European Act:

> In the EEC-parliament and in the European public sphere a lot of people are talking about 'a democratic deficit'. The power is moved away from the elected representatives at the national level, but it has not resurfaced among the representatives at the EEC level. Their proposal is therefore to give the EEC-parliament more power . . . But in Denmark, that culturally belongs to the Nordic countries, most people think it is a bad idea to replace the right to be the master of one's own domain with 16 out of 518 seats in the EEC-parliament . . . If we as voters become dissatisfied with a law passed by the EEC-parliament we can only replace the 16 Danish representatives in the next election. We cannot change the majority in the EEC-parliament.[42]

In a publication from 1990, *Folkestyret og EF* [*The Rule of the People and the EEC*], Bonde repeated that 'the democratic deficit' is about the transference of political power from democratic systems at the national level to a less democratic system at the EEC level: 'All the constitutions of the EEC-countries are built on the principle that a majority of the voters can determine the laws of the land. This is the principle of democracy. But the principle of democracy is eliminated at the very moment when decision-making power is moved from the national parliaments to the EEC.'[43] In other words, 'the democratic deficit' was a key concept in the rhetoric of the leading critic of the EEC in the years before the referendum on the Treaty of Maastricht, and the alternative ideas proposed by Bonde and the People's Movement were tellingly presented as 'Democratic Proposals'.[44]

These examples show what seems to be the general picture: that there was a turnaround from 'democratic deficit' being a key concept in arguments for a stronger role for the European Parliament to being a key concept in arguments for less European integration. It is important to note that there was certainly nothing new in the critique of the EU as undemocratic or less democratic, but in contrast to the earlier period, the idea of a 'democratic deficit' was now much more prominent in the debate, and with the slight 'no' majority in the referendum, as well as the subsequent shock of the French referendum, where only a slight majority of 51 per cent of the voters accepted the Treaty of Maastricht, this period stands out as a transformative period in terms of the conceptual link between 'democracy' and European integration.

Since this period, a large number of publications on democracy and European integration have emerged and the question of the democratic deficit has also been addressed in the research.[45] The key contributions concerning the question of the democratic deficit, by scholars such as Giandomenico Majone, Andrew Moravcsik, Andreas Føllesdal and Simon Hix, are tellingly from the late 1990s and the early 2000s.[46] From this perspective, the years surrounding the Treaty of Maastricht stand out as the real breakthrough for the concept of the democratic deficit. Danish scholarly literature has also addressed this question, and leading scholars have used the theoretical distinction between 'constitutional democracies' and 'majoritarian democracies' to explain the strong emphasis on the democratic problems in the EU that seems to be a common trait in northwestern countries with strong parliamentarian traditions.[47]

Alongside the breakthrough of 'the democratic deficit' and the rise of much stronger scepticism than before, the fall of the Berlin Wall and the prospects of an enlargement of the community also came to play a key role in the emphasis on democracy as a 'core value' of the union. Most notably, functional democratic governance became one of the Copenhagen Criteria in 1993, the new rules established to define whether a country is eligible to join the EU. The fall of the Berlin Wall and the end of communism were also decisive in changing how many key politicians viewed European cooperation. Most importantly, the years around 1990 seem to have ended the old split in the Social Democratic Party. A politician like Ritt Bjerregaard, for instance, in this period changed her opinion from being an opponent of the EEC to a strong supporter of the EU, and later an EU commissioner.

Towards the Present: Democracy and the Nation State

As shown above, the concept of democracy has in the Danish case had a firm place in the argumentation against European integration, typically in the sense that more integration means less democracy. This rhetoric was routinely used by the People's Movement as well as the Junibevægelsen, which was founded in 1992 as an alternative to the People's Movement. Where the People's Movement, with its primary base among left-wing voters, argued, and continues to argue, against the EU as such and against Danish membership, Junibevægelsen was formed as a more pan-political movement of people who supported membership, but who were against further integration. Junibevægelsen was founded by Jens-Peter Bonde and through the 1990s became the leading group against further integration, while Bonde became leader of the dominant group of sceptics in the European Parliament, where he continuously argued that the EU was not democratic enough and that there was a democratic deficit.

The pro-Europe side, basically the Danish political establishment, which has since the early 1990s been irritated and also frightened by the quite substantial group of sceptics in the Danish population, has tried to argue that there is not such a democratic deficit, basically repeating and developing arguments from the 1970s: that the European Parliament has become increasingly stronger and that negotiations by Danish ministers in the European council always take place on the basis of a majority in the Danish Parliament.

But since the turn of the twenty-first century, several important changes have taken place. On the left side of the political spectrum, the old arguments against the EU seem to live on, but on the not-so-hard left, especially in the Socialist People's Party, a much more pro-EU rhetoric has emerged. And among centre-left politicians, the idea of the EU as a European addition to Danish democracy has gained ground. For instance, the current programme of the Social Liberal party Det Radikale Venstre argues in favour of the 'European democracy' in the EU: 'The EU is a historic innovation of democracy at the international level. We want to develop and strengthen the European democracy even further.'[48] From this perspective, a strong EU is increasingly seen as necessary for democratic development in an age dominated by increasingly global and international problems, from strong multinational corporations to climate change. This perception basically resembles the vision promoted by Jens Otto Krag in the early 1970s, and in recent years this view has spread to wider parts of the centre-left.

But this development – to some degree a shift away from identifying democracy with the sovereignty of the nation state – should be seen in the context of other important changes that have taken place on the right side of the spectrum. Since the late 1990s, the Danish People's Party has emerged with Euroscepticism as a key item on its agenda. Today, the Danish People's Party is not against Danish membership, unlike the United Kingdom Independence Party, but, that said, it is certainly the place to find the same kind of rhetoric: bureaucrats in Brussels deciding about your life, power taken from the Danish Parliament to a less democratic labyrinth of power in Brussels and so on.

The first sentence in the first programme of the Danish People's Party (from 1997) states that: 'The primary objective of the Danish People's Party is to reinstate Denmark's independence and freedom and to secure the survival of the Danish nation and the Danish monarchy.'[49] Hence, the Constitution (*grundloven*) was from the very beginning a positive key concept in the rhetoric of the party, seen as the basis of both Danish *folkestyre* and the monarchy.[50] In this vision, democracy is something that thrives within the framework of the Danish constitutional monarchy, guarded by the Constitution and threatened by the EU (among other threats). From the earliest programmes, the Danish People's Party wanted the EU to concentrate on free trade and the protection of nature. It wanted decisions in the EU to be taken exclusively by the Council, with the power of the Parliament reduced; the first programme even argued for the abolition of the European Parliament.[51] Likewise, the role of the Commission should change from that of an executive power to that of an administration, following directions from the Council.

On this basis, the Danish People's Party argued strongly against the Treaty of Amsterdam in 1998 and against joining the euro in 2000,[52] and during this period, the momentum in Danish Euroscepticism shifted from the left to the right, and as a result the ideology behind Danish Euroscepticism shifted to a more national discourse, emphasizing national sovereignty, the Constitution and Danish culture. In the 1980s and 1990s, this type of rhetoric was seen only among individuals and small groups (most notably promoted by Søren Krarup, who also became an MP for the Danish People's Party), but with the coming of the Danish People's Party, it became a wider phenomenon.

It is often argued that rise of the Danish People's Party during the last twenty years has been fuelled more than anything by its opposition to immigration. However, without diminishing the dominant role of immigration, one should not underestimate the party's appeal in relation to the European question. Thus, in 2014, the Danish People's Party became, for the first time, the biggest party in the Danish delegation to the European Parliament. The main line of thought continues to be that democracy is guarded by the Danish Constitution and practised in the Danish Parliament, which is directly responsible to the Danish people. Thus, a typical passage in a recent document (2008) on European affairs produced by the Danish People's Party reads as follows:

> Democracy only lives and functions in the nation state. Only here are politicians directly held accountable to their people; there can only be an open debate where there is a common language that everyone understands; there can only be a political dialogue where there are common media; and trust in democracy can only exist where there is trust between responsible politicians and the individual voter. Democracy means rule of the people [*folkestyre*] – in the EU there is a lot of rule, but there is not a people.[53]

Most recently, a new liberal party, the Liberal Alliance, has become a different voice in the fraction of parties on the right side of the spectrum, and like the Danish People's Party, it is also against further integration. However, more in line with a Thatcherite image of Brussels as a scene of bureaucrats running an over-regulated system, it has not focused as much on democracy and its national roots, but more on the bureaucratic side of the EU. Since the party joined the government in 2016, and its chairman became foreign secretary, this rhetoric has surely waned. In the broader picture, this means that Euroscepticism now comes, at least in Denmark, in a variety of different ideological modes across the political spectrum, from the anti-capitalist left through liberal discontent with regulation to the position of national sovereignty, and the role of the People's Movement is now more or less reduced to left-wing Euroscepticism. In late 2015, this broad coalition of Eurosceptics dealt a significant defeat to the establishment in a referendum on a reform of the Danish exceptions in relation to legal affairs, and one of the things that unified this coalition was the argument that a 'no' vote was a vote in favour of Danish democracy and Danish sovereignty.

All in all, it seems fair to conclude that the conceptual link between democracy and European integration has not, in the Danish case, been driven by the hopes of a truly European democracy. Although positive ideas about the promises of a new age of a European and postnational democracy have been part of the debate during the whole period and may have assumed increasing strength as a counter-discourse to more national positions, the conceptual history of democracy in relation to debates about European integration shows more than anything that the link between democracy and the nation state has not been easy to break up.

Jeppe Nevers is Professor of History at the University of Southern Denmark in Odense. He has written on a variety of topics in modern Danish and European history, including democracy, liberalism and industrial society. His books include *Fra skældsord til slagord: Demokratibegrebet i dansk politisk historie* (2011) and *Det produktive samfund: Seks kapitler af industrialiseringens idéhistorie* (2013). He has also contributed to comparative and collective volumes as well as international journals, and he is a board member of Concepta – Research Seminars in Conceptual History and Political Thought.

Notes

1. EUF Executive Bureau, *Report on General Policy*, in Walter Lipgens and Wilfred Loth (eds), *Documents on the History of European Integration*, vol. 4 (Berlin: Walter de Gruyter, 1991), 45.
2. This reorientation in the constitutional rhetoric of the EU stems from the never-enacted Constitutional Treaty of 2004. Alongside this rhetoric of representative democracy, the Constitutional Treaty presented the principle of 'participatory democracy', including the suggestion that more than one million citizens from a significant number of Member States should be able to propose legislation on issues within the framework of the powers of the commission.
3. Deirdre M. Curtin, *Postnational Democracy: The European Union in Search of a Political Philosophy* (The Hague: Kluwer, 1997).
4. Jan-Werner Müller, *Contesting Democracy: Political Ideas in Twentieth-Century Europe* (New Haven: Yale University Press, 2013), 146–50. See also Martin Conway's chapter in this book.
5. Müller, *Contesting Democracy*, 148–49.
6. Claus Friisberg, *Ingen over og ingen ved siden af Folketinget*, vols 1–2 (Varde: Vestjysk Kulturforlag, 2007), 441.
7. Jeppe Nevers, *Fra skældsord til slagord: Demokratibegrebet i dansk politisk historie* (Odense: University Press of Southern Denmark, 2011), 119–44.
8. Nevers, *Fra skældsord til slagord*, 138.
9. Anita Lehmann, 'Venstres vej til Europa: Venstres Europapolitik, 1945–1960', *Den jyske historiker* 93 (2001), 32–52.
10. P. Nyboe Andersen, *Danmark i Fremtidens Europa* (Holte: EF-Forlaget, 1972), 6.
11. Nyboe Andersen, *Danmark i Fremtidens Europa*, 13.
12. Ibid., 9.
13. *Sådan sagde de om Danmark og EF: Fuldstændig gengivelse af folketingets markedsdebat den 16. december 1971* (Copenhagen: Forlaget Aktuelle Bøger), 119.
14. Jesper Vestermark Køber, *Et spørgsmål om nærhed: Nærdemokratibegrebets historie i 1970'ernes Danmark* (Ph.D. dissertation, University of Copenhagen, 2017).
15. H. Koch, *Hvad er demokrati?* (Copenhagen: Gyldendal, 1945).
16. *Sådan sagde de om Danmark og EF*, 119.
17. E.g. 'Demokrati á la EF', *Det ny Notat* (1)1 (1974), 3. See also David Helin, *30 år i folkestyrets tjeneste – om Folkebevægelsen mod EU's historie, 1972–2001* (Mørke: Grevas Forlag, 2002).
18. E.g. 'Den 2. december vedtager topmøde direkte valg til EF-parlamentet', *Det ny Notat* (25)2 (1975), 4–5.
19. For some early examples, see, for instance, the contributions in Johs. Bøggild et al., *Romtraktaten, Europamarkedet og Danmark* (Holbæk: Forlaget IDAG, 1961).

20. Iver B. Neumann, 'This Little Piggy Stayed at Home: Why Norway is Not a Member of the EU' and Lars Trägårdh, 'Sweden and the EU: Welfare State Nationalism and the Spectre of "Europe"', in Lene Hansen and Ole Wæver (eds), *European Integration and National Identity: The Challenge of the Nordic States* (London: Routledge, 2001).
21. E.g. Søren Krarup: *Fædreland og folkestyre: En kritik af Danmarks nyere historie* (Copenhagen: Gyldendal, 1974).
22. *Sådan sagde de om Danmark og EF,* 227.
23. Ibid., 31.
24. Morten Rasmussen, 'Ivar Nørgaards mareridt: Socialdemokratiet og den Økonomiske og Monetære Union, 1970–1972', *Den jyske historiker* 93 (2001), 73–95.
25. *Sådan sagde de om Danmark og EF,* 106.
26. Ibid., 107.
27. Jens-Otto Krag, 'Danmark og EF', in Jan-Erik Modig and Poul Nielson (eds), *Socialdemokrater fra 6 lande om EF* (Copenhagen: Samlerens Piccolobøger, 1972), 16.
28. Krag, 'Danmark og EF', 17.
29. *Sådan sagde de om Danmark og EF,* 169.
30. E.g. Paula Scalingi, *The European Parliament: The Three-Decade Search for a United Europe* (Westport, CT: Greenwood Press, 1980), 11 (Spinelli), 26 (Monnet) and in relation to arguments in favour of direct election (107–8, 115, 117).
31. E.g. Kyle Keith, 'The European Parliament', *The World Today,* December 1972, 530–37.
32. House of Commons, European Community Secondary Legislation, 24 January.
33. David Marquand: *Parliament for Europe* (London: Jonathan Cape, 1979), 64.
34. Marquand, *Parliament for Europe,* 65. See also 88.
35. E.g. Bill Newton Dunn, *Why the Public Should be Worried by the EEC's Democratic Deficit* (London: European Democratic Group, 1988).
36. See, for instance, the Google Ngram search engine.
37. Vernon Bogdanor, 'The Future of the European Community: Two Models of Democracy', *Government and Opposition* 21(2) (1986), 161–76.
38. Michael Newman, *Democracy, Sovereignty and the European Union* (London: Hurst & Company, 1996), 179.
39. Kurt Francis Madsen, 'Vi skal ikke acceptere rollen som delstat', *Århus Stiftstidende,* 7 December 1990.
40. Henning Asp-Poulsen, 'Demokratisk underskud', *Jyllands-Posten,* 28 November 1991.
41. Arne Hardis, 'Nej'ets mange ansigter', in Jens Maigård (ed.), *Under bekvemmelighedsflag: En kritisk undersøgelse af Folkebevægelsen mod EF og Junibevægelsen* (Frederiksberg: Fiskers Forlag, 1993).
42. Jens-Peter Bonde, *Tænk lidt længere: Udfordringen fra EF's Indre Marked* (Forlaget Notat: Allingåbro, 1989), 81.
43. Jens-Peter Bonde, *Folkestyret og EF* (Allingåbro: Notat, 1990), 9.
44. Bonde, *Folkestyret og EF,* 93–95.

45. Some examples of this international trend are Dimitris N. Chryssochoou, *Democracy in the European Union* (London: I.B. Tauris, 2000); John Pinder (ed.), *Foundations of Democracy in the European Union: From the Genesis of Parliamentary Democracy to the European Parliament* (London: Macmillan, 1999); Christer Karlsson, *Democracy, Legitimacy and the European Union* (Uppsala, 2001); Erik Oddvar Eriksen and John Erik Fossum (eds), *Democracy in the European Union: Integration through Deliberation?* (London: Routledge, 2000); Christopher Lord, *Democracy in the European Union* (Sheffield: Sheffield Academic Press, 1998); Michael Newman, *Democracy, Sovereignty and the European Union* (London: Hurst & Company, 1996); Alex Warleigh, *Democracy in the European Union* (London: Sage, 2003).
46. E.g. Giandomenico Majone, 'Europe's "Democratic Deficit": The Question of Standards', *European Law Journal* 4(1), 5–28; Andrew Moravcsik, 'In Defence of the "Democratic Deficit": Reassessing Legitimacy in the European Union', *Journal of Common Market Studies* 40(4), 603–24; Andreas Føllesdal and Simon Hix, 'Why There is a Democratic Deficit in the EU: A Response to Majone and Moravcsik', *Journal of Common Market Studies* 44(3), 533–62.
47. E.g. Morten Kelstrup, Dorthe Sindbjerg Martinsen and Marlene Wind, *Europa i forandring: En grundbog om EU's politiske og retlige system* (Copenhagen: Hans Reitzels forlag, 2012), 269–70.
48. Retrieved 31 January 2018 from https://www.radikale.dk/content/demokrati.
49. 'Principprogram', Dansk Folkeparti 1997, 6.
50. E.g. 'Fælles værdier – fælles ansvar', Dansk Folkeparti 2001, 12–13.
51. 'Principprogram' (1997), 9.
52. 'Stem dansk, stem nej', Dansk Folkeparti 1998 and 'Bevar kronen – stem dansk', Dansk Folkeparti 2000.
53. 'Europapolitisk oplæg', Dansk Folkeparti 2008.

Bibliography

1974. 'Demokrati á la EF', *Det ny Notat* (1)1, 3.
1975. 'Den 2. december vedtager topmøde direkte valg til EF-parlamentet', *Det ny Notat* (25)2, 4–5.
Asp-Poulsen, H. 1991. 'Demokratisk underskud', *Jyllands-Posten*, 28 November 1991.
Bogdanor, V. 1986. 'The Future of the European Community: Two Models of Democracy', *Government and Opposition* 21(2), 161–76.
Bonde, J-P. 1989. *Tænk lidt længere: Udfordringen fra EF's Indre Marked*. Allingåbro: Forlaget Notat.
———. 1990. *Folkestyret og EF.* Allingåbro: Forlaget Notat.
Bøggild, J. et al. 1961. *Romtraktaten, Europamarkedet og Danmark*. Holbæk: Forlaget IDAG.
Chryssochoou, D.N. 2000. *Democracy in the European Union*. London: I.B. Tauris.

Curtin, D.M. 1997. *Postnational Democracy: The European Union in Search of a Political Philosophy*. The Hague: Kluwer.

Dunn, B.N. 1988. *Why the Public Should be Worried by the EEC's Democratic Deficit*. London: European Democratic Group.

Eriksen, E.O., and J.E. Fossum (eds). 2000. *Democracy in the European Union: Integration through Deliberation?* London: Routledge.

Føllesdal, A., and S. Hix. 2006. 'Why There is a Democratic Deficit in the EU: A Response to Majone and Moravcsik', *Journal of Common Market Studies* 44(3), 533–62.

Friisberg, C. 2007. *Ingen over og ingen ved siden af Folketinget*, vols 1–2. Varde: Vestjysk Kulturforlag.

Hardis, A. 1993. 'Nej'ets mange ansigter', in Jens Maigård (ed.), *Under bekvemmelighedsflag: En kritisk undersøgelse af Folkebevægelsen mod EF og Junibevægelsen*. Frederiksberg: Fiskers Forlag.

Helin D. 2002. *30 år i folkestyrets tjeneste – om Folkebevægelsen mod EU's historie, 1972–2001*. Mørke: Grevas Forlag.

Karlsson, C. 2001. *Democracy, Legitimacy and the European Union*. Stockholm: Uppsala University Library.

Keith, K. 1972. 'The European Parliament', *The World Today*, December 1972, 530–37.

Kelstrup, M. et al. 2012. *Europa i forandring: En grundbog om EU's politiske og retlige system*. Copenhagen: Hans Reitzels forlag.

Koch, H. 1945. *Hvad er demokrati?* Copenhagen: Gyldendal.

Krag, J-O. 1972. 'Danmark og EF', in J-E. Modig and P. Nielson (eds), *Socialdemokrater fra 6 lande om EF*. Copenhagen: Samlerens Piccolobøger.

Krarup, S. 1974. *Fædreland og folkestyre: En kritik af Danmarks nyere historie*. Copenhagen: Gyldendal.

Køber, J.V. 2017. *Et spørgsmål om nærhed: Nærdemokratibegrebets historie i 1970'ernes Danmark*. University of Copenhagen, Dissertation.

Lehmann, A. 2001. 'Venstres vej til Europa: Venstres Europapolitik, 1945–1960', *Den jyske historiker* 93, 32–52.

Lipgens W., and W. Loth (eds). 1991. *Documents on the History of European Integration*, vol. 4. Berlin/New York: Walter de Gruyter.

Lord, C. 1998. *Democracy in the European Union*. Sheffield: Sheffield Academic Press.

Madsen, K.F. 1990. 'Vi skal ikke acceptere rollen som delstat', *Århus Stiftstidende*, 7 December 1990.

Majone, G. 1998. 'Europe's 'Democratic Deficit': The Question of Standards', *European Law Journal* 4(1), 5–28.

Marquand, D. 1979. *Parliament for Europe*. London: Jonathan Cape.

Moravcsik, A. 'In Defence of the "Democratic Deficit": Reassessing Legitimacy in the European Union', *Journal of Common Market Studies* 40(4), 603–24.

Müller, J-W. 2013. *Contesting Democracy: Political Ideas in Twentieth-Century Europe*. New Haven: Yale University Press.

Neumann, I.B. 2001. 'This Little Piggy Stayed at Home: Why Norway is Not a Member of the EU', in L. Hansen and O. Wæver (eds), *European Integration and National Identity: The Challenge of the Nordic States*. London: Routledge, 88–129.

Nevers, J. 2011. *Fra skældsord til slagord: Demokratibegrebet i dansk politisk historie*. Odense: University Press of Southern Denmark.

Newman, M. 1996. *Democracy, Sovereignty and the European Union*. London: Hurst & Company.

Nyboe Andersen, P. 1972. *Danmark i Fremtidens Europa*. Holte: EF-Forlaget.

Pinder, J. (ed.). 1999. *Foundations of Democracy in the European Union: From the Genesis of Parliamentary Democracy to the European Parliament*. London: Macmillan.

Rasmussen, M. 2001. 'Ivar Nørgaards mareridt: Socialdemokratiet og den Økonomiske og Monetære Union, 1970–1972', *Den jyske historiker* 93, 73–95.

Scalingi, P. 1980. *The European Parliament: The Three-Decade Search for a United Europe*. Westport, CT: Greenwood Press.

Sådan sagde de om Danmark og EF: Fuldstændig gengivelse af folketingets markedsdebat den 16. december 1971. Copenhagen: Forlaget Aktuelle Bøger.

Trägårdh, L. 2001. 'Sweden and the EU: Welfare State Nationalism and the Spectre of "Europe"', in Hansen and Wæver (eds), *European Integration and National Identity: The Challenge of the Nordic States*. London: Routledge, 130–181.

Warleigh, A. 2003. *Democracy in the European Union*. London: Sage.

Index

A

absolutism, 28–29, 44, 75, 122, 140, 152, 209, 211, 214, 218
Adams, John, 66
Agrarian League (Finland), 169
alienation, 151, 163, 261, 263–64
Alkio, Santeri, 169–70
Alps, 90–91, 93, 95–96, 240
Althing (Iceland), 89
Ames, Fisher, 26
anachronism, 102, 189
anarchism; anarchists; anarchy, 45, 51–52, 68–69, 71, 143, 152, 194, 213, 272–73
ancien régime, 4, 17
Anglo-American; Anglo-Saxon, 2, 7, 164, 190, 218
Ankersmit, Frank, 42
anti-authoritarianism, 265, 267, 287. *See also* authoritarianism
anti-democratic, 32, 116, 148–52, 164–65, 168, 173, 176, 187, 216, 235–36, 249n16
anti-Semitism, 94
antiquity, 42, 94–95
Antonelle, Pierre Antoine, 21
Arendt, Hannah, 236, 258, 264–265
Aretin, Christoph Freiherr von, 68
Argenson, René Louis d', 18, 67
aristocracy; aristocrats, 4–5, 17–21, 26–27, 42–56, 57n7, 65–72, 91–92, 96–97, 103, 117, 121, 137–39, 196, 210, 214–15, 220. *See also* nobility
Aristotle; Aristotelian, 17, 43, 48, 50, 65–66, 90, 97, 116, 128n14
Aron, Raymond, 246

Asquith, Herbert, 190
assembly, 9, 19, 21, 29–31, 46, 75, 89, 96, 121, 125, 164, 166, 171, 210–11, 266, 289
atheism, 141
Athens, 4, 50, 89–90, 94, 102
Attlee, Clement, 194
Auken, Svend, 287
Austria; Austria-Hungary; Habsburg Empire, 31, 79, 130n33, 147, 182, 208–11, 214–16, 223n2, 223n3, 223n7, 234, 237, 239
Austrian Parliament; *Reichsrat*, 210
authoritarianism, 6, 45, 52, 71, 80, 125, 146, 150, 163, 186, 189, 195–98, 219–20, 237, 241, 247, 259–60, 263–69
autocracy, 6, 57n2, 114, 116, 147, 164–68, 195, 208, 211 223n2, 269
autonomy, 2, 122, 125, 162, 210–11, 217–19, 226n44, 259, 263–72
Avaliani, S, 125
Azaña, Manuel, 145
Azorín (José Martínez Ruiz), 145

B

Babeuf, François-Noël, 'Gracchus', 21, 25
Baden, 31, 37n57
Bagehot, Walter, 51–54, 61n60
balance of power; balanced government, 10–11, 43–45, 49–54, 66, 188
Barker, Ernest, 193
Baroja, Pio, 145
Barriobero, Eduardo, 147
Bastille Day, 29

Batavian Republic, 21
Bavaria, 24
Beard, Charles, 193
Belgium, 24, 46, 144, 147, 234–36, 239, 242. *See also* Low Countries
Beneš, Edvard, 209, 219–222, 223n5–6, 225n32, 226n46–47, 227n57
Bentham, Jeremy, 23, 51–52
Bergson, Henri, 193
Berlin Wall, 23, 236, 291
Bessarabia, 231, 233
Beyerle, Konrad, 166
bicameralism; bicameral parliament; two-chamber system, 21, 46, 48, 121, 216, 282–84
Billaud-Varenne, Jacques Nicolas, 20
Bismarck, Otto von, 185
Bjerregaard, Ritt, 291
Blackstone, William, 47
Blanqui, Auguste, 26
Bluntschli, Johann Casper, 72
Bogdanor, Vernon, 289
Bohemia, 210–211, 215, 220, 224n10
Bolshevism; Bolsheviks, 79, 101, 115, 118, 124–26, 164, 167–76, 186
Bonald, Louis Gabriel Ambroise de, 27
Bonaparte, Napoleon. *See under* Napoleon I
Bonapartism, 71
Bonde, Jens-Peter, 290–291
Bonn, Moritz Julius, 194
Bourbon dynasty, 137, 142
bourgeoisie; bourgeois, 26, 67, 75–77, 80, 99–100, 114, 118, 125–26, 148, 166, 169, 172–75, 188–189, 208, 212, 220–21, 267
Branting, Hjalmar, 99, 163–64, 172
Brater, Carl, 72
Breines, Wini, 262
Britain; British Empire, 4–7, 10, 19, 24–30, 42–48, 50–55, 66–69, 74, 77–80, 92, 97, 114, 139, 160–68, 170–76, 182–85, 189, 193–98, 231–33, 237, 245, 283, 287–89. *See also* England
British constitution; English constitution, 25, 44–47, 50–54, 66
British parliament; House of Commons; House of Lords, 18, 27, 43–46, 184

Brougham, Henry, 52
Brown, Ivor, 190
Brussels, 29, 286, 293–94
Bryce, James, 6, 9, 89, 165, 182–84, 190
Buonarroti, Philippe, 21, 25
bureaucracy, 164, 232–233, 243, 247, 269, 284, 287, 293–94
Burdett-Coutts, William, 166
Burke, Edmund, 4, 19, 43, 52, 68

C
Cadiz, 136
Calvert, Creg, 266
Cámara, Sixto, 141
Campoamor, Clara, 147–48
Cánovas, Antonio, 144
cantons (Switzerland), 17, 24, 88–89, 91–93, 103
Čapek, Karel, 208
capitalism, 2, 169, 173, 193, 198, 221, 242, 263, 268, 270–71, 287, 294
Castelar, Emilio, 142
categorization; categories, 7, 17, 67, 72–73, 97, 266, 271. *See also* typology
Catholic Center Party (Germany), 79, 166
Catholicism; Catholic Church, 19, 27–28, 76, 137–41, 147, 150, 210, 212, 215, 239–42
Cavendish-Bentinck, Henry, 167
censorship, 113, 126, 219
Central Europe, 31, 208, 236
centralization, 21, 211, 233, 281. *See also* decentralization
Certeau, Michel de, 265
Chamberlain, Joseph, 55
chaos and democracy, 32, 43, 68, 71, 140, 146
Chartism, 25, 28–30
Chas, Jean, 45
Chateaubriand, René de, 47
checks and balances, 47–54, 66, 284
Cherbuliez, Antoine-Elisée, 91–92
Chicherin, Boris, 114
Christian Democracy, 33, 238–40, 243, 247
Christianity, 28, 33, 71, 141
church, 27, 139–41, 147, 218, 232

citizen, 5, 32, 91–93, 95, 103, 106n32, 123, 151–52, 179n67, 182, 187, 196, 209–10, 213, 217–18, 223n7, 232, 238, 242–46, 258–61, 264, 270–71, 282–83, 295n2
citizenship, 22, 25, 146, 191, 194, 225n32, 244, 283
city state; *polis*, 72–73
civilization; civilized, 53, 78, 90, 120 195, 208, 213 220, 236
civil society, 2, 7, 198, 232
civil war, 24–25, 45, 52, 94, 163
    of England, 18
    of Finland, 162–74
    of Portugal, 24–25, 28
    of Spain, 24, 28, 149
Cobban, Alfred, 193–94
Cohen, Joshua, 270–71
Cohn, Oskar, 173
Cohn-Bendit, Daniel, 260
Cold War, 7, 102, 104, 232, 235–36
collectivism; collectivity, 189, 217, 220, 239, 264, 268
common good; general good, 18, 22, 93
communism; communists, 1, 6, 23, 28, 76, 95, 100, 143, 148, 175, 192, 198, 212, 218–22, 223n2, 234–40, 245, 249n16, 260, 263, 267, 284, 291
community, 89–90, 96, 171, 232, 240, 244, 262, 281
    national, 78, 212, 226n44, 233
    organic, 78, 212
    See also European Economic Community
comparative perspective; comparative research, 9–10, 161, 165, 168, 175, 190–91
conceptual ambiguity, 8, 42, 116, 162
    entanglement, 68, 90, 192
conceptual history; history of concepts, 7–9, 58n24, 90, 135, 152–53, 233, 257, 294
consensus, 71, 124, 137, 152, 190, 268, 272, 283–84
conservatism; conservatives, 5, 8, 25–26, 46–54, 73–74, 80, 97–100, 103, 114–16, 126, 136–49, 152, 161, 164–70, 174–76, 184, 189, 194, 210, 220, 236, 283–89
conservative liberalism, 5, 48–50, 53, 136

Considérant, Victor, 26
Constant, Benjamin, 47
Constituent Assembly (France), 30
constitution; constitutional, 4–5, 8–10, 18–25, 29–33, 42–56, 65–76, 79–80, 88–92, 96–99, 103, 106n32, 113–18, 121, 125, 135–39, 142–48, 151–53, 160–76, 187–98, 208–11, 214–19, 223n6, 236–37, 241, 281–84, 289–93, 295n2
    dictatorship, 188–89
    monarchy, 5, 25, 30, 46, 75, 113, 144, 148, 161–64, 209, 293
    see also mixed constitution
Constitutional Assembly (Russia), 125
Constitutional Democrats (Russia), 116
constitutionalism, 2, 24, 31, 67, 114
continuity, 73, 93–94, 142, 166–68, 238
convergence, 17, 95, 221, 248
corporatism; corporations, 74, 149, 241–42, 272
corruption, 2, 45, 51, 187, 235
Corsica, 18, 247
Cortés, Donoso, 137
Costa, Joaquín, 145–46
council democracy, 170–71, 259, 262, 267
counter-concepts; antonyms, 97, 117, 125, 162
counter-revolution, 20, 22, 28, 31, 138, 174, 211. *See also* revolution
crisis of democracy, 6, 100, 103, 193–94, 247
critique; criticism, 6, 51, 60n45, 68, 73–77, 99–100, 142, 145, 162, 167, 171–73, 183, 192–93, 213, 216, 219–22, 227n50, 246–47, 257–60, 263, 272, 286, 291
Croatia, 31
Croce, Benedetto, 193
Cuesta, Nemesio Fernández, 142
Cussac y García, Antonia, 144
Czechoslovakia; Czech Republic, 6, 10, 102, 105n5, 109n111, 119, 130n33–34, 196, 208–22, 223n2, 223n5–6, 224n10, 224n12, 226n44, 226n48

D

Dahl, Robert A., 89–90
Dahrendorf, Ralf, 259
Danish Constitution, 283

Danish Parliament (*Folketing*), 284
David, Eduard, 171, 188
Dean, Vera Micheles, 191
decentralization, 32, 211, 261, 267–68, 281. *See also* centralization
degeneration; devolution, 17, 32, 50–52, 65–67, 114, 233, 242
Delbrück, Clemens von, 166
deliberation; deliberative democracy, 32, 46, 150–151, 265, 270–72, 277n78, 286
Delolme, Jean-Louis, 47, 51
demagogy; demagogic, 17, 21, 32, 94, 162, 196, 236–237
democracy
    American, 4–5, 97, 192
    ancient, 88–90, 96–103
    bourgeois, 77, 148, 169, 172–74, 221, 267
    capitalist, 193, 193
    Catholic, 27–28
    constitutional, 33, 223n2
    contested, 7–10, 16, 32, 90, 136, 182–83
    crisis of, 6, 103
    critique of; critics of; discontents of, 11, 196, 244–45, 257
    deliberative, 32, 46, 150–51, 265, 270–72, 277n78, 286
    direct, 32, 66–67, 72, 92–93, 103, 160, 169, 173, 262, 267–70
    economic, 173, 176, 211, 242
    false; *faux*, 67
    future of, 193–94, 220
    global, 7, 217
    liberal, 1–3, 6–7, 13n24, 10, 45, 56, 169, 183–84, 187–89, 197–98, 212, 257, 259
    mass, 5–6, 22, 77, 184–185, 237
    modern, 4, 6–7, 26, 32, 42, 88–89–95, 102, 118, 136, 183–85, 198, 233–34
    national, 8, 11, 90, 217, 282, 288, 294
    Nordic, 9–10, 95–96, 100–104, 170
    organic, 135, 150, 217
        origin of, 2, 88–90, 102
    parliamentary, 6, 13n24, 100–103, 135, 147–49, 152, 161–67, 170–71, 174–75, 186, 189–90, 226n48, 235, 257–61, 290
    participatory, 2, 7–8, 136, 241, 257–60, 266–72, 295n2
    proletarian, 25, 77, 148
    'pure', 4–5, 19–21, 43–47, 53, 66, 69–71, 89, 137, 168
    representative, 3–4, 19, 21, 32, 42, 53, 72, 103, 137, 170, 174, 247, 265, 282, 295n2
    tradition of, 88–90, 99–102, 163, 173, 287
    'true', 1, 6, 21, 93, 174, 247, 286
    Western, 6–7, 9, 162–63, 172, 182–84, 233
Democratic Party
    Austria, 211
    Germany, 184
    Spain, 143
Democratism; *Demokratismus*, 69, 75, 172, 211–213, 267
democratization, 10, 22, 55, 99, 102, 118–25, 139, 151, 161–75, 177n7, 182, 185, 190, 209, 213–14, 221, 257–62, 268–69
democrats, 2–5, 9, 17–20, 24–32, 70, 74–80, 98, 103, 115–26, 140–44, 148–49, 168, 174, 183, 186, 196–97, 211–12, 222, 284
Demosthenes, 26
Denmark, 5–6, 8, 24, 88–90, 144, 169, 241, 281–294
despotism, 43–45, 48, 52, 56, 66, 69
Dewey, John, 187, 191–93, 198, 258
Dickinson, Willoughby, 168
dictatorship, 1, 6, 54, 135, 146, 149, 151–53, 183–98, 220–21, 227n50, 232, 265
    of the proletariat, 76, 118, 125, 170, 174–75, 189, 221
diplomacy; diplomats, 5, 149, 186, 216
direct democracy, 32, 66–67, 72, 92–93, 103, 160, 169, 173, 262, 267–70
Dunn, John, 9, 43
Dutch Constitution, 46–47
Dutch Parliament, 7, 46–47
Dutschke, Rudi, 261

E
Eastern Europe, 5, 28, 31, 198, 220, 222, 235

education, 17, 23–25, 75, 79, 98, 116, 122–24, 138, 145–47, 168–70, 174, 185–88, 193–94, 198, 210, 213–14, 217, 240–45, 268
egalitarianism, 21, 28, 49, 88–89, 96, 104n3, 137–41, 148, 153, 211, 234
elections; electoral process; electoral system; electorate, 20–23, 29–32, 42, 46, 53, 71, 91–92, 96, 115, 120–26, 140–49, 163–67, 170, 186, 196–98, 210–12, 216, 232, 236–40, 243–48, 258–60, 266, 286, 289–90. *See also* franchise; suffrage; vote
Eliot, Thomas S., 1
elites, 2, 55, 136–138, 161–65, 168–70, 185–186, 210, 215, 232, 244
emancipation, 73–74, 136, 165, 193, 212, 222, 234, 243
empire, 71, 140
    Napoleonic, 23
    Russian, 113–114, 120–125, 162
    Second German, 76–77, 80
    Spanish, 145
Engelbert of Admont, 65
Engels, Friedrich, 29, 38n62, 76
England, 5, 18–20, 23, 44, 50, 70, 89, 119, 124, 139. *See also* Britain
Enlightenment; enlightened, 22, 66–68, 72, 209, 218
Enzensberger, Hans Magnus, 261–262
equality, 16–20, 23–26, 30, 33, 67, 71–76, 89–90, 118–23, 139–44, 153, 189, 209, 215, 268, 282
Erlander, Tage, 240
estates, 4, 19, 53, 97–100, 103, 119, 136
ethics; ethical, 73, 80, 193, 214–215, 271–272. *See also* morality
ethnicity, 8, 31, 168–169, 179n67, 210, 216–218, 222
European Economic Community (EEC), 282–91
European Union (EU), 7, 281–83, 290–94, 295n2
executive government; executive power, 44, 52–56, 66, 161, 173, 293
exiles; exile politics, 28–29, 31, 186, 195–197, 215, 220, 237
expectations (horizon of), 8, 29, 68–69, 77, 80, 143–44, 151, 172, 245–46, 257

exploitation, 119, 216, 234, 263–64
extremism, 100, 118, 152, 196–98, 219. *See also* radicalism

F
Fascism, 1, 6, 95, 101, 149, 152, 183–88, 190–96, 218–21, 234
February Revolution (Russia), 115, 123, 126, 161, 172
federalism, 106n26, 144, 281, 289
Ferdinand VII, 137–138
Fernández, Manuel Giménez, 149
Fernández-Miranda, Torcuato, 151
feudalism, 20, 49, 96, 103, 139, 211, 269
Fichte, Johann Gottlieb von, 218
Finer, Herman, 231
Finer, Samuel, 231
Finland, 6, 8, 97, 120, 147, 161–76, 196, 223n2–3
First World War, 6, 77–78, 94–95, 115, 146, 160, 175, 182–90, 194, 198, 208, 214–15, 220
Føllesdal, Andreas, 291
Ford, Guy Stanton, 191
Fox, Charles James, 44, 68
France, 4–7, 10, 17–32, 42–55, 66–78, 92–94, 97, 116, 119, 123, 137–40, 144, 147, 165–66, 196, 208, 219, 222, 231, 233, 235–36, 239, 242–47, 259–63, 266–70, 283, 291
franchise, 21, 23, 25, 27, 31, 71, 190, 211, 241–42. *See also* elections; suffrage; vote
Franco, Francisco, 135, 149–50
Franco-German War, 91
Franke, Emil, 219, 227n52
Franz Joseph, 211
fraternity, 125, 139, 141, 215
freedom (individual/popular/of conscience/of assembly/of the press), 23, 27, 43, 47–49, 66, 73, 80, 88, 91–99, 101–2, 104n3, 105n18, 114, 122, 125, 136, 140–44, 151, 193, 209, 212–14, 219–21, 234–38, 240–41, 245, 247, 265, 282, 293. *See also* liberty
French Parliament, 48–49, 54–55
French Revolution, 4, 17, 19–23, 27, 45–48, 52, 65–69, 74, 93–94, 97, 141, 259
future; future-orientation, 4–5, 9, 20, 26, 32–33, 54, 67–69, 73–75, 80, 90, 94,

113, 116, 141, 144, 160–63, 167, 170–75, 182, 193–98, 220, 227n50, 236, 242, 261–68, 289. *See also* expectations

G
Galiano, Alcalá, 138
Gallego, Jerónimo García, 147
Gallie, W.B., 7
Garrido, Fernando, 143
Gaulle, Charles de, 233, 239
Geijer, Erik Gustav, 96–97, 107n52
gender, 9, 20, 242–43, 246, 268
Geneva, 18–19, 47, 72
Gentile, Giovanni, 186
Gentz, Friedrich, 68
George, David Lloyd, 160, 162, 168, 170
Ger'e, Vladimir, 116
German constitution; Weimar constitution, 75, 164, 168–69, 188
German Parliament; *Reichstag*, 78, 161, 163, 184, 188
Germany, 5, 8, 22–32, 65–80, 89–91, 96, 99, 120, 129n18, 136, 142, 147, 160–76, 177n7, 182–91, 194–97, 208, 211–12, 215–21, 223n3, 226n44, 231, 234–39, 245–46, 258–63, 265–70, 286
Gessen, Vladimir, 117, 121–22
Gladstone, William, 54–55
globalization, 272–273
Glorious Revolution (Britain), 44, 74
Glorious Revolution (Spain), 143
Gorz, André, 247
government (constitutional), 24, 47
    democratic, 2, 22–23, 45, 52, 101, 116, 126, 137, 166, 189, 198, 238, 291
    liberal, 30, 99, 139
    parliamentary, 6, 49–55, 57n7, 59n43, 99, 161–63, 174, 213–14, 236, 261
    popular, 16, 89, 136, 144
    representative, 19, 33, 42, 47–49, 52–55, 57n7, 137, 139
    see also mixed government; self-administration
Graeber, David, 272
Graefe, Albrect von, 164
Great Depression, 192, 194
Greece, 17, 23–24, 26, 42, 69, 89–90, 94, 222, 223n3, 265

Grevensmöhlen, Carl August, 97
Grote, George, 4
Guérin, Daniel, 262
Guizot, François, 5, 9, 23, 32, 43, 49, 52, 59n43, 71, 97, 140

H
Habermas, Jürgen, 246, 259–60, 271–72
Haldane, John Burdon Sanderson, 193
Halifax, Lord Irwin (Edward Wood), 194
Hallendorff, Carl, 165–166
Hammarskjöld, Hugo, 165
Hansen, Mogens Herman, 42
Hansson, Per Albin, 101
Hardenberg, Karl-August von, 22 69, 72
Harney, G.J., 29
Hayden, Tom, 258
Hayek, Friedrich, 231, 247
Hegel, Georg Wilhelm Friedrich, 72–74, 218
Henderson, Arthur, 163
Henke, Alfred, 173
Herder, Johann Gottfried, 218
Heuss, Theodor, 184, 188
hierarchy, 20, 27, 43, 53, 233, 259, 263–72, 287
Hildebrand, Karl, 165–66
Hitler, Adolf, 80, 186, 219–21
Hjärne, Harald, 165–166
Hobson, John A., 193
Hoetzel, Jiří, 217
Hogendorp, Gijsbert Karel van, 47
Hollweg, Theobald von Bethmann, 160
Holocaust, 236
Holy Roman Empire, 17
humanitarianism, 218
human rights, 194–95, 218, 226n44, 237, 249n24, 268, 281–82
Hungary; Austria-Hungary, 31, 208–10, 215–18, 223n2, 224n10

I
Iceland, 89, 102, 105n4
idealism, 190, 216
identity (collective/national/political), 16, 28–30, 91–95, 102, 141–42, 147–48, 209, 240, 268, 281
ideology, 1, 6–7, 65–70, 74–80, 92–93, 100–17, 135, 143, 147–49, 153, 160–62,

166, 172, 175, 177n6, 183, 189, 194, 211–13, 238–40, 244–47, 267–68, 272, 293–94
immigration; immigrants, 187, 246, 258, 293
independence, 6, 31, 100, 136, 162, 164–65, 208, 215, 223n2, 233, 285. *See also* sovereignty
individualism, 142, 183, 189, 192, 220, 242, 245
industry; industrial society, 9, 32, 77, 221, 234, 241, 245–47, 262–63
industrialization, 77, 79, 186, 210, 272
inequality, 118, 120, 246. *See also* equality
intellectuals; *intelligentsia*, 5–6, 78, 95, 115–16, 145–46, 193–95, 209–11, 216, 222, 263–64
interests; interest groups, 18, 46–55, 72–73, 78, 114–18, 171, 185, 209, 214, 219, 232–39, 241, 244–46, 261, 270, 285
internationalism, 29, 76, 171, 175, 221
interwar period, 1, 6, 91, 95, 103, 173, 182–98, 208, 215–22, 226n47, 236, 238, 241, 245, 247, 284
Ireland; Northern Ireland, 6, 25, 27–28, 247, 283, 287
Isabella II, 141–143
Islam; Muslims, 2, 139
Italy, 21–24, 31–32, 68, 89, 138, 144–47, 183–91, 218, 223n3, 231, 235–42, 245

J

Jacobinism, 66, 69–70, 138
Jakobsen, Frode, 286–87
Jeffrey, Francis, 45
Joseph I Bonaparte, 136
Juan Carlos, 151–52
Judaism; Jews, 19, 231, 234, 258–59
July Monarchy (France), 26, 29
July Revolution (France), 24–28, 49, 70
justice, 73, 126, 169, 173, 218, 232, 235, 262, 288
justification, 32, 53, 72, 123, 143, 165, 187, 209, 213–17, 223n6. *See also* legitimation

K

Kaizl, Josef, 211–13
Kant, Immanuel, 22, 66, 69

Kaufmann, Walter Arnold, 258
Kautsky, Karl, 172, 174, 184, 186
Kellett, Ernest E., 193
Kelsen, Hans, 6, 9, 195
Kent, Victoria, 147
Keynesianism, 243
Kjellén, Rudolf, 167
Koch, Hal, 286
Kokoshkin, Fedor, 119–20
Koselleck, Reinhart, 8, 65
Krag, Jens Otto, 288, 292
Kramář, Karel, 211–12
Krarup, Søren, 287, 293
Krause, K.C.F., 142
Kuusinen, Otto Wille, 174

L

Labour Party (Britain), 168, 170, 193, 289
Lagerroth, Fredrik, 99–100
Lamartine, Alphonse de, 67
Lammenais, Félicité de, 27–28
Laski, Harold, 193–94
Lassalle, Ferdinand, 76
Latin America; Spanish America, 136, 145, 191
Laube, Heinrich, 75
law; legislation, 20, 32, 51, 94–96, 106n32, 117, 120–22, 139, 142–50, 165–66, 173, 183, 187, 192, 196, 209–10, 216–20, 232 237, 243, 270, 281, 284, 290. *See also* natural law; rule of law
League of Nations, 184
Ledru-Rollin, Alexandre, 29–30
legislature, 21–23, 25, 44, 116, 130n33, 150, 242
legitimation; legitimacy, 1–3, 8, 20, 29, 45–47, 52–55, 67, 71, 94, 98, 137, 141, 152, 161, 173–75, 192–94, 219–21, 236–37, 243, 270–72, 289–90. *See also* justification
left; left-wing, 8, 23, 26, 30, 49, 70, 76, 79, 92, 99–100, 114–17, 122, 126, 135–36, 141, 145–52, 161–64, 167–76, 189, 211, 216, 219, 234, 237, 244, 247, 258–69, 287–88, 292–94
Leibholz, Gerhard, 189
Lenin, Vladimir Ilyich; Leninism, 114, 118, 125–26, 186, 214, 266

Levellers, 190
Liberalism, 67–70, 74–79, 135–140, 145, 153, 183–97, 210–18, 231, 248
liberal democracy, 1–3, 6–7, 13n24, 10, 45, 56, 169, 183–84, 188–89, 197–98, 212, 257, 259
Liberal Party
  Britain, 168
  Germany, 270
  Spain, 142
  Sweden, 169
Libertarianism, 247
liberty, 20 23–26, 32, 46, 66, 71, 89–93, 96, 100–102, 114, 118, 139, 147, 169, 183, 186, 209, 212, 215, 221, 234, 259, 263, 281. *See also* freedom
Lijphart, Arend, 239
Lincoln, Abraham, 191
Lindsay, Alexander Dunlop, 184, 190–91
Lippmann, Walter, 187, 191
Louis Napoleon, 32, 71
Lovett, William, 29
Low Countries, 234, 240. *See also* Belgium; The Netherlands
Löwenstein, Karl von, 184, 195–97, 237
lower class, 67, 72, 139

M
Macaulay, Thomas Babington, 55
MacDonald, James Ramsay, 170
de Maistre, Joseph, 27–28
Majone, Giandomenico, 291
majority democracy/rule, 6–7, 17, 55, 66, 116–17, 124 146, 168, 172–73, 187, 192, 213, 217–18, 236, 269, 283–86, 290–92
Mäkelin, Yrjö, 174
Mallet, Paul-Henri, 90–91, 96, 104n3, 105n18
Mallock, W.H., 190
Manin, Bernard, 42
Mann, Thomas, 78, 193
Marcuse, Herbert, 260–62, 266
Maritain, Jacques, 193
markets; market forces, 25, 241, 285–89
Marquand, David, 289
Marsilius of Padua, 65
Marxism, 149, 164, 172–73, 213–14, 240, 263–64

Marx, Karl, 29, 38n62, 76, 125, 214
Masaryk, T.G., 208–9, 211–22, 223n5–6, 225n20, 225n25, 225n32, 226n46, 227n50, 227n57
May, Thomas Erskine, 89
masses, 22, 30, 68, 73, 77, 98, 114, 117–22, 125, 149, 161, 165, 172–73, 183–87, 198, 208
mass democracy, 5, 77, 184–85, 237
materialism, 78, 213, 220
Mazower, Mark, 182
Mazzini, Giuseppe, 29
Melucci, Alberto, 268
Mendès-France, Pierre, 244
Mensheviks, 115, 118, 125
Michelet, Jules, 67
Michels, Robert, 214
Middle Ages; medieval, 16, 65, 88, 91–94, 99–101, 106n26, 118, 137–39, 150, 215, 224n10, 234
middle class, 27, 68, 138–39, 211, 245
Mignet, François, 67
military; militarism, 74, 79, 99, 124, 142, 146–47, 152, 182, 194–97, 210, 216, 236–37, 261
Mill, John Stuart, 50, 214
Mills, C. Wright, 260
minorities, 7, 66, 116–17, 136, 145, 166, 173, 210, 213–18, 242, 247, 266, 282
mixed constitution, 4–5, 11, 17–18, 42–56, 57n7, 59n31, 66, 90, 97, 103, 116, 128n14, 136, 176
mixed government, 17, 42–46, 49–56, 57n7
mixed monarchy, 49, 96
mob rule, 4, 44, 55, 138
moderation, moderate, 31, 46–54, 72, 138–42, 148–52, 165, 170–73
Molina, Ramón, 147
monarchy; monarchism, 4–6, 17–26, 29–31, 43–48, 51–52, 60n45, 65–66, 69–72, 75–79, 91–92, 97–100, 103, 107n60, 108n83, 113–16, 136–48, 161–64, 167–72, 176, 182, 210, 233, 236, 263, 293
Montesquieu, Charles-Louis de Secondat, 17–18, 20, 45, 47, 104n3, 121, 286
morality; moral, 20, 29, 55, 73, 78, 91, 102, 105n18, 145, 212–20, 232, 271–72. *See also* ethics

Moravia, 210–11, 215, 220
Moravcsik, Andrew, 291
movement (ideological/national/political/ social), 2, 7–9, 24–28, 58n25, 68, 71, 75–76, 100, 122–23, 137, 143, 150–53, 188, 196, 208–11, 215, 224n10, 231, 239, 245–47, 257–72, 285–87, 290–94
Müller, Jan-Werner, 283–284
Mussolini, Benito, 184, 231
myth; mythification, 78, 138 217, 222

N
Naples, 22–23, 31
Napoleon I; Napoleonic Empire/period/ wars, 4, 20, 22–23, 45–47, 55, 69, 74–75, 136–38, 194
Napoleon III, 52, 71
narrative, 74, 80, 89, 99–101, 105n4, 151, 209, 234
nation; nationality; nation state; nation-building, 4–16, 23–24, 31, 55, 71–78, 89–102, 119–26, 137–44, 150, 160–76, 179n67, 185, 191, 208–22, 224n10, 232–47, 281–94
National Assembly (Germany), 31, 75
National Convention (France), 20, 46, 48
Nationalism; nationalists, 8, 48, 99–100, 122, 125, 194, 212, 215–18, 220–22, 247
natural law, 18, 170, 218
Naumann, Friedrich, 77, 79
Nazism; National Socialism, 95, 101, 185–89, 193–95, 219–21, 226n47, 227n58, 235–37, 284
The Netherlands, 7, 19, 21, 30, 42, 44–47, 53–55, 144–47, 196, 234, 239
Neumann, Franz, 259
Nicholas II, 115
Nieto, Moreno, 141, 145
nobility, 17–21, 28, 46–50, 67, 96–98, 137, 208, 212. *See also* aristocracy
Nordic countries, 10, 88, 96–98, 101–3, 104n3, 287, 290. *See also* Denmark; Finland; Iceland; Norway; Scandinavia; Sweden
Nordic democracy, 9–10, 95–96, 100–104, 170
North America, 19, 66, 231, 237
Norway, 24, 30–31, 88–89, 97, 105n4, 119, 121, 169, 287
Nyboe Andersen, Poul, 285–88

O
O'Brien, Bronterre, 25
ochlocracy, 44, 53, 55
O'Connell, Daniel, 27–28
October Revolution (Russia), 79, 172, 174
oligarchy; oligarchs, 18–19, 44, 48, 65, 70, 74, 138, 144–45, 214
Ollivier, Émile, 71
Orange family, 44, 47
Ortega y Gasset, José, 145, 147
Osipov, I, 120
Ostrogorski, Moisey, 116, 214
Ottoman Empire, 23, 31, 223n2

P
Paasikivi, Juho Kusti, 167
Pagnerre, Louis-Antoine, 141
Paine, Thomas, 26, 51, 68
Palacký, František, 211
Palmerston, Henry John Temple, 51
parliamentarism; parliaments; parliamentarians; parliamentary debate/democracy/government, 6–7, 9, 25–31, 44–45, 58n22, 47–55, 59n43, 68–71, 75, 89, 97–103, 114–16, 120–21, 126, 135–38, 141–42, 145–52, 160–76, 183–90, 193–97, 208–14, 216, 219, 226n47–48, 227n50, 234–39, 242–43, 257–62, 267, 282–93
parliamentarization, 55, 168–70
parliamentary proceedings; parliamentary minutes, 9, 138
participation, participatory democracy, 2, 5–8, 11, 73, 77–78, 88–90, 96, 101–103, 136, 139, 160, 176, 188–90, 236, 241, 246, 257–61, 266–72, 284, 295n2
paternalism, 146, 185, 263
patriotism; patriots, 18–19, 75, 137, 150–51, 163–64, 167, 221, 224n10, 234
peace; peaceful, 26, 45, 68, 72, 78, 93, 146, 163, 171–72, 216, 226n44, 236, 239
peasantry, 27–28, 31, 44, 88, 91, 96–103, 116–19, 125–26, 169–70

people; *demos*; *folk*; *kansa*; *lid*; *narod*; *volk*, 2, 8, 17, 22, 31–32, 44–55, 73–75, 96–103, 114–26, 136–42, 147, 150, 160–76, 179n67, 182–86, 190–97, 209, 212–18, 222, 232–47, 259–63, 281–94
    rule of; power of, 3, 7–8, 11, 18, 29, 53, 66, 68, 72–73, 88–89, 96, 99–100, 117–18, 123–24, 168–74, 217–18, 285–94
    sovereignty of, 22, 192, 284
    will of, 71, 117, 120, 124, 160, 165–66, 172, 192, 232
people's democracy, 1, 212, 235–36, 267
Petrazhitskii, L., 122
Pi y Margall, Francisco, 143
Piedmont, 23, 30
pluralism, 67, 74, 80, 126, 135, 148–53, 213, 234, 240, 265
plutocracy, 1, 165
Poland, 24, 28–29, 119, 122, 211, 223n2–3
polarization, 65–74, 125, 147, 235, 239
political culture, 17, 22, 70, 103, 135–36, 152–53, 161–62, 191, 257
political parties, 2, 6–8, 24, 29–32, 53, 68–71, 74, 77–79, 100–101, 114–18, 121–22, 126, 135, 138, 140–51, 161–75, 184, 190, 195–97, 210–15, 219–221, 232, 236–40, 243, 260–72, 284–94
political science; political theory, 3, 6, 9, 42, 52, 66, 91, 99, 165–67, 185–95, 231–32, 259–60, 270
politicization, 29, 68, 75, 79, 151
Polybius, 17, 43, 48, 50
Populism, 2–3, 7, 27, 56, 238
Port Huron Statement, 258, 261
Portugal, 23–25, 28, 36n36, 223n3
postwar period, 6, 79, 212, 221–22, 231–48, 283–86
Potsdam Conference, 88
Poujade, Pierre, 245
poverty; poor, 22, 27, 72, 93, 138, 262
president; presidential, 78, 88, 141, 164–67, 175, 188, 192, 208–9, 216–21, 223n6, 227n50
Preuß, Hugo, 169
privileges, 18–25, 33, 48, 67, 92, 96, 119, 164, 172, 196, 208

progress; progressive, 3, 11, 25, 32, 45, 50–51, 56, 69, 71–78, 93, 99–100, 114, 117, 119, 139–44, 166–71, 175, 187, 194–95, 209–16, 223n2, 246, 260, 287
propaganda, 141–43, 149, 162–63, 175, 182, 187, 232
proportional representation/voting, 170, 213, 216, 238–39
Protestantism, 73, 210–15, 239
Proudhon, Pierre-Joseph, 38n62
Prussia, 22, 30, 53, 69, 74, 160–64, 166, 170, 176
public opinion, 23, 32–33, 162, 187, 190, 235
Pufendorf, Samuel, 18

R
race, 9, 20, 246
radicalism; radicals, 4–5, 21–33, 51, 55, 60n48, 67, 74–76, 79–80, 93, 96–97, 103, 120, 141–42, 147–49, 164, 169–74, 197, 210–11, 215–16, 234, 245–46, 261, 266, 272. *See also* extremism
Rádl, Emanuel, 217–19, 226n44
Rapant, Daniel, 217
Rataj, Jan, 219
Rathenau, Walther, 79
rebellion; rebels, 149, 197, 261, 266
Reconquest (Spain), 137, 142
referendum; plebiscite, 23, 71, 93, 106n32, 150, 188, 232, 236, 259, 282–91, 294
reform; reformism, 6, 22, 24–27, 30–31, 44, 50–, 69, 72–76, 80, 90, 97–99, 103, 115, 121, 123–24, 145–46, 150–51, 160–75, 184, 189, 192, 211, 214, 240–42, 263, 268, 283, 289, 294
religion, 9, 19, 27, 80, 122, 139–41, 144, 212, 215–17
Rémusat, Charles de, 49–50
representation; representatives, 6, 18, 25, 31–32, 42, 46–49, 52–56, 66–67, 92–98, 101–103, 121, 139–41, 147–50, 160–61, 166, 169–75, 182, 186, 211–13, 217, 238–43, 248, 261, 285–87, 290
representative assembly/democracy/government, 3–4, 19–21, 25, 32–33, 42, 47–49, 52–55, 57n7, 69, 72, 91, 103,

136–39, 149–50, 167–70, 174, 247, 265, 282, 295n2
republicanism; republics, 1, 4–5, 7, 10, 17–32, 44–50, 66–80, 89, 92–97, 102–3, 141–42, 144–53, 167, 171–76, 184–89, 194–96, 208, 216–17, 222, 223n2, 227n50, 233–39, 246, 259–60
Restoration (Netherlands), 47; (France), 23, 27, 47–48, 67, 70; (Spain), 144, 146, 152
revisionism, 161, 170, 173, 176
Revolutions of 1848, 5, 7, 16, 28–32, 43, 72–76, 80, 210–11
Revolution of 1905 (Russia), 113–15, 120, 126, 214
rhetoric, 2–3, 5, 8–11, 27, 31–32, 38n62, 52, 88–91, 95–103, 105n7, 136–38, 148–50, 162, 166–71, 175–76, 214, 219, 238, 246, 249n16, 251n38, 287–94, 295n2
right; right-wing, 70, 77, 92, 100, 115–16, 135–36, 142, 149, 151–52, 161–76, 189, 219, 221, 223n2, 234, 237, 244–47, 292–94
rights, 5, 8–9, 23, 52, 75–76, 92–96, 103, 106n32, 119–25, 135, 140–48, 167–69, 175, 179n67, 182, 189, 196–97, 209–19, 237, 240, 266, 270, 281–82, 290. *See also* human rights
Riklin, Alois, 42, 57n4
Ríos, Fernando de los, 147
Rivera, Miguel Primo de, 146
Robespierre, Maximilien, 4, 20–21, 26, 67
Romania, 223n3, 231
Romanov family, 163
Roosevelt, Franklin Delano, 191–192
Rosanvallon, Pierre, 3, 9, 59n31
Rosenkranz, Karl, 74
Ross, Alf, 241
Rossmann, Michael, 265
Rousseau, Jean-Jacques, 18, 26, 72, 118, 238, 286
Royalism, 70, 74, 97, 103, 136
Royer-Collard, Pierre Paul, 49
Rubio, Carlos, 143
Ruge, Arnold, 74–76, 79
rule of law, 2, 6–11, 47, 54, 66, 147, 183, 209, 271, 282, 284
rural, 27–28, 32, 88–89

Russell, Bertrand, 193
Russia, 5, 8, 10, 28, 97, 102, 113–27, 160–65, 168–75, 182, 186, 208, 214–15, 231
Russian parliament (*Duma*), 114–22

S
Sæter, Ingebrigt, 31
Sagasta, P. Mateo, 144
Salmerón, Nicolás, 141
Samuel, Herbert, 168
Sarlin, Bruno, 169
Sattelzeit, 3, 8, 65
Scandinavia, 30, 44, 88–89, 96, 100–102, 107n52, 196, 215, 222, 234, 237, 239, 250n35. *See also* Denmark; Finland; Iceland; Nordic countries; Norway; Sweden
Scheidemann, Philipp, 78
Schlegel, Friedrich, 69
Schlözer, August Ludwig von, 66
Schmitt, Carl, 9, 188–90, 194, 197, 271
Schotte, Axel, 169
Schmidt-Hartmann, Eva, 212
Schumpeter, Josef, 259
Second World War, 6, 183, 185, 193–94, 198, 233, 238, 243, 257
security, 23, 51, 54, 73, 185, 221, 236
self-administration; self-determination; self-government; self-management; *autogestion*, 27, 75, 89, 100–101, 119, 122–24, 169, 174, 190, 208, 213–17, 234, 247, 261–72, 281
semantics, 9, 65–68, 70–75, 78, 80, 135–36, 148, 153, 188, 194, 213
semantic field, 65–67, 139
Semkovskii, S., 125
senate, 46, 48, 147
separation of powers, 11, 47, 54, 114, 216
Serbia, 215
Sforza, Carlo, 184, 186
Shalland, Lev, 117, 120
Shepard, Walter, 192
Shershenevich, G.F., 122
Shore, Peter, 289
Simon, Ernest, 194
Sismondi, Jean Simonde de, 47
slaves, 89, 96, 122
Slavonic peoples, 211, 215, 218

Slovakia; Slovaks, 209–10, 215, 217–19, 222, 224n10, 225n32
social change, 33, 69, 247, 259, 264
social classes; social groups; social strata, 17, 29, 32, 43, 48, 67–68, 72, 76–79, 119–21, 137–140, 146–48, 152, 166, 170–74, 186, 210–212, 216, 221, 241, 245–246, 260, 264–265, 271
social democracy, 75–79, 99–101, 114–18, 126, 161–66, 169–76, 184–85, 188, 198, 211, 238, 240, 250n35, 259–60, 263, 267, 284–88, 291
Social Democrats (France), 30–31
Social Democratic Party
    Austria, 211
    Czechoslovakia, 211
    Denmark, 284–91
    Finland, 163–66, 172–74
    Germany, 76–79,161–63, 171–73, 188, 260
    Russia, 115–18, 126
    Sweden, 99–101, 164, 169, 172–73
Socialism; socialists, 32, 76–79, 99–100, 114, 119, 125–26, 141–49, 152–53, 163–75, 186, 190, 213, 220–21, 239–40, 247, 263, 285, 292
socialization, 212, 221–22
social liberalism, 77, 287, 292
social justice, 126, 173, 235, 288
social questions, 71, 75, 143, 213
sociology, 58n25, 139, 185, 191, 209, 213, 220–21, 239
solidarity, 73, 75, 114, 149
Sonderweg, 65, 74, 80
sovereignty (national/popular), 7, 20, 22–24, 31, 45–47, 66–68, 75, 98, 137, 140–43, 172, 192–94, 218, 235–36, 241, 283–86, 292–94
Soviets, 125–26
Soviet Union, 191, 221, 231–32
Spain, 7–8, 10, 23–30, 36n32, 36n36, 135–53, 223n3, 234
Spanish constitution, 23, 136, 142
Spanish parliament (*Cortes*), 136, 139–50
stability/instability, 2, 10, 16–17, 30, 33, 43–47, 50–56, 68, 114–16, 144–48, 226n48, 237–38, 246
Staël, Germaine de, 47

Stalin, Joseph, 174, 221
Stalinism, 263
State Council (Russia), 120–121
Stein, Lorenz von, 76
Stein, Peter, 269
St Just, Louis Antoine de, 20
Stresemann, Gustav, 168
Struve, Petr, 120
Suárez, Adolfo, 151–52
suffrage (manhood/universal), 5–6, 9, 27, 30–32, 71, 75–77, 99–100, 120–121, 126, 143–45, 148, 161, 164–65, 172, 208, 212–14, 216
    women's, 120, 147–48, 211
    See also elections; franchise; vote
Suolahti, Hugo, 166
Swartz, Carl, 167
Sweden, 8, 18–19, 88–90, 95–103, 105n4, 107n60, 161–76, 240, 286–87
Swedish Parliament (*Riksdag*), 99–101
Switzerland, 8, 17, 24, 42, 47, 88–96, 102–4, 104n2, 106n26, 107n52, 144, 196, 222
Syndicalism, 213
Szporluk, Roman, 213–14, 219

T
Taylor, Charles, 260
technocracy, 242–43, 263, 288
Tegnér, Esaias, 98
temporalization, 67, 73
theology, 79, 136, 286
Thoma, Richard, 188
Thompson, E.P., 261
Tigranian, Sirakan Faddeevich, 119
Tikhomirov, Lev, 116
Tocqueville, Alexis de, 2, 4, 9, 26, 36n41, 71, 91–93, 97, 138, 191
Tönnies, Ferdinand, 185
Totalitarianism, 54, 101, 185, 188–22, 232
Toye, Richard, 247
trade unions, 232, 239–40, 270
translations, 25, 68, 140–41, 168, 226n46, 259
Treaty of Trianon, 217
Treaty of Versailles, 78, 171
Treitschke, Heinrich von, 77
Troeltsch, Ernst, 79–80
Trotsky, Lev, 186, 266

Truman, Harry S., 88
Turkey, 191
Tuscany, 21, 31
typology, 65, 67, 72. *See also* categorization
tyranny, 6, 17, 19–20, 23, 44, 65, 190, 194
  of the majority, 6, 17, 66

U

unicameralism; unicameral system, 121, 126, 136, 147, 165. *See also* bicameralism
United States, 5, 20, 26, 53, 68–71, 74, 80, 116, 119–23, 145, 161–65, 182–84, 187–94, 198, 215, 221–22, 231, 248, 258–60, 263, 266–68, 270. *See also* America
universalism, 74, 78, 209, 222
urban, 27, 32, 102, 187, 234, 242, 284

V

Valera, Fernando, 146–147
Ventura, Gioacchino, 28
Viking age, 89, 96–97, 101–2
Vile, Maurice, 54
Villiers, Edward, 139
Villiers, Georges, 139
violence, 17, 19, 75, 94, 140–42, 149, 174–75, 215, 234–36, 245–47, 273
virtues, 18–21, 49, 53, 56, 67, 97, 103, 213, 219
vote; voting, 8–9, 19, 24, 27, 31–32, 53, 71, 91, 95 117, 120, 140, 144–45, 150–51, 182, 188, 190, 216, 235–39, 243, 259–60, 269, 283, 290–94. *See also* elections; franchise; suffrage

W

Walpole, Robert, 18
Weber, Max, 161, 185, 215
Weimar Republic, 78–79, 151, 164–73, 184–89, 195–96, 234–35
Weizsäcker, Carl Friedrich von, 271
welfare, 114, 167, 233–34, 237, 241–47
welfare state, 76, 104, 184–86, 268
West; Western, 1, 6–9, 90, 113–16, 126, 162–75, 182–84, 195, 212–18, 232–35, 240, 257, 272
Westarp, Kuno von, 164
Western Europe, 74, 78, 117, 126, 160, 212, 231, 233–40, 242–47
Weston, Corinne Comstock, 51
Whigs, 44–45, 51–52, 74
Whitehead, A.N., 193
Wieland, Christoph, 22
Wilson, Woodrow, 78, 175, 184, 208, 216
women, 8–9, 95, 101, 120, 147–48, 161, 167, 190, 208, 211, 213, 216, 239–40, 242–43
working class; workers, 22, 25, 30–32, 76–77, 116–19, 125–26, 141, 146–48, 170–74, 211, 241–42, 245, 262–64, 268
Wrede, Rabbe Axel, 165

X

xenophobia, 95

Y

Yugoslavia, 223n2–3

Z

Zahra, Tara, 216–17
Zeitgeist; spirit of the age, 26, 69

www.ingramcontent.com/pod-product-compliance
Lightning Source LLC
Chambersburg PA
CBHW051528020426
42333CB00016B/1822